SCAPEGOATING ISLAM

SCAPEGOATING ISLAM

Intolerance, Security, and the American Muslim

JEFFREY L. THOMAS

 PRAEGER™

An Imprint of ABC-CLIO, LLC

Santa Barbara, California • Denver, Colorado

Library of Congress Cataloging-in-Publication Data

Thomas, Jeffrey L., 1964–
    Scapegoating Islam : intolerance, security, and the American Muslim / Jeffrey L. Thomas.
        pages cm
    Includes bibliographical references and index.
    ISBN 978-1-4408-3099-0 (print : alk. paper)—ISBN 978-1-4408-3100-3 (e-book)   1. Muslims—United States.   2. United States—Foreign relations—Islamic countries.   3. Islamic countries—Foreign relations—United States.   4. National security—United States.   5. Terrorism—United States—Prevention.   6. Islamophobia—United States.   7. Hate crimes—United States.   8. United States—Ethnic relations.   I. Title.
    E184.M88.T46 2015
    305.6'970973—dc23   2015025369

ISBN: 978-1-4408-3099-0
EISBN: 978-1-4408-3100-3

19 18 17 16 15   1 2 3 4 5

This book is also available on the World Wide Web as an eBook.
Visit www.abc-clio.com for details.

Praeger
An Imprint of ABC-CLIO, LLC

ABC-CLIO, LLC
130 Cremona Drive, P.O. Box 1911
Santa Barbara, California 93116-1911

This book is printed on acid-free paper ∞

Manufactured in the United States of America

Contents

Introduction

At various times throughout U.S. history, dating back to the founding of the nation, Americans have viewed Islam through the lenses of security. Events involving Muslims overseas and occasionally within the United States raised concerns about U.S. interests abroad and security at home, even if such incidents rarely maintained a hold on American public attention for long. The magnitude of 9/11 and its impact on American perceptions ensure that Islam and Muslims will be associated with security concerns well into the 21st century. The immense changes in U.S. foreign and domestic policies following 9/11—including two wars in Muslim lands, the creation of a vast homeland security enterprise, and the use of inhumane practices that challenge American values—underscore a striking shift in threat perception among policy makers and the public. Moreover, the continued threat posed by al-Qaeda and other Muslim extremist groups will keep Islam on the public agenda, alongside concerns about terrorism and security, for years to come.

This book explores the rise of terrorism and homeland security as dominant issues after 9/11, the inclusion of Islam as a fundament factor in these issues, and the resulting impact on Muslims in America. Chapter 1 provides an overview of America's evolving perspectives on Islam from the colonial era through the 20th century. A central theme throughout this 400-year period is the gradual shift from perceptions of Islam as a threatening presence abroad to a challenge and potential danger at home. Against a background of negative stereotypes of Islam pervasive in Western culture, U.S. military engagements with Muslim peoples overseas during the nation's first 150 years—from the Barbary Wars shortly after the nation's founding to the Moro Rebellion more than a century later—helped sustain American views of Islam as a distant and sometimes threatening adversary. For two and a half centuries, throughout the colonial period and well into America's years as an independent nation, Anglo-American society almost completely overlooked the thousands of African Muslims living among them as slaves.

This view of Islam as a threat abroad began to change in the early and mid-20th century as thousands of African Americans accepted interpretations of Islam that gave them a social identity separate from American society and its legacy of racism. The rise of the Nation of Islam, the Moorish Science Temple, and other African American Muslim movements with separatist agendas raised concerns among some segments of American society that Islam was becoming a dangerous presence within the United States. Such concerns gradually increased with the growth and diversification of America's Muslim population in the last half of the century, along with an increase in terrorist attacks by Muslim militants abroad and the first bombing of the World Trade Center in 1993. Although Islam was not a dominant concern for most Americans or U.S. policy makers at the end of the 20th century, perceptions of Muslims as a potential internal threat to American society were gaining acceptance.

This trend accelerated markedly after 9/11. Chapter 2 provides an overview of the rise of the federal government's homeland security architecture and how the security and law enforcement agencies within this architecture directed their attention toward Muslims in America and, in some cases, toward Muslim Americans living abroad. From surveillance and monitoring to arrest and indefinite detention, U.S. homeland security policies affected thousands of Muslims in the country. The affected groups included U.S. citizens and permanent legal residents, foreign students, visiting family members, and especially foreign nationals without legal immigration status. In addition, federal authorities listed an undisclosed number of Muslim Americans on an expanded No Fly List, while relying on coercive means to recruit others as informants to spy on mosque congregations and Muslim communities. In a few extraordinary cases, missiles fired from drones operated by the U.S. military or the CIA took the lives of Muslim Americans abroad.

In the years after 9/11, state and municipal governments became increasingly important participants in America's expanding homeland security enterprise. State and local efforts to strengthen counterterrorism capabilities beyond Washington, as well as to coordinate homeland security operations and functions with federal authorities, enhanced the security and safety of many local communities. However, in many cases, these efforts relied heavily on coercive and intrusive measures that targeted Muslims. Parallel to these efforts, many state and local governments engaged in discriminatory practices unrelated to security that violated the rights of Muslim Americans, infringing on their ability to freely practice their religion and seeking to marginalize them as participants in American society.

Chapter 3 briefly discusses the expansion of homeland security capabilities outside of Washington. It then provides a detailed assessment of changes in the New York Police Department, the largest municipal law enforcement agency in the country. The NYPD counterterrorism strategy adopted after 9/11 included many aspects that singled out Muslims and resembled—and in some cases went beyond—the coercive law enforcement tactics used by the federal government. Following this discussion, the chapter juxtaposes state and local efforts to enhance public safety, sometimes through coercive and intrusive measures, with discriminatory state and municipal policies and practices that target Muslims without having any connection to homeland security. Such policies and practices have sometimes resulted from confusion about the role of government in protecting religious freedom or from unfamiliarity with Islam, but they are often based on anti-Muslim bias and fear of Islam.

A major driver of changes in public policy affecting Muslim Americans is public opinion. The efforts of responsible public officials, interfaith groups, and numerous civic organizations helped curtail anti-Muslim sentiment for several months after 9/11. However, in subsequent years, the number of Americans with negative views of Islam steadily increased, and a growing percentage of the American public began to express suspicion and intolerance toward Muslim Americans. Chapter 4 outlines these trends, then turns to some of the most important factors that influence public attitudes toward Islam in the post-9/11 environment. Along with the continued threat of terrorist attacks by Muslim militants, images of Muslims presented to American audiences by the news and entertainment media often conform to negative stereotypes. In addition, anti-Muslim activists present Islam as incompatible with American culture and raise fears that Muslim Americans are seeking to impose alien religious values on American society.

The anger and fear that contributed to anti-Muslim sentiments after 9/11 also triggered an increase in discrimination, hate crimes, and other acts of intolerance against Muslim Americans, as well as Christian Arab Americans, Sikh Americans, and others mistaken for being Muslim. As recorded by the FBI, hate crimes targeting Muslims declined after a sharp rise during the first several weeks after 9/11, but remained well above pre-9/11 levels in following years. Chapter 5 provides an account of this rise in intolerance directed at Muslims, including threats and intimidation, violent assaults, murder, killing sprees, and three terrorist plots designed to inflict large-scale destruction and mass casualties on Muslim targets. The chapter then addresses potential motivating factors, in addition to anti-Muslim bias, behind such acts, including the cultural and social factors that encourage some Americans to see the nation's diverse Muslim population as a homogenous group deserving of punishment.

Chapter 6 gives an overview of Muslim participation in American civil society, including the mobilization of Muslim civic organizations after 9/11 to protect the rights of Muslim citizens and to contribute to America's counterterrorism efforts. Muslim civic engagement provides significant advantages both for safeguarding America's democratic principles and for strengthening America's homeland security enterprise, mutually reinforcing complements that form the basis of a community-based approach to security. Such an approach, which relies on trust and cooperation between security and law enforcement officials and the communities they serve, capitalizes on the unique cultural knowledge and community awareness of local residents in localities across the nation. This community knowledge is often key in preventing acts of terrorism and hate crimes or apprehending assailants when prevention fails.

Three themes emerge from these chapters. First, when public and policy perceptions of a social group are dominated by security concerns, fear and intolerance, followed by civil rights abuses, discrimination, and even bias-motivated violence are difficult to contain. Second, the emergence of these factors undermines America's commitment to democratic principles, such as freedom of religion and equal protection under the law, and it allows those who would devalue these principles to gain greater influence in society. Third, protecting civil rights and countering terrorism and extremist influence are not only compatible objectives in the long run but also necessary components of an effective homeland security strategy. Security arrangements that do not safeguard civil rights, or ones that actively subvert them, undermine trust and cooperation between the state and the public and call into question the legitimacy of the state's approach to homeland security.

CHAPTER 1

America's Evolving Perspectives on Islam: From Threat Abroad to Challenge at Home

For most of Anglo-American history, from the rise of British colonies along North America's eastern seaboard to the early 20th century, Americans generally saw Islam as an exotic and dangerous foreign presence confined to distant lands. This view was mistaken, for Muslims were a fundamental part of colonial America dating back to the 16th century, when European powers opened the trans-Atlantic slave trade. For three and a half centuries, slave ships transported African men and women to the Americas, including people from predominantly Muslim regions of West and Central Africa. However, Anglo-American colonists—and, later, U.S. citizens—remained largely unaware of the religion and other cultural characteristics of the people who lived among them as slaves.

Similarly, Americans barely noticed the relatively small number of Muslims who immigrated from southern Europe and the eastern Mediterranean region to the United States after the Civil War. Not until after World War I, when Muslims in America started to become politically and socially active, did the American public and U.S. policy makers take note of Islam as a religion and social force within U.S. borders. From that point forward, events both abroad and within the United States increasingly placed American Muslims in the spotlight. No longer existing as a hidden presence in society, Muslims in America became an object of government scrutiny and U.S. policy with growing frequency throughout the 20th century.

America's Colonial Inheritance from Europe

A broadly consistent Western perception of Islam began to emerge long before the British colonization of North America, dating back at least to the time of the Crusades. In 1095, while speaking at the Council of Claremont, Pope Urban II issued his call to defend the Byzantine Empire from encroaching Muslim armies. As Christians across much of Europe rallied to the pope's call, the vague impressions that most Europeans had of Muslims coalesced into an image of Muslims as fanatical followers of a false religion and usurpers of Christian lands. Robert the Monk drew on this image as he chronicled the First Crusade in his *Historia Iherosolimitana* (*History of the First Crusade*), a widely disseminated work that promoted a view of the Crusades as heroic campaigns against the enemies of Christendom.[1] European literature sustained and elaborated upon this perception throughout the late Middle Ages. Medieval romances and legends of battles between Christian and Muslim knights propagated the view that Muslims were a violent and dangerous enemy that threatened Christian civilization.[2] As Europe emerged from the Middle Ages, the fall of Constantinople to the Ottoman Turks in 1453 appeared to give credence to such fears.

Almost half a millennium after Pope Urban II's call to arms, the Ottoman Empire's advance into southern Europe elicited an expansion of these themes. After the Ottomans captured Belgrade and laid siege to Vienna in the early 16th century, prophesies of doom at the hands of the Turks became increasingly popular. These prophecies often included references to the book of Revelation and depictions of the Prophet Mohammad as the Antichrist.[3] European literary romances placed a renewed emphasis on Muslims, usually referred to simply as "Turks" by this point in time, as a powerful force threatening Christian Europe. In addition, as the Protestant Reformation challenged the authority of Rome, invoking fear of a Turkish invasion became a means of mobilizing mass protest for change. In German-speaking Europe, a genre of popular pamphlet (the *Türkenbüchlein*), including three booklets written by Martin Luther, relied on this method of demonizing the Turks (and Muslims in general) to create a sense of urgency for religious reform.[4]

As the Ottoman Empire expanded into southern Europe, the Spanish, the Portuguese, and the Dutch—followed later by the English and the French—began to colonize the Americas. Not surprisingly, colonial settlers brought European notions of Islam with them—in some cases as firmly held convictions, in others as roughly formed ideas about a people and religion in faraway lands. Just as in Europe, historical and quasi-historical accounts helped perpetuate negative stereotypes. In his widely read *Book of Martyrs*, devoted primarily to recounting Catholic persecution of Protestants, English cleric John Foxe (1516–1587) wrote at length about the cruelty of the Turks and compared Turkish atrocities against Christians with the Roman treatment of the early Christians, centuries before.[5] Later, English lecturer Humphrey Prideaux (1648–1724) produced his biography of Mohammad, *The True Nature of the Imposture Fully Displayed in the Life of Mahomet*. It became the most influential treatise on Islam in the English colonies. By the mid-1700s, this anti-Muslim work, which portrayed Mohammad as a fraud and a tyrant, had been reproduced in eight editions to meet demand in English-speaking North America.[6]

Popular European fiction also carried anti-Muslim views to the colonies. In his masterpiece *Paradise Lost*, John Milton described Satan as an Ottoman sultan and depicted fallen angels as Muslim warriors. Meanwhile, Voltaire's play *Fanaticism, or the Prophet Mahomet* debuted in North America in 1780. Writing the play to praise secularism and warn against religious intolerance, Voltaire followed common Western thinking at the time and chose Mohammad and Islam to represent intolerance and religious fanaticism.[7] By the time of U.S. independence, stereotypical Western depictions of Muslims were widely incorporated in numerous genres of fiction, from dramatic plays and poems to romantic tales of the Orient. These stories were increasingly written by American authors rather than imported from Europe.[8]

By the close of the colonial period, Barbary captivity narratives had emerged as one of the most popular genres of fiction among English speakers in North America. Throughout the colonial period, pirates from Morocco and the Ottoman provinces of North Africa captured thousands of merchant ships in the Mediterranean Sea and northern Atlantic Ocean. As a common practice, they took crew and passengers captive to serve as slaves and to extort ransom. As early as 1625, Barbary pirates captured North American vessels. Before the end of the century, biographical accounts of sailors captured and enslaved by Muslim pirates became popular in Europe and the colonies. Fictionalized versions of these accounts appeared in novels, plays, and operas on both sides of the Atlantic. By the early 19th century, publishers in North America made available more than 100 Barbary-related captivity narratives. The account of Captain James Riley, who was captured after his ship ran aground off the coast of Morocco, sold nearly a million copies.[9]

At the outset of U.S. independence, popular fiction and historical literature helped ensure that the United States was home to many of the same preconceived ideas and stereotypes of Islam that developed in Europe over the previous 700 years. Few Americans had visited Muslim lands, and Islam was rarely a prominent topic of concern in the country. Nevertheless, the cultural references and popular images of Islam that Europeans brought with them to North America and the ones that North American colonists developed in subsequent years remained active in the newly independent nation. Literary accounts of the Muslim world commonly described a collection of exotic and dangerous lands characterized by violence, religious zeal, corrupt rulers, piracy, and maltreatment of Christians and other non-Muslims.

Islam as a Foreign Policy Matter in Early America

For the first 150 years after U.S. independence, U.S. policies directed toward Muslims both reflected and reinforced the view of Islam as a distant, exotic, and sometimes threatening presence abroad. From the outset of independence to the early 20th century, policy makers and much of the general public perceived relations between Muslims and American society as a foreign policy matter, an issue to be addressed by diplomats and, occasionally, the U.S. Navy. Although only periodically at the forefront of U.S. foreign policy during this period, predominantly Muslim states and peoples—from North Africa to Southeast Asia—appeared primarily as challenges to U.S. interests overseas.

The Barbary Wars

At the time of U.S. independence, the Barbary Coast, stretching more than 2000 miles along the Mediterranean shores of North Africa, was dominated by four Muslim states. Three of these states—Algiers, Tunis, and Tripoli—were nominally ruled by Constantinople as tributaries of the Ottoman Empire. In reality, they exercised substantial autonomy. Morocco remained an independent kingdom with its own emperor. Largely free to determine their own foreign policies, all four Barbary States practiced a centuries-old tradition of piracy, including capturing merchant crew members to keep as slaves until—and unless—Barbary rulers collected ransom for their captives' release. By the time Britain began colonizing North America, thousands of Europeans were held captive in North Africa.[10]

Beginning in 1662, Britain attempted to mitigate this threat by negotiating a series of treaties with the Barbary States, a precedent that other European powers followed. Typically, such treaties required European governments to pay ransom for the release of captives and to provide annual tribute to ensure continued safe passage of their merchant ships through the Mediterranean and North Atlantic. The parties abided by the treaties irregularly, with European powers often delaying payment and sometimes encouraging piracy against rival European states. Meanwhile, North African raiders continued to selectively capture merchant ships and crews.[11] The Barbary pirates also preyed on Anglo-American vessels trading with Europe. In 1625, Moroccan corsairs seized a merchant ship from the North American colonies, the first ship sailing from North America to be captured by the Barbary States. Two decades later, the crew aboard a ship built in colonial Massachusetts fought off an Algerian pirate ship in what was possibly the first naval battle fought by Anglo-Americans.[12]

As the American Revolution approached, the number of North American merchant vessels visiting Europe's Mediterranean ports reached between 80 and 100 ships annually. Other than their own armaments, these merchants relied on precarious British treaty arrangements with the Barbary States as well as British naval ships on patrol for protection. The American Revolution disrupted even these tenuous protections. The 1783 Treaty of Paris, which marked the official end of hostilities between Britain and the rebellious colonies, brought an end to British rule in North America. To the misfortune of American merchants, it also ended the British navy's protection of American merchant ships and the imperfect immunity from pirate raids that British tribute to the Barbary States provided.[13] The following year, Morocco seized the USS *Betsy* and held the crew captive until receiving $30,000 in ransom 9 months later. The following year, Algiers seized the U.S. merchant ships *Maria* and *Dauphin*, holding some of the crew captive for more than 10 years.[14] In 1793, Algerian corsairs captured 11 U.S. vessels over a 3-month period, taking 120 Americans captive.[15]

In response to these attacks, the newly established United States entered into negotiations with the North African rulers. By 1797, the U.S. government concluded treaties with all four Barbary States, guaranteeing free passage for American ships in the Mediterranean and North Atlantic. The treaty with Morocco required no U.S. payments or annual tribute.[16] Treaties with the other North African states, however, required substantial payments from the United States. The treaty with Tripoli required a one-time payment of $56,000, while the treaty with Tunis required the United States to pay $107,000 and to subsequently provide $20,000 in annual tribute. The treaty with Algiers required a payment of $642,000 (20 percent of U.S. federal government annual expenditures) in exchange for more than 100 American captives; it also required an annual tribute of more than $21,000 in naval stores.[17]

These treaties bought just three years of peace. In 1800, Tripoli seized the USS *Catherine* and demanded a renegotiation of its treaty with the United States. Tripoli released the ship in return for payment, but it rejected new treaty arrangements offered by the U.S. envoy and threatened war if the United States did not agree to a new treaty more favorable to Tripoli.[18] In response, the United States launched a military campaign against Tripoli. Beginning in 1801 and continuing for the next four years, the United States—now armed with a growing navy—bombarded the city of Tripoli, blockaded Tripoli's port, and organized a land assault with U.S. Marines and an army of mercenaries recruited in Egypt.[19] In 1805, Tripoli agreed to a new treaty much less favorable than the one offered before the start of the war. The United States agreed to pay $60,000 in exchange for more than 300 U.S. sailors captured when their ship ran aground in Tripoli's harbor but was not required to pay annual tribute.

Shortly after the United States reached a new peace agreement with Tripoli, corsairs from Algiers renewed attacks on U.S. merchants, seizing several ships and their crews for ransom. The danger to American vessels increased sharply when, during the War of 1812, Algiers sided with Britain and declared war on the United States. Following the 1814 Treaty of Ghent that formally ended hostilities with Britain, the United States declared war on Algiers and sent two naval squadrons to the Mediterranean. In the summer of 1815, U.S. Navy detachments secured agreement with Algiers, gaining the release of 10 American prisoners, receiving $10,000 in compensation from the government of Algiers, and ending annual U.S. tribute payments. The U.S. Navy coerced similar agreements with Tunis and Tripoli, ending U.S. tribute payments to the Barbary States for good.[20] The conclusion of hostilities brought an end to one of most immediate problems facing the newly independent United States, a 30-year-long challenge—from the end of the Revolutionary War to 1815—that resulted in the seizure of at least 36 merchant ships and about 700 U.S. sailors.[21]

The Sumatra Expeditions

Less than two decades after the end of the Barbary Wars, the United States faced another challenge from pirates in a predominantly Muslim region of the world—this time in Southeast Asia. In 1831, the U.S. merchant ship *Friendship* set anchor off the town of Quallah Battoo on the northwest coast of Sumatra. While the captain and some of the crew were ashore, pirates raided the ship, killed three crew members, and plundered the vessel. The captain and remaining crew gained the help of sailors anchored about 25 miles away and retook the *Friendship*. To deter future attacks on U.S. merchant ships, President Andrew Jackson diverted the USS *Potomac*, a navy frigate headed for China, to Sumatra. The crew of the *Potomac* stormed three forts around Quallah Battoo and set fire to the town. The next day, the ship bombarded a fourth fort in the town, killing about 100 inhabitants. The naval ship departed when the remaining residents promised not to assault U.S. vessels in the future.[22]

This military action did not end Sumatran piracy against U.S. ships, however. In 1833, the merchant ship *Derby* fought off a pirate ship while anchored outside of the Sumatran town of Trabangunchute. Five years later, Sumatran pirates raided the U.S. merchant ship *Eclipse* while it was similarly anchored off Trabangunchute, killing the captain and plundering the vessel. The plundered stores were divided between the towns of Quallah Battoo, Muckie, and Soo Soo. In response, two U.S. navy ships paying a port call at Ceylon sailed to Sumatra. After negotiations failed to gain restitution for the *Eclipse*, the navy ships fired on the restored forts at Quallah Battoo. They then sailed to the town of Muckie and, after talks there failed as well, bombarded the town. Sailors aboard the U.S. vessels then landed and burned down the town and its surrounding forts, after allowing the inhabitants to evacuate. The ships sailed back to Quallah Battoo and secured $2,000 in restitution for the *Eclipse* and an agreement from the residents not to harass U.S. merchant ships in the future.[23]

The Moro Rebellion

At the turn of the 19th century, the United States confronted another challenge in Southeast Asia. In 1898, at the conclusion of the Spanish-American War, Spain surrendered a large part of its remaining overseas colonial possessions to the United States, including Puerto Rico, Guam, Cuba (as a U.S. protectorate), and, in exchange for a $20 million payment, the Philippines. The arrival of U.S. soldiers in the Philippines the following year, and the prospect of continued rule by an outside power, sparked a nationalist uprising for independence across much of the northern Philippine islands. The United States defeated the nationalists in a three-year war that cost the lives of 4,200 U.S. soldiers, more than 20,000 Filipino combatants, and as many as 200,000 Filipino civilians, who died primarily from famine and disease.[24]

Throughout the conflict with Filipino nationalists, the United States focused on putting down resistance in the predominantly Christian northern islands of the Philippines, where nationalist leader Emilio Aguinaldo had broad support. To the south, in southern parts of Mindanao Island and on the Sulu Archipelago, the United States allowed substantial autonomy for the predominantly Muslim inhabitants. Commonly called "Moros" at the time, based on the common Spanish term for Muslims, the people of the region comprised a mix of 13 linguistic cultural groups unified to some degree by a common Islamic identity.[25] During the last decades of Spanish rule in the Philippines, the Sultanate of Sulu, covering more than 300 islands of the Sulu Archipelago, was allowed to exercise a significant degree of independence.[26] At first, the United States emulated this arrangement after assuming control of the Philippines. In 1899, U.S. General John Bates and Sultan Jamal-ul Kiram II signed the Bates Agreement. It allowed Moro law and culture to prevail on the Sulu Archipelago in exchange for recognition of U.S. sovereignty over the region. This agreement served as the basis for a series of informal power-sharing agreements between the United States and local Muslim leaders throughout the southern Philippine islands.[27]

These agreements secured relative peace in the south, despite periodic clashes between Moros and U.S. military personnel, as U.S. forces battled nationalists in the north. However, the agreements with Muslim leaders were also a source of intense criticism among American detractors of U.S. policy in the Philippines, in large measure because they permitted the continuation of the traditional Moro practices of slavery and polygamy.[28] In addition, as was the norm for centuries, competing Moro clans frequently conducted raids against one another, engaged in piracy off the coast, and fought with Christian and pagan Filipinos. They also occasionally attacked Americans soldiers, surveyors, and road-building crews.[29] With the end of major fighting in the northern Philippines in 1902, the United States took stronger measures to police the southern islands and to eliminate Moro practices that ran counter to American norms. As part of this strategy, southern Mindanao and the Sulu Archipelago were combined administratively to create a new Moro Province. This new province was placed under the authority of an American military governor. Subsequently, slavery was abolished in the province, and a legal code modeled after U.S. law was imposed.[30]

In response to this encroachment on local autonomy and culture, a Moro insurgency arose in the southern Philippines. Guerrilla attacks on U.S. encampments and personnel, including suicide attacks (*juramentados*) against U.S. detachments, elicited a series of punitive raids by

U.S. forces against Moro strongholds. In 1906, a large group of Moro fighters and their families gathered at a fortified crater of Bud Dajo, a dormant volcano. After months of negotiation failed to convince the Moros to leave, U.S. forces stormed the position. They killed several hundred Moros, including a large number of women, children, and family members of Moro fighters. After this assault, large-scale resistance to U.S. rule subsided until 1911, when the American military governor attempted to institute a new law requiring Moros to surrender their firearms and cease carrying their traditional swords and spears. This attempt to disarm the Moro population resulted in renewed fighting, including a second battle at Bud Dajo in 1911 and another large battle along the summits of a second dormant volcano, Bud Bagsak, in 1913. Both battles, won by the U.S. military and allied Filipino militia, resulted in the death of several hundred Moro fighters and dozens of their family members.[31]

The Battle of Bud Bagsak was the last major battle against the Moros involving a significant number of U.S. soldiers. Fighting continued afterward, but it primarily involved Moro insurgents battling constabulary forces comprising mostly Filipinos loyal to the U.S.-administered government. When Congress passed the Jones Act of 1916, which set a course for eventual Filipino independence, the bulk of U.S. military forces had already withdrawn from the Philippines, and a civilian colonial administration had replaced the U.S. military governorship.[32] By the time the Philippines attained independence in 1946, the Moro rebellion had been conflated in the minds of many Americans with the nationalist uprising in the predominantly Christian northern Philippines. However, the counterinsurgency campaign against the Moros, occurring after the suppression of the Filipino nationalist movement, constituted the first prolonged U.S. encounter with a Muslim population and culture.

The Perdicaris Affair

During the early stages of the Moro rebellion, and almost 100 years after the Barbary Wars, the United States faced another captivity crisis in North Africa. In May 1904, a group of armed men broke into a villa just outside of the Moroccan city of Tangier and kidnapped the owner, American expatriate Ion Perdicaris, along with his stepson, a British citizen. The perpetrators of this act were Mulai Ahmed el-Raisuli and his followers, who were engaged in a long-running conflict with Abd-er-Rahman Abd-el-Saduk, the local ruler of Tangier and a powerful ally of the Sultan of Morocco. In return for the release of his captives, el-Raisuli demanded $70,000 in indemnity from el-Saduk, the dismissal of el-Saduk as local ruler of Tangier, and the surrender of two districts of the city to the control of el-Raisuli and his followers. He also demanded guarantees from the U.S. and British governments that they would force the Moroccan government to honor the terms of any agreement reached in negotiations over the release of Perdicaris and his stepson.[33]

President Theodore Roosevelt responded aggressively to this hostage crisis. He ordered seven warships to sail to Moroccan waters and sent an additional five warships to stand by off the coast of Portugal. When negotiations between the Moroccan government and el-Raisuli appeared to falter, Roosevelt approved a set of guidelines, sent by the secretary of state to the U.S. consul general stationed in Tangier, which included the ultimatum, "This government wants Perdicaris alive or Raisuli dead." The message was promptly released to the press as a display of U.S. resolve on the matter. Whatever the effects of U.S. efforts at intimidation, the Moroccan government came to terms with el-Raisuli in June 1904, paying him $70,000 and releasing some government prisoners in exchange for the release of Perdicaris and his stepson.[34]

U.S. Relations with the Ottoman Empire

For more than a century after U.S. independence was won, the Ottoman Empire was the dominant Muslim political entity in world affairs. Throughout this period, with the exception of war against the Barbary pirate states—three of which were nominally Ottoman tributaries—U.S. engagement with the Ottoman Empire was based primarily on trade. Not until 1830, when the United States and the Ottoman government began negotiating a treaty of naval navigation and commerce, did the two states establish formal diplomatic relations. The U.S. diplomatic mission at Constantinople was not upgraded to the status of an embassy with a U.S. ambassador until 1906.[35] During this period, the fate of the declining Ottoman Empire and the future of its territorial possessions in southern Europe played a major role in the foreign policies of European powers. These issues sometimes figured prominently in the news that reached American audiences, usually with a sharply anti-Turkish bias.[36] However, except for trade relations, the United States remained at a distance from the changes gradually bringing about the end of the centuries-old Ottoman Empire.

This political remove from events in the Ottoman Empire broke down in the mid-1890s, as Turkish efforts to put down a growing ethnic Armenian independence movement escalated into a series of massacres, costing the lives of tens of thousands of Armenians.[37] Sporadic violence continued into the 20th century, leading to violent clashes and massacres on a much larger scale. After entering World War I in 1914, the Ottoman Empire faced resistance from ethnic Armenians, many of whom joined the opposing Russian army or joined guerrilla groups fighting for an independent Armenia. In response, the Ottoman government initiated the mass deportation of Armenians from Anatolia in 1915. Whether officially sanctioned or undertaken on the initiative of military commanders in the field, large-scale massacres accompanied this persecution. According to some estimates, more than a million Armenians died from direct violence, starvation, exposure, and disease during what is often called the Armenian genocide.[38]

Anti-Armenian violence during this period resulted in an influx of several thousand Armenians into the United States and broad public condemnation of Ottoman actions.[39] The Ottoman Empire's treatment of ethnic Armenians also received growing media attention in the United States. By the early stages of World War I, U.S. newspapers provided extensive coverage of the conditions of Armenians under Ottoman rule, including 145 stories in the *New York Times* in 1915 alone. In addition, by the beginning of World War I, Protestant missionaries from the United States had established a significant presence in the Ottoman Empire, where they operated hospitals and more than 400 schools for a total of 25,000 students. The principal beneficiaries of their services were Christian Armenians.[40] Attacks against missionary property and reports from missionaries of atrocities committed against the Armenian population fueled negative public sentiments in the United States toward the Ottoman Empire.

Beginning with the initial large-scale attacks on Armenians in the mid-1890s, the U.S. government sought to protect U.S. citizens in the Ottoman Empire and protested the destruction of property that belonged to missionaries serving the Armenian community in Anatolia. As anti-Armenian violence escalated in the first years of World War I, the Department of State and the U.S. ambassador in Constantinople, Henry Morgenthau, condemned the treatment of Armenians and vigorously protested Ottoman policies. Ambassador Morgenthau also played a prominent role in relief efforts, encouraging private donors in the United States to provide funds to assist Armenians in Anatolia.[41] Diplomatic entreaties with the Ottoman government on behalf of the Armenian population continued until April 1917, when the United States declared war on Germany, the Ottoman Empire's ally. In response to this move, the Ottoman government severed diplomatic relations with the United States, ending formal

U.S.-Turkish ties until the establishment of diplomatic relations between the United States and the new Republic of Turkey in 1927.

The Early Muslim Presence in North America

From the time the United States gained independence in the 18th century to the early 20th century, the prevailing view of Islam as a religion and culture distant from American shores was supported by the sporadic— often sensational—news and information reaching Americans. It especially came from news accounts and fiction related to U.S. involvement with the Muslim world. At the turn of the 18th century, America's decades-long struggle with the pirate states of North Africa revived the Barbary captivity narrative as a popular genre and helped perpetuate the image of Muslim lands as exotic and dangerous.[42] A century later, the Perdicaris affair in North Africa and the Moro rebellion halfway around the world in Southeast Asia, both of which were featured prominently in newspapers across the United States, reinforced this image.[43] After World War I and the Armenian massacres, negative images of Turks were ubiquitous in newspapers, magazines, popular fiction, school lessons, and church sermons.[44]

These depictions of Muslims presented Islam and its adherents as far removed from American society. However, long before the American Revolution and throughout the proceeding centuries, Muslims were an integral part of America, first as African slaves, and then as small but growing immigrant communities. Policy makers rarely took note of this "hidden" Muslim population, but the policies they enacted profoundly affected Muslims within and beyond American shores.

The Trans-Atlantic Slave Trade

During the century after Christopher Columbus landed in the New World in 1492, Spain and Portugal, Europe's dominant naval powers at the time, established colonies throughout much of South America. The Portuguese focused on colonizing Brazil on the Atlantic coast, while the Spanish steadily extended their control northward along the Pacific coast into Central America and southern areas of North America. As gold mining operations and colonial sugar plantations expanded in Spanish and Portuguese America, European traders transported African slaves to the New World to meet the demand for labor. For most of the 16th century, this trans-Atlantic trafficking in African men and women concentrated on the growing plantations of South America and the West

Indies, especially in Portuguese Brazil.[45] However, as early as 1527, Este-vancio (or Estaban), a slave from Morocco, became possibly the first African—as well as the first Muslim—to set foot on North American soil. After surviving the wreck of a Spanish vessel in the Gulf of Mexico with three other crew members, Estevancio traveled across much of the southern part of North America, including modern-day New Mexico and Arizona.[46]

Almost 100 years after Estevancio's travels in southwestern North America, the British colonies along the Eastern Seaboard began relying on forced African labor. In 1619, at the colony of Jamestown in Virginia, the crew of a Dutch warship traded 20 indentured servants from Africa for supplies from the British colonists, the first documented case of Africans subjected to forced labor in Anglo-America. They joined the ranks of many other indentured servants from Europe, serving as forced laborers for a predetermined length of time before being set free. As the number of forced laborers from Africa increased in the British colonies over the next several decades, indentured servitude for Africans evolved into chattel slavery based on race, which defined African slaves as property bound to their owners for life.[47] For 200 years, from 1619 until the United States banned the importation of slaves into the country in 1808, this trans-Atlantic trade brought nearly 500,000 African men and women to North America as slaves.[48]

The religion of Africans transported to North America during these two centuries was of little concern to either slave traders or slave owners, with the exception of a few slave owners who wanted to introduce Christianity to their charges. As a result, much knowledge about the religious beliefs of North America's early African diaspora has been lost to history. However, a large—if indeterminate—number of slaves were certainly Muslim. Most of the African slaves transported to North America came from West Africa, including regions where Islam played a significant role, either as the dominant religion or as the religion of large minority populations. Historian Michael Gomez calculates that approximately 50 percent of African slaves brought to the British colonies and the United States, about a quarter of a million people, came from areas where Muslims lived and, in some cases, ruled. Historian Allan Austin estimates that, during the final 100 years of the slave trade, between 30,000 and 40,000 Muslims were transported to North America as slaves.[49]

On rare occasions, individual Muslim slaves became well known in Anglo-America. One such case involved Ayuba Suleiman Ibrahima, a member of a prominent Muslim family from northwest Africa, who impressed colonial Americans during the 1730s with his sharp mind, high educational status, and literacy in Arabic. Known as Job Ben Solomon to the colonists, he eventually gained his freedom with the help of James Oglethorpe, founder of the colony of Georgia. He then traveled to England, where he was elected to the prestigious Spalding Gentlemen's Society, before returning to Africa.[50] Similarly, Abdul Rahman Ibrahima, son of a Muslim leader in northwestern Africa, briefly became a celebrity in North America after he was captured by an enemy clan in Africa and sold into slavery. He labored for several decades in Mississippi before being freed at the request of the Sultan of Morocco and the intercession of President John Quincy Adams.[51] A handful of other Muslim slaves became well known locally, such as Omar Ibn Said in North Carolina, Yarrow Mamout in northern Virginia, and Bilali Mohammad and Salih Bilali on the coastal islands off Georgia.[52]

Despite the examples provided by these exceptional men, Anglo-Americans remained largely ignorant of the tens of thousands of Muslims who lived among them as slaves. In some cases, early American leaders defended the rights of non-Christians, including Muslims. In 1784, in a letter requesting wage laborers to work on his Virginia home, George Washington wrote: "If they are good workmen, they may be of Asia, Africa, or Europe. They may be Mahometans [Muslims], Jews, or Christians of any Sect, or they may be Atheists."[53] Similarly, reflecting on his efforts to promote religious freedom, Thomas Jefferson expressed his belief that religious freedom should be available to "the Jew and the Gentile, the Christian and the Mahometan [Muslim], the Hindoo [Hindu], and the Infidel of every denomination."[54] However, as historian Denise Spellberg points out, both presidents used Muslims as hypothetical examples to demonstrate their view that people holding even exotic religious beliefs were entitled to the free exercise of religion. They and most of their fellow Americans remained unaware of the large Muslim population already in the country.[55]

Muslim Immigration before World War I

Throughout most of the 19th century, immigrants entering the United States came from predominantly Protestant and Catholic regions of the world, especially Ireland, Germany, Scandinavia, and Canada. Beginning in the 1890s, large numbers of immigrants from Eastern Europe and Southern Europe arrived on American shores, adding communities of Jews and Orthodox Christians to the ranks of first-generation Americans.[56] During the last quarter of the century, immigrants from the Ottoman Empire's eastern Mediterranean region—modern-day Lebanon, Syria, Jordan, and Palestine—began to arrive. From 1880 to 1900, nearly 35,000 people from this region immigrated to America. Over the next 30 years, this number increased nearly 10-fold, as more than 325,000 people left the Ottoman Empire's eastern Mediterranean shores for America.[57]

Like their European counterparts, most immigrants from Ottoman lands at the turn of the 19th century were Christian, but a significant minority was Muslim. A precise count of the number of Muslims who left the Ottoman Empire for America during this period is unobtainable, primarily because U.S. immigration officials classified most people from the region as being from "Turkey in Asia" or labeled them "other Asians" without noting their religion or ethnicity.[58] In addition, many Muslims from the region attempted to pass themselves off as Christian, both to avoid Ottoman government restrictions on the emigration of Muslims from the empire and to more easily assimilate into American society. Based on imperfect Ottoman records from the time, Turkish historian Kemal Karpat estimates that between 27,000 and 36,000 Muslims emigrated from the Ottoman Empire to the United States from 1860 to the beginning of World War I in 1914. Joining them during the late 1800s and early 1900s were smaller contingents of Muslims from Eastern Europe, the Balkans, the Caucasus, Yemen, and the Punjab in northern India.[59] By the mid-1920s, approximately 60,000 Muslims had immigrated to the United States.[60]

Just as Muslims from various regions of the world sought entry into the United States, the U.S. Congress enacted immigration restrictions. These restrictions began with the Chinese Exclusion Act of 1882, designed to reduce the number of Chinese laborers in the country, and steadily grew to include broad barriers to immigration from regions other than Western Europe.[61] In 1891, Congress barred polygamists or "persons who admit their belief in the practice of polygamy" from immigrating to the United States. This measure directly affected adherents to Islam, which permits Muslim men to take as many as four wives.[62] In 1917, Congress enacted two additional restrictions: a requirement that prospective immigrants pass a literacy test and the designation of "Asiatic Barred Zones." The latter restriction, although not aimed specifically at Muslims, cut off immigration from British India and Southeast Asia, regions with large Muslim populations.[63]

Beginning in 1921, Congress erected a quota system designed to further reduce immigration from non-Western regions of Europe. The Quota Act of 1921 established an annual number of immigrants allowed into the United States, based on a percentage of foreign-born residents who were living in the country in 1910. Three years later, the National Origins Act of 1924 lowered the ceiling for immigration further, limiting the number of immigrants from any one country to just 2 percent of the number of people from that country who were living in the United States in 1890. The following year, immigration fell by 50 percent, with three-quarters of new arrivals coming from Western and Northern Europe.[64] For the next 40 years, until immigration reform eliminated this race-based quota system, Muslim immigration to America remained limited, as did immigration of other non-Christian religious groups and non-European ethnicities.

Black Muslim Activism: Islam as a Domestic Challenge

As immigration into the United States declined in the early 20th century, a large-scale internal migration within the country began. This internal migration was spearheaded by African Americans moving from the South to escape Jim Crow segregation laws and to find work in industrializing cities in the North, the Midwest, and the West. During World War I, military conscription and the decline in immigration from abroad created labor shortages for the emerging factories and manufacturing plants. Beginning in 1915 and continuing for the next six decades, more than 6 million African Americans moved from the South. Often referred to as the "Great Migration," this mass movement of people led to the growth of black urban communities in New York, Chicago, Philadelphia, Detroit, Los Angeles, and other cities outside of the South. In 1910, about 90 percent of African Americans lived in the South, the large majority of them in rural areas. By the 1970s, only half of the African American population lived in the South, and less than a quarter lived in rural areas.[65]

The growth of new black urban centers during the first decades of the Great Migration led to an increase in political and social activism among African Americans trying to improve their living conditions and assert their rights as U.S. citizens. It also abetted the desire for new social identities distinct from mainstream American society's view of African Americans as the descendants of slaves and second-class citizens. In addition, the loss of familiar rural cultural norms and the demands of the new urban environment created, among many new migrants from the South, the need for a new vision of their place in history and their role in society. For many, Islam, with its multiethnic and multicultural history, offered such an alternative vision.[66]

The Emergence of African American Islamic Movements

In the early 1920s, visitors from other parts of the world began presenting Islam as a viable path for African Americans longing for a new social identity. In 1920, Muhammad Sadiq, an Indian missionary from the Ahmadiyya sect of Islam, took his message to Detroit, Chicago, and other cities with growing black populations. He became a harsh critic of racism in America and focused his efforts on African Americans.[67] Sadiq argued that Islam was a fundamental part of Africa's past that was taken from Africans when they were enslaved. He endorsed Black Nationalist movements, including Marcus Garvey's United Negro Improvement Association (UNIA), and he convinced a number of Marcus Garvey's followers to convert to Islam.[68] Two other prominent foreigners joined Sadiq's efforts: Sudanese-born Satti Majid and Egyptian-born Duse Mohamed Ali. Satti Majid founded a number of Muslim social welfare societies, including the Islamic Benevolent African Society and the Society of Africans in America, while taking his message to New York, Buffalo, Detroit, and Philadelphia.[69] His peer, Duse Mohamed Ali, spent 10 years lecturing throughout the United States and, in 1922, became head of the African Affairs department in Marcus Garvey's UNIA.[70]

As Muslim visitors from overseas introduced Islam to black America, African American converts to Islam established Muslim-based black activist movements. The first prominent example was Noble Drew Ali, founder of the first mass religious movement based on Islam in America. Born Timothy Drew in North Carolina, he migrated northward and established the Canaanite Temple in Newark in 1913.[71] He later renamed his organization the Moorish Science Temple of America and, in 1925, relocated his headquarters to Chicago.[72] Ali taught that Africans, including members of the African diaspora in America, were Moors, the descendants of an Asiatic Muslim people. He claimed to be the last of a long line of prophets and that his mission was to teach African Americans their true genealogy and true religion. By the late 1920s, Ali's movement had gained tens of thousands of members, with congregations in Detroit, Philadelphia, Pittsburg, Milwaukee, Cleveland, Baltimore, and other cities.[73]

As the Moorish Science Temple expanded, a schism emerged within its leadership. Friction reached a breaking point when Noble Drew Ali's business manager, Claude Green, declared himself Grand Sheikh and, with the aid of a faction within the movement, tried to take control of the movement. In March 1929, Greene was shot and stabbed to death. Police arrested Ali and several of his followers in connection with Green's murder. Ali was released on bail but died of unknown causes in July 1929.[74] Although it was divided among competing factions and splinter groups, the movement Ali founded persisted and continued to attract African Americans in the country's urban centers and, increasingly, in parts of the South.

A follower of Noble Drew Ali, Muhammad Ezaldeen, later developed his own set of teachings based on Islam and attracted a large African American following. After becoming associated with the Moorish Science Temple, Ezaldeen traveled to Egypt to study Islam more intensively. Upon his return to the United States, he taught a version of Islam that incorporated a belief that African Americans were the Arab Asiatic descendants of Ham, son of the biblical figure Noah. He claimed they could reclaim their Hamitic Arab identity through Islam. Between 1938 and 1941, he and about 140 followers founded an agricultural commune in rural New York State to create a self-sufficient community based on Islamic precepts. Shortly afterward, he founded Addeynu Allahe (Arabic for "the Religion of God") Universal Arabic Association, or AAUAA.[75]

In the summer of 1930, a year after the death of Noble Drew Ali, Wallace Fard Muhammad founded the Lost-Found Nation of Islam in the Wilderness of North America (later shortened to Nation of Islam).[76] Fard Muhammad first appeared as a public figure in Detroit, claiming to be a prophet. He taught that African Americans were members of the lost—and now found—ancient tribe of Shabazz, which lived in Mecca before being enslaved and taken into exile by white people centuries before. He claimed his mission was to teach African Americans about their preslave Muslim heritage and to prepare them for an approaching apocalyptic war with the white race.[77] Over a four-year period, Fard Muhammad gained about 8,000 followers in Detroit.[78] He was arrested for inciting violence through his teachings and, in May 1933, was forced to leave Detroit by the police. He found refuge in Chicago, but he disappeared the following year and was never seen in public again.[79]

After Fard Muhammad's disappearance, his most prominent disciple, Elijah Muhammad, became leader of the Nation of Islam. Born Elijah Poole in Georgia, he moved to Detroit as a young man and joined the Nation of Islam.[80] In 1932, he established a temple for the Nation of Islam in Chicago. From this base, Elijah Muhammad provided Fard Muhammad sanctuary until the latter's disappearance. Once the founder of the Nation of Islam left the scene, Elijah Muhammad moved the headquarters of the organization to Chicago and steadily expanded its membership in urban areas throughout the North and Midwest.[81] The Nation of Islam eventually operated 75 temples and claimed a million members across the United States.[82]

The Beginning of FBI Counterintelligence

In the early stages of the Great Migration, as African Americans were beginning to encounter and develop forms of liberation theology based on Islam, the federal government was developing advanced domestic intelligence and counter-espionage capabilities. In 1908, at President Theodore Roosevelt's instructions, the attorney general established an investigative division within the Department of Justice.[83] This division, given the title Bureau of Investigation the following year, steadily grew in size and authority over the next decade. In 1917, during World War I, the Bureau gained primary responsibility for countering acts of espionage and sabotage in the United States. At this time, the bureau launched its first nationwide domestic counter-espionage operations, conducting surveillance on dissidents and arresting people deemed subversive or suspected of being spies.[84]

After World War I, the Bureau of Investigation continued to expand its intelligence operations, and J. Edgar Hoover, a man who would later lead the organization for several decades, rose swiftly through the bureau's bureaucracy. In 1919, a group of anarchists attempted to assassinate several public officials, including members of Congress, Supreme Court Justice Oliver Wendell Holmes, and Attorney General Mitchell Palmer.[85] In response, Attorney General Palmer directed Hoover, who had joined the bureau just two years earlier, to coordinate efforts to round up subversive elements. Over the next several months, Hoover oversaw raids to detain anarchists, communists, and other radicals in New York, Chicago, Detroit, Cleveland, Pittsburgh, and a dozen other cities (the infamous "Palmer raids").[86] Five years later, in 1924, Hoover was appointed director of the bureau, an organization with 650 employees in Washington, D.C., and field offices in nine cities. By the end of the decade, under Hoover's leadership, the bureau expanded its presence to 30 field offices across the country.[87]

At this time, the Bureau of Investigation began to take note of African American Muslim groups. Noble Drew Ali taught his followers to remain loyal to the U.S. government, but many of them agitated publically for political change, especially in Chicago, attracting the attention of both local police and federal law enforcement.[88] In 1931, the bureau initiated its first clandestine surveillance operations against the Moorish Science Temple.[89] Over the next 10 years, the Nation of Islam also attracted attention. In 1932, Robert Harris, an apparently mentally unstable follower of Fard Muhammad, stabbed a boarder in his house in Detroit to death as part of a human-sacrifice ritual.[90] Five years later, police arrested Nation of Islam member Verlene Ali for allegedly preparing to sacrifice his wife and daughter.[91] Sociologist Erdmann Beynon added to concern about the group when he published a sensationalist article about the Nation of Islam called "The Voodoo Cult among Negro Migrants in Detroit" in 1938.[92] The following year, J. Edgar Hoover's agency, which had been renamed the Federal Bureau of Investigation in 1935, began surveillance of the Nation of Islam.[93]

Wartime Domestic Counterintelligence

During World War II, the FBI launched a broad initiative to assess the threat posed by African American dissident organizations, including black Muslim groups.[94] In 1942, the bureau opened an investigation called "Foreign-Inspired Agitation among the African Negroes," which mobilized 56 field offices to assess efforts by Germany and Japan to cause racial agitation among African Americans. The findings of this investigation formed the basis of the FBI's *Survey of Racial Conditions in the United States* (or RACON, for Racial Conditions), a 730-page report completed in September 1943.[95] This report created a profile of African American organizations with pro-Japanese sympathies and catalogued Muslim groups popular among African Americans.[96] After completing its initial report, the FBI continued surveillance activities for 18 months and gave the entire operation the code name "RACON."[97]

During this investigation, the FBI found no evidence of widespread collusion between African American Muslim organizations and Japanese provocateurs. However, concerns about such collusion, while exaggerated, were not manufactured. During World War II, pro-Japanese sympathies were prevalent in several Black Nationalist movements in the United States. The idea that a Japanese invasion of the United States would be a form of liberation for African Americans by fellow people of color became popular in some African American circles.[98] In the 1930s, shortly before the United States entered the war, Augustus Muhammad, an assistant minister to Elijah Muhammad in Chicago, left for Detroit to lead a group called Development of Our Own, which was an African American organization sympathetic to the Japanese cause.[99] The FBI identified several other pro-Japanese African American organizations operating during the war, including the Pacific Movement of the Eastern World, the Ethiopian Pacific Movement, and the Original Independent Benevolent Afro-Pacific Movement of the World.[100]

The FBI also identified the Moorish Science Temple and the Nation of Islam as being organizations with pro-Japanese sympathies. Based on these suspicions, the bureau investigated the Moorish Science Temple for wartime sedition in several cities extending from the Midwest to the South. In 1942, the FBI conducted raids on the homes of African American Muslims suspected of pro-Japanese sympathies in Detroit, Chicago, Milwaukee, and parts of New Jersey. Several members of the Moorish Science Temple were indicted for teaching that the Japanese were fighting a war of liberation for the Asiatic race. According to the group's ideology, this included African Americans.[101]

Further raising suspicion, several African American leaders and their followers refused to register for the draft to fight for a country that prevented them from exercising many of their basic rights as American citizens. In 1942, authorities arrested Elijah Muhammad and his son, Emmanuel. They were acquitted of sedition but were convicted of refusing to register for the draft and were sentenced to four years in prison. In addition, 70 other members of the Nation of Islam were arrested for refusing to register for the draft, along with 15 members of the Moorish Science Temple who refused to register.[102] To avoid arrest while protesting conscription, members of Muhammad Ezaldeen's AAUAA registered as conscientious objectors on the grounds that they could not eat food prepared by the military, and they could not be expected to fight against their own people (counting Japanese as fellow members of the "dark race").[103] In the end, 18 African Americans were convicted of sedition or conspiracy to commit sedition under the Espionage Act. About 200 others were convicted of refusing to register for the draft.[104]

Civil Rights Era Domestic Counterintelligence

In the years after World War II, the Cold War between the United States and the Soviet Union became a dominant security concern for the FBI. This was especially true for J. Edgar Hoover, who harbored animosity for communist and socialist activists dating back to his days working with Attorney General Mitchell Palmer during World War I. The emergence of the civil rights movement in the late 1950s, accompanied by the rise of the New Left and antiwar movement in the 1960s, added to Hoover's concerns about politically left-leaning activists and their potentially subversive influence on American society. To counter this threat, Hoover initiated a series of counterintelligence initiatives to disrupt and discredit leftist movements and their leaders. Expanding far beyond surveillance and criminal investigation, these counterintelligence programs (designated COINTELPROs by the FBI) were designed to sow friction and distrust within and between targeted organizations, ruin the public reputations of their leaders, and harass their members.

The first of these counterintelligence programs began in 1956 with an attack on the Communist Party USA and allied groups (COINTELPRO-CPUSA). As part of the initiative, the FBI sent anonymous hate mail to thousands of suspected communists and socialists in the United States, subjected them to tax audits by the Internal Revenue Service, and forged documents to encourage infighting among their leaders.[105] Over the course of the next 15 years, the FBI initiated 11 additional counterintelligence programs against activist groups and dissident organizations, including operations targeting the Socialist Workers Party (COINTELPRO-SWP) and antiwar groups and left-leaning activists (COINTELPRO-New Left).[106] At the instruction of President Lyndon Johnson, the FBI also launched a campaign against the Ku Klux Klan (COINTELPRO-White Hate Groups), the only counterintelligence program during this period directed at right-wing agitators.[107]

Long before the FBI launched these formal counterintelligence programs, the bureau conducted clandestine operations against African American civil rights leaders and organizations, beginning a pattern that would continue for decades. Since World War I, the FBI had spied on most prominent African American leaders. In 1941, it began investigating the National Association for the Advancement of Colored People, with a special focus on the organization's links to the Communist Party.[108] By the early 1960s, the FBI was engaged in attempts to undermine Martin Luther King Jr. and his organization, the Southern Christian Leadership Conference (SCLC). FBI agents conducted electronic surveillance of Martin Luther King Jr.'s office and hotel rooms while investigating SCLC employees and monitoring the organization's finances.[109]

The Nation of Islam, a target of FBI scrutiny since the 1930s, did not escape attention during these operations against African American leaders and organizations. In 1955, the FBI produced a brief on the Nation of Islam and distributed it to field offices across the country. The brief referred to the Nation of Islam and "the Muslim Cult of Islam" (abbreviated MCI) and described it as "an especially anti-American and violent cult."[110] The brief concluded that the "MCI is a fanatic Negro organization purporting to be motivated by the religious principles of Islam, but actually dedicated to the propagation of hatred against the white race ... The aims and purposes of the MCI are directed at the overthrow of our constitutional government, inasmuch as Cult members regard it as an instrument of the white race."[111]

Shortly after issuing this report, the FBI began wiretapping Elijah Muhammad's Chicago residence and, later, his second home in Arizona.[112] The FBI also launched a series of clandestine initiatives against the Nation of Islam, including electronic surveillance, planting negative stories in the media, and infiltrating the organization with informants.[113] As part of these efforts, the FBI briefed journalists on the Nation of Islam to present it as a danger to society and conducted a media campaign to discredit Nation of Islam founder Fard Muhammad in newspapers and popular newsmagazines.[114] The FBI also sent anonymous letters to Clara Muhammad, Elijah Muhammad's wife, exposing his many extramarital affairs.[115]

In 1965, the FBI produced another brief on the Nation of Islam for federal agents in the field. This brief claimed that Nation of Islam members, motivated by fanatical antiwhite and antigovernment beliefs, would likely seize upon the opportunity presented by a national emergency to endanger public safety and national security. The brief asserted, "The FBI must determine the identities, whereabouts, and activities of these individuals constituting a threat . . . and must develop sufficient information and evidence to sustain appropriate action against such individuals or to control their movements and activities in the event of a national emergency."[116] Two years later, in August 1967, Hoover issued a memorandum to 23 FBI field offices across the country, instructing agents to "expose, disrupt, misdirect, discredit, or otherwise neutralize the activities of black nationalist, hate-type organizations, their leadership, spokesmen, membership, and supporters."[117]

This 1967 memorandum formally initiated a new counterintelligence program, this time targeting groups designated by the FBI as Black Nationalist-Hate Groups (COINTELPRO-BNHG).[118] In his memorandum, Hoover specified several groups to target, including the Congress of Racial Equality, the Revolutionary Action Movement, the Student Nonviolent Coordinating Committee, and Martin Luther King Jr.'s Southern Christian Leadership Conference. Hoover also designated the Nation of Islam as a Black Nationalist hate group and singled out Elijah Muhammad as a danger to American society.[119] In 1968, George Moore, director of the FBI's newly created Racial Intelligence Section, issued a set of long-range goals to 41 field offices to carry out the counterintelligence program. These goals included preventing unification among specified African American groups, discrediting Black Nationalist leaders in the eyes of African Americans, and undermining their efforts to recruit youth.[120]

As part of this counterintelligence initiative, the FBI increased operations against the Nation of Islam. For the next three years, FBI agents continued to send anonymous letters about Elijah Muhammad's philandering to his family members and continued to use journalists to spread disinformation about the Nation of Islam in the news media.[121] The FBI also began sending anonymous letters to Elijah Muhammad accusing his ministers of malfeasance, while planting informants inside mosques to spread rumors about Nation of Islam members and leadership. More dangerously, the FBI promoted disinformation to encourage strife between Black Nationalist groups. Such tactics succeeded in fostering a series of violent confrontations in San Diego between the Black Panther Party and a group called the United Slaves, resulting in three known deaths. In at least six cities, the FBI attempted to cause similar conflict between the Black Panthers and the Nation of Islam, with limited success.[122]

In March 1971, three years after the FBI launched its coordinated counterintelligence initiative against African American organizations, a group of activists who called themselves the Citizens' Commission to Investigate the FBI broke into an FBI office in Media, Pennsylvania, and stole thousands of documents. Among these documents were detailed accounts of COINTELPRO activities. This break-in is the only known action by the group, whose members were never apprehended. Over the course of the next several months, they mailed batches of select documents to Congress, reporters, and groups targeted by the FBI. The news media reported widely on the revelations contained in the documents.[123] One month after the break-in, Hoover ordered an abrupt end to all COINTELPRO operations.[124]

The Growing Presence of Muslims in America: Islam as a Security Concern

At the height of the FBI's COINTELPRO activities, the United States entered a period of rapid ethnic, cultural, and religious diversification. In 1965, Congress passed the Immigration and Naturalization Act. This law eliminated the national-origins quota system created in 1924 and established two new priorities for U.S. immigration policy: reuniting families and encouraging individuals with desired occupational skills to immigrate to the United States.[125] With the passage of this act, immigrants came to the United States from across the world, altering the ethnic and religious demographics of the country over the course of the following decades. Immigration from Latin America experienced the most significant increase, but a large number of new arrivals also came from predominantly Muslim countries in Asia, particularly India, Pakistan, and Bangladesh.[126] Accompanying them was an influx of immigrants from the Middle East. In total, from 1960 to 1990, the number of immigrants from predominantly Muslim regions rose from roughly 135,000 to about 870,000—an increase of more than 600 percent.[127]

Alongside rising immigration, the United States experienced an influx of foreign visitors, both as consequence of and a contributing factor to accelerating globalization. As a result, tourists, business travelers, temporary workers (both legal and illegal), and foreign nationals visiting relatives in the United States steadily increased in numbers. During the second half of the 20th century, the number of visitors to the United States increased 100-fold, reaching 24 million visitors in 1997.[128] In addition, the number of foreign students attending American colleges and universities rose sharply. From 1971 to 2000, the number of student visas issued by the Department of State rose from 6,500 to 315,000. By 2003, more than half a million foreign nationals were studying in the United States.[129]

Muslims constituted a significant portion of the growing foreign student population in the United States. The number of students from the Middle East had been rising steadily since the end of World War II, growing from about 2,700 in 1948 to more than 13,500 in 1965.[130] In subsequent decades, the Middle East, particularly the oil-producing Persian Gulf states, remained a principal source of foreign students studying in America.[131] Students from India, a country with a minority Muslim population larger than the populations of most majority-Muslim nations, also contributed to this rise in foreign students. By the end of the first decade of the 21st century, the United States was host to nearly 40,000 students from the Middle East and North Africa; about 13,000 from the predominantly Muslim Southeast Asian countries of Malaysia and Indonesia, and more than 112,000 from the South Asian countries of India, Pakistan, and Bangladesh.[132]

This growth and diversification of the Muslim population in America increased the range of cultural influences, attitudes, and interests—including political and social causes—of Muslims in the country. For federal authorities and some segments of U.S. society, this development created perceptions of heightened risk to national security. Such perceptions were enhanced by concerns that many Muslims in the country, influenced by events overseas, might be pursuing causes contrary to U.S. interests.

Containing Palestinian Activism

In September 1972, eight militants from a group called Black September, a faction of the Palestine Liberation Organization, infiltrated Olympic Village in Munich during the Olympic Games. They then stormed the complex housing the Israeli delegation to the games, killing 2 Israelis and taking 11 members of the delegation hostage. The next day, all of the hostages, along with five of the hostage takers and one German police officer, died in a failed German rescue operation. News media in the United States and around the world covered the terrorist attack and reported on the day-long negotiations between the members of Black September and German authorities. News of the violent climax, including the deaths of nine Israelis who were either shot to death or burned alive when one of the terrorists ignited the helicopter they were in with a grenade, was broadcast to audiences globally.[133]

Following this act of terrorism, President Richard Nixon initiated Operation Bolder to disrupt pro-Palestinian activism in the United States and, more broadly, to prevent Arab foreign nationals from engaging in subversive activities in the country. During this three-year operation, the FBI compiled dossiers on politically active Arab Americans, especially those engaged in Palestinian causes, and engaged in wiretapping and other surveillance measures to monitor their activities.[134] In October 1972, FBI agents raided the offices of several Palestinian American groups across the country. They also broke into the office of the Arab Education League in Dallas and stole a membership list from the office safe. The FBI used this list to identify suspected agents of the Palestine Liberation Organization's Fatah faction and forced them out of the country.[135] In addition, immigration officials, aided by the CIA and the FBI, screened all Arab foreign nationals applying for visas to enter the United States.[136] Several dozen of the foreign Arab nationals who were already in the country were deported for visa violations.[137]

Countering the Threat from Iran

Shortly after President Nixon initiated Operation Bolder, another crisis that originated overseas heightened security concerns in the United States. Beginning in early 1978 and escalating throughout the year, a series of demonstrations and violent protests in Iran threatened the regime of Shah Mohammad Reza Pahlavi, a longtime U.S. ally. By the summer of that year, violence quickly spread across much of the country. The Shah left Iran in January 1979, later entering the United States to receive medical treatment for lymphatic cancer. In his absence, Iranian religious leader Ayatollah Ruhollah Khomeini, who had lived in exile for more than 10 years, returned to Iran and assumed leadership of the unfolding revolution. Following a national referendum in April, revolutionary forces declared the creation of the Islamic Republic of Iran with a theocratic government led by Khomeini.[138]

In November 1979, as tensions between the new Iranian regime and the United States escalated, an Iranian crowd stormed the U.S. embassy in Tehran and captured several dozen American diplomats and embassy employees. The Iranians freed women, non-Americans, and African American employees of the embassy, but they kept 52 of the Americans hostage for more than a year. Tensions rose higher after an aborted rescue operation by the U.S. military became public in April 1980. Throughout the 444-day hostage crisis, nightly television news coverage and intensive reporting in print media about the U.S.-Iranian standoff reached audiences across America. In January 1981, after lengthy negotiations, an oil embargo imposed on Iran by the United States, a U.S. promise to release $8 billion in frozen Iranian assets, and the invasion of Iranian territory by the Iraqi military, Iran released all 52 U.S. hostages.[139]

Fearing possible pro-Iranian espionage, sabotage, or terrorist attacks in the United States during the hostage crisis, President Jimmy Carter ordered his attorney general to launch the Iranian Control Program, an initiative to screen Iranian students across the United States. This initiative required all Iranian nationals in the country on student visas to register with the Immigration and Naturalization Service by December 1979.[140] Each student was required to provide proof of residence, evidence of full-time school enrollment, and a passport with a valid visa. At that time, Iranian students in America, numbering almost 57,000, constituted the largest group of foreign students in the country.[141] During this initiative, more than 3,000 Iranian nationals were ordered to leave the country, although only 445 departures were actually verified.[142]

Countering a Diverse Terrorist Threat

Shortly after the release of American hostages from Iran, the threat of terrorism against Americans escalated in the Middle East. In April 1983, a suicide bomber drove a truck loaded with 2,000 pounds of explosives into the U.S. embassy in Beirut, Lebanon, killing nearly 60 Lebanese and Americans.[143] Five months later, suicide bombers attacked barracks housing U.S. Marines and French paratroopers, who were stationed in Beirut as part of multinational forces aiding the Lebanese government during the Lebanese civil war. The attacks on the barracks killed 241

Americans and 58 French military personnel.[144] These suicide attacks accompanied the beginning of a decade-long hostage-taking crisis in Lebanon, during which militants kidnapped dozens of Westerners, including several Americans.[145]

Along with attacks in Lebanon, terrorists active in the Middle East and further north in the Mediterranean region struck U.S. targets during the 1980s. Militants from different terrorist organizations bombed the U.S. embassy in Kuwait in late 1983, killed U.S. Navy Seaman Robert Dean Stethem onboard a hijacked TWA airliner in 1984, and executed American passenger Leon Klinghoffer aboard the hijacked cruise ship *Achille Lauro* in 1986.[146] Two years later, Libyan operatives placed a bomb aboard Pan American flight 103, en route to New York from London. The bombing caused the aircraft to explode over Lockerbie, Scotland, killing 11 people on the ground and all 259 people aboard, including 189 Americans. It was the deadliest terrorist attack against U.S. civilians until the terrorist attacks of 9/11.[147]

During the last decade of the 20th century, fears that such acts of terrorism would reach American shores rose steadily, beginning with U.S. military intervention in the Persian Gulf. In August 1990, the Iraqi regime of Saddam Hussein invaded neighboring Kuwait, seizing the country's extensive oil reserves. In response, the United States deployed more than 500,000 military personnel to Saudi Arabia to prevent a further Iraqi incursion across the Saudi border. In January of the following year, the United States led a multinational military coalition to expel Iraqi forces from Kuwait. During the same month, the administration of President George H. W. Bush imposed special registration requirements for certain foreign visitors entering the United States. Fearing that either Iraqi agents or individuals who opposed U.S. intervention in the Middle East might enter the country to commit terrorist acts, Attorney General Richard Thornburg required that all temporary (nonimmigrant) visitors bearing Iraqi or Kuwaiti travel documents be registered, fingerprinted, and photographed at their point of arrival to U.S. territory. This policy began a series of port-of-entry registration requirements employed throughout the 1990s, aimed exclusively at visitors from predominantly Muslim countries.[148]

In early 1993, two unconnected acts of terrorism by Muslim militants heightened fears of Islamic extremists conducting operations on American soil. In January, Pakistani immigrant Mir Aimal Kansi fired on cars entering CIA headquarters in Langley, Virginia, during the morning rush hour. Using an AK-47 semiautomatic rifle, he killed two people and wounded three. The following month, a diverse network of extremists, comprising U.S. citizens and foreign nationals, detonated a truck bomb beneath the World Trade Center in New York, killing 6 people and injuring more than 1,000.[149] Some members of the terrorist network that carried out this first bombing of the World Trade Center, almost a decade before 9/11, went on to develop a second plot to destroy targets throughout the New York City metropolitan area. Authorities discovered their plot and arrested members of the network before they could launch their attacks.[150]

Later in 1993, the administration of President Bill Clinton applied port-of-entry registration requirements for a growing list of foreign visitors considered to pose a potential risk to U.S. national security. That year, Attorney General Janet Reno renewed the special registration for nonimmigrant visitors with Iraqi passports. She also extended this requirement to visitors from Sudan.[151] The inclusion of Sudanese visitors stemmed from concern about Sudan's support for international terrorist groups, including al-Qaeda. Two years earlier, at the invitation of the ruling Sudanese National Islamic Front, Osama bin Laden had taken up residence in Sudan. From this new base of operation, he established training camps for militants who wanted to aid Muslim causes around the world, including Muslim-based insurgencies from Bosnia in southern Europe to the Philippines in Southeast Asia.[152] Bin Laden also condemned the United States for intervening in the Middle East and called for attacks on U.S. forces in the region.[153]

In 1996, Attorney General Reno expanded special registration measures to include visitors with Iranian and Libyan passports.[154] This expansion of registration requirements occurred as U.S. relations with both Iran and Libya, already sharply negative, deteriorated further. Concerned that both countries were trying to obtain weapons of mass destruction or the ability to manufacture them, the United States led international efforts to curtail their ability to do so. In addition, the United States sought to counter Iranian and Libyan support for international terrorist activity. These efforts led, in July 1996, to Congressional passage of the Iran and Libya Sanctions Act. This act required the president to impose economic sanctions on foreign companies that invest $40 million or more annually in either country.[155] As tensions rose following the passage of the sanctions law, the attorney general imposed port-of-entry registration requirements on nonimmigrant visitors from Iran and Libya, hoping to prevent potential acts of espionage or terrorism within the United States.[156]

As U.S. officials worked to contain the potential threat from Libya and Iran, Osama bin Laden issued a new challenge to the United States from Afghanistan, where he had reestablished a base of operation after being expelled from Sudan in 1996. In February 1998, he led a coalition of militants in urging Muslims anywhere in the world to kill Americans wherever and whenever they could. Six months later, al-Qaeda initiated a global terrorist campaign against the United States. In August 1998, al-Qaeda operatives conducted suicide bombings against the U.S. embassies in Nairobi, Kenya, and Dar-es-Salaam, Tanzania. Together, the explosions killed 224 people and injured nearly 5,000. In December of the following year, U.S. customs officers arrested Ahmed Ressam, an Algerian national residing in Canada, as he transported explosives across the U.S.-Canadian border. Ressam, who had received training at an al-Qaeda training camp in Afghanistan, planned to bomb a terminal at Los Angeles International Airport on New Year's Eve. Almost a year after Ressam's capture, al-Qaeda launched a suicide attack via boat, killing 17 sailors aboard the USS *Cole*, a navy destroyer making a port call at Aden, Yemen.[157]

By the end of the 20th century, Americans had a long tradition of viewing Islam and Muslims as a potential threat. Such concerns remained latent through most of U.S. history, generally rising to the forefront of public consideration and U.S. policy formulation only during times of real or perceived crisis. However, they exercised growing influence over policy makers and the public in the final decades of the century. Throughout the 1980s and 1990s, the growth of Islamic extremism in the Middle East and elsewhere in the Muslim world, underlined by terrorist attacks and plots against the United States, steadily strengthened American perceptions of Islam as a security issue. This trend would accelerate sharply in the first years of the next century.

CHAPTER 2

9/11 and the New Homeland Security Paradigm

The terrorist attacks of 9/11 moved both terrorism and Islamic extremism to the forefront of American fears about threats abroad and, most importantly, security at home. In one of the boldest acts of terrorism in modern history, al-Qaeda operatives turned four hijacked commercial airliners into weapons of immense destruction. The attack on the World Trade Center caused the collapse of both Twin Towers and destroyed much of the surrounding neighborhood in Lower Manhattan, killing more than 2,700 people. The attack on the Pentagon destroyed a section of the building and killed more than 180 people. The crash of United Airlines Flight 93 in western Pennsylvania, apparently caused deliberately by the hijackers when passengers and crew tried to retake control of the aircraft, killed all 44 people aboard. With nearly 3,000 people killed in the worst terrorist attack in American history, public fear, anger, and demand for action—as well as a swift and sweeping response from the U.S. government—were inevitable.

The Homeland Security Enterprise

Three days after 9/11, Congress passed the Authorization for the Use of Military Force, authorizing the president to use "all necessary and appropriate force against nations, organizations, or persons he determines planed, authorized, committed, or aided the terrorist attacks."[1] This unprecedented legislation empowered the president to use military force against unspecified nations and nonstate actors. A month after the law's passage, the United States initiated military action against al-Qaeda and the Taliban in Afghanistan, beginning what would become America's longest war. A year later, Congress passed a resolution authorizing the use of force against Iraq, in part to prevent weapons of mass destruction, falsely believed to be held by the Saddam Hussein regime, from falling into the hands of terrorists. In March 2003, the U.S. military launched operations in Iraq, beginning a second war that would last almost a decade.

As the United States engaged enemies abroad, the federal government also began a massive reorganization to secure U.S. borders and to prevent terrorist attacks on American soil. In November 2001, Congress voted to establish the Transportation Security Administration (TSA) within the Department of Transportation. With this act, TSA assumed responsibility for airport screening (previously performed by private security firms contracted by the airlines), expanded airport checkpoints and random canine-assisted searches, and placed armed air marshals on thousands of international and domestic flights.[2] In addition to civil aviation security, TSA gained responsibility for securing hundreds of ports and tunnels, thousands of train stations and public bridges, thousands of miles of public waterways, and millions of public roads across the United States.[3]

One year later, in November 2002, Congress passed the Homeland Security Act, establishing the Department of Homeland Security (DHS). The creation of this new department initiated the largest federal government reorganization since the creation of the Department of Defense under President Truman.[4] Over the next few years, nearly a quarter of a million federal employees were assigned to DHS, as it absorbed 22 existing federal agencies and hired thousands of new employees. Among the agencies transferred to DHS were the newly created TSA, the U.S. Secret Service, the Federal Protective Service, the Federal Emergency Management Agency, and the U.S. Coast Guard. In addition, DHS took charge of immigration enforcement and border protection. This restructuring placed nearly half of all federal law enforcement officers under DHS command, while giving the new department responsibility for preventing terrorist attacks, coordinating emergency preparedness and response, securing the nation's transportation system, protecting critical infrastructure and cyberspace, and securing 7,000 miles of land borders and 95,000 miles of maritime borders.[5]

The urgent need to strengthen the federal government's counterterrorism capabilities extended to the intelligence community, which received withering criticism for its failure to detect al-Qaeda's plans before 9/11.

The position of director of national intelligence was created to integrate foreign and domestic intelligence from the nation's multiple intelligence agencies, while the National Counterterrorism Center was created to integrate and analyze terrorism-related intelligence.[6] In addition, the Federal Bureau of Investigation was reorganized as a dual intelligence and law enforcement agency, reporting to both the attorney general and the new director of national intelligence. The FBI's National Security Branch, created in 2005, assumed primary responsibility for domestic counterterrorism and intelligence activities, as the FBI doubled the number of agents it deployed in the field.[7]

On top of these changes, the U.S. government created new agencies and offices or repurposed existing ones to work on counterterrorism and intelligence. These government agencies and offices ranged in size from the massive Department of Homeland Security to small intelligence teams within existing agencies. An investigation by reporters at the *Washington Post* revealed that, in the decade after 9/11, more than 1,000 federal government entities and nearly 2,000 private companies contracted by the government engaged in counterterrorism or intelligence work requiring top-secret security clearance.[8] Adjustments and additions to these security structures continued for years. In 2012, the Department of State elevated its office for coordinating counterterrorism activities to a larger Bureau of Counterterrorism.[9] Two years later, the director of national intelligence announced the creation of the National Counterintelligence and Security Center to better integrate U.S. counterintelligence and security operations.[10]

As America's homeland security enterprise expanded, the post-9/11 perception of American vulnerability led policy makers to adopt a new approach to counterterrorism, with fewer restrictions and less deference to civil rights. Six weeks after the attacks, Congress passed the USA PATRIOT Act, an acronym for the awkwardly named Uniting and Strengthening America by Providing Appropriate Tools Required to Intercept and Obstruct Terrorism Act (henceforth, the Patriot Act). Among the many contentious provisions of the law, the Patriot Act allowed expanded use of "roving wiretaps" to monitor the communications of targeted individuals as they changed locations or communications devices, while easing restrictions on "trap and trace" orders and the use of "pen registers" to allow authorities to trace the sources and destinations of phone calls, e-mails, and other electronic communications. The law also allowed federal authorities to search private residences without notifying the owners or occupants for up to 90 days after the search (so-called sneak-and-peak searches).[11]

The Patriot Act further expanded the scope of federal surveillance through a provision on National Security Letters. Laws passed before 2001 allowed federal authorities, under restricted circumstances, to issue National Security Letters to private companies. These letters required private companies to provide investigators with certain customer records, such as telephone records, credit records, and financial business records. The Patriot Act expanded this power, allowing the FBI to issue such letters without obtaining search warrants in cases related to international terrorism. Under the new law, organizations that received National Security Letters were required to provide the information without informing the suspect under investigation. The use of such letters escalated sharply after 9/11. In 2000, the FBI issued 8,500 National Security Letters. In 2006, five years after the passage of the Patriot Act, the FBI issued almost 50,000 National Security Letters.[12]

Alongside this enhanced authority for domestic spying, the federal government initiated specific programs to capture information on U.S. citizens and legal residents. Two such initiatives—the Terrorism Information and Prevention System (TIPS) and the Total Information Awareness (TIA) Program—surpassed the level of intrusion that Congress or the public would tolerate, despite heightened fear of terrorism. The TIPS program sought to recruit millions of American workers in unique positions, due to the nature of their jobs, to report on suspicious activities of their fellow citizens. The TIA Program attempted to erect a broad electronic data-mining system operated by the Defense Advanced Research Projects Agency, an agency within the Department of Defense. Congress ended both programs within a year of their start dates.[13]

In contrast to these misfires, other domestic surveillance programs persisted for years after 9/11. The National Security Agency (NSA) began initiatives shortly after 9/11 to capture phone conversations and Internet traffic, without warrants or court orders, between persons in the United States and people abroad suspected of having ties to terrorist organizations. The NSA also launched programs to collect telephone and Internet metadata—such as cell phone identification signatures, numbers dialed, length of conversations, e-mail addresses, and Web sites visited—generated by Americans across the United States.[14] At the same time, the FBI began collecting profiles of people identified by the Nationwide Suspicious Activities Reporting Initiative, a joint DHS-FBI program, and then storing these profiles in the FBI's new Guardian database. Through this system, the FBI built a large repository of individuals who, although not accused of committing crimes, were suspected of engaging in suspicious behavior, possibly related to terrorism. Within ten years after 9/11, the Guardian database held profiles of more than 160,000 individuals.[15]

Parallel to the collection of data on millions of U.S. citizens, the federal government launched initiatives to monitor foreign students and visitors in the United States. In January 2003, DHS and the Department of State jointly launched the Student and Exchange Visitor System (SEVIS), replacing an earlier system operated by immigration authorities to track foreign visitors. Through this upgraded system, the federal government began monitoring all foreigners participating in approved U.S. education or exchange programs and tracking their U.S. addresses, their enrollment, and their continued participation in educational programs.[16] One year later, DHS deployed U.S. Visitor and Immigration Status Indicator Technology (US-VISIT) at airports and seaports around the country. Through this initiative, DHS began recording the biometric identifiers (digital fingerprints and photographs) of foreign nationals entering the United States and checking these identifiers against lists of known criminals and suspected terrorists.[17]

Homeland Security and Muslims in America

The scale and reach of the post-9/11 homeland security enterprise in the United States, and Americans' willingness to tolerate increased intrusion into their private lives, underlined the shift in perceptions about the vulnerability of American society. Terrorism was now seen as the principal threat to the United States, and Islamic extremism was the primary source of that threat. Policies implemented to protect the homeland after 9/11 reflected this thinking, with consequences, sometimes dire, for thousands of Muslims in America, including U.S. citizens, legal residents, students, visitors, and especially foreign nationals residing in the country illegally.

Arrest and Detention

Among the most immediate and sweeping initiatives directed at Muslims in the United States was the federal government's broad policy of arrest and detention of people with even the most tenuous potential connection to the 9/11 attacks. Arrests began immediately after 9/11 as the FBI, in cooperation with other law enforcement agencies, initiated the largest criminal investigation in U.S. history. This investigation, code-named PENTTBOM (short for Pentagon-Twin Towers-Bombing), included the arrest and questioning of hundreds of individuals who authorities determined might have been involved in, or had knowledge of, the terrorist attacks. Within two months of 9/11, authorities arrested more than 1,200 U.S. citizens and foreign nationals. The exact number remains unknown; the Department of Justice stopped updating the number of PENTTBOM arrests after two months because tracking the statistics of those arrested across the country became too daunting.[18]

Many of those arrested were questioned and released. More than 700 others, all of them Muslim foreign nationals residing illegally in the United States, were designated by the FBI as being of special interest to the PENTTBOM investigation and detained pending further scrutiny, some for prolonged periods of time. In almost all cases, the apparent links between the detained individual and terrorism were vague, tenuous, or nonexistent. According to an internal review released in 2003 by the Department of Justice, "Many of the persons arrested as part of the PENTTBOM investigation were aliens unlawfully present in the United States either because they entered this country illegally or because they entered legally but remained after their authorization to do so had expired. *It is unlikely that most if not all of the individuals arrested would have been pursued by law enforcement authorities for these immigration violations but for the PENTTBOM investigation*"[19] (emphasis added). Nevertheless, during the 11 months following 9/11, the FBI determined that 762 Muslim foreign nationals guilty of immigration violations should be detained as potential terrorists pending further investigation.[20]

Lacking sufficient legal basis (probable cause) to incarcerate most of these special-interest detainees for terrorism-related offenses, federal officials co-opted immigration laws to keep the individuals in custody. Immigration authorities arrested many of these suspects, often with an FBI agent present, and sent most to immigration detention facilities.[21] Under normal circumstances, with approximately 11 million illegal aliens residing in the United States, an individual arrested for a minor immigration violation would be released on bond, and most illegal aliens would be allowed to leave the country voluntarily to avoid formal deportation orders. In addition, federal law requires that any noncitizen who enters the country legally but fails to maintain legal immigration status be deported within 90 days of a removal order.[22] In the case of special-interest detainees, however, authorities practiced an unofficial "hold until cleared" policy for several months, requiring that no detainee be released, deported, or allowed to leave the country before being cleared by the FBI of any connection to terrorism.[23] The Department of Justice also kept the identities and locations of special-interest detainees secret and ordered all immigration hearings for them to be closed, with family members and members of the press barred from attending.[24]

While immigration authorities retained custody of the majority of special-interest detainees, the FBI designated 184 of them as being "of high interest" to the PENTTBOM investigation. These high-interest detainees were placed in high-security federal prisons around the country. The largest contingent, 84 men arrested in the New York City area, was transferred to the Metropolitan Detention Center in Brooklyn. Detainees held at this facility faced a pattern of abuse by corrections officers. An investigation by the inspector general at the Department of Justice found that Muslim foreign nationals held at the facility during the PENTTBOM investigation were subjected to racial slurs and threats, unnecessary strip searches, excessive use of handcuffs and leg irons, and 23-hour lockdowns in solitary confinement. Some were slammed into walls and otherwise physically abused by corrections staff.[25]

For all special-interest detainees, the average length of time to be cleared of links to terrorism was 80 days, with 18 cases requiring more than 6 months and one case requiring more than 8 months.[26] In the end, this policy resulted in the deportation of hundreds of Muslim foreign nationals for immigration violations but resulted in no terrorism-related charges.[27] In one tragic case, the FBI arrested Muhammed Rafiq Butt, a Pakistani man who had overstayed his visa. FBI agents soon determined that he was of no interest to the PENTTBOM investigation and transferred him to immigration authorities, who then confined him to a county jail in New Jersey. During a standard deportation hearing, Butt agreed to leave the country without contest. However, after being held in custody for 30 days, Butt died in jail from a congenital heart defect before departing for his native Pakistan.[28]

In January 2002, while the PENTTBOM investigation continued, the Department of Justice initiated the Absconder Apprehension Initiative, a more targeted program to detain foreign nationals residing illegally in the country. This program directed immigration authorities, the FBI, and the U.S. Marshals Service to detain, question, and deport approximately 314,000 fugitive aliens who had been ordered deported previously but had failed to comply with removal orders. Immigration authorities forwarded the names of these fugitive aliens (known as absconders) to the FBI's National Crime Information Center to facilitate this multiagency operation. Although the large majority of absconders were from Latin America, the Department of Justice ordered law enforcement officials to focus on 6,000 individuals from predominantly Muslim countries.[29]

The desire to arrest and deport absconders, foreign nationals who had already been ordered to leave the country, is understandable even in times of relative calm. At a time of widespread fear that al-Qaeda cells might be preparing to launch attacks in the United States, the presence of thousands of absconders in the country elevated the desire to remove them or at least account for them. Their presence, along with that of several million other foreign nationals in the country illegally, unquestionably made the jobs of law enforcement and security professionals more difficult. However, these concerns should be weighed against the opportunity costs of diverting manpower and resources required to make tracking down absconders a priority without sufficient intelligence to indicate that such a strategy would enhance security. Moreover, by giving priority to the arrest and questioning of Muslim absconders, the federal government created a separate class of illegal immigrants, based on religious and ethnic profiling. This policy set a risky precedent, potentially undermining the U.S. commitment to equal treatment under the law.

In the end, neither special-interest detentions nor the Absconder Apprehension Initiative yielded significant counterterrorism benefits, and no terrorists were discovered through either program. Nevertheless, similar polices followed. In March 2003, the U.S. government launched Operation Liberty Shield, a nationwide multiagency initiative to guard against terrorist attacks as U.S. forces prepared for the invasion of Iraq.[30] As part of this operation, DHS ordered the automatic detention of asylum seekers from 33 designated countries in which authorities believed al-Qaeda to be active. All of these designated countries had large Muslim populations. Under normal circumstances, people seeking political asylum are screened and, if they meet certain criteria (such as having family or other ties to the community) are released while their asylum requests are evaluated. Under Operation Liberty Shield, asylum seekers from the designated countries were to be detained for the duration of their asylum proceedings, estimated by DHS officials to last six months or more. Authorities terminated this detention requirement shortly after it began, possibly due to protests from human rights groups and the limited efficacy of such detention policies.[31]

The following year, the federal government launched another initiative to apprehend foreign nationals residing illegally in the United States. From May 2004 to February 2005, immigration authorities spearheaded Operation Front Line, an initiative to disrupt potential terrorist plots timed to coincide with the 2004 presidential election and 2005 presidential inauguration. This operation targeted more than 2,500 illegal aliens as potential national security threats. More than three-quarters of these targeted individuals were from Muslim-majority countries.[32] By the conclusion of the operation, authorities had arrested 504 people. Most of those arrested were charged with minor immigration violations; none was charged with a terrorism-related offense.[33]

Alongside initiatives targeting Muslim foreign nationals in the country illegally, U.S. counterterrorism strategy after 9/11 relied on the long-standing material witness statute to detain suspected terrorists, including U.S. citizens. The material witness statute, passed in 1984 to aid the prosecution of organized crime leaders, allows authorities to detain a witness who has information relevant to a criminal case to ensure that the witness does not flee before testifying in court. Similar to the use of immigration law to incarcerate individuals without probable cause, authorities co-opted the material witness statute as a tool to detain suspects for further investigation, even in the absence of evidence that the suspects had committed or witnessed criminal activities.[34] Use of the material witness statute for this purpose violates the spirit—if not the letter—of the law. As stated by federal judge Gerard Lynch, "A material witness warrant secures a witness's presence at trial or grand jury proceeding. It does not authorize a person's arrest and prolonged detention for purposes of investigative interrogation."[35]

Nevertheless, after 9/11, federal authorities began using material witness warrants liberally as a means of preventive detention in terrorism-related investigations. By 2005, according to a report issued by Human Rights Watch, at least 70 men living in the United States (all but one of them Muslim) were detained on material witness warrants in connection with terrorism-related investigations. Because authorities did not charge them with criminal offenses, these material witness detainees were not informed of their right to remain silent, and most were interrogated without an attorney present. One-third of the detainees were held for at least two months, and some were held for more than six months, including two Indian nationals who were detained for more than a year. Of these 70 material witness detainees, 17 were U.S. citizens. The government ultimately charged 29 of these detainees with crimes, but only nine charges were related to terrorism. The rest were released or deported for immigration violations.[36]

Two stark examples of how federal authorities used the material witness statute as a tool for preventive detention involved two Muslim men, Abdullah al-Kidd and Brandon Mayfield, both U.S. citizens. In the case of al-Kidd, authorities suspected him of aiding suspected terrorist Sami Omar al-Hussayen, a doctoral student from Saudi Arabia, studying at the University of Idaho. In March 2003, FBI agents arrested al-Kidd using handcuffs and shackles as he prepared to board a flight to Saudi Arabia, where he planed to study Arabic.[37] Rather than charging al-Kidd with a crime, authorities claimed he had information essential to the prosecution of al-Hussayen, whom they accused of providing material support to terrorists. After holding al-Kidd for more than 2 weeks in three different high-security prisons, during which time he was repeatedly strip-searched, authorities placed al-Kidd on supervised release until al-Hussayen's trial 14 months later. Prosecutors never called al-Kidd to testify at the trial, which ended in al-Hussayen's acquittal.[38]

Similarly, in May 2004, the FBI executed a material witness warrant against Brandon Mayfield, a retired U.S. Army officer living in Oregon. The FBI suspected Mayfield of involvement in the March 2004 bombing of commuter trains in the Spanish capital of Madrid, which killed 191 people and injured nearly 2,000. Authorities apparently drew erroneous conclusions about Mayfield's involvement in the attack from the faulty reading of fingerprints found at the scene of the bombing.[39] After failing to establish probable cause to charge Mayfield, despite more than a month of wiretapping his home and covertly searching his home and office, the FBI arrested him as a material witness. Authorities held Mayfield in solitary confinement for two weeks while they continued their investigation, releasing him only after Spanish investigators matched the fingerprints found at the scene of the attack to another suspect. Mayfield later won a $2 million settlement from the U.S. government and a formal letter of apology.[40]

Surveillance and Monitoring

Alongside new detention policies and procedures, federal authorities initiated a series of measures to track and question Muslim foreign nationals in the United States, based largely on their religion and ethnicity. During the first several weeks after 9/11, the Department of Justice worked with immigration officials to compile a list of approximately 8,000 foreign nationals, currently visiting or residing temporarily in the United States, who authorities believed might possess information about terrorist activities. This list comprised individuals whose demographic and visa information was similar to that of the 9/11 hijackers, such as age, gender, passport-issuing country, date of entry into the United States, and type of visa.[41] With about two dozen exceptions, all individuals named on the list were legally present in the United States, unlike absconders or special-interest detainees arrested in connection with the PENTTBOM investigation.

In November 2001, Attorney General John Ashcroft initiated a multiagency effort to interview certain individuals named on this list of foreign nationals. For the next year and a half, the FBI conducted thousands of interviews in cooperation with other federal law enforcement agencies, such as the Drug Enforcement Administration and the U.S. Secret Service, as well as local police departments across the country. Because of manpower shortages within the FBI, due largely to the ongoing PENTTBOM investigation, employees of the Internal Revenue Service and even the U.S. Postal Service were also dispatched to conduct interviews. Launched in two phases, this program targeted nearly 5,000 individuals for interviews beginning at the end of 2001 and about 3,000 individuals beginning in March 2002. All the subjects of these interviews were males between the ages of 16 and 33. All were from predominantly Muslim countries.[42]

These interviews were designed as information-gathering sessions, not criminal investigations. Nevertheless, during the first few months of the interview process, authorities arrested nearly 20 people after interviewing them, 3 on criminal charges unrelated to terrorism and the rest for immigration violations. The interviews were also officially voluntary, with subjects allowed to refuse to answer certain questions or to decline participation altogether. However, an evaluation by the Government Accountability Office found that a large number of those interviewed did not perceive the process as voluntary. Concerned that they might be denied visa-extension requests or permanent resident status, many felt compelled to comply with interview requests, and many participated with attorneys or immigrant-rights advocates present to advise them.[43]

During subsequent years, the FBI launched several other interview initiatives targeting Muslims in the United States. As the initial effort to question foreign nationals was ongoing, the FBI launched an interview program aimed at Iraqi Americans and Iraqi immigrants. This second program, codenamed Operation Darkening Clouds, began in March 2003, at the outset of U.S. combat operations in Iraq. Over the next several months, FBI agents across the country interviewed approximately 11,000 people of Iraqi origin to assess the risk of a terrorist attack and other forms of retaliation against the United States in response to the invasion of Iraq.[44] No arrests associated with this operation were disclosed to the public.[45]

In May 2004, the FBI spearheaded another large-scale initiative to interview Muslims in the United States. Roughly coinciding with efforts to detain illegal aliens under Operation Front Line, this interview initiative was designed to gather intelligence about potential terrorist attacks during the Democratic and Republican National Conventions in the summer of 2004 and during the presidential election in November.[46] Once again, law enforcement authorities sought interviews with people across the country based largely on their ethnicity and religion. Although the FBI claimed this round of interviews would be based on solid intelligence or investigative leads rather than demographic data, the program focused specifically on Muslim Americans and Muslim foreign nationals residing legally in the United States.[47]

Eight years later, the FBI launched yet another interview initiative directed almost exclusively at Muslims. In April 2011, as U.S. and allied forces began an air campaign in Libya to aid rebels seeking the overthrow of the regime of Muammar el-Qaddafi, FBI agents began interviewing Libyans residing in the United States to uncover any spies working for the el-Qaddafi regime or any terrorists affiliated with extremist groups in Libya. Over the course of this program, the FBI interviewed more than 800 Libyan students, visitors, immigrants, and other people living permanently or temporarily in the country.[48]

Alongside these interview initiatives, the attorney general announced a program, beginning in September 2002, to register nonimmigrant visitors deemed to pose a potential security risk to the United States. Called the National Security Entry-Exit Registration System (NSEERS), this initiative imposed a special-registration requirement on visitors with temporary visas from 25 countries. All countries on the NSEERS list had predominantly Muslim populations, with the exception of Eritrea, which is roughly evenly divided between Christians and Muslims, and North Korea, a country from which few if any visitors were expected.[49]

Upon arriving in the United States, all male visitors from these countries who were 16 years of age or older were photographed, fingerprinted, and interviewed by immigration officials. After staying in the country for a month, they were required to report to immigration authorities within 10 days and provide proof of compliance with their visa restrictions. For the remainder of their stay in the United States, those required to participate in the special registration program had to notify authorities of any change of address, report to an immigration office upon request, and notify officials of their departure from the country. Willful failure to comply with the special registration requirements was considered a failure to maintain legal visa status, which constituted grounds for deportation.[50]

In addition to tracking targeted foreign visitors upon their arrival in the United States, the NSEERS program established a call-in system for foreign visitors who met the NSEERS criteria but were already in the country. This call-in system required targeted foreign nationals to register at a designated immigration office and submit to being fingerprinted, photographed, and interviewed. From November 2002 to April 2003, more than 80,000 men from Muslim-majority countries participated in this call-in system. Authorities determined that approximately 13,500 of these visitors were outside of legal visa status and initiated deportation proceedings against them.[51] In one case of mass detention, authorities arrested more than 400 people attempting to register at an immigration office in Los Angeles but released all except 20 over the next several days.[52]

As it absorbed several federal agencies and programs related to homeland security, the newly created Department of Homeland Security assumed responsibility for immigration enforcement, including the NSEERS program. In December 2003, DHS announced the suspension of NSEERS, but for another eight years it retained both the list of designated countries and the discretion to reactivate the registration process. In 2011, officials announced the formal termination of the NSEERS program, citing the implementation of several automated data-collection systems that capture entry and exit information about foreign visitors (regardless of nationality), making manual registration of men from predominantly Muslim countries unnecessary.[53]

Another tool used by the federal government to monitor people suspected of posing a threat to homeland security is the terrorism watch list. In fact, several federal agencies maintain different watch lists that include suspected or potential terrorists. Among these lists, the National Counterterrorism Center maintains the Terrorist Identities Datamart Environment (TIDE) database. The TIDE database contains the names of several hundred thousand people (nearly a million according to some sources) suspected of involvement in international terrorism or having links to foreign terrorist organizations. The FBI's Terrorism Screening Center combines names listed on the TIDE database with the FBI's list of suspected domestic terrorists to compile the Terrorism Screening Database (TSDB), a large amalgam of all suspected and known terrorists—foreign and domestic—who threaten the United States. People named on the TSDB form the basis of two of the most controversial terrorism watch lists: the No Fly List and the Automatic Selectee List, both managed by the Transportation Security Administration.[54]

The No Fly List contains the names of individuals who are deemed a direct threat to civil aviation. These individuals are automatically denied permission to board commercial flights that are bound for the United States, are scheduled to fly over U.S. airspace, or are operated by a U.S.

airline. The Automatic Selectee List contains the names of individuals who must undergo additional security screening, from body searches to questioning by federal officers, before being allowed to board such flights.[55]

Before 9/11, the FBI and the Federal Aviation Administration jointly maintained a precursor to today's No Fly List. This pre-9/11 list held fewer than 20 names. By the end of 2004, the TSA's No Fly List and Automatic Selectee List held a combined total of more than 20,000 names, with commercial airlines alerting TSA officials as often as 30 times per day about passengers whose names appeared to be on one of the lists. As might be expected, considering the exponential increase in the size of these watch lists over just a few years, numerous mistakes occurred. Among the many misidentifications, the late Senator Edward Kennedy and two of his Congressional colleagues, Representative John Lewis and Representative Don Young, found themselves named on the No Fly List.[56]

Muslims and people with names that appear Arabic are especially vulnerable to mistaken identity or special scrutiny. In 2004, British musician Yusuf Islam (known as Cat Stevens before his conversion to Islam) discovered that authorities had placed him on the No Fly List. Aviation officials diverted his flight, bound for Washington, D.C., from London with 249 passengers aboard, to Bangor International Airport in Maine. Federal agents took the musician into custody and questioned him for several hours before placing him on a return flight to the United Kingdom.[57] Authorities have never publicly revealed the reason for Yusuf Islam's treatment, and he traveled to the United States in subsequent years without incident. In a similar case, a year after Yusuf Islam's expulsion from the country, airline officials in San Francisco barred Rahinah Ibrahim, a Malaysian citizen who earned her doctoral degree at Stanford University, from boarding a flight to Malaysia via Hawaii. Federal authorities cleared her to fly back to Malaysia but revoked her visa shortly afterward. Not until 2012, after a six-year court battle, did she learn that U.S. officials mistakenly placed her name on the No Fly List due to a clerical error.[58]

The size of the No Fly List surged again after December 2009, when a Nigerian citizen acting on behalf of al-Qaeda in the Arabian Peninsula attempted to detonate a bomb aboard an international flight bound for Detroit. An evaluation by the Government Accountability Office found that the number of U.S. citizens and legal permanent residents named on the No Fly List more than doubled in the year following this failed attack.[59] Numerous Muslim Americans subsequently discovered that the

U.S. government had labeled them national security threats and placed their names on the No Fly List.

In some cases, Muslims residing in the United States traveled abroad and then discovered that they could not fly home because they had been placed on the No Fly List while they were abroad. In several such cases, U.S. citizens and legal residents had to fly to neighboring Mexico or Canada and then travel over land to reenter the United States. In February 2010, Steven Washburn, a U.S. citizen and air force veteran who had converted to Islam, was prevented from boarding a U.S.-bound flight from Ireland. Three months later, he flew to Mexico via Brazil, and then he crossed into the United States by land.[60] Similarly, in June 2012, Iranian American Kevin Iraniha, a student attending school in Costa Rica, was barred from boarding a flight home to San Diego. After FBI agents informed him that he could not fly home, Iraniha flew to Mexico and walked across the border into the United States.[61] The Department of Homeland Security later acknowledged that several others prevented from boarding flights back to the United States had flown to Mexico or Canada and then traveled over land across the border.[62]

In 2010, the American Civil Liberties Union filed suit against the U.S. government on behalf of 10 U.S. citizens and permanent residents, all Muslims, named on the No Fly List. Three other Muslims later joined the lawsuit. In all 13 cases, federal authorities refused to tell the plaintiffs why their names were on the No Fly List or what they could do to have their names removed.[63] Several of the plaintiffs found themselves unable to board flights home until the government allowed them a one-time waiver to board an approved flight back to the United States. Some claimed the FBI used the No Fly List as a means of pressuring them into informing on Muslim communities in the United States. Nagib Ali Ghaleb, barred from returning home to San Francisco from Yemen, claimed that FBI agents offered to remove his name from the No Fly List if he agreed to become an informant.[64] Similarly, Marine Corps veteran Ibraheim Mashal alleged that after he was blocked from boarding a domestic flight from Chicago to Spokane, the FBI asked him to become an informant in exchange for having his name removed from the No Fly List.[65]

In separate lawsuits, other Muslims living in the United States allege that U.S. officials offered to remove their names from the No Fly List in exchange for cooperating with federal authorities. In 2012, Yonas Fikre, a U.S. citizen from Oregon, claimed that FBI agents questioned him while he was traveling abroad and informed him that he was on the No Fly List. According to Fikre, the FBI offered to remove his name from the list and provide him with financial compensation if he became an informant at a prominent mosque in Portland, Oregon.[66] He subsequently sought political asylum in Sweden and filed suit against the U.S. government.[67] In 2014, four other Muslims residing in the United States filed a joint lawsuit alleging that federal officials used the No Fly List as a tool to pressure them into becoming informants. The four men—Jameel Algibhah of New York, Naveed Shinwari of Connecticut, Awais Sajjad of New Jersey, and Muhammad Tanvir of New York—claimed FBI agents offered to remove their names from the list and, in some cases, provide monetary compensation if they agreed to serve as informants at mosques and in Muslim neighborhoods.[68]

Later in 2014, a federal judge ruled that the government was violating the constitutional rights of U.S. citizens and permanent residents by refusing to provide an effective means for them to challenge their inclusion on the No Fly List. As a result, in 2015, federal authorities announced a revised redress procedure. Previously, individuals who believed they were listed on the No Fly List could appeal to the Department of Homeland Security, but the federal government was not required to divulge whether they were named on the list or what they could do to have their names removed if they were included on the list. Under the revised system, any U.S. citizen or permanent resident who is prevented from boarding a commercial flight is entitled to receive, upon request, a letter explaining his or her status on the No Fly List. In some cases, such individuals are also entitled to receive an explanation for why they are named on the list. However, as a security precaution, federal authorities retain the prerogative to refuse to provide information about why some individuals are named on the No Fly List.[69]

Targeting Islamic Charities

After 9/11, uncovering and eliminating terrorist financing networks became another priority of the U.S. government. Within two weeks of the 9/11 attacks, President George W. Bush issued an executive order authorizing the seizure of all assets belonging to persons who committed terrorist acts against the United States or who posed a serious risk of committing such acts in the future. This directive designated individuals and organizations to be sanctioned, including al-Qaeda and affiliated groups, and tasked the secretary of state with designating additional foreign persons and entities that posed a terrorist threat to the nation. The executive order also authorized the secretary of the treasury to seize all assets of individuals and entities that 1) are owned by, or act on behalf of, designated terrorist organizations, 2) provide support to such organizations, or 3) are otherwise associated with foreign terrorists that threaten the nation. The order explicitly mentioned providing financial support and donations to designated terrorists as prohibited acts that warranted the seizure of assets.[70]

A month after the president issued this executive order, Congress passed the Patriot Act, which contained additional measures to combat terrorism financing. Prior to 9/11, federal law prohibited individuals or organizations from knowingly providing material support, including financial backing, to further terrorist activities. The Patriot Act strengthened penalties for providing such support, increasing the maximum sentence from 10 to 15 years in most cases, as well as authorizing life sentences when perpetrators provided support for terrorist acts that resulted in the deaths of victims. Laws enacted before 9/11 also authorized the Office of Foreign Assets Control (OFAC), an office within the Department of the Treasury, to order the seizure of assets owned by any organization or individual found to be supporting terrorist activities. The Patriot Act expanded this power, allowing OFAC to preemptively freeze the assets of any organization under investigation for aiding terrorists, even before OFAC determined whether the organization was in violation of the law.[71]

Armed with these enhanced powers, federal authorities launched a campaign against U.S.-based charities suspected of supporting terrorist organizations abroad. In December 2001, federal agents raided the offices of the three largest Islamic charities in the country: the Texas-based Holy Land Foundation for Relief and Development, the Illinois-based Benevolence International Foundation, and the Michigan-based Global Relief Foundation. Authorities seized the assets of all three charities, effectively putting them out of business. In the case of the Holy Land Foundation, five of the charity's leaders were convicted in 2008 of numerous criminal counts, including providing material support to the terrorist group Hamas. They were given prison sentences ranging from 15 to 65 years.[72] In 2003, after being detained for 16 months (much of the time in solitary confinement), the director of the Benevolence International Foundation pled guilty to channeling charitable donations to aid Muslim insurgents in Chechnya and Bosnia. He received an 11-year prison sentence. Although authorities did not charge employees of the Global Relief Foundation with terrorism-related offenses, they detained the head of the foundation for immigration violations and deported him to Lebanon in 2003.[73]

Authorities later moved against three other U.S.-based Islamic charities suspected of supporting terrorist activities: Al Haramain Islamic

Foundation in Oregon, Islamic American Relief Agency-USA in Missouri, and the Goodwill Charitable Organization in Michigan. Federal authorities seized the assets of all three, forcing them out of business. In addition to these cases, OFAC opened an investigation of KindHearts for Charitable Humanitarian Development, a Muslim charity established the year after 9/11. Authorities froze the organization's assets in 2006, announcing their suspicion that KindHearts had resumed the illegal financing activities previously performed by the Holy Land Foundation and the Global Relief Fund. This act forced KindHearts to close its doors, although OFAC never a made a final determination regarding the charity's relationship with terrorist groups abroad.[74]

During the first eight years after 9/11, federal agents raided six other Muslim charities in the United States. Authorities did not seize their assets or charge any of these six charities with supporting terrorism. However, two of the charities, Help the Needy, based in New York, and Care International, based in Massachusetts, shut down operations after their leaders were indicted for misusing charitable funds.[75] A federal court later convicted the executive director of Help the Needy for tax fraud, money laundering, and other offenses related to the transfer of funds to Iraq during the 1990s in violation of U.S. sanctions in place at the time. Another court found three leaders of Care International guilty of tax code violations and other charges in connection with their efforts to aid insurgencies abroad. None of these convictions included providing material support to terrorists or abetting acts of terrorism.[76]

By the end of 2014, U.S. government action had forced the closing of nine Islamic charities in the United States. Investigators uncovered some illegal activities, such as aiding insurgencies abroad and circumventing sanctions against Iraq in the 1990s, but only three of the charities ever faced criminal prosecution for aiding terrorists.[77] Meanwhile, a combined total of $20 million in assets seized from Islamic charities in the United States remained in a government bank account.[78]

Extrajudicial Imprisonment and Interrogation

As federal authorities expanded the use of criminal law, immigration law, and financial sanctions to combat terrorist activities, they also initiated a rapid expansion of extrajudicial measures, beyond the reach of the U.S. judicial system, to face the challenge posed by al-Qaeda and allied extremists. Among the most immediate concerns was what to do with militants and suspected terrorists captured on the battlefield in Afghanistan or elsewhere, including in the United States. Prior to 9/11, the criminal justice system maintained an impressive record for dealing with terrorism cases. In fact, several extremists inspired by the brand of jihadist violence espoused by Osama bin Laden, including some with direct links to al-Qaeda, were serving sentences in U.S. prisons at the time of the 9/11 attacks. Ramzi Yousef and five other perpetrators of the 1993 World Trade Center bombing were serving life sentences in federal prison. Omar Abdel Rahman was serving time in federal prison with nine fellow conspirators for planning attacks, thwarted by law enforcement, on targets throughout New York City in 1994. Similarly, Ahmed Ressam was incarcerated for his failed attempt to bomb a terminal of Los Angeles International Airport on New Year's Eve of 1999.

After 9/11, the criminal justice system continued to provide an important means of incarcerating terrorists. In the first post-9/11 case against a member of al-Qaeda, federal authorities pursued criminal charges against Zacarias Moussaoui, a French national arrested in the United States on immigration charges in August 2001. Also in 2001, U.S. prosecutors pressed criminal charges against John Walker Lindh, a U.S. citizen captured in Afghanistan while fighting for the Taliban. Additionally, Richard Reid, a British citizen apprehended in December 2001 during a failed al-Qaeda plot to bring down a U.S.-bound passenger plane, faced criminal prosecution in civilian court. Traditional criminal prosecutions for terrorists continued in subsequent years, from the prosecution of Iyman Faris for plotting to cause the collapse the Brooklyn Bridge in 2003 to the prosecution of Dzhokhar Tsarnaev for his role in the Boston Marathon bombing in 2013. During the decade after 9/11, federal prosecutors obtained 376 convictions related to terrorism, an 87 percent conviction rate (based on cases resolved by September 11, 2011).[79]

However, despite the success rate of criminal prosecutions in terrorism cases, President Bush and his advisors were unwilling to rely solely on civilian courts—with their reliance on probable cause, rules of evidence, and the potential for acquittal—to confine suspected terrorists. Nor was the Bush administration willing to be constrained by traditional rules and methods of interrogation to extract information from suspected terrorists. Instead, federal authorities created a parallel system of imprisonment and interrogation that lay largely outside the bounds of the criminal justice system and extended across several countries. This system afforded the U.S. government a means of detaining suspected terrorists without probable cause, sometimes in secret locations, and facilitated the use of brutal interrogation techniques that violated the Geneva Conventions and the Uniform Code of Military Justice. Legal scholar Jonathan Hafetz has referred to this parallel detention system as America's post-9/11 "global detention system."[80]

The most visible manifestation of this detention system appeared on January 11, 2002, as the first combatants captured in Afghanistan and neighboring Pakistan arrived at the U.S. Naval Station at Guantanamo Bay, Cuba. Citing his authority as commander in chief and the authority granted to him by the Authorization for the Use of Military Force, President Bush asserted the right to detain al-Qaeda and Taliban members who were not U.S. citizens at locations outside of U.S. territory, where he believed they would be beyond the jurisdiction of the U.S. criminal justice system. In addition, he asserted that members of al-Qaeda and Taliban were "unlawful combatants" who did not qualify as prisoners of war and who were not subject to the rights and protections set forth in the Geneva Conventions.[81] Over the next several years, the U.S. military interned a total of 779 detainees at Guantanamo Bay, never more than 700 at any one time.[82] Some were captured on the battlefield or arrested near conflict zones in Afghanistan or Pakistan; others were seized in distant countries thousands of miles away.

Although less well known than Guantanamo Bay, the U.S. military also operated a detention facility at Bagram Airfield in Afghanistan's Parwan province. The U.S. military began confining detainees at the Bagram Theater Internment Facility, a converted aircraft machine plant, in January 2002. Over the next seven years, the prison population at Bagram reached as many as 600 detainees. Most of those confined at the facility were Afghans, primarily members of the Taliban or other insurgents captured on the battlefield in Afghanistan. However, dozens of detainees were non-Afghans, including some seized in other countries and then transferred to Bagram.[83] The U.S. military eventually moved the detainees to a new facility near Bagram Airfield called the Parwan Detention Facility, where the number of detainees grew rapidly to more than 3,000.[84]

Along with these military detention sites, President Bush authorized the CIA to operate a secret detention program. Through this program, the CIA captured or took custody of suspected terrorists and transported them to secret detention sites (or "black sites") outside of the United States. Black sites were located in cooperating countries around the world, including Lithuania, Poland, Romania, Morocco, Thailand, and Afghanistan. The CIA held detainees at black sites in these and possibly other countries as enemy combatants, for years in some cases. Many were interrogated and subsequently transferred to Guantanamo Bay for indefinite detention. President Bush acknowledged the existence of the program in September 2006, claiming that the CIA had secretly detained approximately 100 suspected terrorists.[85]

Deprived of the legal protections given to traditional criminal suspects or prisoners or war, several detainees interned at U.S. military facilities or CIA black sites were subjected to brutal interrogation techniques. Such techniques were reserved primarily for high-value detainees suspected of having information critical to U.S. counterterrorism efforts. They included being held in stress positions for prolonged periods, exposure to extreme temperatures, confinement in a box, prolonged sensory deprivation, simulated drowning (waterboarding), and being led to believe that severe pain or death was imminent for the detainee or his or her family. These and other interrogation methods used on enemy combatants violated both the Uniform Code of Military Justice and the U.S. Army Field Manual, which set forth rules for U.S. military personnel involved in the interrogation of prisoners.[86]

Another component of the U.S. global detention system relied on outsourcing the detention and interrogation of terrorism suspects to third countries. This policy arose from the previous practice, dating back more than a century, of kidnapping fugitives abroad and bringing them to the United States to stand trial. Used sparingly through most of U.S. history, the practice became more systematic under President Ronald Reagan, who issued a directive in 1986, authorizing federal law enforcement agencies to apprehend wanted fugitives and transfer them to the United States. Termed "rendition to justice," this tactic was generally limited to suspects hiding in locations abroad where the U.S. government could not secure custody through extradition. President Bill Clinton expanded this program to include the transfer of suspected terrorists to third countries for criminal prosecution. This strategy allowed the CIA to capture suspected terrorists whom the U.S. justice system would have difficulty prosecuting, due to insufficient evidence or other reasons, and then to turn them over to foreign governments. In most cases, the countries that took custody of such suspects had issued warrants for their arrest or had already tried and convicted them in absentia. Under President Clinton, the CIA's legal counsel approved each rendition operation.[87]

Within days of 9/11, President Bush loosened the rules regulating renditions, authorizing the CIA to capture suspected al-Qaeda-linked terrorists and transfer them to the custody of foreign governments without advance approval of the White House or the CIA's own legal counsel. Under the new rules, the CIA began transferring captured terrorism suspects to third countries, irrespective of whether warrants had been issued for the suspects.[88] Rendition (also called "extraordinary rendition" under President Bush) shifted from an extrajudicial method of transferring fugitives to U.S. custody or to foreign countries for criminal prosecution to a method of transferring suspects to the custody of foreign governments for indefinite detention and interrogation. Many of the countries that agreed to take suspected terrorists, such as Syria, Egypt, and Uzbekistan, were well known for practicing torture against prisoners in their custody.[89]

Throughout President Bush's two terms in office, thousands of individuals passed through this international detention and interrogation system, either in the custody of the U.S. military, the CIA, or cooperating foreign governments. Most suspects were foreign nationals captured outside of the United States. Almost all U.S. citizens arrested for terrorism-related activities, alongside most foreign terrorism suspects arrested on U.S. soil, found themselves in the U.S. criminal justice system. Four exceptions to this pattern arose shortly after 9/11, two involving Americans and two involving foreign nationals arrested in the United States.

The first American enemy combatant case began when the U.S. military took custody of Yaser Hamdi, who was captured with Taliban forces in Afghanistan in late 2001. In January of the following year, Hamdi was transferred to Guantanamo Bay. After three months, U.S. officials discovered that Hamdi was born in Louisiana and held dual U.S.-Saudi citizenship. Authorities abruptly transferred him to the navy brig in Norfolk, Virginia and then moved him to the navy brig in Charleston, South Carolina. He remained incarcerated there as an enemy combatant for the next two years, most of the time in solitary confinement.[90] Hamdi is the only publically known American captured abroad to be held as an enemy combatant and the only known American to have spent time imprisoned at Guantanamo Bay.

Shortly after authorities transferred Hamdi to the navy brig in Charleston, the FBI arrested Jose Padilla as he returned to the United States from a trip to Pakistan. A U.S. citizen of Puerto Rican origin, Padilla spent a troubled youth in Chicago, where he was placed in juvenile detention for four years after being convicted of gang-related violence. He had an equally troubled early adulthood in Florida, where he accumulated a criminal record of assaults and thefts. After serving time in a Florida jail, Padilla became increasingly attracted to Islam and formally converted to the religion in 1994. After his conversion, he gradually became drawn to an extremist subculture within Florida's Muslim community. In 1998, he moved to Egypt and then to Pakistan. Two years later, he attended sessions at an al-Qaeda training camp in Afghanistan and, in the spring of 2002, received instructions from the al-Qaeda leadership to prepare for attacks in the United States.[91]

Authorities learned of Padilla's plans and, in May 2002, arrested him on a material witness warrant as he disembarked at Chicago O'Hare International Airport. The following month, days before Padilla's defense attorney was scheduled to challenge Padilla's detention in court, President Bush declared Padilla an enemy combatant and instructed the secretary of defense to take him into military custody. Authorities transferred Padilla overnight to the same navy brig in Charleston where Hamdi was detained. He remained confined in Charleston, most of the time in solitary confinement, for three and a half years.[92] Padilla is the only publically known U.S. citizen arrested in the United States to be detained as an enemy combatant.

Attorneys for Hamdi and Padilla separately challenged the U.S. government's claim that it had the authority to detain their clients indefinitely without charge or due process. Their cases eventually reached the Supreme Court, which issued a decision on both cases in June 2004. Regarding Hamdi, the Court ruled that the Authorization for the Use of Military Force, passed by Congress in 2001, allowed the president to detain U.S. citizens who were captured while fighting American forces in Afghanistan for the duration of the conflict. However, the Court also ruled that U.S. citizens, even when incarcerated as enemy combatants, could not be denied due process and had the right to contest their detention in court. This decision established that the global detention system erected after 9/11, although mostly beyond the reach of civilian courts, was not completely outside the bounds of the U.S. justice system. In the Padilla case, the Supreme Court refused to rule on the merits of the case, stating that the defense team had improperly filed his complaint in New York, instead of Charleston, where he was confined.[93]

Three months later, rather than provide Hamdi with due process as required by the Supreme Court's ruling, the U.S. government decided to release him to Saudi Arabia on the conditions that he agree to renounce his U.S. citizenship, agree not to leave Saudi Arabia for five years, and agree not to enter the United States for 10 years. Hamdi accepted the terms, was transferred to Saudi Arabia in October 2004, and was promptly released from custody by Saudi authorities.[94] Similarly, after Padilla renewed his challenge to indefinite detention without trial, this time filed properly in South Carolina, the U.S. government filed criminal charges against him and transferred him to the federal prison system. In August 2007, Padilla was convicted of terrorism-related offenses in civilian court.[95]

Along with U.S. citizens Hamdi and Padilla, two foreign nationals arrested on U.S. territory found themselves in the post-9/11 extrajudicial detention system. The first case involved Ali Saleh Kahlah al-Marri, a dual Qatari-Saudi national who entered the United States on a student visa. Like Jose Padilla, al-Marri was an aspiring terrorist with links to al-Qaeda. Between 1998 and 2001, he received training at al-Qaeda camps in Afghanistan and, in 2001, agreed to assist al-Qaeda operations in the United States. On September 10, 2001 (one day before 9/11), he arrived in the country and set up residence in central Illinois. In December 2001, authorities arrested al-Marri on a material witness warrant and later indicted him for committing credit card fraud and identity theft and for making false statements to authorities. In June 2003, less than a month before al-Marri's scheduled trial in federal court, President Bush declared him an enemy combatant and ordered him transferred to the navy brig in Charleston, where both Hamdi and Padilla were confined.[96]

Al-Marri, who was held in solitary confinement for much of his time in the brig, challenged the legality of his detention. His case gradually moved through the federal court system, stretching beyond President Bush's second term and into the first term of President Barack Obama. In December 2008, the Supreme Court agreed to hear al-Marri's case. The following month, the newly inaugurated President Obama instructed the attorney general, the secretary of defense, and other federal officials to review al-Marri's detention. Subsequently, three months before the scheduled Supreme Court hearing of al-Marri's challenge, the Obama administration announced its intention to file criminal charges against al-Marri in civilian court. In April 2009, al-Marri pled guilty to providing material support to al-Qaeda and received a sentence of eight and a half years in federal prison.[97]

One year after the 9/11 attacks, federal agents arrested another foreign national on U.S. soil and placed him in extrajudicial detention. In September 2002, authorities detained Maher Arar, a Canadian resident with dual Canadian-Syrian citizenship, at New York's John F. Kennedy International Airport. Arar was passing through New York, where he planned to change planes as part of a return trip to Montreal from travels abroad. Alerted (inaccurately) by Canadian officials that Arar was affiliated with al-Qaeda, U.S. authorities detained him for two weeks in New York and then transferred him to Syrian custody. After his rendition to Syria, Arar was confined to a small cell (seven feet high, six feet long, and three feet wide), beaten with cables, threatened with electric shock, and subjected to other forms of torture. In October 2003, after finding no evidence that Arar was linked to al-Qaeda or terrorist activities, the Syrian government released him. In September 2006, a Canadian inquiry found that Arar had no connection to terrorism. The following year, the Canadian government agreed to pay Arar $11.6 million for its part in his rendition and torture.[98]

In addition to erecting a formal, if partly covert, extrajudicial detention and interrogation system, the U.S. government initiated an informal policy of detention by proxy. In such cases, the United States avoided taking custody of terrorism suspects, relying instead on cooperating governments to arrest, detain, and interrogate them, often with U.S. investigators witnessing or participating in interrogations. In 2011, the FBI admitted to the broad outlines of this policy in response to an inquiry by an investigative journalist at *Mother Jones*. As published in *Mother Jones*, the FBI stated:

> There are occasions when the FBI has carefully reviewed information and elected to share that information with foreign law enforcement services. At times, those services may decide to locate or detain an individual or conduct an investigation based on the shared information. Additionally, there have been instances when foreign law enforcement have detained individuals, independent of any information provided by the FBI, and the FBI has been afforded the opportunity to interview or witness an interview with the individual.[99]

During the Bush presidency, at least two U.S. citizens, both Muslim, were detained and interrogated abroad with possible U.S. participation. The first case involved Amir Mohamed Meshal, a U.S. citizen of Egyptian origin who was born and raised in New Jersey. In January 2007, Ethiopian forces invaded Somalia to prevent the Islamic Courts Union, the predecessor of the extremist movement al-Shabaab, from consolidating control over the country. Meshal, who had traveled to Somalia the previous year, attempted to escape Ethiopian forces by fleeing across the border into Kenya. Along with several dozen others, he was seized at the border and transferred to a Nairobi prison. While in Kenyan custody, Meshal was questioned several times by FBI agents who did not uncover sufficient evidence to charge him with a crime. In February 2007, Kenyan authorities deported Meshal back to a part of Somalia controlled by Ethiopian forces. He was then transferred to Ethiopia and detained at a secret prison in Addis Ababa, where FBI agents again questioned him.[100] In May 2007, after four months in Kenyan and Ethiopian prisons, Meshal was released and returned to the United States. American authorities never charged Meshal with a crime.[101]

The following year, Naji Hamdan, a naturalized U.S. citizen from Lebanon, found himself in a similar situation, this time detained by authorities in the United Arab Emirates. Beginning in 1999, after a thwarted plot to bomb a Los Angeles airport terminal, the FBI questioned Hamdan on numerous occasions. In 2006, Hamdan moved to the United Arab Emirates with his family. In the summer of 2008, the FBI summoned him to the U.S. embassy in Abu Dhabi for additional questioning. Six weeks later, Emirati authorities seized Hamdan and held him in a secret detention facility for three months, where Hamdan claims he was interrogated and tortured, on at least one occasion with the participation of an unidentified American. Emirati authorities subsequently pressed criminal charges against him and, in October 2009, convicted him of terrorism-related offenses and deported him to Lebanon. The U.S. government, which denied involvement in Hamdan's detention, never filed charges against him, despite an extensive investigation of his Los Angeles business and overseas activities.[102]

Two days after taking the oath of office in January 2009, President Obama issued a series of executive orders designed to reform America's detention and interrogation policies. He ordered the closure of all CIA black sites and instructed officials to close the detention facility at Guantanamo Bay within one year. He also banned brutal interrogation tactics, limited CIA interrogation techniques to methods outlined in the U.S. Army Field Manual, and ordered full compliance with the Geneva Conventions for enemy belligerents held in U.S. custody.[103] In August 2009, following a review of U.S. interrogation policy, President Obama approved the creation of a multiagency High-Value Detainee Interrogation Group, administered by the FBI, to interrogate al-Qaeda-linked terrorism suspects using noncoercive techniques.[104]

President Obama's reform efforts, however, ran into serious obstacles. Shortly after the president took office, Congress barred the White House from using federal funds to transfer Guantanamo Bay detainees to the United States or to acquire facilities in the United States to house such detainees. Congress also passed legislation requiring a court order or a national security waiver before the release of any detainee from Guantanamo Bay to another country.[105] With these restrictions in place, the Obama administration made halting progress toward its goal to move Guantanamo detainees to other locations and shut down the facility. Transfers came to a virtual halt in 2011 and did not resume again until 2014, during President Obama's sixth year in office. That year, the military transferred 28 detainees to the custody of other countries, the largest number of transfers since 2009. With 127 detainees remaining at Guantanamo at the end of 2014, the Obama administration began accelerating plans to transfer dozens more.[106] However, with both houses of Congress controlled by Republicans, who strongly opposed plans to close the Guantanamo detention facility, the pace of such transfers remained in doubt.

In addition, the U.S. military retained custody of enemy combatants at the detention facility near Bagram Airfield for several more years. Despite White House attempts to transfer them to third countries, few foreign governments proved willing to take the detainees or to provide sufficient guarantees about preventing them from engaging in terrorist activities in the future.[107] In March 2013, the U.S. military transferred control of most of the detention facility to the Afghan government, retaining custody of approximately 60 non-Afghans held without trial or prisoner-of-war status. Not until the end of 2014 did the U.S. military end its detention program in Afghanistan and transfer all remaining prisoners to the custody of Afghan authorities.[108]

Other key elements of the post-9/11 detention-and-interrogation regime remained in operation under President Obama. As early as August 2009, White House officials disclosed that the president would retain the option to hand over suspected terrorists to foreign governments for interrogation, although the Department of State would be given more authority to ensure that such detainees were not abused.[109] In addition, elements of black-site detention methods persisted under the new administration. In 2011, U.S. forces captured Ahmed Abdulkadir, a Somali national, in international waters off the coast of Yemen. He was detained and questioned in secret for two months aboard a U.S. Navy vessel before being transferred to New York to stand trial for aiding al-Qaeda-affiliated terrorist groups.[110] Similarly, in 2013, Abu Anas al-Libi was captured by U.S. Special Forces in Libya and taken aboard a U.S. Navy vessel offshore. He was interrogated for nine days before being transferred to New York to stand trial for his part in the 1998 bombings of U.S. embassies in Nairobi and Dar-es-Salaam.[111]

In many respects, the cases of Abdulkadir and Anas al-Libi resemble detentions at CIA black sites, which President Obama ordered closed in 2009. Both detainees were captured abroad, and both were interrogated at secret locations without access to legal counsel and without being notified of their right not to incriminate themselves. However, some critical factors distinguish the secret detention of Abdulkadir and al-Libi from CIA black-site detentions practiced in previous years. Both were confined by the U.S. military, not the CIA, and both were interrogated by the FBI under rules consistent with the Geneva Conventions (according to the Obama administration). Moreover, they were detained in secret for several days or weeks, not years, and they were subsequently transferred to civilian custody to stand trial instead of being moved to a military prison for indefinite detention.

More closely matching the Bush administration's detention and interrogation tactics is the Obama administration's alleged use of proxy detentions. In at least three cases, U.S. citizens may have been subjected to this tactic. In January 2010, security agents in Yemen shot and wounded Sharif Mobley, a U.S. citizen from New Jersey, and then took him into custody. While in detention, Mobley was questioned several times by U.S. officials. Two months after his arrest, Mobley killed a hospital security guard and wounded another guard in an unsuccessful attempt to escape.[112] At some point in 2014, Yemeni authorities transferred Mobley to an undisclosed location and did not allow him to participate in a court hearing regarding his case. According to Yemeni officials, his transfer to secret detention was coordinated with the United States.[113]

In two similar cases, foreign governments detained and interrogated U.S. citizens with alleged participation of U.S. officials. In 2010, Kuwaiti authorities detained Gulet Mohamed, a U.S. citizen from Virginia. After interrogating him for a week, they transferred Mohamed to a deportation facility, where he was questioned several times by FBI agents before being allowed to return to the United States in January 2011.[114] Six months later, authorities in the United Arab Emirates arrested Yonas Fikre. As discussed above, he claimed the FBI offered to remove his name from the No Fly List if he agreed to become an informant. Emirati authorities held Fikre for three months, interrogating him about alleged terrorism-related activities with, he claimed, the participation of U.S. officials.[115]

Targeted Killing and Collateral Casualties

Alongside extrajudicial detention and interrogation, the U.S. government initiated a policy of targeted killing aimed at al-Qaeda and Taliban leaders. Six days after 9/11, President Bush authorized the CIA to kill high-value terrorists anywhere in the world linked to the 9/11 attacks. The following year, the United States carried out its first killing of an al-Qaeda-linked suspect using a remotely piloted aircraft, or drone, armed with air-to-surface missiles. This drone strike took place in November 2002, when a CIA-operated Predator drone fired a missile at a vehicle traveling through the desert of Yemen. The missile strike killed the intended target, Abu Ali al-Harithi, who was suspected of overseeing the al-Qaeda suicide-bombing operation against the navy destroyer USS *Cole* in 2000.[116]

The strike against al-Harithi also killed five other people riding in the vehicle, including a U.S. citizen named Kamal Derwish (also known as Ahmed Hijazi).[117] Derwish, who spent most of his life in the Middle East, had been involved with al-Qaeda for a number of years before his death. In 1997, he was expelled from Saudi Arabia for extremist activities. Four years later, in the summer of 2001, he recruited a group of Yemeni Americans from Lackawanna in New York State to receive training at an al-Qaeda camp.[118] After the November 2002 drone strike, U.S. officials claimed that the CIA did not intentionally target Derwish and described his death as collateral damage from the strike against al-Harithi.

Nearly two years later, in June 2004, the CIA conducted its first known drone strike in Pakistan, killing Taliban commander Nek Mohammed. During the next three and a half years, the CIA slowly expanded its drone program in Pakistan, conducting 10 known strikes, before escalating in 2008 to an estimated 35 drone strikes against militants in Pakistan.[119] This escalation coincided with the initiation of "signature strikes," which target groups of people who, although their identities are not known, display patterns of behavior (or signatures) associated with terrorist or insurgent activities.[120] Additionally, as the United States expanded its counterterrorism operations in Pakistan, U.S. forces conducted a small number of attacks in Somalia using drone-fired missiles, missiles fired from navy ships and fighter aircraft, as well as raids by attack helicopters and special operations forces.[121]

Under President Obama, the targeted killing of militants continued to expand, reaching nearly 300 drone strikes in Pakistan during his first term of office. President Obama also authorized a more aggressive targeting of al-Qaeda in Yemen, overseeing approximately 60 drone strikes and fighter aircraft strikes against targets in the country during his first term.[122] During President Obama's second term in office, the United States began a gradual de-escalation of drone strikes but continued to rely on them to eliminate al-Qaeda and Taliban militants. By the end of 2014, the United States had conducted several hundred drone strikes in Pakistan and Yemen, exacting a heavy toll on al-Qaeda and the Taliban. Estimates of the number of deaths vary, ranging from nearly 2,000 to more than 3,000 militants killed. Estimates on the number of civilians killed in these strikes range from 350 to more than 1,000.[123]

For nearly nine years after the incidental killing of Kamal Derwish, U.S. counterterrorism operations resulted in no known deaths of Americans suspected of involvement with al-Qaeda or allied terrorist groups, and no U.S. citizen was deliberately targeted. Circumstances changed in 2011, when President Obama ordered the assassination of Anwar al-Awlaki, a militant working with al-Qaeda in the Arabian Peninsula. Born in New Mexico to parents who emigrated from Yemen, al-Awlaki became attracted to Islamic theology as an adult and became an imam, preaching at mosques in Colorado, California, and Virginia. He also became increasingly attracted to radical interpretations of Islam. Beginning in the late 1990s, he met on several occasions with al-Qaeda operatives, including at least three of the men who would carry out the 9/11 attacks. He left the United States in 2002, eventually moving to Yemen, where he grew increasingly hostile to America and began inciting violence in his writings and in video messages distributed on CDs and online.[124]

President Obama's national security team eventually concluded that al-Awlaki was instrumental in directing attacks on the United States, including the attempted suicide bombing of a passenger plane over Detroit on Christmas Day in 2009.[125] After extensive interagency deliberations, the Office of Legal Council in the Department of Justice issued a classified memorandum providing a legal justification for the targeted killing of Americans without trial in countries with which the United States was not at war. The memo concluded that, in the case of al-Awlaki, such a step was legal because he was a belligerent in al-Qaeda's terrorist campaign against the United States, he posed a significant and imminent threat to Americans, and it was not feasible to capture him.[126] In 2011, President Obama took the extraordinary step of ordering the killing of al-Awlaki. In September of that year, a barrage of drone-fired missiles struck a convoy of vehicles in Yemen's Jawf Province, killing four people, including al-Awlaki.[127]

Among the other three people killed in the strike on al-Awlaki was another American, Samir Khan. A naturalized U.S. citizen from Saudi Arabia, Khan grew up in New York City before moving to Charlotte, North Carolina, with this family. He became attracted to extremist ideas in his teenage years and, as a young adult, began disseminating militant views through online jihadist forums. In 2009, Khan moved to Yemen and became an author and editor for *Inspire*, the English-language online magazine of al-Qaeda in the Arabian Peninsula. His death two years later, according to the White House, was an unintended consequence of the drone strike that specifically targeted al-Awlaki.[128]

The following month, another drone strike in Yemen killed Abdulrahman Anwar al-Awlaki, the 16-year-old son of Anwar al-Awlaki. Born in Denver, Colorado, Abdulrahman left the United States with his father in 2002 as a young boy. He was living with his mother in Sanaa, Yemen's capital, when he left unannounced to search for his father in the Yemeni countryside. A few days after he began his search, his father died in a drone strike about 90 miles away. Two weeks later, a barrage of drone-fired missiles struck an outdoor eating venue in Yemen's Shabwa district, killing about a dozen people, including Abdulrahman. The intended target of the strike was Ibrahim al-Banna, a senior al-Qaeda leader from Egypt. However, the intelligence that led to the attack was faulty; al-Banna was not present at the site of the missile strike and remained unharmed. According to U.S. officials, the killing of Abdulrahman was another tragic case of collateral damage from an (albeit misdirected) attack on a legitimate al-Qaeda target.[129]

About four weeks later, in November 2011, another American died in a drone strike, this time in Pakistan. This attack, rather than targeting a specific individual, was a signature strike aimed at a group engaged in activities that identified them as Taliban insurgents. Of the dozen people killed in the strike, one was Jude Kenan Mohammad, an American from Raleigh, North Carolina, who left the United States to join militants in Pakistan. Before leaving for Pakistan, Mohammad became involved with a group of Muslim extremists in North Carolina who planned to launch attacks in the United States and abroad, including an attack on the Marine Corps base in Quantico, Virginia. Afterward, while in Pakistan, Mohammad helped recruit militants for al-Qaeda and the Taliban.[130]

A little more than three years later, a pair of signature strikes from drone-fired missiles took the lives of three more Americans. In January 2015, a CIA-operated drone launched a missile at an al-Qaeda compound near the Afghanistan-Pakistan border. Among those killed in the missile strike was Ahmed Farouq, a senior figure in an al-Qaeda-affiliated group known as al-Qaeda in the Indian Subcontinent (AQIS). Born in New York, Farouq held dual U.S.-Pakistani citizenship, but he left the United States as a young child and never returned. Tragically, the missile strike that killed him also took the lives of two hostages being held at the compound: U.S. aid worker Warren Weinstein and Italian aid worker Giovanni Lo Porto. The CIA did not know the hostages were located in the compound and did not learn of their deaths until months later.[131]

A few days after the missile strike that killed Farouq and the two hostages, a second drone strike targeted a gathering of al-Qaeda operatives in the same vicinity. The strike killed Adam Gadahn, a California-born U.S. citizen. Gadahn, also known as Azzam al-Amriki (Azzam the American), converted to Islam in the late 1990s during his teenage years. He then traveled to Pakistan, where he joined al-Qaeda. In subsequent years, he became a prolific propagandist and spokesman for al-Qaeda, producing online videos for English-speaking audiences. In 2006, a U.S. federal court indicted him for treason and the U.S. government offered a reward of up to $1 million for information leading to his capture.[132] Gadahn's death brought the number of Americans killed by U.S. drone strikes to eight, including six known militants and two innocent civilians.

The deaths of three Americans by drone-launched missiles in early 2015 marked more than 13 years of U.S. counterterrorism efforts formulated and carried out in the shadow of the post-9/11 homeland security paradigm. The successes and failures of U.S. counterterrorism policies during that time have highlighted the tradeoffs between civil rights and homeland security. Co-opting and distorting immigration law to detain and investigate Muslim foreign nationals residing illegally in the United States helped federal authorities address a legitimate immigration concern. However, this strategy also resulted in a large diversion of resources to pursue a policy based on religious and ethnic profiling, while yielding no significant counterterrorism benefits. Similarly, the subversion of the material-witness statute to serve as a tool for counterterrorism allowed authorities to detain and investigate aspiring terrorists Ali Saleh Kahlah al-Marri and Jose Padilla before they could do harm, but it also abetted the mistreatment of Abdullah al-Kidd and Brandon Mayfield, U.S. citizens detained and interrogated without due process.

At the same time, the creation of a detention and interrogation system largely beyond the reach of the U.S. civilian system of justice, combined with the use of drone strikes and other means of targeted killing to eliminate suspected terrorists, has sharply curtailed al-Qaeda's ability to conduct terrorist operations against the United States. However, along with the capture and mistreatment of foreign nationals overseas and the deaths of hundreds of foreign civilians as collateral damage, these strategies have resulted in the inhumane treatment of innocent civilians, such as Canadian citizen Maher Arar, who spent a year being tortured after U.S. authorities transferred him to Syrian custody. Such strategies have also led to the deliberate execution of at least one U.S. citizen, Anwar al-Awlaki, without giving him the chance to contest the order to execute him in a court of law.

These and numerous other uncomfortable tradeoffs during America's ongoing campaign to secure the homeland constitute a trend that is likely to continue for years into the future. All Americans, along with all foreign nationals visiting or residing in the United States (as well as many abroad), are potential subjects to the negative consequences of these tradeoffs, from surveillance without warrants to arrest and interrogation without probable cause and even assassination. Within the United States, Muslim Americans will continue to bear the brunt of these consequences. As long as efforts to defend the homeland against Islamic extremists clash with the goal of guaranteeing civil rights, Islam and those who practice the faith will remain on the borderline between two Americas—a pluralist society committed to democratic principles and a nation defending itself against the threat of terrorism.

CHAPTER 3

Homeland Security and the Muslim Experience at the State and Local Levels

The Homeland Security Enterprise Beyond Washington

As the federal government expanded its homeland defense and counterterrorism capabilities, changes at the state and local levels steadily strengthened the ability of state, county, and municipal governments to participate in the nation's growing homeland security enterprise. In state capitals throughout the United States, governors and state legislatures took steps to enhance the ability of authorities at the state and local levels to address threats posed by terrorism, natural and industrial disasters, and other emergencies. Shortly after 9/11, all 50 states, the District of Columbia, and several U.S. overseas territories established departments to coordinate and manage homeland security activities. Together, they also created hundreds of new agencies—and expanding existing ones—to counter threats to homeland security.[1] Within a decade of 9/11, state and local government entities working on homeland security and counterterrorism numbered nearly 1,200.[2]

Many of these changes were guided and assisted by the federal government, which provided billions of dollars in assistance to improve planning, training, and intelligence gathering, while strengthening security for high-value assets and critical infrastructure. Among the most visible indications of the federal government's influence in state and local homeland security activities was the rapid rise of fusion centers. Operated by the states and municipalities, fusion centers were established to foster collaboration among intelligence, law enforcement, homeland security, and emergency management officials across federal, state, and local jurisdictions. With support and guidance from the Department of Homeland Security, each of the 50 states established one or more fusion centers, as did several municipalities, such as Boston, Chicago, Detroit, Los Angeles, Dallas, Houston, and other cities. Within 10 years of the creation of the Department of Homeland Security, 79 federally recognized fusion centers were up and running.[3]

Alongside the rise of fusion centers, the rapid increase in FBI-led Joint Terrorism Task Forces after 9/11 highlighted the role federal authorities played in guiding the development of homeland defense capabilities beyond Washington. Established and operated by the FBI, these multiagency task forces were designed to bring together state and local officials, local law enforcement, FBI agents, and officials from numerous other federal agencies to coordinate counterterrorism efforts.[4] The FBI established its first Joint Terrorism Task Force in 1980 in New York City and steadily increased the number to 34 task forces over the next two decades. This expansion accelerated after 9/11 as the number of Joint Terrorism Task Forces climbed to more than 100, quadrupling the number of officials from various levels of government working together on counterterrorism. In 2002, the FBI's newly created National Joint Terrorism Task Force assumed responsibility for managing task forces in the field.[5]

The post-9/11 expansion of the homeland security enterprise beyond the nation's capital left the states with a collection of federal, state, county, and municipal agencies and departments engaged in homeland defense. A two-year investigation by the *Washington Post* revealed that, by 2010, nearly 4,000 government organizations located outside of Washington, D.C., were performing homeland security missions. Not surprisingly, a large proportion these organizations were located in large and populous states, such as California (home to nearly 360 homeland security organizations) and Texas (with more than 320). This growing network of homeland security agencies also gained a significant presence in small states such as Rhode Island (with 21 homeland security organizations) and Delaware (with 24), as well as sparsely populated states such as Wyoming and South Dakota (each with 28).[6]

Law Enforcement and the Special Case of the NYPD

Much of the homeland security capacity-building at the state and local levels focused on local law enforcement, which remained a dominant player in countering criminal activity within U.S. borders. Federal agencies, excluding military personnel, employ about 120,000 full-time law enforcement officers authorized to make arrests and carry firearms.[7] These federal agents are spread out among dozens of agencies operating across the country, from the FBI and the Drug Enforcement Administration to the U.S. Postal Inspection Service and the National Park Service. However, the law enforcement manpower of the federal government is dwarfed by the number of police officers at the state and local levels. Together, the nation's roughly 18,000 state and local law enforcement agencies employ more than 750,000 full-time officers with arrest powers.[8]

The large majority of these law enforcement officers work for municipal and county police departments, sheriff offices, and police forces with special jurisdictions (such as college campus police and local public transportation police). Less than 10 percent work for state police forces.[9] Consequently, local law enforcement agencies have played a central role in strengthening domestic counterterrorism capabilities. Since the 9/11 attacks, many municipal and county police departments have created divisions dedicated to counterterrorism, such as the Homeland Security Division of the Los Angeles County Sheriff's Department, the Criminal Investigations and Homeland Security Division of the Houston Police Department, and the Miami-Dade County Police Department's Homeland Security Bureau. In just the first year after 9/11, more than a quarter of metropolitan area police departments across the nation set up specialized counterterrorism units.[10]

The Department of Defense has played an important role in amplifying the firepower available to local police forces as they have expanded their counterterrorism capabilities. As far back as 1987, during the administration of President Ronald Reagan, the Pentagon established an office dedicated to facilitating the transfer of surplus military equipment to civilian law enforcement agencies. As mandated by law, this new office gave priority to civilian agencies working to combat the illegal narcotics trade. Ten years later, with the support of President Bill Clinton, Congress passed a law creating the Law Enforcement Support Program (often called the "1033 Program," after the section of the National Defense Authorization bill in which the program was defined). Through this program, the U.S. military increased the transfer of military equipment to civilian law enforcement throughout the country.[11]

After 9/11, the transfer of military equipment accelerated as local police forces accepted growing volumes of supplies and weapons, including automatic rifles, .50 caliber machine guns, grenade launchers, aircraft, and armored vehicles. By 2014, the Department of Defense had transferred more than $5 billion in military equipment to civilian agencies, including nearly $500 million worth of supplies and weapons in 2013 alone. According to the Pentagon's Defense Logistics Agency, more than 8,000 local law enforcement agencies have received surplus military equipment, although private groups such as the American Civil Liberties Union claim that recipient agencies number at least 17,000.[12] In addition, grants from the Department of Justice and the Department of Homeland Security have allowed law enforcement authorities to purchase additional billions of dollars in material.[13]

Among local police forces, New York City's police department moved most aggressively to establish a counterterrorism capability. As the largest police force in the United States, the NYPD fields more than 36,000 officers with arrest powers, nearly three times the number of FBI agents and more officers than the next four largest U.S. metropolitan police forces combined.[14] Following 9/11, the NYPD shifted a large portion of this officer corps to counterterrorism operations, increasing the number of officers assigned to counterterrorism from a few dozen to several hundred. In 2002, New York City Police Commissioner Ray Kelly assigned primary responsibility for protecting the city from terrorist attack to the police department's newly recruited deputy commissioner for counterterrorism and deputy commissioner for intelligence. The former position was filled by Michael Sheehan, a former U.S. ambassador-at-large for counterterrorism and the former commander of a U.S. Special Forces hostage rescue unit. The latter position was filled by David Cohen, former deputy director of operations at the CIA.

Together, the two new deputy police commissioners oversaw an increase in counterterrorism personnel, unrivaled in any other police department in the United States. As head of the NYPD's newly established Counterterrorism Bureau, Sheehan took charge of the first new bureau created by the NYPD in more than three decades. Along with enhancing the police department's ability to deploy counterterrorism units across the city's five boroughs, he assumed responsibility for coordinating NYPD activities with the FBI's Joint Terrorism Task Force based in the city. Under his watch, the number of NYPD officers assigned to the task force rose from 17 to more than 100. By contrast, when Cohen took command of the NYPD Intelligence Division, he assumed control of a division created long before 9/11. At his direction, the division grew from a collection of officers whose principal task was protecting dignitaries visiting the city to one of the world's largest counterterrorism agencies controlled by a municipal government, with nearly 600 officers.[15]

Despite its growing counterterrorism capabilities, the NYPD faced a series of constraints on its ability to use them in the months immediately after 9/11. In addition to limits set by the U.S. Constitution and federal laws that restrict the activities of all police departments, the NYPD had abided by a special set of limitations for 16 years. In 1985, to settle a civil suit filed by civil rights lawyer Barbara Handschu and a group of political activists, New York City agreed to a set of rules restricting police investigations (the Handschu Guidelines). In accordance with these guidelines, the NYPD agreed not to investigate constitutionally protected speech and other activities unless police had information that a crime was being committed or was imminent. The police department also agreed to use undercover officers only when doing so was essential to an investigation—not just to monitor certain groups—and to avoid keeping dossiers on people without specific information of criminal activity. As part of the agreement, a three-person oversight committee, comprising two senior police officials and one civilian appointed by the mayor, reviewed each police request to open an investigation.[16]

Following the 9/11 attacks, the NYPD argued for a relaxation of the Handschu Guidelines, claiming that the restrictions on investigations could prevent police from discovering activities that, while lawful, were part of a terrorist's or terrorist group's preparations for an attack against the city.[17] In response, a federal district judge ordered less restrictive rules for police investigations, including lifting the requirement that police have knowledge of specific criminal activity before investigating individuals or groups.[18] In addition, the new rules curtailed the power of the oversight committee created in 1985, limiting it to reviewing investigations after they had begun, with no power to decide which people, groups, or activities police could investigate.[19] The revised guidelines took effect in 2003, allowing the NYPD to initiate a broad expansion of its intelligence operations. This expansion included a special focus on Muslims living in New York City and surrounding areas, sometimes well beyond the city limits.

To construct demographic maps of targeted areas, the NYPD sent plainclothes officers (referred to as "rakers" within the police department) into neighborhoods throughout the city to gather intelligence on Muslim-owned businesses as well as on restaurants, cafes, bookstores, and other establishments frequently visited by Muslim patrons. Rakers also picked up informal news and rumors in neighborhoods with large numbers of Muslim residents by entering into casual conversations with cab drivers, food-cart vendors, and others working on New York City streets.[20] These plainclothes officers were not officially undercover officers, because they did not assume false identities, but neither did they identify themselves as law enforcement officials. Their activities were supported by the NYPD's Terrorism Interdiction Unit, which the police department created to help recruit, train, and manage informants. To recruit informants to spy on Muslim neighborhoods, the Terrorism Interdiction Unit often resorted to coercive tactics, such as pressuring Muslim residents arrested for various reasons to become informants in exchange for having charges dropped.[21]

In addition to spying on predominantly Muslim neighborhoods, the NYPD conducted surveillance of Muslim students at the many universities and colleges in the region. In the years after 9/11, the police department placed undercover officers and informants in Muslim student associations at several New York institutions, including St. Johns University, Brooklyn College, Baruch College, City College of New York, Hunter College, La Guardia Community College, and Queens College. Also, officers in the NYPD's Cyber Intelligence Unit monitored the websites, blogs, and online forums operated by Muslim student groups at Columbia University, New York University, and other institutions of higher education.[22] By 2006, the NYPD had investigated 31 Muslim student groups and had identified 7 of them as groups "of concern" due to their conservative religious views.[23]

The NYPD also conducted a sweeping surveillance operation aimed at mosques throughout the New York City metropolitan area. Spearheading this initiative, the Intelligence Division began photographing mosques and their surroundings, collecting license plate numbers of worshippers' cars, listing the ethnic composition of congregations, and installing hidden cameras in light posts outside of mosques.[24] Through these methods, the police department spied on hundreds of mosques over a wide area. By 2006, the NYPD had conducted surveillance on more than 250 mosques, cataloguing the demographic characteristics of their congregations as well as the habits and behavior patterns of mosque staff and worshippers.[25]

To enable undercover officers and informants to conduct more in-depth spying operations against specific mosques, the police department began categorizing some mosques as terrorism enterprises. After the loosening of the Handschu Guidelines in 2003, the NYPD created a new category of investigation called the "Terrorism Enterprise Investigation." Under the rules for these types of operations, the NYPD could investigate any organization if the police department believed it included two or more people involved in a terrorist act or violent crime.[26] Once the NYPD initiated such an investigation, it could deploy undercover officers and informants (referred to as "mosque crawlers") with recording devices to designated mosques in order to record sermons and conversations among congregants. The NYPD also placed informants on decision-making boards within mosques and engaged in other intrusive surveillance techniques. Within eight months of adopting the revised guidelines for investigations, the NYPD Intelligence Division had initiated at least 10 Terrorism Enterprise Investigations targeting mosques. Many of these investigations continued for years, even though police failed to uncover evidence of illegal activity.[27]

In many cases, officers conducting intelligence operations found themselves operating far beyond the limits of New York City. Some members of the Demographics Unit conducted surveillance in suburban neighborhoods of Long Island; others operated across the state line in Newark, New Jersey. Surveillance operations against Muslims also took NYPD intelligence officers as far as Pennsylvania and Massachusetts. Often, the targets of such operations were mosques miles from New York City as well as Muslims in student groups outside the borders of New York State.[28] The NYPD's Cyber Intelligence Unit assisted in these operations, monitoring the online activities of Muslim groups at the University of Pennsylvania, Syracuse University, and Yale. In one bungled operation, NYPD officers conducting surveillance on Muslim students at Rutgers University were exposed when a building superintendent stumbled upon their safe house across from the campus. Fearing that the NYPD surveillance equipment might belong to terrorists planning an attack, the superintendent called the local police.[29]

An expansion of the NYPD's counterterrorism capabilities and operations after 9/11 was neither surprising nor unwarranted. New York City received the brunt of the 9/11 attacks, suffering more than 2,700 deaths and many thousands more wounded, including many police officers, firefighters, and other first responders. In subsequent years, New York remained a highly prized target among terrorists seeking to conduct attacks against America. Nevertheless, as with the federal government's national counterterrorism policies, the actions taken by New York City authorities to secure the city have entailed significant costs. Among these costs are the erosion of restrictions on domestic spying, the expansion of coercive methods to recruit informants, and a general downgrading of hard-won guarantees against violations of basic civil rights (as reflected in the weakening of the Handschu Guidelines).

In addition, implicitly designating Muslims as persons of interest without evidence of criminal—or even suspicious—activity risks incorporating religious and ethnic profiling into policing strategy, undermining the police department's commitment to equal treatment under the law. This strategy also risks jeopardizing the trust and cooperation of the city's large and diverse Muslim population, possibly the NYPD's most valuable counterterrorism asset. The loss or weakening of this asset would undercut both New York City's and—due to the city's unfortunate role as a highly desired terrorist target—the nation's counterterrorism efforts.

Discriminatory Policies and Practices

New York City's efforts to build a counterterrorism capability remain unmatched by any other municipality in the United States. Nonetheless, since 9/11, communities across the nation and the political leaders who represent them at the state, county, and municipal levels have developed their own views about threats to homeland security. These views, sometimes sharply at odds with the federal government's designs, have steadily influenced the nature and content of laws enacted and policies advanced beyond Washington, D.C. In the post-9/11 environment, concern about terrorism and violent extremism has played a dominant role in this process, with fear of Islamic extremism a persistent factor.

In many cases, state and local leaders have attempted to balance concerns about terrorism with a determination to protect civil rights. During the four years following passage of the Patriot Act by the U.S. Congress, eight states and nearly 400 municipalities signed variations of a resolution declaring that provisions of the Patriot Act violated fundamental American values.[30] Additionally, the chiefs of police in Detroit and Portland, Oregon, declined to allow their cities' police officers to participate in the 2001–2003 FBI-led initiative to interview thousands of Arab and Muslim foreign nationals residing temporarily in the United States.[31] From 2005 to 2010, Portland municipal authorities also declined to participate in the FBI's Joint Terrorism Task Force set up in the city. They cited concerns that city officials lacked the ability to verify that the task force was not violating the rights of Portland residents.[32]

In other cases, concerns about civil rights, especially the rights of Muslim Americans, have played a more limited role in decision making. At times, policy making has been distorted by misunderstandings about the role of government in upholding religious freedom and the rights of religious minorities. Such distortions may be compounded by unfamiliarity with Islam, coupled with a failure to take many Islamic practices as seriously as those of other, more familiar religions. At other times, policies and legislation at the state and local levels have been based on overtly negative perceptions of Islam. In several cases, public officials have displayed open hostility toward Islam and bigotry toward Muslims. As a result, polices and laws covering a patchwork of counties, cities, and townships—and sometimes entire states—have disregarded the religious rights of Muslim Americans. Some have treated Islam as a hostile ideology and Muslims as a foreign and unwelcome presence in American society.

Bias against Appearance and Dress

Among the types of discrimination that state and local authorities have practiced against Muslims since 9/11, the most common have revolved around forms of dress and appearance that distinguish Muslims from their non-Muslim fellow citizens. Head coverings frequently worn by Muslim women, along with the women who wear them, have been primary targets for this type of discrimination. In keeping with the Koran's injunction to dress modestly, many Muslim women wear head coverings in public or in the presence of men other than their immediate relatives, as do many women of other religions, including Orthodox Jews, Amish, Mennonites, and Orthodox Christians. Such coverings worn by Muslim women range from headscarves that cover the head and neck while leaving the face uncovered (the hijab) to full head coverings that hide the entire face except for the eyes (the niqab). Although rarely seen in the United States, some Muslim women wear full-body veils that conceal the body from head to foot (the burka).

The U.S. Constitution and federal law protect the right of women to voluntarily wear religious head coverings (Islamic or otherwise) in most circumstances, just as they protect the right of all U.S. citizens and residents to wear religious garments. Whether motivated by religious conviction, custom, or a desire to express a Muslim identity, 60 percent of Muslim women in America take advantage of this right and choose to wear some form of head covering (usually a hijab) at least some of the time. More than a third of Muslim American women wear head coverings whenever they are in public.[33] Nevertheless, several states and localities have instituted policies and regulations that proscribe wearing head coverings in some public settings, sometimes in a manner that forces women to choose between their religious convictions and participating in society as employees, students, and citizens.

One of the earliest post-9/11 cases of discrimination involving Muslim head coverings began in 2002, when the New York Metropolitan Transportation Authority (MTA) prohibited its employees from wearing nonregulation head coverings when operating buses or subway trains, or when performing other work-related tasks requiring contact with the public. An investigation by the Department of Justice's Civil Rights

Division determined that the MTA was selectively enforcing its dress code to target Muslim and Sikh employees, who often wore headscarves or turbans. The Civil Rights Act of 1964 prohibits religious discrimination in employment, including employment by state and local agencies, and requires employers to make reasonable accommodations for their employees' religious beliefs and practices unless doing so would cause undue hardship to the employer. Despite this legal requirement, the MTA took various punitive measures against Muslim and Sikh employees who continued to wear religious head coverings. By contrast, MTA authorities allowed other employees to wear nonregulation headgear, such as ski caps and baseball caps, without incident.[34]

One year after the MTA began enforcing this policy, the school district of Muskogee, Oklahoma, suspended 12-year-old Nashala Hearn for wearing a headscarf in accordance with her Islamic faith. The school had previously granted permission for Nashala to wear a hijab; however, on September 11, 2003 (the second anniversary of 9/11), the school principal abruptly ordered Nashala to remove her headscarf in compliance with the school district's dress code. In the following weeks, school officials twice suspended Nashala for continuing to wear a hijab at school. While federal law and the First Amendment to the Constitution (as interpreted by the courts over the past two centuries) prohibit public schools from promoting religion, they also bar public schools from restricting religious practices unless the practices in question would significantly disrupt the classroom, and any such restriction must apply to all students equally. In violation of these principles, school authorities targeted Nashala and her religious attire, despite the fact that she had worn a hijab at school in the past without disrupting school activities. Also, the school had previously made numerous exceptions to its dress code for nonreligious hats and head coverings, and regularly allowed students to wear non-Islamic religious attire.[35]

During the next decade, many state and local government agencies across the nation interfered with the right of Muslim women to freely exercise their religion by banning head coverings in certain venues, sometimes requiring women to remove their head coverings in public. In New Jersey, the Essex County Department of Corrections first suspended and then fired corrections officer Yvette Beshier for refusing to comply with a prohibition against wearing head coverings at work.[36] In Georgia, officials at the Douglasville municipal courthouse refused to allow Miedah Valentine to enter the courtroom while wearing a hijab. When she protested, Valentine was detained, handcuffed, and held for several hours in a cell for contempt of court.[37] Following this incident, complaints that Muslim women with head coverings were barred from entering courthouses throughout Georgia prompted civil rights lawyers at the Department of Justice to open a statewide civil rights inquiry.[38]

State and local officials have also violated the religious rights of Muslim men by selectively enforcing rules regarding appearance. Maintaining beards and wearing skullcaps (kufis) have long been common religious practice among some Muslim men in the United States. However, on several occasions after 9/11, state and municipal government agencies have refused to make accommodations to allow public employees to keep beards or wear kufis. The New York Department of Correctional Services, for example, abruptly prohibited one of its employees, a Muslim corrections officer named Abdus Samad Haqq, from wearing a kufi while on duty. Corrections officials ignored the fact that Haqq had worn a kufi for several years without disruption while working at the corrections department.[39] Similarly, the School District of Philadelphia abruptly instituted a policy requiring male employees with beards to keep their facial hair trimmed to no more than a quarter inch long. No accommodation was made for security officer Siddiq Abu-Bakr, a Muslim who had worn a longer beard while on duty in accordance with his religious beliefs for more than 20 years.[40]

Another case arose in Philadelphia when the city's fire department refused to accommodate a firefighter's conviction that his religious faith required him to maintain a beard. In 2001, Muslim recruit Curtis DeVeaux shaved his beard after accepting a position at the fire department in order to conform to department's requirement that all firefighters remain clean-shaven. The ban on beards was designed as a safety measure, primarily to avoid facial hair from interfering with the operation of the department's respirators. Three years after being hired, DeVeaux learned of firefighters elsewhere in the country who wore beards, despite using the same basic equipment as the Philadelphia fire department. DeVeaux subsequently grew a beard and made both informal and formal requests for an exemption on religious grounds to the prohibition on beards. Without responding to his requests, fire department officials suspended DeVeaux without pay and informed him that he would be fired if he did not shave his beard within 30 days. In addition to disregarding DeVeaux's religious beliefs, fire department officials ignored the common practice of allowing firefighters with unusual facial features to take a respiratory fit test to demonstrate their ability to use the equipment safely.[41]

Bias against Religious Practice

Alongside appearance and dress, prayer and other forms of worship have been at the center of disputes between local government authorities and Muslim Americans. The Civil Rights Act of 1964 and other federal laws as well as the U.S. Constitution protect the right of Americans to pray and worship in accordance with their sincerely held religious beliefs under most circumstances. Accordingly, employers are required to make reasonable accommodations for their employees' beliefs about prayer and worship, unless doing so would cause significant hardship to the employer. Similarly, public schools are prohibited from promoting prayer or worship, but they must allow students to pray or worship independently, unless the form of worship in question would disrupt classroom or school activities.

Despite these requirements, Muslim public employees and students in different localities have found their rights to pray and worship curtailed by policies at the state, county, and municipal levels. In the first several months after 9/11, intervention by the Department of Justice's Civil Rights Division was required to settle a dispute in Plano, Texas. In this case, school district officials refused to continue arrangements to allow a Muslim employee to worship in accordance with his religious convictions. For many years, the school district had provided one of its bus drivers with a work schedule that allowed him to attend Friday prayer services. However, the bus driver's supervisor abruptly cancelled this arrangement, and the school district refused to reverse the decision until a legal settlement required school officials to resume the previous accommodation.[42]

In another school case, this time affecting students, the Lewisville Independent School District in Texas declined to accommodate Muslim students' needs to say prayers in a manner consistent with their religious beliefs. Although school officials allowed clubs and other groups to gather during lunch hour, they refused to allow Muslim students to assemble during lunch for midday prayers. A request by Muslim students for the use of an empty classroom or other unused space to say prayers during lunch was rejected, as was a subsequent request to allow students to kneel in the corner of the cafeteria for prayer. Once again, intervention by federal civil rights authorities prompted school officials to agree to an accommodation, which permitted Muslim students to pray in a designated space, similar to arrangements the school district had regularly made for other groups.[43]

In addition to prayer, the Muslim practice of making the pilgrimage to Mecca in Saudi Arabia (the hajj) has been a source of conflict. An annual event that brings together millions of Muslims from around the world, the hajj takes place during the last month of the Islamic calendar. Islamic practice requires that all adult Muslims perform the hajj at least once in a lifetime, as long as they are physically and financially able to do so. Nevertheless, the school district of Berkeley, Illinois, declined a request by middle school teacher Safoorah Khan for time off to make the hajj. In the spring of 2008, Khan informed the principal of her school that she planned to perform the hajj during the following school year. In the summer, she made a formal request for unpaid leave to perform the pilgrimage in December. After the school district declined her request, Khan submitted a second request with an explanation of the importance of the hajj to Muslims. The school district declined her request a second time and informed her that the matter would not be considered further. Khan subsequently resigned from her teaching position to perform the pilgrimage.[44]

Religious Bias in Government-Run Institutions

Among those most vulnerable to discriminatory policies are people confined to state-run prisons and other institutions. To guard against unnecessary restrictions on their religious practices, Congress passed the Religious Land Use and Institutionalized Persons Act (RLUIPA) in 2000. This law prohibits government authorities from imposing any regulation that places a substantial burden on an institutionalized person's religious practice, unless the regulation serves a compelling state interest and is the least restrictive means of advancing that interest. As stipulated in the law, if an institutionalized person can demonstrate that a regulation infringes significantly on his religious practice, the burden then falls on the institution to show that the restriction is needed to further a compelling public interest and that less restrictive measures would not be effective.[45] Muslims serving sentences in state prisons and county jails across the country have invoked this law to ensure their ability to practice their religion. In just five years after 9/11, more than 70 cases of alleged discrimination against Muslim prisoners reached the federal courts, nearly 3 times the number of cases involving infringement on Christian religious practices during the same time period.[46]

As in cases involving religious bias in school, the workplace, and public spaces, discrimination against Muslims at government institutions often revolves around appearance and dress. In 2006, officers at the Santa Ana Courthouse in Orange County, California, required Souhair Khatib, a Muslim immigrant from Lebanon, to remove her hijab despite her repeated objections. After forcing her to remove her headscarf, officers placed Khatib in a holding facility to await a hearing regarding previous misdemeanor violations. She was forced to appear before the judge later that day without her hijab.[47] In a similar case in 2008, the Maricopa County Sheriff's Office in Arizona arrested Eman Mabrouk, a Muslim woman, and detained her overnight pending her arraignment the next day. Officers on duty forced Mabrouk to remove her headscarf during her detention, without offering her an alternative head covering approved by the prison.[48] In contrast to these cases, the federal prison system and several other state prison systems allow women to wear state-approved head coverings for religious reasons.

Muslim men have also been denied the freedom to dress or groom in accordance with their religion in state and local detention facilities. In 2013, a federal court ruled that Texas prison officials had violated RLUIPA when they denied Muslim inmate Willie Lee Garner permission to maintain a quarter-inch beard, even though the Texas prison system allows several thousand prisoners with skin conditions to wear such beards.[49] The following year, the Supreme Court agreed to hear a similar RLUIPA case, this one involving Gregory Holt, a Muslim prisoner in an Arkansas state prison. In this case, prison officials also denied a prisoner in their custody permission to grow a quarter-inch beard, despite the fact that beards were permitted for other inmates under certain conditions without disruption of the prison's operations.[50] The Supreme Court ruled unanimously that the Arkansas policy violated the right of Holt and other Muslims to practice their religion.[51]

Other RLUIPA cases revolve around access to religious literature and materials. In one illustrative case in 2011, investigators at the Department of Justice's Civil Rights Division determined that authorities at the Sullivan County Jail in Tennessee were illegally denying Muslim prisoners access to the Koran and other religious items, such as prayer rugs.[52] In another case during the same year, the Department of Justice filed suit against the Berkeley County Detention Center in South Carolina for violations involving Jewish and Muslim inmates. At their discretion, Berkeley County prison officials sometimes allowed inmates to receive religious texts delivered in person by friends or family members. However, officials exercised this prerogative in an arbitrary manner and, in a case of blatant discrimination, denied Muslim inmate JaMichael Howard access to a Koran delivered to the facility specifically for his use. By contrast, prison authorities distributed copies of the King James Bible to prisoners at no cost and allowed inmates to buy other versions of the Bible available for purchase at the facility.[53]

Bias against Houses of Worship

Hostility toward religious minorities, in addition to fostering discrimination against individuals, is often directed at entire congregations and the most visible symbol of their presence—their houses of worship. Although attitudes and practices vary substantially across jurisdictions, several state and local governments throughout the United States have enacted laws and policies that impede religious groups trying to exercise their right to gather for worship or perform other religious activities. Such discrimination is commonly found in land-use decisions, particularly decisions regarding zoning requests made by religious congregations seeking to construct new houses of worship or expand existing ones. In some cases, religious groups in general are treated worse in zoning decisions than comparable secular groups. At other times, local zoning and land-marking decisions target congregations of specific religions. In these cases, the targets of discrimination are often groups from minority religions and new or unfamiliar denominations.[54]

To protect religious communities from such discrimination, Congress included prohibitions against religious bias in land-use decisions in the Religious Land Use and Institutionalized Persons Act. In addition to protecting the rights of institutionalized persons, RLUIPA prohibits zoning laws and ordinances that discriminate based on religion or that unjustifiably infringe on the freedom of religious groups to assemble. Similar to the protections it provides to institutionalized individuals, RLUIPA makes it unlawful to implement any land-use regulation that imposes a substantial burden on any religious community's ability to assemble unless authorities can demonstrate that the regulation 1) is necessary to advance a compelling public interest and 2) is the least restrictive means of advancing that interest.[55] Provisions of the law also bar authorities from completely excluding religious assemblies from any jurisdiction and prohibit unreasonable limits on religious buildings or other physical structures.

Despite the legal protections provided in RLUIPA, religious bias in local land-use decisions remains an obstacle to the free exercise of religion in many localities. In the decade after 9/11, Muslim congregations opened nearly a thousand mosques and Islamic community centers across the United States, most without notable opposition from local governments or communities.[56] However, on several occasions, discriminatory zoning policies have targeted Muslim congregations seeking to build or expand mosques and Islamic centers. At times, brazen expressions of anti-Muslim bigotry have accompanied local denials of zoning requests to build such facilities. More often, such anti-Muslim sentiments are combined with—and sometimes disguised as—concerns about traffic, parking, and increased noise levels that would presumably result from the new construction. From 2001 to 2011, the Department of Justice's Civil Rights Division opened 28 investigations of possible anti-Muslim discrimination in local land-use decisions.[57]

One of the earliest cases began just weeks after 9/11. In October 2001, the Albanian Associated Fund, representing about 200 families of Albanian ancestry, purchased vacant land in Wayne Township, New Jersey, and applied for a permit to build a mosque on the property. In response, the township abandoned its standard practice of allowing applicants for new construction to resolve outstanding technical issues after approval of a site plan, stating that no permit would be issued until all issues—technical and otherwise—were resolved. For several years, Wayne Township authorities refused to issue a decision on whether to allow the mosque to be built, even though the township's own regional planner submitted a report in 2003 stating that the site and architectural plans for the mosque complied with the township's specifications. In 2006, the township halted consideration of zoning for the mosque and initiated eminent domain proceedings to seize the property, declaring a desire to preserve the property as open space. Only civil action in federal court halted the seizure of the Albanian Associated Fund's land.[58]

Two years later, a Muslim congregation of approximately 1,250 people purchased land in Henrico County, Virginia, and requested that the county rezone the property to allow construction of a mosque. At that time, the county had more than 200 churches but no mosque. As a result, Muslim residents rented temporary space at various locations for worship, at significant cost to worshippers. Although the county had never previously turned down a rezoning application from a Christian church, and no other suitable land was available for sale in Henrico County to build a mosque, county officials declined the Muslim congregation's request. Moreover, county officials involved in the decision made derogatory comments about Islam and, in one instance, suggested that the Muslim congregation develop a plan to perform charitable work in order to be a good neighbor, even though the county had never made a similar request to a non-Muslim denomination.[59]

Similarly, in 2009 and 2010, officials in the town of Lilburn, Georgia, twice denied rezoning requests from the Dar-e-Abbas Islamic Center to allow construction of a 20,000-square-foot mosque. In the absence of a suitable house of worship, congregants of Dar-e-Abbas performed religious services in a deteriorating 2,000-square-foot house (one-tenth the size of the proposed mosque) located on the contested site between a Baptist church and a Hindu temple. An investigation by civil rights lawyers at the Department of Justice determined that Lilburn had regularly granted similar rezoning requests from non-Muslim religious groups and that officials on the town planning committee declined the request from Dar-e-Abbas in order to appease anti-Muslim sentiments expressed by some of the town's residents.[60]

Since 9/11, local governments have also attempted to prevent Muslim groups from expanding existing facilities to meet the demands of growing Muslim communities. Two early cases arose in Illinois. In the village of Morton Grove, a Muslim community center operated out of an unused elementary school it had purchased in 1989. In addition to using the space as a Muslim school, the center regularly held prayer services during the week, convening students for prayer in the gymnasium during the day and permitting Muslim residents in the area to gather in the gymnasium for prayer on Friday evenings. In 2002, the center applied for a permit to build more classrooms for the school and to construct a mosque at the site large enough to accommodate about 600 congregants. Amid strong resistance to the expansion by some residents—including acts of vandalism—municipal officials rejected the expansion plans, despite the obvious need for upgraded facilities. A federal civil rights suit against Morton Grove, along with mediation by the Department of Justice's Community Relations Service, was required before municipal authorities allowed expansion of the community center to proceed.[61]

Also in Illinois, authorities in the village of Berkeley rejected a proposed expansion of a local mosque to service a growing Muslim community. In 1982, the Albanian American Islamic Center purchased property in Berkeley and began holding services in a former school building at the site. As the only Islamic institution in Berkeley and the only mosque in Illinois catering to Albanian immigrants, the Islamic center gained a large congregation. During prayer services, worshipers often spilled out of the designated prayer room, into the hallways of the school building. In January 2004, the Islamic center submitted an application to expand the facility and remodel the exterior in order to give the building a mosque-like appearance. Municipal officials rejected the application, prompting the Islamic center to submit three revised proposals over the next three years. Berkeley officials rejected all three applications, ultimately allowing the expansion only after federal authorities opened a RLUIPA investigation of the matter.[62]

Two similar cases arose in Georgia and California, both requiring intervention by the Department of Justice before Muslim congregations were able to proceed with expansion plans. In the California case, municipal officials in the town of Lomita in Los Angeles County rejected the proposed upgrading of the Islamic Center of the South Bay in March 2010. Due to the small size and layout of the Islamic center's facilities, many congregants had to pray outside in tents and in small annex buildings scattered across the property. The Islamic center submitted an application to construct a prayer hall large enough for the congregation to pray together, along with washing facilities, a library, classrooms, and office space. Citing traffic concerns, the city council denied permission for the expansion, despite the fact that a study conducted by municipal staff had concluded that the proposed project would actually improve traffic and parking in the neighborhood.[63]

Two months later, in May 2010, the city of Alpharetta, Georgia, denied permission for the Islamic Center of North Fulton to expand its facilities to accommodate a congregation that had grown more than 20-fold over the previous decade. In 1998, the Islamic center began holding prayer services for a congregation of 25 Muslim residents. In 2010, with the congregation numbering about 600 people, the center requested permission to erect a main prayer hall and a smaller community hall on the property. Despite the need for upgraded facilities, city officials refused to grant permission for the project. In previous years, the city had approved the construction of similarly sized churches, including two churches on the same road as the Islamic center.[64]

In August 2014, federal officials took action in a similar case, filing a lawsuit against St. Anthony Village in Minnesota for violating the civil rights of the Abu Hiraira Islamic Center. After purchasing a business center in St. Anthony, the Islamic center applied for approval to repurpose the building's basement as a space for worship. The St. Anthony city council voted to deny the request, despite the fact that the city allowed nonreligious groups to assemble in the same vicinity. The denial left the Abu Hiraira congregation without a site large enough for prayer services, forcing members to continue praying at various sites in the Minneapolis-St. Paul region. At some locations, congregation members had to pray in entry halls and hallways, while also attending services in shifts, due to the small size of the facilities.[65] In December 2014, local officials reached a legal settlement with the Islamic center, allowing space in the building to be used for a mosque and classrooms.[66]

Countering the "Sharia Threat"

For centuries, Sharia (which means "the path" or "the way") has provided Muslims with guidelines for how to conduct themselves in accordance with the teachings of the Koran and the sayings and deeds of the Prophet Mohammad. Historically, interpretations of Sharia among Muslims have been highly contested and have varied widely. Over the centuries and throughout the world today, Muslim communities and individuals have adopted versions of Sharia in conformity with their religious beliefs, often in sharp contrast with other versions. In all cases, Sharia provides a moral code of conduct that observant Muslims strive to live by, just as many Christians seek to live their lives based on the moral lessons found in the Bible and the teachings of Jesus Christ.

In the popular American imagination, however, Sharia is often viewed as an oppressive legal code based on premodern moral precepts. Many Americans believe some of the harshest interpretations of Sharia—the forced marriage of underage girls, the stoning to death of women for adultery, and amputation of limbs for thieves—are required by Islamic practice. Since 9/11, anti-Muslim activists have taken advantage of this popular perception to misrepresent Islam as a religion and to stoke fear that Muslim Americans seek to impose a violent and intolerant version of Sharia on the country. Among the most active of such agitators has been David Yerushalmi, an American lawyer and the founder of the Society of Americans for National Existence (SANE). Yerushalmi initiated his anti-Sharia campaign by posting a proposed law on his organization's website that would make observing Sharia a felony punishable by up to 20 years in prison. Later, after failing to make progress at the federal level, he and his supporters began focusing on state legislatures, with the hope of convincing states across the country to ban any consideration of Sharia in state judicial proceedings.[67]

Bans on considering Sharia—or any other religious code—in court may seem innocuous, since the U.S. Constitution already prohibits courts from imposing religion or religious practices. However, in addition to unfairly singling out a specific religion and its adherents, adoption of any such measure would distort the judicial process and violate the First Amendment to the U.S. Constitution, which proscribes laws that prohibit the free exercise of religion. Many Americans live their lives in accordance with religious traditions and often make legal arrangements based on religious law and custom. Orthodox Jews often use rabbinical courts to obtain divorces and resolve business disputes, while Catholics frequently turn to diocesan tribunals for marriage annulments and other matters. Similarly, observant Muslims commonly rely on religious authorities to decide legal, business, and family disputes. Courts in the United States routinely settle disputes regarding contracts drafted on the basis such arrangements, as long as they do not violate secular law or the U.S. Constitution.[68]

Notwithstanding the common use of religious law and custom in everyday life, anti-Sharia activists began achieving results in 2010. In April of that year, the Oklahoma legislature voted to allow a referendum on a proposed amendment to the state constitution (the Save Our State Amendment) that would ban state courts from considering international law and Sharia law in their proceedings. The amendment, which was put before voters the following November, stated, "The courts shall not look to the legal precepts of other nations or cultures. Specifically, the courts shall not consider international law or Sharia law."[69] The proposed amendment passed with 70 percent of the vote.

Two days after the amendment's approval, Oklahoma City resident Muneer Awad, the executive director of the Oklahoma chapter for the Council on American-Islamic Relations, filed a lawsuit claiming the amendment violated his right to freely exercise his religion.[70] A federal district court found that Awad's claim deserved consideration and barred the state from implementing the new amendment until the merits of the case could be decided in court. A federal appeals court upheld this temporary ban on the amendment, stating that state authorities "did not know of even a single instance where an Oklahoma court had applied Sharia law or used the legal precepts of other nations or cultures, let alone that such applications or uses had resulted in concrete problems for Oklahoma."[71] Subsequently, a federal court ruled in favor of Awad and struck down the Oklahoma amendment as a violation of the U.S. Constitution.[72]

Taking note of this failure in the courts, supporters of anti-Sharia measures tried different tactics to pass state laws that would survive constitutional scrutiny. Rather than singling out Sharia or Islam, anti-Sharia activists in some states began proposing legislation that would bar state courts from considering religious laws in general. In Arizona, state lawmakers who favored anti-Sharia legislation introduced a measure to bar state courts from implementing or using tenants of any sectarian law. The measure specifically listed Catholic canon law, Jewish Halacha law, and karma as banned from court consideration.[73] Similarly, the South Dakota legislature considered, and ultimately passed, a law prohibiting state courts and government agencies of the state from enforcing "any provisions of any religious code."[74]

In other states, lawmakers attempted to draft anti-Sharia legislation that would survive a challenge in court by broadening proposed bans to encompass all foreign laws while omitting any reference to religion. The language of proposed measures varied across states, but most sought to ban state courts and state-level government agencies from applying or enforcing any foreign law if doing so would violate citizens' rights under the state constitution or the U.S. Constitution. In some cases, lawmakers proposed laws that would invalidate any court decision based in whole or in part on a legal system that did not recognize the same rights as the state constitution or the U.S. Constitution. In two states, Florida and North Carolina, state legislators opposed to Sharia narrowed language in their proposed laws to ban courts from considering foreign laws that dealt specifically with family matters, such as marriage, divorce, and child custody.[75]

Through these types of bans on foreign laws, anti-Sharia advocates sought to avoid charges of religious bias, while broadening support for their proposals. By excluding mention of religion, they attempted to avoid directly challenging citizens' First Amendment right to freely exercise their religious beliefs, while also avoiding explicitly discriminating against any one religion or any group of religions. Such proposed laws, however, remained focused primarily on Islamic law and custom. In Louisiana, for example, the coauthors of a proposed foreign-law ban justified their bill by citing attempts by Muslim immigrants to invoke Sharia law during court cases. In Kansas, a state legislator attempted to gain support for a measure banning foreign laws by telling her colleagues that voting for the bill was important to prevent the encroachment of Sharia in the state. In Florida, the cosponsor of a proposed foreign-law ban compared Sharia to a "dreadful disease" and distributed booklets titled *Shari'ah Law: Radical Islam's Threat to the U.S. Constitution.*[76]

By the end of 2014, state lawmakers in at least 34 states had introduced more than 100 bills and constitutional amendments to ban consideration of foreign or religious laws in state courts or government agencies. These states were spread across all regions of the country, from Florida in the southeast to Alaska in the far northwest. Below is a regional breakdown of states in which legislators proposed measures to prevent state courts from considering foreign or religious laws.

In eleven of these states (listed below), anti-Sharia activists succeeded in marshalling measures through the state legislatures.

TABLE 3.1 States in Which the State Legislators Have Proposed Laws Banning Foreign or Religious Laws

Southeast	Midwest	West	Northeast
Alabama	Indiana	Alaska	Maine
Arkansas	Iowa	Arizona	New Jersey
Florida	Kansas	Idaho	New Hampshire
Georgia	Michigan	New Mexico	Pennsylvania
Kentucky	Minnesota	Utah	Vermont
Louisiana	Missouri	Washington	
Mississippi	Nebraska	Wyoming	
North Carolina	South Dakota		
Oklahoma			
South Carolina			
Tennessee			
Texas			
Virginia			
West Virginia			

Sources: Faiza Patel and Amos Toh, "The Clear Anti-Muslim Bias Behind Anti-Shariah Laws," *Washington Post*, February 21, 2014; Bill Raftery, "Bans on Court Use of Sharia/International Law," Gavel to Gavel, February 5, 2014, www.GavelToGavel.us; Pew Research Center, *State Legislation Restricting Use of Foreign or Religious Law* (April 2013), www.pewforum.org.

TABLE 3.2 States That Have Passed Laws Banning Foreign or Religious Laws

Alabama	Idaho	Missouri	South Dakota
Arizona	Kansas	North Carolina	Tennessee
Florida	Louisiana	Oklahoma	

Sources: Omar Sacirbey, "Anti-Sharia Bill Passed in North Carolina without Governor Pat McCrory's Signature," *Huffington Post*, August 27, 2013; Pew Research Center, *State Legislation Restricting Use of Foreign or Religious Law* (April 2013), www.pewforum .org; Amos Toh and David Barkey, "Anti-Muslim Bigotry Taints Ban on Foreign Laws," *Washington Post*, May 16, 2014; "More States Move to Ban Foreign Law in State Courts," *USA Today*, August 4, 2013, www.usatoday.com.

In the case of Oklahoma, after the courts struck down the state's 2010 prohibition against Sharia, the legislature passed another measure in 2013 that barred courts and administrative agencies from basing decisions on foreign laws that do not grant individuals the same rights guaranteed by the U.S. Constitution and the state constitution of Oklahoma.[77] During the same year, the Missouri state legislature voted in favor of a bill restricting the use of foreign laws, although the governor subsequently vetoed the measure.[78] In Idaho, the state legislature passed a nonbinding resolution requesting that the U.S. Congress enact a federal law banning the use of foreign or international law in domestic courts across the United States.[79] The last measure to pass before the end of 2014 was a ballot initiative in Alabama. This initiative called for an amendment to the state constitution banning state courts from considering foreign laws that would violate the state's public policy or the rights of the state's citizens. The measure passed with more than 70 percent of the popular vote.[80]

As with federal legislation and policies designed to enhance homeland security and counter the threat of terrorism, measures pursued at the state and local levels have often intruded on the rights of American citizens. Muslim Americans have borne the brunt of these intrusions. From warrantless surveillance and monitoring by local police to efforts aimed at excluding Muslim institutions from certain jurisdictions, state and local authorities have often ignored—or attempted to proscribe—the rights of Muslims to freely practice their religion. In some cases, such actions have resulted from ignorance or confusion about guarantees on freedom of religion contained in federal law and the U.S. Constitution. However, in many cases, laws and policies affecting Muslims at the state and local levels have arisen from anti-Muslim bias and intolerance, with little consideration of their actual impact on security at the municipal, state, or national level.

CHAPTER 4

Climate of Fear

In the immediate aftermath of 9/11, fear, anger, and uncertainty pervaded American society. These emotions persisted for years afterward, sometimes dropping into the background of public awareness, but never fading away. They frequently reemerged when events at home or abroad underscored the continuing threat of terrorism. This persistent concern about terrorism, especially terrorism motivated by Islamic extremism, had a profound effect on U.S. perceptions of Islam and Muslims, including Muslim Americans. Before 9/11, most Americans had few thoughts about Islam and only passing awareness of Muslim Americans. Negative stereotypes of Islam abounded. However, like most aspects of national culture, they were transmitted to members of society through movies, books, peer-group influences, popular culture, and other indirect means, often without triggering critical appraisal or strong awareness of their presence. The attacks of 9/11 abruptly changed that pattern, first by providing a salience to Islam never before experienced by the American public and, second, by providing a new opportunity to frame the way Americans perceive and understand Islam and Muslims.

Evolving Attitudes toward Islam

Unfavorable perceptions of Islam have had an enduring presence in the West, dating back centuries before the founding of the United States and persisting throughout American history. These perceptions often exercised a degree of influence on American popular attitudes, even as most of the public remained disengaged from the topic of Islam and formed no firm opinions about the religion or its adherents. At times, when Islam or some segment of the world's Muslim population became salient—such as during the Ottoman Empire's massacre of ethnic Armenians early in the 1900s or during the Iran hostage crisis later in the century—negative sentiments rose to the surface. Such events also contributed to long-running perceptions of Islam as potentially dangerous and removed from American principles and norms. However, events that placed Islam in the public spotlight appeared sporadically throughout most of American history and failed to spark sustained, widespread hostility toward Islam or Muslims.

In keeping with this trend, nearly a decade before the 9/11 attacks, most Americans were largely ambivalent or indifferent about Islam. In mid-February 1993, two weeks before the first bombing of the World Trade Center, a *Los Angeles Times* poll found that significantly more than half of Americans (64 percent) had no opinion about Islam. When asked what came to mind when thinking about Islam, a plurality of respondents (37 percent) answered, "Nothing" or "I don't know."[1] However, during the rest of the decade, terrorist attacks targeting America—from the 1998 bombing of U.S. embassies in Kenya and Tanzania to the failed effort to bomb Los Angeles International Airport on New Year's Eve in 1999—placed terrorism, Islamic extremism, and Islam in general on the public agenda. In 2001, the 9/11 terrorist attacks focused the American public's attention on Islam to a degree that no previous event in history had achieved. Following the attacks, the ranks of Americans with no opinion about Islam receded, dropping to 13 percent in October 2001 and remaining at similarly low levels for the rest of the decade.

Almost immediately after 9/11, as many Americans began focusing on Islam and Muslims, President George W. Bush led efforts to ensure that the terrorist attacks did not give rise to widespread anti-Muslim animosity. Three days after the 9/11 attacks, he presided over a prayer service at the Washington National Cathedral, with all four living former presidents—Gerald Ford, Jimmy Carter, George H.W. Bush, and Bill Clinton—in attendance. At his insistence, Imam Muzammil Siddiqi of the Islamic Society or North America led the opening prayer service.[2] Three days later, the president met with Muslim leaders at the Islamic Center of Washington, D.C. In public remarks outside the mosque, he spoke against anti-Muslim bigotry, making the following statement:

America counts millions of Muslims amongst our citizens, and
Muslims make an incredibly valuable contribution to our country . . . Those who feel like they can intimidate our fellow citizens
to take out their anger don't represent the best of America, they
represent the worst of humankind, and they should be ashamed
of that kind of behavior. This is a great country. It's a great country because we share the same values of respect and dignity and
human worth. And it is my honor to be meeting with [Muslim]
leaders who feel just the same way I do. They're outraged, they're
sad. They love America just as much as I do.[3]

Others joined President Bush's efforts, including several influential
religious organizations that sponsored interfaith campaigns to prevent
anger over 9/11 from fueling anti-Muslim hostility. Among the most
prominent were the World Council of Churches, the World Jewish Congress, and the Interfaith Council on Metropolitan Washington.[4] Together,
these efforts appear to have succeeded to a remarkable degree, at least
in the short term. After 9/11, as people who previously had no opinion
about Islam formed impressions of the religion, many initially developed
positive views. In October 2001, a *Washington Post*-ABC News opinion
survey found that a plurality of Americans (47 percent) had a generally
favorable opinion of Islam. Those with a negative opinion constituted
almost 40 percent of the public.[5] Although both positive and negative
perceptions of Islam rose, as the proportion of the American public that
professed no opinion declined, the relatively high favorability rating
Islam received just one month after 9/11 was remarkable.

Although this surprising result may have mitigated the public backlash against Muslims in the United States after 9/11, it did not hold firm
during the rest of the decade. In proceeding years, as the effects of efforts
by President Bush and others to curb anti-Muslim sentiment receded,
the percentage of Americans who held favorable views of Islam steadily
declined. According to *Washington Post*-ABC News polling results, by
2010, those with a favorable view of Islam had dropped to 37 percent
of the public, while those with an unfavorable opinion had risen to 49
percent. During this period, Americans leaned increasingly toward negative impressions of Islam, even though a large proportion of the public
lacked basic knowledge of the religion. Americans professing to have
no opinion about Islam constituted a small fraction of the public (13
percent) in 2010, despite the fact that more than half of Americans (55
percent) acknowledged that they did not have a basic understanding of
the teachings and beliefs of Islam.[6]

TABLE 4.1   American Public Perceptions of Islam

	October 2002	September 2003	March 2006	March 2009	September 2010
Unfavorable View of Islam	33%	38%	46%	48%	49%
Believe Islam Encourages Violence	23%	34%	33%	29%	31%

Source: *Washington Post*-ABC News Polls, *Washington Post* Public Opinion Poll Archive, www.washingtonpost.com/wp-srv/politics/polls/poll-archive.html.

Throughout the decade, a similar pattern emerged regarding popular American perceptions of Islam's relation to violence. A year after 9/11, in October 2002, while nearly a quarter (23 percent) of Americans believed mainstream Islam encouraged violence against non-Muslims, more than half (53 percent) regarded Islam as a peaceful religion. Another quarter of the public expressed no opinion on the matter. Public opinion on this question fluctuated over the next nine years, but opinion surveys revealed a long-term increase in the number of Americans who viewed Islam as a violent religion. By September 2010, the percentage of Americans who believed Islam to be a peaceful religion (54 percent) remained almost unchanged, but the proportion of the public that believed Islam encouraged violence against non-Muslims rose to almost a third.[7]

Opinion polls conducted jointly by the Pew Research Center and the Pew Forum on Religion and Public Life revealed a similar pattern during the years after 9/11. According to Pew survey data, in March 2002, a quarter of the U.S. public believed that Islam was more likely than other religions to encourage violence among its believers. By August 2010, the proportion of Americans who shared this view had increased to 35 percent.[8] An opinion poll commissioned by *Time* magazine that same year indicated that an even larger percentage of Americans associated Islam with violence. According to *Time*'s survey data, in August 2010, a plurality of 46 percent of Americans believed Islam was more likely to encourage violence against nonbelievers than other religions.[9]

Several other opinion polls conducted in the years after 9/11 demonstrated a reservoir of concern about Islam and violence among much of the public. A 2004 poll from the Council on American-Islamic Relations found that 26 percent of Americans believed Islam taught violence.[10] Similarly, a national survey led by sociologist Robert Wuthnow shortly after 9/11 revealed that 47 percent of Americans associated Islam with the word "fanatical" and 40 percent associated Islam with the word "violent."[11] In 2010, an opinion poll conducted by Zogby International and the Arab American Institute found that 46 percent of Americans believed Islam taught hate.[12] Four years later, the Pew Research Center revisited the issue of Islam's relation to violence, finding in September 2014 that 50 percent of Americans believed Islam was more likely than other religions to encourage violence among its believers.[13]

Alongside this pattern of evolving post-9/11 attitudes toward Islam, a parallel trend emerged regarding the country's attitudes toward Muslim Americans. According to a Pew opinion survey conducted in March 2001, five months before the 9/11 attacks, 45 percent of the public held a favorable opinion of Muslims in the United States, while 24 percent held an unfavorable view and 31 percent expressed no opinion. Two months after the 9/11 attacks, 59 percent of Americans expressed a favorable view of Muslim Americans and 17 percent expressed a negative view. The number of people with no opinion declined to 24 percent. Pew researchers found a clear indication that President Bush's call for tolerance was a major factor in this change. Among conservative Republicans, President Bush's primary base of support, those expressing a favorable opinion of Muslim Americans rose from 35 percent in March 2001 to 64 percent the following November.[14]

As with American views on Islam in general, the sharp rise in positive perceptions of Muslim Americans immediately after 9/11 did not go unchallenged in subsequent years. From November 2001 to August 2007, Pew survey data revealed a relatively small decline in those with favorable views of Muslims in America (from 59 percent to 53 percent), coupled with a larger increase in those with an unfavorable opinion (from 17 percent to 29 percent).[15] In later years, other opinion surveys indicated a continued decline in the public's attitudes toward Muslim Americans. Caution is necessary when comparing surveys from different polling organizations since different methodologies can yield significantly different results. However, the magnitude of the changes in public attitudes measured by a variety of polls is substantial. *Time* magazine's 2010 poll found that public opinion about Muslim Americans was evenly split, with 44 percent expressing a favorable view and 43 percent expressing an unfavorable view.[16] The Arab American Institute later released the results of two polls that indicated a continued downward trend in public attitudes toward Muslim Americans, with 40 percent expressing a favorable opinion in 2012 and just 27 percent expressing a favorable opinion in 2014.[17]

TABLE 4.2   The American Public's Views of Muslim Americans

	November 2001	March 2002	June/ July 2003	July 2005	August 2007	August 2010	June 2012	June 2014
Favorable	59	54	51	55	53	44	40	27
Unfavorable	17	22	24	25	29	43	41	45
No Opinion	24	24	25	20	18	14	19	28

Sources: Arab American Institute; Pew Research Center and Pew Forum on Religion and Public Life; *Time* magazine.

Militant Islam and the Terrorist Threat

In addition to raising Islam as a salient topic for the American public, the 9/11 terrorist attacks strongly influenced how Americans approached this topic in subsequent months and years. As millions of Americans began developing more fully formed opinions about Islam, heightened awareness about Islamic extremism and its role in inspiring terrorist acts was unavoidable. This awareness was maintained in the years afterward by long U.S. counterinsurgency campaigns in Afghanistan and Iraq as well as the rise of violent extremist movements (some allied to al-Qaeda), notably in North Africa, the Middle East, and South Asia. More than a decade after 9/11, the rise of the terrorist network in Iraq and Syria referred to as the Islamic State demonstrated the persistence of Islamic extremism as a social force in some parts of the world.

Alongside these factors, a number of high-profile terrorist attacks around the world highlighted the threat presented by Muslim militants. Bombings in Bali, Indonesia, in 2002, followed by the 2004 bombing of commuter trains in Madrid and the 2005 suicide bombings in London, demonstrated the capacity of religious extremism to inspire spectacular acts of violence against civilian populations. For years afterward, public attention was directed toward such horrific attacks as the four-day assault in 2008 on Mumbai by the terrorist group Lashkar-e-Taiba, the 2013 attack on a shopping mall in Nairobi by the Somalia-based group al-Shabaab, and the massacre of more than 140 children and teachers at a school in Peshawar in 2014 by the Pakistani Taliban (Tehrik-i-Taliban Pakistan). The attack on the U.S. diplomatic mission in Benghazi, Libya, in 2012, which killed U.S. Ambassador Christopher Stevens and three other Americans, underscored the fact that Americans were high on the list of targets.

Parallel to these attacks abroad, al-Qaeda attempted to follow 9/11 with new attacks against targets in the United States and against U.S.-bound passenger planes. In December 2001, British citizen Richard Reid, who received training and instruction from al-Qaeda, tried to bring down a passenger plane bound for Miami from Paris. Once the plane was in flight, he attempted to detonate a bomb hidden in his shoe but was subdued by passengers and crew before he could ignite the bomb.[18] His foiled attack elevated fears about airline safety and resulted in a policy requiring passengers to remove their shoes at security checkpoints before boarding commercial flights. This requirement continues to serve as a reminder that commercial airliners remain highly prized targets for al-Qaeda and allied extremists.

In August 2006, five years after Richard Reid's failed terrorist attack, British police arrested eight men trained and instructed by al-Qaeda to detonate explosives aboard at least seven commercial flights traveling from London to cities in Canada and the United States. The assailants planned to smuggle liquid explosives disguised as beverages onto the aircraft and then detonate them over the Atlantic Ocean. Had they succeeded, the attacks would have killed as many as 1,500 passengers and crew.[19] Their failed attempt, like Richard Reid's thwarted attack, resulted in a new security measure, this one barring passengers from carrying containers holding more than a few ounces of liquids or gels into airliner cabins. This new regulation served as yet another reminder to millions of air travelers about the threat of terrorism motivated by al-Qaeda's brand of militant Islam.

Three years later, on Christmas Day 2009, Nigerian national Umar Farouk Abdulmutallab launched yet another attack designed to bring down a passenger plane, this time aboard an airliner traveling from Amsterdam to Detroit. Trained and instructed by al-Qaeda's affiliate in Yemen, al-Qaeda in the Arabian Peninsula (AQAP), Abdulmutallab tried unsuccessfully to detonate explosives sewn into his underwear as the flight prepared to land at Detroit Metropolitan Airport. The explosives ignited in flames rather than exploding, giving passengers and crew time to restrain him.[20] This failed terrorist attack highlighted for Americans the continued threat from al-Qaeda and affiliated groups more than eight years after 9/11.

Along with these attacks launched from overseas, Muslim terrorist groups recruited people living in the United States to launch attacks from within the country. In September 2009, three months before the failed attempt to bring down a passenger plane over Detroit, authorities arrested members of an al-Qaeda cell instructed to conduct a suicide bombing in the New York City subway system. The three al-Qaeda operatives, two originally from Afghanistan and one originally from Bosnia, were either U.S. citizens or legal permanent U.S. residents. All three had trained for their mission in al-Qaeda camps in Pakistan.[21] Eight months later, in May 2010, Faisal Shahzad attempted to detonate a car bomb in New York's Times Square. The bomb failed to detonate because of faulty construction, and the assailant was arrested as he attempted to depart the United States aboard a commercial flight to Pakistan. Shahzad, a naturalized U.S. citizen from Pakistan, received training and financing to carry out the attack from the Pakistani Taliban.[22]

In other cases, Muslim extremists who lacked direct affiliation with any terrorist organization carried out attacks in the United States. In July 2006, Naveed Haq, a naturalized U.S. citizen from Pakistan, opened fire with two semiautomatic handguns on the office of the Jewish Federation of Greater Seattle, killing one person and injuring five others.[23] Three years later, Abdulhakim Muhammad, an American convert to Islam, shot two soldiers outside an army recruiting station in Little Rock, Arkansas, killing one and wounding the other.[24] Later that year, in November 2009, Army Major Nidal Hasan, an American-born U.S. citizen of Palestinian descent, opened fire on fellow soldiers at Fort Hood in Texas. Hasan's attack killed 13 people and wounded 32.[25]

Four years after Nidal Hasan's mass shooting, another sensational terrorist attack underlined the threat posed by extremists associated with militant interpretations of Islam. In April 2013, Tamerlan and Dzhokhar Tsarnaev, brothers of Chechen origin who had immigrated to the United States years earlier, detonated two bombs near the finish line of the Boston Marathon. The nearly simultaneous explosions killed 3 bystanders and wounded approximately 275 other people. The brothers eluded capture until they were confronted by police in the suburb of Watertown four days later. Tamerlan was killed in the confrontation, and the gravely injured Dzhokhar was apprehended several hours later.[26]

These and other attempts to carry out terrorist attacks against the United States, combined with the immense impact of 9/11, ensured that terrorism and Islamic extremism (as well as Islam in general) remained at the top of the public agenda for years after 9/11. An NBC News-*Wall Street Journal* poll found that, in September 2014, almost half of Americans (47 percent) believed the nation had become less safe in the years since 9/11, compared to only about a quarter (26 percent) that believed the nation had become more secure. Americans who believed the country had become less safe had more than doubled since September 2002, just one year after the 9/11 attacks.[27] Based on data from Zogby Analytics and the Arab American Institute, this rise in pessimism about America's vulnerability to terrorist attack in 2014 occurred as favorable public attitudes about Islam declined to their lowest levels since before 9/11.[28]

Framing Islam in the Media

The 9/11 attacks and subsequent efforts by Islamic extremists to strike American targets pushed Islam onto the public agenda. However, they were not the only factors influencing how Americans would approach Islam as a topic or what assumptions Americans would make about the religion and its adherents, including their fellow citizens who happened to be Muslim. In the immediate aftermath of 9/11, the efforts of President Bush and other influential public figures to stave off, or at least limit, an anti-Muslim backlash had a demonstrable effect on public opinion. In the following months and years, however, American attitudes toward Islam and Muslims were increasingly shaped by other aspects of American culture and society, none more important than the news and entertainment media.

News Media

Heavy news reporting on terrorism and Islamic extremism was inevitable after 9/11, and ongoing efforts by terrorists to strike American targets at home and abroad guaranteed the continuation of such news coverage for years afterward. In the aftermath of 9/11, the news media played an essential role in informing a shocked public that had been largely unaware of the danger posed by al-Qaeda or even of the group's existence. The news media also served as an important source of information for the large majority of Americans who were uninformed about Islam and the world's more than 1.5 billion Muslims. As with reporting on any major event or issue, news reporting on these topics required journalists, correspondents, and editors to filter vast quantities of information. They drew attention to some elements, while excluding others in order to present a coherent narrative.[29] Whether by design or simply the nature of the news business, the news media provided some of the most powerful and enduring frames through which most Americans thought about and understood Islam, Muslims, and their relationship to extremism and violence.

In one of the first and most comprehensive efforts to measure news coverage of Islam and Muslims after 9/11, scholars Brigitte Nacos and Oscar Torres-Reyna compared news reports during the six months before

9/11 with reporting during the six months after 9/11. Looking at coverage provided by the major broadcast news programs (ABC News, CBS News, and NBC News), as well as major cable news networks (CNN and Fox News), they found—as expected—a sharp rise in reporting on Islam and Muslims (as well as Arabs) after 9/11. Stories mentioning these subjects rose from only 188 in the six months before 9/11 to more than 1,400 in the six months afterward. In a parallel examination of print media news during the same time period, Nacos and Torres-Reyna found similar results regarding reporting on Muslim Americans and Arab Americans. Their analysis of the major newspapers in New York City (the *New York Times*, the *New York Post*, and the *Daily News*) and a national daily newspaper (*USA Today*) revealed an increase in stories devoted to Muslim and Arab Americans, which rose from a combined total of 59 to more than 650.[30]

Evaluating the content of this reporting, Nacos and Torres-Reyna found a shift toward more balanced and informative reporting after 9/11, with a trend toward positive presentations of Muslims and Arabs living in the United States. Just as the Bush White House attempted to mitigate anti-Muslim sentiments after 9/11, the print media in their study generally attempted to provide nuanced presentations, often with care taken to avoid stereotypes and gratuitous negative imagery. During the 12 months before 9/11, approximately a quarter of the depictions of Muslim and Arab Americans in the newspapers were positive or supportive, while about two-thirds were negative. In the six months after the terrorist attacks, positive and supportive depictions increased to more than 40 percent, while negative portrayals declined to less than 25 percent.[31]

In addition, after 9/11, the four newspapers examined in the study placed greater emphasis on contextualizing news about Muslim and Arab Americans, providing a more sophisticated and comprehensive discussion than found in most news reports before 9/11. Nacos and Torres-Reyna discovered that, during the six months before the 9/11 attacks, only about 30 percent of news reports on Muslim and Arab Americans were thematic stories that explained events in a broad social context. By contrast, about 60 percent of news reports during this period were episodic in nature, describing the details of immediate events without providing the background information necessary for an informed understanding. During the six months after 9/11, thematic reporting on Muslim and Arab Americans rose to about 50 percent, while episodic news stories declined to about 40 percent. Alongside this trend, after 9/11, reporters and editors at the four newspapers selected Muslim

Americans far more frequently to interview and to serve as sources for reports on Islam and Muslims, rather than relying on non-Muslims to discuss these topics.[32]

These post-9/11 news media trends, like the Bush administration's efforts to counter anti-Muslim sentiment, may have helped mitigate the rise in anti-Muslim attitudes during the first several months after 9/11. However, Nacos and Torres-Reyna discovered that these trends did not persist. In an analysis of news coverage during the first several weeks before and after the first anniversary of the 9/11 attacks, they found that positive portrayals of Muslim and Arab Americans in the four newspapers they examined had declined to 21 percent, while negative portrayals had risen to 43 percent. A similar change was apparent in television news coverage. Furthermore, in both print and television news, a trend toward associating Muslim and Arab Americans with terrorism began to emerge as stories accusing them of supporting terrorism rose from 4 percent during the six months after 9/11 to 14 percent during the weeks around the first anniversary of the attacks.[33]

Alongside this decline in positive reporting on Muslim and Arab minorities, other news media trends that appeared in the aftermath of 9/11 began to fade. Among the four newspapers examined in their study, Nacos and Torres-Reyna found that thematic coverage declined to 20 percent in the weeks around the first anniversary of 9/11, while episodic coverage increased to about 65 percent. Also, both in print and television news, the trend toward giving Muslim and Arab Americans a larger voice in news reports on Islam began to weaken. In the weeks around the first anniversary of 9/11, reports on Islam that cited Muslim or Arab Americans as sources declined as news organizations began edging back toward the pre-9/11 pattern of relying on non-Muslims to discuss news and events about Islam.[34]

Ten years after Nacos and Torres-Reyna first published their findings, the international media research institute Media Tenor conducted an extensive analysis of U.S. news coverage of Islam and Muslims. Examining more than 430,000 stories on primetime television news from 2007 to 2013, Media Tenor researchers found an overwhelming trend toward negative depictions of Islam, with 75 percent of news stories containing unfavorable portrayals of Islam or Muslims. Most of the remaining news stories were neutral in tone, with very few positive reports about Islam appearing. Throughout this period, stories about terrorism and violence dominated news coverage involving Islam. Among news stories in which Islam played a prominent role, the top five topics were international terrorism, international conflict, political unrest, domestic terrorism, and civil war.[35] Despite the fact that the overwhelming majority of world's Muslims do not live in conflict zones or engage in violence, the nature of the news business guaranteed a primary focus on violence and turmoil in the Muslim world.

Much of such news coverage focused on attempts by Muslim militants from abroad to strike American targets, such as Richard Reid's attempt to bring down an airliner with a shoe bomb and Umar Farouk Abdul-mutallab's attempt to detonate a bomb sewn into his underwear in a passenger plane over Detroit. Coverage also focused heavily on the long U.S. counterinsurgency campaigns in Afghanistan and Iraq, a number of sensational terrorist attacks in different regions of the world, and the rise of Muslim terrorist insurgencies such as al-Shabaab in Somalia and Boko Haram in Nigeria. Among the most evocative news reports involving Muslims abroad were depictions of riots in response to insults to Islam or the Prophet Mohammad. The publication of offensive cartoons depicting the Prophet Mohammad in the Danish newspaper *Jyllands-Posten* in 2005 sparked protests in several cities. Most of these protests were peaceful, but news stories reaching American audiences focused heavily on violent riots in Lebanon, Iran, Pakistan, and Syria as well as the destruction of the Danish embassy in Damascus.[36]

Two additional events sparked similar violent protests. In 2011, Terry Jones, the leader of a small evangelical church in Florida, declared the Koran "guilty of crimes against humanity" and burned a copy of the Muslim holy book. In response to his mock trial, a mob stormed the United Nations compound in the Afghan city of Mazar-e Sharif, killing seven United Nations workers and five Afghans.[37] During the summer of the following year, an amateur filmmaker posted portions of a low-quality, homemade video titled *The Real Life of Mohammad* (also known as *The Innocence of Muslims*), which depicted the Prophet Mohammad as a lecherous man who made up passages of the Koran to justify his immoral behavior.

In response to these provocations, Muslims protested outside U.S. embassies in several countries, and a riot erupted in Sydney, Australia.[38] Common American perceptions regarding these events were captured in the September 2012 edition of the magazine *Newsweek*, which featured on its cover a photograph of angry Muslim men chanting with raised fists under the headline "Muslim Rage."[39] The *Newsweek* cover highlighted the fact that a significant fraction of the world's Muslims was primed for violent protest against Western insults to Islam, while saying nothing about the fact that large numbers of Muslims protested peacefully and that the overwhelming majority of Muslims did not protest at all.

Regarding events in the United States, the majority of news coverage concerning Muslim Americans after 9/11 revolved around terrorism. In addition to reporting extensively on successful terrorist attacks by Nidal Hasan at Fort Hood and the Tsarnaev brothers in Boston, the news media provided substantial coverage of failed terrorist plots. During the first few years after 9/11, the exploits of al-Qaeda-trained terrorist Jose Padilla, a U.S. citizen who was originally accused of planning to detonate a radiological device (a "dirty bomb") somewhere in the United States, received significant coverage. Also, the arrest of a group of Yemeni Americans from Lackawana in New York State, originally accused of constituting an al-Qaeda sleeper cell, garnered much media attention. In later years, the news media focused heavily on a plot by three Muslim immigrants to conduct a suicide bombing on a New York City subway train and on Faisal Shahzad's failed attempt to detonate a car bomb in Times Square less than a year later.

News reporting on these and similar events is hardly surprising. Any professional and competent news organization providing coverage for national audiences would report on U.S. wars overseas, major international events, and attempted large-scale terrorist attacks against the United States. Regrettably, however, such events received heavy coverage as the brief post-9/11 trend toward thematic coverage gave way to the familiar pre-9/11 pattern of episodic coverage of stories involving Islam and Muslims. Offering in-depth reporting on potential causes for the descent of some Muslims into violent extremism, and how these individuals contrast with the overwhelming majority of Muslims in the United States and abroad, may run counter to the demands of the news industry. However, providing such context is essential for promoting a broad understanding of terrorism and violent extremism rather than fueling fear and mistrust of Muslims in general.

Compounding the effects of heavy news reporting about terrorism and violence associated with Islam, news organizations provided scant coverage of Muslim efforts to counter extremism and terrorism. Charles Kurzman notes that, during the first 12 years after the 9/11 attacks, members of the U.S. Muslim community were responsible for bringing to the attention of law enforcement authorities more than 50 Muslim Americans suspected of terrorism-related activity. This number constitutes more than a quarter of cases in which authorities publicly identified the initial tip that led to the arrest of Muslim American terrorist suspects.[40] Additionally, Muslim leaders, religious scholars, and organizations in the United States have issued numerous condemnations of terrorism. Charles Kurzman and Sheila Musaji, the founding editor of *The American Muslim* journal, have compiled separate lists of such statements by Muslim leaders and Islamic scholars, both from the United States and abroad.[41] However, lacking the newsworthiness of more rousing stories, such Muslim efforts to delegitimize terrorism are scarcely reported in the mainstream news media and only briefly reported when they are mentioned.[42]

Entertainment Media

Like the rest of American society, Hollywood inherited many of the stereotypes and caricatures of Islam and Muslims found in the Western tradition. From the early days of the film industry, stereotypical images of Islamic lands and Muslim peoples dominated representations of Islam in American movies. In an extensive study of American films, mass communications scholar Jack Shaheen analyzed nearly 1,100 movies, all released between 1896 and 2001, featuring Arab characters (who were generally equated with Muslims). Only a handful contained Arab heroes, with the vast majority presenting Arab characters as villains prone to brutality and religious fanaticism and frequently engaging in abusive treatment of women. Shaheen also found that movie producers often inserted stereotypical and dislikeable Arab characters in films that had nothing to do with Arabs or Muslims, a device Shaheen called "bad Arab cameos." At least 250 feature films released before 9/11 used such gratuitous cameos.[43]

After 9/11, negative depictions of Arabs and Muslims (still often presented as synonymous) retained a large presence in American films. In an analysis of more than a hundred feature-length films released in the first six years after the 9/11 attacks, Shaheen found a continued reliance on images of Arabs and Muslims as villains (now often depicted as terrorists), religious radicals, and unprincipled characters. Popular movies such as *Secondhand Lions* (2002), *Hidalgo* (2004), and *The Kingdom* (2007) featured American heroes battling evil Arab characters in the Middle East, while *Red Mercury* (2005), *The War Within* (2005), and *The Stone Merchant* (2006) depicted Muslims engaged in terrorist plots or brutal acts of violence against Westerners in Europe and America. In addition, Shaheen discovered that about one quarter of the post-9/11 feature films he examined contained gratuitous anti-Arab or anti-Muslim slurs or scenes that depicted Arabs in demeaning ways, even though the films had nothing to do with Arabs or Muslims.[44]

Shaheen also discovered some notable exceptions to these trends. In the post-9/11 environment, some producers attempted to provide audiences with a more responsible treatment of Islam and a more balanced and sophisticated portrayal of Muslims. As a result, Shaheen found 29 Hollywood movies that presented diverse, nuanced, and even positive images of Muslims and Islam, such as *Kingdom of Heaven* (2005), *Syriana* (2005), and *The Kite Runner* (2007). Some films released after Shaheen completed his evaluation of post-9/11 movies, such as *Traitor* (2008) and *Body of Lies* (2008), presented Muslim characters as heroes and critical allies in America's efforts to counter terrorist groups targeting the West. Consequently, in feature films released in the years after 9/11, American audiences continued to receive negative images of Muslims that corresponded to disparaging stereotypes along with a smaller set of positive, or at least more complex, depictions.[45]

During this period, television programs reaching American audiences displayed many of the same negative Arab and Muslim caricatures as post-9/11 Hollywood films. Following the pattern established decades before 9/11, Arabs and Muslims often appeared as violent, brutal, and fanatical characters. Such representations of Muslims were especially prevalent in reruns of television programs produced before 9/11, which aired frequently in subsequent years as television networks sought content for an expanding spectrum of channels. Negative depictions of Muslims, most often Arabs, also appeared in numerous television shows produced after 9/11. Virtually all of the major broadcast and cable networks presented post-9/11 programs with Muslim characters that conformed to traditional negative stereotypes.

Shortly after 9/11, television writers and producers expanded negative depictions of Muslims to encompass Muslim Americans in the post-9/11 environment. Beginning with the 2002–2003 season, television networks introduced a new type of Muslim character—the neighbor who appears to be a loyal American but who is actually a terrorist plotting an attack against America. Shaheen's analysis uncovered more than 50 television programs that used this type of character, including prominent shows such as *24* (2001–2011), *Criminal Minds* (2005–ongoing), *NCIS* (2003–ongoing), *Sleeper Cell* (2005–2006), and *The Unit* (2006–2009).[46]

In a separate examination of post-9/11 entertainment media, Evelyn Alsultany, a scholar of American culture and media studies, uncovered several devices used by television writers and producers to diversify depictions of Muslims. Among the most prominent were creating patriotic Muslim American characters, showing sympathy for the hardships faced by Muslim Americans after 9/11, and humanizing terrorists to contextualize their descent into violence. Alsultany also uncovered a device she termed "flipping the enemy," in which a suspected Muslim terrorist turns out either not to be a terrorist or to be the pawn of a non-Muslim villain.[47] These devices often allowed more diverse presentations of Muslim characters.

As Alsultany pointed out, however, whether Muslim characters on television conform to negative stereotypes or present more sophisticated representations of Muslims, since 9/11, they have usually been characters in stories revolving around terrorism and extremism. From the 2001 premiere of the long-running show *24* to the first airing of the show *Homeland* in 2012 and afterward, television writers and producers have generally portrayed Muslims as villains, heroes, or other types of characters primarily to advance narratives about terrorism.[48] As a result, at least as much as Hollywood films, American television since 9/11 has framed Islam and Muslims as important first and foremost because of their role—sometimes positive, but more often negative—in America's ongoing struggle against terrorism.

Anti-Muslim Activism

The continuing threat of terrorism since 9/11, the extensive news coverage of this threat, and the methods and media frames used to present it to the public have provided Americans with numerous images of Islam that correspond to and expand on traditional negative stereotypes. Such representations of Islam have found additional access to American audiences through the entertainment media, which relies heavily—although no longer exclusively—on standard formulas for depicting Muslims. In the case of news media outlets and popular entertainment media, perpetuating and expanding negative perceptions of Islam and Muslims has rarely been a goal. Rather, it has more commonly been a side effect of business practices prevalent in the news and entertainment industries, the expectations of American audiences, and undeniable newsworthiness of terrorist attacks and plots targeting America.

By contrast, anti-Muslim activists have deliberately promoted negative perceptions of Islam and Muslims, including Muslim Americans, either out of deeply held convictions about the dangers of Islam, political opportunism, or both. The origins of such activism predate 9/11 but have expanded significantly in the years afterward, providing additional frames through which to interpret Islam and understand the actions of Muslims at home and abroad. The impact of such activism on popular attitudes toward Islam is difficult to measure and almost impossible to separate from other influential factors. However, the expansion of anti-Muslim activism after 9/11 corresponds to declining public perceptions of Islam over the course of the following years.

Founding Ideas of Contemporary Anti-Muslim Activism

Although negative stereotypes of Islam are rooted in centuries of Western religious and political thought, some of the most important aspects of contemporary anti-Muslim activism arose during the decade before 9/11. Historian Bernard Lewis introduced one of the cornerstones of such activism in his 1990 article, "The Roots of Muslim Rage," published in *The Atlantic*. In this article, Lewis argued that the Islamic world constitutes a civilization that has clashed with Christendom (or the West) for more than a millennium and that the rise of Islamic extremism in the 20th century is largely a reaction to the decline of the Islamic world in both absolute terms and in comparison to the West. He further argued that large and growing segments of the Muslim world seek to reassert the historic greatness of Islamic civilization achieved by Muslim empires during the golden age of Islam (corresponding to Europe's Middle Ages) and to push back Islam's historic rival, the West. After 9/11, Lewis promoted this theme in lectures, articles, and two widely read books, *What Went Wrong? The Clash between Islam and Modernity in the Middle East* (2002) and *The Crisis of Islam: Holy War and Unholy Terror* (2004).

Explaining his view on Islam's relations with the West, Lewis wrote:

> The struggle between these rival systems has now lasted for some fourteen centuries. It began with the advent of Islam, in the seventh century, and has continued virtually to the present day. It has consisted of a long series of attacks and counterattacks, jihads and crusades, conquests and reconquests. It should by now be clear that we are facing a mood and a movement far transcending the level of issues and policies and the governments that pursue them. *This is no less than a clash of civilizations*—the perhaps irrational but surely historic reaction of an ancient rival against our Judeo-Christian heritage, our secular present, and the worldwide expansion of both.[49] (Emphasis added)

Shortly after Lewis published this article, political scientist Samuel Huntington developed a broader thesis based on Lewis's concept of a clash of civilizations. In his seminal article, "The Clash of Civilizations?" published in *Foreign Affairs* (1993) and later in a book titled *The Clash of Civilizations and the Remaking of the World Order* (1996), Huntington described a world divided into distinct civilizations, including Western, Islamic, Confucian, Japanese, Hindu, Slavic-Orthodox, Latin

American, and possibly African. He argued that major conflicts in the future would "occur along the cultural fault lines separating these civilizations from one another." Echoing Lewis's idea of enduring conflict between Islam and the West, Huntington claimed that "conflict along the fault line between Western and Islamic civilizations has been going on for 1,300 years" and "is unlikely to decline" in the near future.[50]

Parallel to this "clash of civilizations" thesis, another idea emerged in the 1990s that, while compatible with the contentions of Lewis and Huntington, pointed to a different source of danger from the Muslim world. During the same year that Lewis published "The Roots of Muslim Rage," Daniel Pipes published an article in *The National Review* titled "The Muslims Are Coming! The Muslims Are Coming!" In this article, Pipes, who received a doctorate in history from Harvard University, argued that the Muslim threat to America comes from two sources: hostile Islamic states abroad and Muslim extremists living in the United States. Pipes identified the latter threat as the greater danger to America and claimed that the West was not engaged in a clash of civilizations but a battle against militant Islam that had infiltrated Europe and the United States.[51]

In presenting his "enemy within" thesis, Pipes stated that mainstream Islam was compatible with Western values, but militant political Islam was an ideology deeply inimical to non-Muslims and especially hostile to the West.[52] Pipes estimated that a minority of perhaps 10 percent of Muslims ascribed to this extremist ideology, but his vision of Islamic extremists infiltrating the United States was expansive, encompassing the leadership of most major Muslim American organizations, a majority of mosques in the country, and most of the Muslim newspapers and communal organizations operating in America. In a 1997 article, Pipes claimed that among Muslims, "fundamentalists dominate in the United States, to the point that moderates hardly have a voice."[53] He warned that this extremist segment of America's Muslim populations was pursuing a largely nonviolent strategy to impose Islamic principles defined by Sharia on America.[54]

Unlike Lewis and Huntington, Pipes adopted an activist—rather than strictly scholarly—role. In the early 1990s, he founded the nonprofit Middle East Forum, along with its flagship online publication, *The Middle East Quarterly*, to promote American interests in the Middle East and help protect Western values from Islamic encroachment at home. He also published numerous articles in other publications, gave interviews and lectures, and appeared on several major news shows to promote his views. Within weeks after 9/11, he published an article in *Commentary* claiming that "the Muslim population in this country is not like any other group, for it includes a substantial body of people . . . who share with the suicide hijackers a hatred of the United States and the desire, ultimately, to transform it into a nation living under the strictures of militant Islam."[55] The following year, he launched a project called Campus Watch to monitor professors at colleges around the country, with an emphasis on identifying academics he believed to be apologists for militant Islam.[56] In 2006, he launched a project called Islamist Watch to combat radical Islam in the United States and other Western countries.[57]

As Daniel Pipes began propagating his views in the early 1990s, another proponent of the enemy-within argument entered the discussion. In 1994, Steven Emerson, a former senior editor at *U.S. News and World Report* and a former correspondent for CNN, produced and narrated a documentary film titled *Terrorists among Us: Jihad in America* for the PBS series *Frontline*. Like Pipes, Emerson argued that the majority of Muslims in America presented no threat, but a significant segment of the Muslim American population held extremist views and conspired to subvert America's democratic system. Also like Pipes, Emerson's view of this militant minority was expansive. Writing after 9/11, he claimed, "Mainstream Islamic groups are actually radical organizations that teach and imbue their followers with a hatred of the United States and Israel . . . These groups control the mosques, the Islamic newspapers, the Islamic schools, and the Islamic leadership."

In 1995, Emerson founded the nonprofit Investigative Project on Terrorism to investigate and track the activities of Islamic extremist groups as well as mainstream organizations he believed were serving as fronts for radical Muslim groups. After 9/11, he published two books, *American Jihad: The Terrorists Living Among Us* (2003) and *Jihad Incorporated: A Guide to Militant Islam in the U.S.* (2006). He also produced a second documentary called *Jihad in America: The Grand Deception* (2012). Emerson has also presented his views before congressional committees and in numerous interviews on television news programs. In 2014, on the same day that the 9/11 Memorial Museum opened, the Investigative Project on Terrorism placed a full-page ad in the *New York Times* proclaiming, "Still here. Still free. But for how long? Stop Islamist groups from undermining American security, liberty, and free speech."[58]

The Post-9/11 Anti-Muslim Network

After the 9/11 terrorist attacks, a number of activists began promoting versions of the clash-of-civilizations and the enemy-within theses.

Among the first to take up this cause was David Horowitz, a long-time conservative activist who founded the Center for the Study of Popular Culture in 1988. Renamed the David Horowitz Freedom Center in 2006, this institute was repurposed after 9/11 to "combat efforts of the radical left and its Islamist allies to destroy American values and disarm the country as it attempts to defend itself in a time of terror."[59] Horowitz has taken an uncompromising stand on the dangers of Islam, declaring in a speech at Brooklyn College that "Islam is a religion possessed by hate, violence, and racism."[60] His center's online journal, *FrontPage Magazine*, presents news and commentary warning readers about the dangers of liberal ideas and militant Islam, while the center's online database, DiscoverTheNetworks.org, describes the agendas of those Horowitz believes are pursuing liberal or Islamic causes.

Alongside these outlets, the David Horowitz Freedom Center sponsors the online journal *Jihad Watch*, which monitors Muslim extremist activities abroad and supposed efforts by Islamic radicals in the United States to "infiltrate and subvert Western institutions and civic life."[61] The director of *Jihad Watch*, Robert Spencer, emerged shortly after 9/11 as a staunch critic of the encroachment of Islam on American society. During an interview on C-SPAN, he claimed that Islam is "the only religion in the world that has developed a doctrine, theology, and legal system that mandates violence against unbelievers and mandates that Muslims must wage war in order to establish the hegemony of the Islamic social order all over the world."[62] Spencer has also published several books promoting his ideas, including *The Truth about Muhammad: Founder of the World's Most Intolerant Religion* (2007) and *Stealth Jihad: How Radical Islam Is Subverting America without Guns or Bombs* (2008).

In 2010, Robert Spencer joined with political activist Pamela Geller to establish a project called Stop Islamization of America (SIOP). Geller, creator of the conservative blog *Atlas Shrugs*, promotes the idea that Islam is incompatible with Western values, calling Islam "an extreme ideology, the most radical and extreme ideology on the face of the Earth."[63] She has also stated, "I don't think that many Westernized Muslims know when they pray five times a day that they are cursing Christians and Jews five times a day. . . . I believe in the idea of a moderate Muslim. I do not believe in the idea of a moderate Islam."[64] Geller received attention in the mainstream news media when, working with Spencer through their Stop Islamization of America initiative, she played an instrumental role in organizing resistance to the construction of an Islamic community center a couple of blocks from the site of the World Trade Center in Lower Manhattan. This effort raised her stature among anti-Muslim activists and made her—at least briefly—a public figure identifiable beyond anti-Muslim circles.

The idea for a new Islamic community center in Lower Manhattan came from Imam Feisal Rauf and his wife, Daisy Khan. In 2009, they announced plans for a community center, later named Park51, which would include a performing arts center, movie theater, exercise facilities, and restaurants, all open to the public. The center would also contain a mosque in one section of the building. In response to this project, Geller and Spencer organized a series of protests during the summer of 2010, culminating on the ninth anniversary of 9/11 with a "September 11 Rally of Remembrance."[65] During this campaign, Geller labeled the proposed community center "the Ground Zero Mosque" because of its location near the site of the World Trade Center. At one of the protest rallies, she declared, "It is unconscionable to build a shrine to the very ideology that inspired the jihadist attackers at Ground Zero."[66]

In addition to organizing protest rallies, Geller and Spencer used their Stop Islamization of America initiative to sponsor a series of advertisements disparaging the proposed community center on New York City buses and subway trains. The ads featured an image of an airplane headed toward a burning World Trade Center juxtaposed with an image of another building labeled: "WTC Mega Mosque. Why Here?" Geller also directed and produced a documentary film titled *The Ground Zero Mosque: Second Wave of the 9/11 Attacks* and published two books, *Stop the Islamization of America: A Practical Guide to the Resistance* (2011) and *Freedom or Submission: On the Dangers of Islamic Extremism and American Complacency* (2013).[67] In addition, as the 2012 presidential election season approached, she and Spencer co-authored *The Post-American Presidency: The Obama Administration's War on America*, a book proposing, among other things, that President Obama was subverting America with pro-Islamic policies.

Following their campaign against Park51, Spencer and Geller created a second project named the American Freedom Defense Initiative to resist what they called "treason committed by national, state, and local government officials, the mainstream media, and others in their capitulation to the global jihad and Islamic supremacism."[68] Through this initiative, Spencer and Geller launched a series of ad campaigns targeting public transportation systems in cities across America, including New York, Chicago, San Francisco, and Washington, D.C. Among the ads they placed was one featuring a photograph of a British citizen suspected of joining the Islamic State in Syria alongside the statement, "Yesterday's moderate is today's headline. It's not Islamophobia, it's Islamorealism."

Geller stated in an interview that the ad was meant to "point up the uselessness of the distinction between 'moderate' and 'extremist' Muslims."[69] Another ad featured a photo of Adolf Hitler meeting with the Grand Mufti of Jerusalem with the caption: "Islamic Jew-Hatred: It's in the Quran."[70]

Parallel to these efforts, another organization, the Center for Security Policy, began to focus heavily on the supposed dangers of Islam. Founded and directed by Frank Gaffney, who served as assistant secretary of defense under President Ronald Reagan, the Center for Security Policy operated for many years as a conservative nonprofit institute focused on a range of national security issues, including Islamic extremism. After 9/11, Gaffney turned the center's attention more resolutely to the threat of militant Islam within the United States, emphasizing the encroachment of Islamic legal codes. In 2010, he released a report titled *Sharia: The Threat to America*. This report rejected the idea that Sharia is a highly contested concept that forms the basis of how all observant Muslims believe they should behave. Instead, the report described Sharia as a totalitarian ideology that commands or condones honor killing, female genital mutilation, and warfare to spread the faith. The report further claimed that most Muslim organizations in the country were fronts for militant Islam and that a network of Muslim extremists was working in secret to impose Sharia on the United States.[71]

Gaffney secured the collaboration of several notable figures to work with him on this report, including James Woolsey, former director of the Central Intelligence Agency; William Boykin, former deputy undersecretary in charge of intelligence at the Department of Defense; and Harry Edward Soyster, former director of the Defense Intelligence Agency. Other contributors included Andrew McCarthy, a former chief assistant U.S. attorney who helped prosecute the perpetrators of the 1993 World Trade Center bombing, and John Guandolo, a former FBI agent specializing in counterterrorism. Another contributor to the report was David Yerushalmi, founder of the Society of Americans for National Existence (SANE). Yerushalmi emerged after 9/11 as a leading advocate for the use of litigation to pursue social objectives, a strategy he calls "lawfare." Since establishing SANE in 2006, he has pursued this strategy, through lawsuits against the federal government and Muslim organizations, to counter what he perceives to be the threat of Sharia subverting American values.[72] Alongside this strategy, Yerushalmi launched two initiatives to expose and counter this threat, one aimed at mosques in the United States and another directed at state legislatures.

Yerushalmi initiated the first of these efforts shortly after founding SANE with a proposal to make observing Sharia a felony with a sentence of 20 years in prison. Once he realized that the U.S. Congress was unlikely to pass any such measure, Yerushalmi turned his attention to the state level. Moderating his aims, he drafted a narrower model law called American Laws for American Courts, which would prohibit state courts from considering Sharia in legal proceedings.[73] Yerushalmi launched the second of his principal initiatives in 2008 with financial support from the Center for Security Policy. Through this initiative, called "Mapping Sharia: Knowing the Enemy," SANE investigators presented themselves as Muslims to attend prayer services at 100 mosques around the country. At the project's conclusion, they claimed to have found that more than 80 percent of the mosques they visited displayed texts advocating violence.[74] Later, Yerushalmi claimed that his research made clear that militants had not perverted Islamic law but were following an authoritative doctrine that seeks global hegemony.[75]

During the same year that Yerushalmi founded SANE, Rabbi Raphael Shore, a Canadian-Israeli film producer and writer, established the Clarion Fund (later renamed the Clarion Project). With the stated mission of exposing the dangers of Islamic extremism, the organization began providing news and analysis of extremist Muslim groups around the world, with a strong focus on the supposed threat of militant Islam in the United States.[76] The Clarion Project acknowledges that not all Muslims accept radical interpretations of Islam and identifies on its website a handful of groups it calls "progressive Muslim organizations" that have a positive influence.[77] Nevertheless, the Clarion Project claims that Islamic extremists maintain a network of interconnected organizations across America. This network, according to the Clarion Project, attempts to expand Sharia in the public sphere through nonviolent means. Researchers at the Clarion Project have identified more than 100 organizations throughout the United States, including some of the largest mainstream Muslim organizations in the country, which they believe participate in this network.[78]

In 2007, the Clarion Project produced the documentary film *Obsession: Radical Islam's War against the West*, featuring images of terrorist attacks in different parts of the world, Muslim leaders denouncing America, and Muslim children reciting poetry celebrating suicide bombings.[79] The following year, during the presidential election season, the Clarion Project distributed DVD versions of the film inside the inserts of 70 Sunday newspapers across 14 electoral battleground states. Copies of the film reached more than 28 million households and religious institutions.[80]

During the same year, the Clarion Project released a second film titled *The Third Jihad: Radical Islam's Vision for America*, which posits that Islamic extremists are engaged in a multifaceted struggle to subdue the West. According to the film, this struggle includes efforts to infiltrate and undermine American from within, a strategy termed "cultural jihad."[81]

Shortly after the founding of the Clarion Project, Brigitte Gabriel established the grassroots organization Act for America to educate and mobilize Americans against the threat of militant Islam.[82] Many years earlier, Gabriel, a Maronite Christian from Lebanon, found refuge in Israel after she was injured in a bombing in her village. She later immigrated to the United States. Her view of Islamic militants in America, like that of many others who ascribe to the enemy-within thesis, is especially broad. During a political rally in Texas, she claimed, "America has been infiltrated on all levels by radicals who wish to harm America. They have infiltrated us at the CIA, at the FBI, at the Pentagon, at the State Department."[83] She published two books: the *New York Times* bestseller *Because They Hate: A Survivor of Islamic Terror Warns America* (2008) and *They Must Be Stopped: Why We Must Defeat Radical Islam and How We Can Do It* (2010). She has also propagated her views at hundreds of lectures at churches, synagogues, and conferences.[84]

To reach citizens across the United States, Gabriel's organization has recruited thousands of volunteers organized into local chapters. According to the Act for America website, by the end of 2014, the organization boasted 280,000 members and nearly 900 chapters.[85] Through this large network, Act for America informs the public and political leaders about what Gabriel believes to be the dire threat of Sharia to American democracy. During a statewide campaign in Oklahoma to ban Sharia, she donated $60,000 to provide automated phone calls and a series of radio ads to support the ban.[86] Also, during the campaign to block construction of the Park51 community center, Gabriel delivered, via news conference, a national petition opposing the project to New York Mayor Michael Bloomberg. In 2011, Act for America distributed thousands of copies of two instructional booklets: *Sharia Law for Non-Muslims*, directed at elected officials and other leaders across the country, and *Understanding the Threat of Radical Islam*, a 60-page illustrated booklet targeting teenagers.[87]

Impact of Anti-Muslim Activism

During the decade after 9/11, anti-Muslim activists formed a loose network to collaborate and amplify their efforts, often sharing financial resources and providing one another with legal and other expertise.[88] In an extensive study of the growth and collaboration of this network, researcher Nathan Lean outlined how a core group of activists methodically nurtured anti-Muslim sentiment, achieving a significant impact on public perceptions after years of effort.[89] In 2011, the Southern Poverty Law Center, a civil rights organization dedicated to fighting bigotry in America, released a brief outlining the activities of this network. According to the brief, "The apparent surge in popular anti-Muslim sentiment in the United States has been driven by a surprisingly small and, for the most part, closely knit cadre of activists."[90] That same year, two nonprofit institutes, the Center for American Progress and People for the American Way, released separate reports detailing how this network promotes fear of Islam.[91]

To examine the impact of this anti-Muslim network on public perceptions, sociologist Christopher Bail analyzed the influence of 120 civil society organizations on news media coverage about Islam in the years after 9/11. Using an innovative technique relying on plagiarism software, Bail compared more than 1000 press releases from these organizations with more than 50,000 news reports. He found that that the large majority of social organizations released statements with positive or neutral messages about Islam, but only a small fraction of such statements received coverage in the news media. As an illustration, during the first two years after the 9/11 attacks, 12 Muslim American organizations issued a total of 27 statements condemning terrorism. The national news media almost completely ignored these condemnations, however, providing brief mention of only two. Furthermore, Bail found that a handful of anti-Muslim organizations dominated news coverage. Using messages based on fear and anger, this small network accounted for nearly half of all civil society organizations that exerted influence on the news media's representation of Islam and Muslims.[92]

One notable success for this network was to frame efforts to build the Park51 community center in Lower Manhattan as an attempt to signify Islam's triumph at one of the sites of the 9/11 attacks. In fact, without the frame of Islamic triumphalism, plans to build an Islamic institution in the neighborhood would not have been especially noteworthy. A large Muslim community has resided in the neighborhood for years, and two mosques provide services for worshippers in the area.[93] Nevertheless, anti-Muslim activism brought national attention and opposition to the project, largely by presenting Park51 as a new Muslim presence encroaching on the neighborhood around the site of the World Trade Center. In the summer of 2010, at the height of the controversy, a *Time* magazine poll revealed that 61 percent of Americans opposed the construction of Park51 and a plurality of 44 percent believed that building a mosque near the site of the World Trade Center would be an insult to those who died there on 9/11.[94] A Pew Research Center poll the same year similarly found that only 34 percent believed Park51 should be allowed.[95]

Rousing public opposition to Park51, in addition to bringing national attention and significant public opposition to the proposed community center, may have contributed to an increase in antimosque activity around the country. In an effort to map such activities across the United States, the American Civil Liberty Union recorded a sharp increase in incidents targeting mosques beginning in 2010, from about 10 incidents in 2009 to about 40 in 2010. Such incidents included efforts by local authorities to halt construction or expansion of mosques, organized resistance by citizens of local communities to resist mosque construction or expansion, and several cases of vandalism, desecration, and property destruction.[96] A similar study by the Pew Center on Religion and Public Life found a significant increase in efforts by local governments or community citizens to halt the construction or expansion of mosques in 2010.[97]

The most controversial case, aside from resistance to the Park51 project, was a campaign to halt construction of an Islamic community center in Murfreesboro, Tennessee, about 30 miles outside of Nashville. Like opposition to Park51, the Murfreesboro project attracted nationwide attention in 2010 and became a symbolic issue for those opposed to the presence of Islam in American society. Following approval of the project by the county planning commission in 2010, local residents filed a lawsuit to halt construction, claiming that Islam was a political ideology and the proposed Islamic center, therefore, could not be considered a place of worship as defined by the county zoning ordinance.[98] During deliberations on the proposal, protestors gathered outside the county courthouse with signs that said, "Remember 9/11," and, "Islam is not a religion." Intervention by the Department of Justice and the federal courts was required to overcome the opposition of anti-Muslim activists and allow the project to proceed.[99]

Organized and coordinated activism also helped present Sharia as a draconian body of religious law and a threat to American democracy. Although David Yerushalmi and his allies did not persuade the U.S. Congress to consider banning Sharia, they did have a degree of success at the state level. By the end of 2014, more than 30 state legislatures had introduced measures to ban consideration of foreign or religious laws. Many of these bills used the language proposed in Yerushalmi's model law. Eleven state legislatures passed such bills, although a measure passed by the legislature of Missouri was subsequently vetoed by the governor. More importantly for Yerushalmi and his supporters, controversy surrounding anti-Sharia legislation raised public awareness of a previously obscure issue, Islamic jurisprudence, and framed it as a threat to America. Yerushalmi stated in a 2012 interview, "If this thing passed in every state without any friction, it would not have served its purpose. The purpose was heuristic—to get people asking this question, 'What is Sharia?'"[100]

Anti-Muslim Bias and Electoral Politics

As anti-Muslim activists gained a degree of influence on public opinion, their views began influencing national politics and election campaigns. The signs that anti-Muslim sentiment would enter U.S. politics began to emerge shortly after 9/11. Despite the efforts of President Bush to limit anti-Muslim bigotry, some conservative politicians adopted rhetoric disparaging of Islam almost immediately after the 9/11 attacks. In 2001, referring to police stopping Muslim drivers on the road, Congressman John Cooksey of Louisiana infamously stated during a radio interview, "Someone who comes in that's got a diaper on his head and a fan belt wrapped around that diaper on his head, that guy needs to be pulled over."[101] Similarly, Congressman Saxby Chambliss of Georgia (later elected to the Senate) joked to a group of police officers in 2001 that the best antiterrorism measure for his district would be to "arrest every Muslim that crosses the state line," a statement for which he later apologized.[102]

This type of anti-Muslim rhetoric continued in subsequent years, especially among Republican leaders and candidates for office attempting to appeal to conservative elements of the electorate. In 2004, Congressman Peter King of New York, chairman of the House Homeland Security Committee, claimed that extremists controlled 80 to 85 percent of mosques in the country.[103] Three years later, Congressman Tom Tancredo of Colorado offered that the best means of deterring another terrorist attack on the United States would be to threaten a retaliatory strike against Mecca and Medina, thereby holding all Muslims responsible for the actions of Islamic extremists.[104] That same year, after winning election to represent the Fifth Congressional District of Minnesota, Keith Ellison, the first Muslim elected to Congress, announced plans to take the oath of office using a copy of the Koran originally owned by Thomas Jefferson (now kept by the Library of Congress). Commenting on his announcement, Congressman Virgil Goode of Virginia declared that Ellison's plan to use the Koran was "a threat to the values and beliefs traditional to the United States."[105]

In 2008, anti-Muslim sentiment entered the presidential election campaign between Senators Barack Obama and John McCain. Dating at least as far back as 2006, chain e-mails began circulating, claiming that Obama was a Muslim and indicating this was an undesirable and potentially dangerous trait for a national political figure. In 2007, *Insight Magazine* published an article, later highlighted on Fox News, claiming that Obama attended a Muslim religious school in Indonesia as a child.[106] Meanwhile, despite Obama's repeated assertions that he was a Christian, conservative radio and television talk show hosts repeated the rumor that he was a Muslim, often underscoring that his middle name was Hussein.[107] Calling Obama a Muslim as an epithet continued throughout the 2008 presidential campaign.

In 2010, at the height of the Park51 controversy, anti-Muslim rhetoric in electoral politics increased markedly. That year, Renee Ellmers, a candidate for one of North Carolina's congressional seats, launched a television campaign ad featuring a narrator stating, "After the Muslims conquered Jerusalem, Cordoba, and Constantinople, they built victory mosques. And now, they want to build a mosque near Ground Zero."[108] After the narration, Ellmers appears in the ad and asserts, "The terrorists haven't won, and we should tell them in plain English, 'No, there will never be a mosque at Ground Zero."[109] Another North Carolina candidate for Congress, Ilario Pantano, made a similar statement in June 2010, claiming, "The suggestion that this mysteriously funded mosque is anything other than a permanent demonstration of Islam's march on the West is naive at best . . . It is about marking religious, ideological, and territorial conquest."[110]

Further south, Allen West, a congressional candidate from Florida, made headline news during the 2010 congressional election season with several inflammatory comments about Islam. At one point, he declared that Keith Ellison represented the antithesis of the principles upon which the United States was founded. Later, during a fundraising event, he stated, "Islam is a totalitarian theocratic political ideology. It is not a religion . . . [Islam is a] very vile and very vicious enemy that we have allowed to come into our country."[111] Using similar rhetoric, Lou Ann Zelenick, a candidate running for one of Tennessee's congressional seats, claimed that the proposed Islamic center in Murfreesboro was "part of a political movement designed to fracture the moral and political foundation of Middle Tennessee."[112]

In 2011, after a decade of post-9/11 anti-Muslim activism, bias against Islam again emerged as a factor in presidential electoral politics, this time as a tactic used overtly by candidates running for the Republican nomination. In the spring of that year, a reporter asked candidate Herman Cain if he would be comfortable appointing a Muslim to his cabinet or as a federal judge. Cain responded, "No, I would not. And here's why: There is this creeping attempt to gradually ease Sharia law and the Muslim faith into our government."[113] Later, Cain asserted during a television interview that any community has the right to ban mosques because "Islam is both a religion and a set of laws—Sharia law."[114] Shortly afterward, Cain apologized for making disparaging statements about Islam, but he later acknowledged that he accepted the view that the majority of Muslims hold extremist views.[115]

Even more forcefully than Herman Cain, presidential contender Newt Gingrich relied on anti-Muslim sentiment to elevate his campaign for the Republic nomination. Gingrich had already begun to establish his credentials as an advocate for resisting the encroachment of Islam in America society. In 2010, he released a film titled *America at Risk*, which he produced and narrated, to warn of the infiltration of militant Islam. That same year, during a speech at the American Enterprise Institute, Gingrich warned, "Stealth jihadis use political, cultural, societal, religious, intellectual tools; violent jihadis use violence. But, in fact, they're both engaged in jihad, and they're both seeking to impose the same end-state, which is to replace Western civilization with a radical imposition of Sharia."[116] The following year, in the midst of his campaign for the nomination for president, Gingrich compared the construction of Park51 near the site of the World Trade Center with Nazis placing a sign near the Holocaust Museum in Washington, D.C.[117]

Later in the campaign season, during the summer of 2012, five Republican Members of Congress—Michele Bachmann of Minnesota, Trent Franks of Arizona, Louie Gohmert of Texas, Tom Rooney of Florida, and Lynn Westmoreland of Georgia—sounded the alarm about Muslim extremists infiltrating the U.S. government. To induce action on their concerns, they sent letters to the inspectors general at the Department of State, Department of Defense, Department of Homeland Security, and other government agencies. In their letters, they asked whether Muslim extremists could be inserting themselves in positions within the federal government. Bachmann singled out Huma Abedin, deputy chief of staff for Secretary of State Hillary Clinton, as a potential extremist. They stood by their accusations despite widespread criticism, including a denunciation by Senator John McCain during a speech on the Senate floor.[118]

Nearly two years later, the advocacy group South Asian Americans Leading Together released a report documenting 78 cases of bigoted political speech directed at Arabs and South Asians during a three-year period beginning in January 2011. In more than 90 percent of these incidents, the biased remarks were motivated by anti-Muslim sentiment. Politicians running for national office were responsible for nearly two-thirds of these incidents, while state and local politicians accounted for about one-third.[119] A few months after the release of this report, John Bennett, a member of the Oklahoma state legislature, claimed that the goal of Muslims was "the destruction of Western civilization from within." Speaking at a forum attended by more than 100 constituents, he further stated that Islam is "a cancer that must be cut out of the American society."[120]

The steady advance of anti-Muslim rhetoric in American politics, whether presented out of sincere conviction or political opportunism, underscores the consolidation of negative perceptions of Islam among some segments of American society. The 9/11 attacks instantly raised the salience of Islam for the U.S. public, priming Americans to accept new understandings of Islam or to deepen existing attitudes that were often only loosely held. Subsequent events, including wars overseas and terrorist activity at home and abroad, kept Islam on the public agenda. Over time, anti-Muslim activists succeeded in inserting their views into mainstream discourse, framing Islam and Muslims for many Americans who were forming strong impressions about these subjects for the first time.

By the end of the first decade of the 21st century, the early work of government officials, concerned citizens, and several civil society organizations to curb anti-Muslim sentiments had largely faded. Meanwhile, both news and popular media had returned to familiar pre-9/11 patterns of presenting stereotypes and unfavorable depictions of Muslims, with some notable exceptions. In this environment, anti-Muslim activists, including politicians willing to mobilize support through displays of anti-Muslim bias, frequently captured the public spotlight as well as a degree of public support. Although they remain a minority voice, they are no longer relegated to the margins of society and will likely have a corrosive effect on American attitudes as long as Islam remains on the public agenda.

CHAPTER 5

Hate Crimes and Anti-Muslim Violence

The 9/11 Backlash

On the morning of September 12, 2001, in the village of Bridgeview outside of Chicago, protestors gathered in the predominantly Arab American and Muslim neighborhood surrounding the Bridgeview Mosque Foundation. As the site of one of the region's largest mosques and Islamic community centers as well as two Islamic schools, the institution regularly attracted nearly 2,000 worshippers for Friday prayers and provided education for more than 600 students. For three straight days after 9/11, protestors attempted to march on this prominent symbol of Islam in America.[1] On the second night, as many as 700 protestors gathered, some waving American flags while others shouted anti-Muslim and anti-Arab insults.[2]

In response, more than 100 local and state police sealed the area and established checkpoints to ensure that only residents had access to the neighborhood.[3] In time, as the number of protestors dwindled and the danger of a mob storming the Mosque Foundation subsided, law enforcement authorities withdrew most of their officers, and neighborhood activities began returning to normal. However, extra police patrols continued around the neighborhood for several weeks, and mosque officials hired an off-duty police officer to stand guard at the front door. The Islamic schools remained closed for a week, and outdoor recess was cancelled for an extended period to ensure the safety of the students.[4]

The siege of the Bridgeview Mosque Foundation and the surrounding neighborhood was not representative of reactions everywhere in the country. In the first few months after the attacks, positive public perceptions of Muslim Americans increased as responsible civic organizations and public figures worked to minimize the inevitable anti-Muslim backlash. As evidence of a backlash against Muslim Americans grew, civil rights coalitions and interfaith partnerships began mobilizing to blunt the effects of growing anger against groups and individuals perceived—correctly or falsely—to be associated with Islam. In many instances, non-Muslims joined their Muslim neighbors to protect mosques and other Islamic sites from vandalism and other acts of intolerance. Nonetheless, events in Bridgeview underscored a sharp rise in anti-Muslim sentiment in some segments of society following 9/11, including a willingness to engage in open expressions of anti-Muslim bigotry. For the next decade and beyond, this new normal of heightened antipathy for Islam fostered—and continues to foster—intolerance, discrimination, and violence against Muslims and those perceived to be Muslim.

Hate Crimes and Ethnoviolence

In the behavioral sciences, aggression is defined as any behavior designed to cause physical or psychological harm to others against their will.[5] Acts of aggression directed at persons because of their ethnicity, religion, or another group characteristic are commonly referred to as hate crimes or bias crimes, and the tool most frequently used to quantify such acts in the United States is the FBI's annual hate crimes statistics report. According to the FBI's report covering 2001, hate crimes targeting Muslims spiked 1,700 percent that year, increasing from 28 incidents in 2000 to 481 incidents in 2001.[6] Anti-Muslim hate crimes captured in the FBI's statistics for 2001 include nearly 400 assaults and acts of intimidation, along with almost 150 acts of arson and vandalism targeting property. Several hate crime incidents involved more than one criminal offense, including elements of both assault and destruction of property. According to the FBI's data, more than 330 known offenders took part in bias-motivated crimes targeting Muslims, Muslim-owned businesses, and Islamic institutions during 2001.[7]

The rate of anti-Muslim hate crimes declined after the initial wave of incidents during the first several weeks after the 9/11 attacks, but it did not return to pre-9/11 levels.[8] For the next 12 years, from the beginning of 2002 through 2013, anti-Muslim hate crimes recorded by the FBI occurred at an average annual rate of roughly 140 incidents, from a low of 105 cases in 2008 to a high of 160 cases just 2 years later.[9] This post-9/11 rise in hate crimes against Muslims prompted the Department of Justice to create a special 9/11 backlash crime task force. By 2007, the task force had investigated more than 800 incidents involving violence, threats, vandalism, and arson against people perceived by the assailants to be Muslim.[10] For 2013, the FBI recorded 135 anti-Muslim hate crime incidents, including two homicides and more than 100 assaults, with no indication that this post-9/11 pattern would subside in the near future.[11]

Despite the sharp increase in anti-Muslim hate crimes recorded by the FBI after 9/11 and their stubborn persistence in the years since, the FBI's hate crime statistics capture only a portion of hostile acts directed at Muslims. In large part, the reasons for this shortfall lie in the legal definition of hate crimes. In the American judicial system, an act motivated by bias (a bias incident) must meet demanding criteria before being classified as a hate crime. First, it must be a criminal act that would be illegal regardless of whether prejudice and intolerance were motivating factors. Hostile acts that do not violate the law, such as disseminating anti-Muslim hate speech that does not include a specific and credible threat, are not considered hate crimes. Second, the criminal act (or predicate offense) must be clearly motivated, at least in part, by prejudice. If the motives of assailants are ambiguous or unknown, even when anti-Muslim bias is strongly suspected, crimes against Muslims may not be classified as hate crimes.[12]

TABLE 5.1   Anti-Muslim Hate Crime Incidents

1996	27	2005	128
1997	28	2006	156
1998	21	2007	115
1999	32	2008	105
2000	28	2009	107
2001	481	2010	160
2002	155	2011	157
2003	149	2012	130
2004	156	2013	135

Source: Federal Bureau of Investigation, *Hate Crime Statistics* (annual reports for the years 1996 through 2013), www.fbi.gov/about-us/cjis/ucr/ucr-publications#Hate.

Alongside the restricted legal definition of hate crimes, problems with collecting information limit the effectiveness of using hate crime statistics to gauge the magnitude of bias-motivated aggression. In accordance with the Hate Crime Statistics Act of 1990, the FBI collects data for its annual hate crime statistics report from federal, state, and local law enforcement agencies across the nation. All agencies that report data to the FBI do so on a voluntary basis. No enforcement mechanism exists to compel law enforcement agencies at the state and local levels, where the large majority of hate crimes are adjudicated, to collect hate crime statistics or to provide them to the FBI. As a result, the FBI statistics provide an incomplete survey of hate crimes committed nationwide.[13]

Compounding this problem, hate crime laws and the capacity to assess them vary widely across jurisdictions. This divergence leads to differences in how bias is defined and which categories of bias are covered. Most states include crimes motivated by bias against race, religion, and ethnicity in their hate crimes statutes, but only a few follow the federal government's model of including bias against a victim's gender, sexual orientation, or gender identity.[14] In addition, a wide disparity exists in the capacities of state and local law enforcement agencies to collect hate crime data. Many agencies at the state and local levels lack systematic means of recording and tracking hate crimes, lack the resources to follow up on crime reports to verify motives, and lack a clear definition of hate crimes.[15] Consequently, data on hate crimes passed on to the FBI vary in consistency and quality.

Systemic underreporting by victims, perhaps the most intractable problem with collecting hate crime data, further reduces the accuracy of the FBI's hate crime statistics. According to the Bureau of Justice Statistics (BJS) at the Department of Justice, the pattern since 9/11 indicates that less than half of hate crime incidents are reported to local police. The Department of Justice uses the term "victimization" to refer to any incident in which a single individual or a single household is targeted for a bias-motivated crime. For crimes against households, such as burglary or vandalism, each household affected is counted as a single victimization. According to BJS estimates, during the four-year period from 2003 through 2006, only 46 percent of hate crime victimizations were reported to local police departments. During the following five-year period, from 2007 through 2011, the share of hate crime victimizations reported to police declined to 35 percent.[16] As a result, information about most hate crimes during these periods never reached local law enforcement agencies, much less the FBI.

The magnitude of the difficulties faced by the FBI in collecting hate crime data is further reflected in disparities between numbers reported in the FBI's hate crime statistics reports and numbers reported in the National Crime Victimization Survey (NCVS). The NCVS, administered jointly by the Bureau of Justice Statistics and the U.S. Census Bureau, provides national crime rate estimates based on annual interviews with a representative sample of households (comprising approximately 160,000 individuals in 2013). The NCVS includes information on non-fatal crimes against persons and households, whether or not the crimes were reported to police. It does not include data on homicides, crimes against individuals under the age of 12, and crimes against institutions, such as churches and mosques.[17]

Among the crimes included in the NCVS are criminal acts perceived by victims to be motivated by bias against them because of their race, religion, ethnicity, gender, sexual orientation, gender identity, or disability. For the first 10 years that the NCVS included hate crimes data, from 2003 through 2012, estimates for the number of hate crime victimizations averaged more than 250,000 annually.[18] This estimate far exceeds the annual average of approximately 7,000 hate crime incidents recorded in the FBI's hate crimes statistics reports for the same period.[19] Data on crimes targeting specific religious groups, such as Muslims, are not provided in the NCVS. However, 28 percent—or more than 80,000—of hate crime victimizations in 2012 were perceived by victims to be motivated by bias against their religion. This figure dwarfs the nearly 1,100 hate crime incidents motivated by religious bias that the FBI recorded in its hate crime statistics report for the same year.[20]

To avoid some of the limitations associated with the legal concept of hate crimes, many social scientists and criminologists advocate using a broader framework to provide a more complete picture of bias-motivated aggression. In the mid-1980s, sociologist Howard Ehrlich offered perhaps the most widely used alternative framework with his concept of ethnoviolence. As defined by Ehrlich, this concept encompasses all acts of aggression motivated by prejudice against a group and designed to cause physical or psychological injury to members of that group. Such acts include violent assaults intended to cause bodily harm or destruction of property as well as verbal abuse, intimidation, harassment, and other hostile acts that do not involve physical violence. Also, the targets of ethnoviolence may be members of any socially defined group, not just ethnic groups as the term might imply.[21]

Ehrlich's framework covers legislatively defined hate crimes, while also encompassing acts of aggression that do not violate the law.

Constitutionally protected acts of bigotry and bias, such as engaging in some forms of hate speech, fall under the definition of ethnoviolence. Similarly, Ehrlich's model is not restricted to legislatively defined categories of bigotry, such as bias based on race or religion, but includes acts of aggression targeting any group based on that group's physical or social characteristics. For example, ethnoviolence includes attacks on people because they are homeless or live in a particular area, acts that could not be prosecuted as hate crimes under federal law because bias against place of residence or lack of residence is not specifically identified in hate crime law. Also, the ethnoviolence designation avoids the implication that perpetrators must harbor hatred for their victims. As Ehrlich recognized, many perpetrators engage in ethnoviolence as acts of conformity to peer pressure or as impulsive acts of anger, rather than as hatred of a targeted group.[22]

In the aftermath of 9/11, several civil rights and advocacy groups used broader measurements of bias incidents, such as Ehrlich's ethnoviolence model, to gain a better accounting of the 9/11 backlash against Muslim Americans than provided by the FBI's hate crime statistics. Based on an extensive review of media accounts across the nation, the advocacy group South Asian American Leaders of Tomorrow (SAALT) identified 645 bias incidents targeting Muslims and Americans of Middle Eastern and South Asian origin during the first week after 9/11. Harassment and threats constituted more than two-thirds of these incidents, while assailants used weapons in 27 cases and engaged in vehicular assault in 5 cases.[23] In the following weeks and months, other organizations reported similar cases. In mid-October 2001, the Muslim Public Affairs Council reported 800 bias incidents targeting Muslims, and in the middle of November 2001, the American-Arab Anti-Discrimination Committee reported more than 1,100 cases of bias directed at Muslims and Arabs.[24]

Early in the following year, the Council for American-Islamic Relations (CAIR) released a report identifying 1,717 anti-Muslim incidents that occurred during the five-month period between September 11, 2001 and the end of February 2002. These incidents included discrimination at school and the workplace, false arrests and intimidation by authorities, threats and harassment in public places, and more than 300 acts of violence.[25] Later that year, Human Rights Watch issued a report pointing to a total of more than 2,000 backlash incidents reported by Arab and Muslim groups in the United States.[26] More than a decade after 9/11, the civic group SAALT reported continued hostility, well beyond pre-9/11 levels, directed at Muslims as well as Sikhs, Hindus, and people of Middle Eastern and South Asian ancestry.[27]

Together, these and other reports on bias incidents after 9/11 suggest that acts of anti-Muslim aggression have a much broader impact on society than indicated by official FBI hate crime data. From acts of intimidation and vandalism to violent physical assault and even murder, the 9/11 backlash has affected Muslim Americans across the nation as well as people who are mistaken for being Muslim, including Sikhs, Hindus, Jews, Arab Christians, people of other religions, and people of no religion. Such acts, although directly targeting individuals who belong to the socially defined group "Muslims," are fundamentally expressions of intolerance toward the group as a whole. Whether perpetrators act out of personal conviction or the desire to conform to social pressure and peer-group demands, bias-motivated acts targeting Muslim individuals serve to belittle, intimidate, or ostracize all Muslims in a community or throughout the country. Anti-Muslim bias incidents may also be designed to achieve more far-ranging consequences, such as terrorizing Muslims within a community, coercing Muslims to leave a neighborhood or region, or making Muslims across the nation believe they are an unwelcome presence in American society.

Threats and Intimidation

During the first several weeks after 9/11 and continuing at lower levels of intensity for years afterward, countless cases of verbal abuse, harassment, and public bullying of Muslims occurred across the country. To begin an accounting of such incidents, sociologist Lori Peek gathered information from 140 Muslim Americans, most of them living in the New York City metropolitan area, from late September 2001 through the end of 2003. About 80 percent of participants reported that they had been verbally harassed in the months after 9/11 or had been in the immediate vicinity of friends or family members who had been targets for abuse. Participants in the study also reported an increase in nonverbal expressions of hostility, such as intimidating stares and angry gestures.[28]

In the aftermath of 9/11 and continuing today, verbal abuse has often escalated to physical intimidation, with assailants spitting on Muslims, pushing and shoving them in public spaces, pulling off their headscarves and kufis, and throwing things at them when walking down the street. In some cases, such acts of intimidation have come close to crossing the line between harassment and criminal assault. In one of many such incidents, a Muslim student at Arizona State University was pelted with eggs during the first week after 9/11.[29] In another case shortly after the 9/11 attacks, angry customers at a Walmart in the city of Laramie in

Wyoming chased a Muslim woman and her children from the store.[30] Years later, in September 2007, a group of teenagers pelted Muslims with rocks as they exited a mosque after Friday prayers in Columbus, Ohio.[31] In October 2010, police arrested a woman and charged her with malicious harassment for kicking and shoving two Somali women and then slamming a car door on one of the victims at a gas station in Burien, Washington.[32]

In addition to individuals, Islamic institutions and Muslim civic organizations have also experienced verbal harassment and acts of intolerance since 9/11. Across the country, such organizations have received phone calls and e-mails containing racial slurs and insults to Islam. They have also received statements suggesting that Muslims must be happy about the 9/11 attacks and that Muslims should be expelled from the country. In October 2002, at the Islamic Center of Honolulu, an unknown person or persons littered the grounds with hundreds of pamphlets proclaiming that Muslims should be killed for supporting terrorism. During the summer of 2003, in the city of College Park in Maryland, assailants burned a cross in front of a mosque, creating a precedent that would be emulated a year later when perpetrators burned a cross in the yard of an Arab family in Edmonds, Washington.[33] In July 2006, at the Lewiston-Auburn Islamic Center in Maine, an assailant rolled a pig's head into the mosque during prayer services.[34]

Acts of intimidation targeting Islamic organizations have also taken the form of vandalism and desecration of religious sites. In the years since of 9/11, vandals have desecrated several Muslim gravesites and defaced mosques across the country with swastikas, graffiti, and offensive statements. Among the numerous cases of such acts, vandals painted "Jesus is Lord and Allah is the Devil" outside a mosque in the town of Canejo in California, a Star of David on a mosque in the city of Charleston in South Carolina, and graffiti associating congregants with Osama bin Laden at a mosque in Augusta, Georgia. Vandalism has also included graffiti with threatening statements such as "You will all die," which assailants painted on a mosque in Bridgeport, Connecticut, as well as "Muslims Burn Forever" and "Die Pigs," which assailants painted in seven-foot-tall letters on the walls of the All Dulles Area Muslim Society in Sterling, Virginia.[35]

Vandals have also attacked businesses and shops they believed to be owned by Muslims, often shattering storefront windows and sometimes wrapping notes containing threats around the rocks and other items used to break the glass.[36] In communities across the United States, Islamic bookstores, Middle Eastern grocery stores and restaurants, Arab and

South Asian street vending stations, and convenience stores with Muslim proprietors have become targets. At times, vandals have systematically targeted businesses in predominantly Muslim and Arab neighborhoods or in urban areas with large Muslim populations. During the first few days after 9/11, a series of attacks targeted Afghan and Iranian restaurants with bottles and rocks in the San Francisco Bay Area, while a mob in Chicago shattered the windows of several Arab-owned shops in an area of the city with a large number of Arab residents.[37]

Along with having to endure expressions of hostility and acts of vandalism, individual Muslims, Islamic institutions, and Muslim-owned organizations across America have received threats of impending attacks. During the week after 9/11, the Islamic Center of Southern California evacuated patrons and staff after receiving several threats, including an e-mail threatening to execute the center's director.[38] Several other mosques and Islamic centers at locations throughout the country received death threats during the same week. In numerous other cases, perpetrators issued bomb threats or threats to commit arson.[39] In Janesville, Wisconsin, an Arab-owned restaurant received a threatening note in the mail containing a substance meant to resemble anthrax.[40] In the town of West Babylon in New York, police arrested a man who brought a homemade pipe bomb to an apartment building and told residents he planned to bomb an Arab.[41]

Assailants have also issued threats against students and staff at Islamic schools, forcing many to cancel classes. In the immediate aftermath of 9/11, the Salam School at the Islamic Society of Milwaukee and the Granada Islamic School in Santa Clara cancelled classes after receiving threats.[42] In Tucson, Arizona, an Islamic charter school closed temporarily after motorists and passersby shouted at students and staff. In Henderson, Nevada, authorities apprehended an assailant who was threatening students at the Omar Haikal Islamic Academy with pepper spray.[43] Also, on college campuses across the country, local chapters of the Muslim Students Association have received threats and warnings, including a letter mailed to the association's chapter at the University of California at Berkeley declaring on behalf of the people of Sacramento, "We will defeat and destroy you."[44]

Violent Assaults

Along with open expressions of intolerance, vandalism, desecration of religious sites, and threats of violence, Muslims in America have also experienced a rise in violent assaults designed to inflict bodily harm.

Violence motivated by bigotry tends to be especially brutal, employing physical force primarily to cause harm rather than subdue a victim, steal possessions, or compel the victim to comply with a demand.[45] Post-9/11 attacks on Muslims have not been exceptions. Such attacks have included gang beatings and assaults with baseball bats, golf clubs, screwdrivers, knives, firearms, and motor vehicles.[46] In one attack within days of 9/11, three assailants threw bleach into the eyes of an Arab shopkeeper in the Little Arabia neighborhood of Cleveland, Ohio.[47] In another case a few weeks later, a perpetrator forced an elderly Persian couple to walk into oncoming traffic in Huntington Beach, California. A neighbor rescued the couple before they were injured.[48]

Like other acts of intolerance, anti-Muslim violence rose sharply immediately after 9/11.[49] The advocacy group SAALT identified 52 violent assaults against Muslims as well as Arabs and South Asians in the first week after the 9/11 attacks.[50] Violent assaults targeting Muslims and those perceived to be Muslims declined in frequency after several weeks, but they continued for years with the same level of brutality that characterizes most bias-motivated violence. Among the many examples, in October 2002, assailants shouted derogatory comments about Islam as they stabbed a worshipper leaving a mosque in Lemon Grove, California. In September 2008 in Dayton, Ohio, assailants sprayed a toxic substance through the window of a mosque, targeting a room where infants and children were being kept while their parents performed Ramadan prayers.[51] Two years later, an assailant who later pled guilty to attempted murder, slashed the neck and face of a Bangladeshi taxi driver in New York City after learning that the driver was Muslim.[52]

As with incidents of vandalism, mosques and Islamic centers became targets of choice for assailants seeking to damage institutions associated with Islam. In some cases, the perpetrators may have intended to cause property damage without harming people, but they chose methods of destruction that posed serious risks to human lives and safety. Firearms proved to be common weapons for such attacks, as assailants fired on mosques in states across the country.[53] In two cases, one in the borough of Landsdale in Pennsylvania and the other in the Miami suburb of West Kendall in Florida, assailants fired more than 50 shots at mosques and property on mosque grounds. In another incident, gunshots struck San Diego's largest mosque while worshippers performed morning prayers.[54] No casualties resulted from these attacks, but the assailants succeeded in causing significant damage and terrorizing Muslim congregations.[55]

Arson proved to be another common method of striking Islamic institutions across the country, including a number of attacks that resulted in the complete destruction of their targets. In the years after 9/11, arsonists destroyed or caused serious damage to mosques at numerous sites, including Stockton, California; Corvallis, Oregon; Toledo, Ohio; Houston, Texas; Wichita, Kansas; Joplin, Missouri; Savannah, Georgia; and Columbia, Tennessee, where assailants also painted swastikas and the phrase "white power" on the mosque grounds.[56] In Jacksonville, Florida, one or more perpetrators threw a homemade firebomb at the Islamic Center of Northeast Florida while worshippers were praying inside. In Falls Church, Virginia, arsonists destroyed a school bus parked outside the Dar al-Hijra Islamic Center while children played in the center's playground.[57] On the other side of the country, a man attempted to set fire to cars parked outside a Seattle mosque, and then he drew a gun and fired on members of the congregation who interrupted his plot.[58]

Assailants also used their vehicles as weapons to strike mosques and Islamic centers. During the first week after 9/11, a man drove a Ford Mustang through the entrance of the Grand Mosque at the Islamic Center of Cleveland, the largest mosque in Ohio. The attack collapsed the front wall of the mosque and caused up to $100,000 in damage. No one was inside the building at the time of the attack; only the driver was injured.[59] In a similar incident during the same week, a man drove his car repeatedly into the Evansville Islamic Center in Indiana while shouting anti-Muslim slurs.[60] Six months later, a man deliberately crashed his truck into the Islamic Center of Tallahassee on the campus of Florida State University. Although this attack failed to cause serious injuries, it occurred just 30 minutes before evening prayers, narrowly missing an opportune time to inflict casualties.[61]

Alongside Islamic institutions, the homes and businesses of Muslims often became targets for potentially deadly anti-Muslim violence. In some cases, armed assailants fired shots into the homes of Muslim families and Muslim-owned establishments; in others, they used explosives and flammable substances against their targets, placing the lives of owners and customers at risk. In March 2003, as the United States prepared to launch military operations in Iraq, perpetrators threw bottles of explosives into the backyard of an Iraqi family in Phoenix, Arizona.[62] During the same month, assailants used explosives to destroy a van parked outside the home of its owners, a Palestinian family living in Burbank, Illinois.[63] In a case in Salt Lake City, an arsonist set fire to a Pakistani-owned restaurant while patrons dined inside. Customers and staff extinguished the fire before it spread throughout the restaurant.[64]

Bias-Motivated Murder

Among the numerous anti-Muslim assaults after 9/11, assailants committed several bias-motivated homicides against Muslims or people they perceived to be Muslim, especially people of Middle Eastern and South Asian origin. The first such case to be confirmed by authorities occurred four days after 9/11, when Frank Roque shot Balbir Singh Sodhi five times as the victim tended plants in front of a gas station he owned in the Phoenix suburb of Meza. Although Sodhi was a Sikh, Roque apparently mistook Sodi's turban and beard as signs that the gas station owner was Muslim.[65] After killing Sodhi, Roque embarked on a shooting spree, shooting at a Lebanese man at a nearby gas station and then firing on a house owned by an Afghan family.[66] Hours before launching his attacks, Roque declared at a local bar that he planned to "kill the rag-heads responsible for 9/11."[67] During his arrest, Roque shouted, "Go ahead, arrest me and let those terrorists run wild!"[68]

On the same day that Frank Roque killed Balbir Singh Sodhi in Arizona, white supremacist Mark Stroman began a series of murders and attempted murders in Texas. Stroman's first victim was Waqar Hasan, the Pakistani owner of a Dallas-area grocery store, where Stroman shot and killed him. Six days later, Stroman critically wounded Rais Bhuiyan, a man from Bangladesh who was working at a Dallas gas station when Stroman shot him in the face, leaving him blind in one eye. Two weeks after shooting Bhuiyan, Stroman carried out his last attack. In early October 2001, he shot and killed Vasudev Patel, the Indian owner of a convenience store in Mesquite, Texas.[69] After his arrest, Stroman gave a televised interview from jail, proclaiming, "We're at war. I did what I had to do."[70]

A year and a half later, Larme Price began a killing spree in the New York City boroughs of Queens and Brooklyn. In early February 2003, he shot and killed three of his victims: John Freddy, a man of Indian descent who immigrated to the United States from Guyana; Sukhjit Khajala, another man of Indian ancestry; and Albert Kotlyar, an immigrant from Ukraine. Price did not strike again until late March, when he shot and killed Mohammed Abdo Nasser Ali, a shopkeeper from Yemen. After shooting Ali, Price shot and wounded Yakoob Aldailam, another Yemeni man who worked in the same store. Price turned himself in to the police a few days later, admitting that he was motivated by the urge to kill people from the Middle East in retaliation for 9/11, apparently unaware that his first three victims were from other parts of the world.[71]

In addition to these clear cases of bias-motivated murder, several homicides committed in the years after 9/11 manifested mixed, ambiguous, or unknown motives that may include anti-Muslim bias. As one example, in mid-September 2001, Brent David Seever shot and killed Ali Almansoop, a Yemeni man, in Lincoln Park, Michigan. Jealousy was apparently one of the motivating factors behind the crime; Almansoop had been romantically involved with Seever's former girlfriend, and Seever had been stalking her before the murder. These facts prompted prosecutors to focus on jealousy as Seever's motive. However, Seever also indicated that he targeted Almansoop to retaliate for the 9/11 attacks. Immediately before killing Almansoop, Seever expressed rage about 9/11 and, following his arrest, claimed that one of his motives for killing Almansoop was revenge for the terrorist attacks.[72]

Similarly, potentially mixed motives may have played a role in the murder of Jawed Wassel, a filmmaker born in Afghanistan. In early October 2001, Nathan Powell stabbed and beat Wassel to death, then packed his dismembered body into boxes in preparation for disposal. Powell, a producer who was working with Wassel on a forthcoming film, apparently killed Wassel following a business dispute. After his arrest, Powell claimed that Wassel had been working with the Taliban and had threatened to kill Powell and his family. He subsequently told a reporter during a prison interview that all foreign-born Muslims should be expelled from the country.[73]

In a number of other cases, unidentified assailants took the lives of Muslims, or people they may have believed to be Muslim, for reasons that remain unknown. Three cases with similar circumstances took place in California during the first several weeks after 9/11. Three days after the terrorist attacks, one or more perpetrators shot and killed Adel Karas, an Egyptian-born Christian, in a grocery store he owned in the city of San Gabriel.[74] Later in the month, assailants shot and killed Abdo Ali Ahmed at a store he owned in the town of Reedley in central California. Two days before his death, Ahmed discovered a note on the windshield of his car that declared, "We are going to kill all (expletive) Arabs."[75] The following month, unidentified perpetrators shot and killed Syrian-born Ranez Younan at a convenience store he owned in San Fernando Valley.[76] Police uncovered no signs of robbery or theft at any of the three stores and identified neither the perpetrators nor motives for the attacks.

Across the country, other homicides—perpetrated by unknown assailants and potentially motivated by anti-Muslim bias—occurred at various types of locations, including public spaces, the workplace, and the victims' homes. Two widely reported cases occurred almost a decade apart, one targeting a Somali man in Minneapolis and the other targeting a Jordanian man in California's San Bernardino County. In October 2001, an unidentified assailant assaulted a Somali man named Ali Warsame Ali at a Minneapolis bus stop, beating him unconscious. Ali was taken to the hospital, where he died several days later. His murder occurred both during the initial post-9/11 spike in anti-Muslim violence and during a wave of bias incidents targeting the 40,000-strong Somali immigrant community in Minneapolis. Anti-Somali sentiments in the city may have been sparked by news reports that local Somalis were funding terrorist groups connected to al-Qaeda.[77] Nearly eight years later, in June 2009, unknown arsonists set fire to a house in the California town of Yermo, killing homeowner Ali Abdelhadi Mohd. An immigrant from Jordan, Mohd had returned to his temporarily vacant house to clean up anti-Arab and white supremacist graffiti scrawled on the property.[78]

In several other incidents, assailants used deadly force against Muslim victims for reasons that investigators could not determine, even after apprehending the perpetrators. In 2002, in a neighborhood of Brooklyn with a large immigrant community from Bangladesh, Mizanur Rahman and Mohammed Hossain were beaten to death in separate incidents, in both cases by a gang of assailants.[79] Police apprehended two suspects in the murder of Rahman but were unable to determine if bias was a factor in the assault.[80] In October 2006, Manuel Urango shot and killed Alia Ansari, an Afghan woman, as she was walking with her three-year-old daughter in Fremont, California. Following his arrest, Urango did not give a reason for his actions, and investigators did not discover a motive for the crime.[81] In March 2014, Jeffrey Caylor shot and killed Hassan Alawsi, a refugee from Iraq, in the parking lot of a Home Depot in Sacramento. Police arrested him shortly afterward, but they could not determine a clear motive for the murder. Prosecutors initially declined to add a hate crime violation to charges against Calor but said they reserved the option to do so later, pending further investigation.[82]

In New York City, more than a decade after 9/11, an assailant embarked on a five-month killing spree against people of Middle Eastern origin, similar to the murders committed by Larme Price in 2003. In July 2012, 64-year-old Salvatore Perrone shot and killed his first victim, an Egyptian-born Muslim man named Mohamed Gebeli. The following month, he stabbed Isaac Kadare, an Egyptian-born Jewish man, in the neck and then shot him in the head. In November, Perrone shot and killed his last victim, Rahmatollah Vahidipour, a Jewish man from Iran. All three victims were killed in stores they owned and operated in Brooklyn. Perrone, who was arrested shortly after committing his last murder, had no known connection to the victims, and his motive for the murders remained unclear as his trial began in 2013.[83]

At the close of 2014, another possible hate crime took the life of a Muslim American. In December of that year, Ahmed Aden, a Christian man from Somalia, deliberately drove his SUV into a Muslim teenager outside a mosque in Kansas City. The victim, 15-year-old Abdisamad Sheikh-Hussein, died of his injuries in the hospital. Aden admitted to intentionally killing the victim, but he claimed he did so because he mistook the teenager for someone who had threatened him several days earlier. However, worshippers at the mosque identified Aden as a local resident who frequently made violent threats against Muslims. Weeks before the crime, several residents reported seeing an SUV resembling Aden's vehicle with threatening and offensive messages painted on it, including the statement, "Islam is worse than Ebola." State authorities charged Aden with murder, and federal officials opened a hate crime investigation of the incident.[84]

Large-Scale Terrorist Plots Targeting Muslims

During the first 12 months after 9/11, authorities also uncovered two terrorist conspiracies targeting Muslim Americans. Like many hate crimes, these conspiracies included plans to engage in especially brutal attacks against members of a socially defined group the perpetrators held in contempt. However, in contrast to most hate crimes and acts of ethnoviolence, both of these conspiracies involved complex plots to strike multiple targets and cause mass casualties. The principal objective in both cases was to send a message to Muslims throughout and potentially beyond the borders of the United States.

The first of these terrorist conspiracies began to take shape almost immediately after 9/11. Within weeks of al-Qaeda's attack on the World Trade Center and the Pentagon, members of the Jewish Defense League (JDL), a Jewish nationalist organization with a history of violence, began collaborating to strike Muslim and Arab targets in the Los Angeles metropolitan area. Irving David Rubin, national chairman of the JDL, joined with his lieutenant, Earl Leslie Krugel, to select targets and methods of attack. They recruited a third JDL member, Danny Gillis, to conduct surveillance of potential targets and construct explosive devices. The conspirators first decided to bomb the offices of the Muslim Public Affairs Council in downtown Los Angeles but later altered their plans, instead deciding to bomb the King Fahd Mosque and the district office of U.S. Representative Darrell Issa, a Christian of Lebanese descent.

The King Fahd Mosque, located in Culver City in western Los Angeles, regularly served about 1,000 worshippers.[85]

This 2001 plot continued a 30-year pattern of JDL terrorist activity. Founded in 1968, the JDL has since launched numerous terrorist attacks against persons, institutions, and foreign governments engaged in activities deemed by the group to be anti-Semitic. The group has initiated attacks—sometimes with firearms or homemade bombs—against foreign diplomats and consulates in the United States, against neo-Nazi and other far-right groups, against Arab and Muslim activists, and against other Jewish groups seen by the JDL as acting contrary to Jewish interests.[86] Law enforcement authorities identified members of the JDL as suspects in the 1985 bombing of the California headquarters of the American-Arab Anti-Discrimination Committee, which resulted in the death of the organization's director, Alex Odeh.[87] In 1994, JDL member Baruch Goldstein, a U.S.-born doctor living in Israel, entered a mosque in the West Bank city of Hebron and fired on worshippers with an automatic rifle, killing 29 people and wounding 125.[88]

In October 2001, before the JDL cell could launch its attacks in Los Angeles, fellow conspirator Danny Gillis told law enforcement authorities about the plot and became an informant for the FBI. In December, an FBI-led Joint Terrorism Task Force arrested his partners, Rubin and Krugel. During a search of Krugel's home, investigators found explosives, bomb components, bomb-making instruction manuals, and several firearms.[89] A year later, before the case went to trial, Rubin committed suicide by slashing his throat with a razor and jumping from the balcony of the Metropolitan Detention Center in Los Angeles.[90] Krugel subsequently pled guilty to charges related to the terrorist plot and received a 20-year prison sentence. In 2005, another inmate, who may have been motivated by white supremacist views, struck Krugel in the head with a cinder block, killing him.[91]

Eight months after authorities arrested the JDL conspirators in Los Angeles, police in Florida uncovered another terrorist plot targeting Muslim Americans. In August 2002, while responding to a call about a domestic disturbance at a residence near the Florida city of St. Petersburg, sheriff's deputies discovered an extensive arsenal along with plans to attack Islamic sites throughout the state. During a search of a townhouse owned by Robert Goldstein, a podiatrist at a local medical office, deputies found fully automatic machine guns, sniper rifles, other assorted firearms, 25,000 rounds of ammunition, grenades, rocket launchers, more than 20 homemade bombs, and a 5-gallon gasoline bomb with a timer. They also discovered plans for assaults on 50 mosques and Islamic educational and cultural centers. Among the attack plans were instructions for an assault on an Islamic center that involved bombing facilities at the site and then detonating explosives in the center's parking lot and playground to kill fleeing survivors.[92]

After their search of the Goldstein residence, police arrested Goldstein and his wife, Kristi, who had called police to the scene in the first place because her husband was becoming increasingly violent, and she feared for her safety.[93] During the following investigation, authorities discovered that Goldstein planned to attack Islamic sites on the first anniversary of 9/11 to retaliate for al-Qaeda's attacks on the United States and for Palestinian terrorist attacks against Israel. Their investigation also led police to arrest two other suspects associated with the plot: Michael Hardee, another local doctor who helped plan the attacks, and Samuel Shannahan, a firearms dealer who provided some of the weapons for the planned attacks. Kristi Goldstein pled guilty to firearms violations. The four conspirators received prison sentences ranging from 37 months for Kristi Goldstein to 151 months for Robert Goldstein.[94]

Nearly 13 years later, federal authorities uncovered another plot to inflict mass casualties on Muslim Americans. In April 2015, FBI agents arrested Robert Doggart in Tennessee following a sting operation during which Doggart discussed plans with FBI informants to attack a small Muslim community in rural New York State called Islamberg. Doggart claimed the residents of Islamberg were planning a terrorist attack and that the community "must be utterly destroyed." In recorded phone conversations, in meetings with informants, and on his Facebook page, Doggart outlined plans to gather a militia to conduct an armed assault on the community. Following his arrest, he pled guilty to the federal offense of communicating threats across state lines, a crime punishable by up to five years in prison.[95]

Mobilization: From Bigotry to Violence

Identifying a common set of factors that motivate people to engage in hate crime violence is difficult, both because of the wide diversity of those who commit such acts and because a large number of bias crimes are committed anonymously, with the perpetrators never being identified. By definition, bias always plays a role, but it is insufficient to explain why some biased individuals decide to commit acts of property destruction, violent assaults, and even murder. Most expressions of intolerance do not involve physical violence, and many bigots and racists never engage in violent attacks against members of the groups they despise. Bigotry and hatred are compelling forces, but other contributing factors are necessary to explain the descent into violence.

Adherence to a racist or xenophobic ideology may impel some hate crime offenders to engage in violence, especially when combined with membership in an organized hate group, such as a neo-Nazi or white supremacist organization. However, based on cases in which the assailants have been identified, available evidence suggests that most hate crime offenders lack strong political affiliation or ideological commitment. And most perpetrators of hate crimes are not affiliated with organized hate groups. Regarding anti-Muslim incidents, on several occasions, vandals have painted swastikas and white supremacist statements on mosques and Islamic centers, but such offenses are often expressions of intolerance in an extreme form rather than the work of organized hate groups. A common (but not universal) characteristic of hate crime offenders is their willingness to engage in extraordinary acts of bigotry despite their lack of dedication to causes or political movements that would explain their actions.[96]

In this respect, most hate crimes differ from terrorism, another extreme form of violence often compared to violent hate crimes. The FBI defines terrorism as the "unlawful use of force or violence against persons or property to intimidate or coerce a government, the civilian population, or any segment thereof in furtherance of political or social objectives."[97] Similarly, the National Consortium for the Study of Terrorism and Responses to Terrorism (START), a University of Maryland research center partly funded by the Department of Homeland Security, defines terrorism as the "threatened or actual use of illegal force and violence by non-state actors to attain political, economic, religious, or social goals through fear, coercion, or intimidation."[98] Attacks that conform to these definitions are usually planned, often as part of sustained campaigns to advance political causes.

As demonstrated by the Jewish Defense League's 2001 plot to strike Arab and Muslim targets in the Los Angeles area and by Robert Goldstein's 2002 plot to attack Muslim targets in Florida, violence inspired by bias can overlap with acts of terrorism. In both cases, the plotters were motivated by anti-Muslim bigotry and a desire to advance what they perceived as Jewish nationalist or pro-Israel causes. However, such overlap between hate crimes and terrorism is not the norm. In 2012, a team of social scientists at the University at Albany-SUNY released the results of an extensive analysis comparing terrorism and hate crimes in the United States from 1992 to 2008. Using data from START's Global Terrorism Database and FBI hate crimes statistics, they found that only about 3 percent of terrorist attacks in the United States were recorded as hate crimes during the 17-year period under examination. This study, which compared 505 terrorist attacks with more than 130,000 hate crimes, included controls to limit the effects of underreporting of hate crimes.[99]

Nevertheless, terrorism and violent hate crimes, in addition to tending toward especially brutal acts, have at least one basic characteristic in common: the violence inflicted on the victims is also aimed at a larger community. Acts of terrorism target noncombatants to intimidate or coerce a government, a population, or some other third party to advance a political or social agenda. Similarly, hate crimes directly target individual members of a social group but indirectly send a message of intolerance to the entire group. The victims of hate crimes are selected because of their symbolic value as representatives of their entire social group.[100] In all such cases of bias-motivated aggression, perpetrators make two central decisions, usually aided by cultural and social cues. First, they identify a group they believe deserves punishment or is acceptable to punish, often because some segments of society encourage aggression against the group. Second, they decide to be the instrument of that punishment.

Defining the Enemy

Defining the world's Muslims as a cohesive group requires an enormous degree of oversimplification and blurring of distinctions. Comprising about 1.6 billion people, nearly a quarter of the world's population, Muslims are dispersed throughout Asia, Europe, the Middle East, North Africa, and sub-Saharan Africa, with smaller but still significant numbers living in North America, Latin America, and the Caribbean.[101] Muslims around the world speak more than 80 major languages and differ significantly in their religious practices, interpretations of their faith, and levels of religious commitment.[102] Nearly 15 centuries old, Islam has spread throughout the world, picking up cultural influences and distinctions while diverging into different and often competing schools of thought, sects, and interpretations, much the same way that Christianity has evolved.

Categorizing Muslims as a single homogeneous social group is equally problematic when referring to Muslims within the United States, home to one of the most diverse Muslim populations within any single country. Based on a Pew Research Center survey released in 2011, Muslim Americans number about 2.75 million, slightly less than one percent of the total U.S. population. This number includes approximately 1.8 million adults, 63 percent of whom were born abroad and 15 percent of whom are second-generation Americans. These relative newcomers to America trace their origins to more than 77 countries. They are racially diverse, with many identifying themselves as either white, black, Asian, Hispanic, mixed, or belonging to some other racial designation, with no one racial category constituting a majority.[103] A Gallup survey conducted in 2009 concluded that Muslim Americans were the most racially diverse of the major religious groups in the United States.[104]

Constructing a social category broad enough to encompass the diversity of Muslim Americans results in a category that is exceptionally broad and that overlaps with other major social categories, including racial, ethnic, native-born or immigrant, religiously observant or non-practicing, and many others. However, throughout U.S. history, Americans have been exposed to simplified images and descriptions of Muslims that disregard or downplay differences among the many peoples and cultures of the Muslim world. These depictions have formed the basis for how many Americans see their fellow citizens who happen to be Muslim. Such images are found in America's cultural inheritance from Europe, in biased interpretations of America's encounters with Muslim societies abroad, in the news and entertainment media, and, especially in recent years, in depictions of Muslims terrorists and religious extremists. After 9/11, anti-Muslim activists and some political figures contributed to reductive perceptions of Muslims and Islam.

Through socialization—growing up in the United States and participating in American culture—almost all Americans encounter the central images and descriptions used to construct the social category called "Muslims." During this process of social categorization, Americans also learn the generalizations used to define this category, including negative stereotypes. These stereotypes may be enthusiastically embraced, consciously rejected, or, more commonly, unconsciously internalized by Americans before they reach adulthood. Unless they are countered by other influences, such as interacting with Muslims or learning about Islam from informed sources, these stereotypes are likely to be incorporated into the mental models, or schemas, through which individuals view and understand Muslims and Islam.

A schema defining any social group is most influential when a precipitating event or series of events activates the schema in the minds of individuals. Such activation brings the stereotypes contained in the schema to the surface of consciousness or, in the case of people who have already embraced the stereotypes, deepens previously held perceptions.

For most individuals, major events and crises that give the social group defined by a schema immediate and heightened relevance are likely to activate the schema. The terrorist attacks of 9/11 unquestionably gave the social category "Muslims" salience for virtually all Americans. Many Americans dismissed or resisted the negative stereotypes of Muslims that such heightened relevance brings to the surface, but others embraced the stereotypes as an explanation for why 19 Muslim men would engage in such an act of mass murder. For some, the event provided proof that Muslims, not just al-Qaeda and its supporters, were the enemy.

Writing four decades ago, sociologist Stanley Cohen labeled this type of reaction "moral panic." As he observed, the actions of some members of a socially defined group may lead many in society to define the entire group as a threat. In any such case, things associated with the group may come to symbolize the threat, while behaviors commonly displayed by the group—although barely noticed or seen as benign previously—may be redefined as deviant behavior, a process Cohen termed "sensitization."[105] In this manner, since 9/11, mosques, Islamic centers and schools, people wearing headscarves or kufis, Muslims praying, and other images symbolic of Islam, although previously unremarkable, have come to be interpreted as threatening by some elements of American society. Compounding this problem, as criminologist Lu-Win Wang has noted, hostility directed at a particular social group communicates to others that mistreating members of that group is acceptable and possibly desirable.[106] Accordingly, anti-Muslim aggression may encourage others to take similar action.

Such periods of heightened hostility toward Muslims in America predate 9/11. As Muslim Americans increased in number and visibility during the late 20th century, they became targets of aggression arising from adverse events overseas. The 1973 Arab-Israeli war and associated Arab oil embargo against the United States, along with the 1979 Iran hostage crisis, sparked hostility toward Muslims, Arabs, Iranians, and other Middle Easterners.[107] In the 1980s, terrorist attacks by Hezbollah, Hamas, and other Muslim terrorist groups contributed to sporadic cases of anti-Muslim and anti-Arab violence.[108] In the early 1990s, additional acts of aggression targeting Muslims followed Iraq's invasion of Kuwait, including beatings, vandalism, and at least two arson attacks on mosques, one in Brooklyn and one in Yuba City, California.[109]

By the middle of the 1990s, many Americans viewed Muslims and Islam with suspicion both abroad and, especially after the 1993 World Trade Center bombing, at home. The degree to which this sentiment could influence public attitudes and behaviors toward Muslim

Americans was displayed by events after the 1995 Oklahoma City bombing, which destroyed the Alfred P. Murrah Federal Building and killed 168 people.[110] For two days after the bombing, Muslims suffered verbal abuse, workplace harassment, death threats, bomb threats, and physical assaults. These bias incidents declined after news emerged that right-wing extremist Timothy McVeigh was responsible for the bombing, but attacks on Muslims continued at lower rates throughout the year. Foreshadowing the types of attacks that would occur in greater numbers after 9/11, assailants targeted mosques and Islamic centers for vandalism, drive-by shootings, and arson attacks.[111] The Muslim advocacy organization CAIR recorded nearly 300 cases of aggression toward Muslim Americans during the year after the Oklahoma City bombing, including 29 acts of physical violence.[112]

Widening the Net

Incorporating all Muslims, or even the much smaller number of Muslim Americans, into a cohesive social category requires overlooking differences among individuals, ethnic groups, and religious practices on an enormous scale. Blaming this socially constructed category for the 9/11 terrorist attacks requires an even more stubborn ability to suppress readily available information and disregard competing facts. However, in addition to taking these steps, many perpetrators of anti-Muslim violence have taken the additional step of broadening the social category of Muslims to include people unaffiliated with Islam. This third step, an example of a process Stanley Cohen termed "widening the net," often arises from cases of mistaken identity, as perpetrators target people they believe appear to be Muslim.[113] In such cases, assailants may single out anybody who matches their image of a Muslim.

Anti-Muslim violence inflicted on non-Muslims is often directed at persons matching symbolic cues, such as being of Middle Eastern or South Asian descent, speaking Arabic, or wearing head coverings that appear Islamic.[114] As sociologist Victoria Munro has pointed out, people who to fit the perpetrators' image of Muslims may become stand-ins for terrorists, just as Asians of all ethnicities often became stand-ins for Japanese during World War II. This new category of Muslim-looking people may include Arab Christians, South Asian Hindus, Sikhs, Latinos, non-Muslim African Americans, and anyone with a headscarf or prominent beard.[115] In the months after 9/11, as violence in Los Angeles that appeared to be aimed at Muslims expanded to include a large number of non-Muslims, Los Angeles County officials created a special hate crime classification called "9/11-related hate crimes." This category of hate crimes provided authorities with a means of grouping together bias-motivated crimes related to the 9/11 backlash, regardless of the ethnicities and religions of the victims.[116]

During the years after 9/11, several people belonging to faiths other than Islam became victims of backlash violence, including victims of highly publicized shooting sprees. The first victim of Frank Roque, the killer who began his shooting spree in the Arizona town of Meza four days after 9/11, was a Sikh man. Similarly, the two men Mark Stroman killed during his shooting spree in the Dallas area shortly after 9/11 included one who was Hindu. More than a decade later, Salvatore Perrone killed three victims of Middle Eastern origin in New York City, including two Jewish men. One month after Perrone killed his last victim, Erika Menendez, a woman with a history of mental illness, murdered Sunando Sen, a Hindu man of Indian origin. Menendez pushed Sen onto the tracks in a New York subway station, where an oncoming train struck and killed him. Apparently conflating Hindus and Muslims, she later told investigators that she assaulted Sen because she blamed Hindus and Muslims for destroying the Twin Towers on 9/11.[117]

Additionally, along with mosques, non-Muslim houses of worship have frequently become targets of what appears to be anti-Muslim aggression. Assailants have targeted Hindu and Sikh temples at several locations across the nation with threats, harassment of worshippers, vandalism, and arson. Perpetrators have also targeted Coptic Christian churches and other churches with Arab congregations, possibly to strike out against Arab Americans or out of the mistaken belief that all Arabs are Muslims. In one case during the first week after 9/11, vandals struck a synagogue in Tacoma, Washington, leaving graffiti blaming Zionists for the 9/11 terrorist attacks. A week later, the synagogue was the target of a failed arson attack.[118]

Because of the turbans and beards traditionally worn by Sikh men and the head coverings often worn by Sikh women, Sikh Americans are often mistaken for Muslims. Since Frank Roque's killing of Balbir Singh Sodhi, other hate crime offenders have apparently made this mistake. In the first several weeks after 9/11, a man burst into the car of Swaran Kaur Bhullar, a Sikh woman, while she was stopped at a traffic light in San Diego and slashed her in the head.[119] Later that year, two assailants armed with metal rods beat Surinder Singh Sidhi in a liquor store he owned in Los Angeles, calling him Osama bin Laden during the assault.[120] After the initial increase in anti-Muslim violence in 2001, assailants continued to target Sikhs in what appear to be cases of anti-Muslim bias, although authorities have often been unable to identify the offenders or conclusively determine their motives.

Among the many cases of possible anti-Muslim violence committed mistakenly against Sikhs, in August 2002, unknown assailants in San Francisco shot and killed taxi driver Sukhpal Singh Sodhi. The victim was the brother of Balbir Singh Sodhi, who was murdered by Frank Roque the previous year.[121] In subsequent years, other Sikh victims of possible 9/11 backlash violence include Dalvir Sangha, a postal worker shot and injured as he delivered the mail in Sacramento; Gurdeep Singh Saluja, shot and killed while working at a gas station in Miami; and Inderjit Singh Jassal, shot and killed while working at a convenience store in Phoenix.[122] Almost a decade after 9/11, in March 2011, unknown assailants shot and killed two elderly Sikh men, Surinder Singh and Gurmej Atwal, as the victims were on their daily walk in Elk Grove, California.[123]

Eleven years after 9/11, violence against Sikh Americans took the form of a mass shooting designed to inflict multiple casualties. In August 2012, Michael Wade Page entered a Sikh temple in Oak Creek, Wisconsin, during religious services and fired on worshippers with an automatic weapon. Page killed six people and wounded four in the temple. He then shot and injured a police officer outside the temple before turning his gun on himself and committing suicide. Page left behind no note or testament explaining his actions, and investigators could not reach a definitive conclusion regarding his motives.[124] A longtime activist in white supremacist, neo-Nazi, and extremist Christian circles, Page may have been motivated by racist sentiments to strike out against a symbol of nonwhite and non-Christian presence in America. Like several previous hate crime offenders, he may also have been driven by anti-Muslim bigotry to attack a house of worship he mistook for a mosque and to kill individuals he incorrectly believed to be Muslim.

Following the Oak Creek shooting, the Sikh American Legal Defense and Education Fund (SALDEF) commissioned a study to assess the American public's views of Sikhism and Sikh Americans. Conducted by the Stanford Peace Innovation Lab at Stanford University during the summer of 2013, the study found pervasive misunderstandings about Sikh identity and biased attitudes toward symbols of the Sikh religion, especially turbans, beards, and uncut hair. Approximately half of Americans surveyed associated turbans with Muslims and believed Sikhism to be a sect of Islam. Overall, the study concluded that a strong cultural bias against Sikhs exists among Americans with little knowledge of Sikhism but also among more educated Americans with a stronger understanding of Sikhs and the Sikh religion. Among the pool of more informed Americans polled in the survey, more than 20 percent said they would become angry or experience an adverse reaction if they encountered a stranger wearing a turban.[125]

These findings indicate an inclination to associate Sikhs with Islam and to incorporate symbols of Sikhism, especially the turban, into anti-Muslim bias and hostility. They also open the door to an alternative explanation for some instances of anti-Sikh violence. The finding that a significant minority of relatively well-informed Americans—one in five—expresses bias toward Sikhs indicates that much anti-Sikh hostility may be based on social trends broader than anti-Muslim animosity. Just as Michael Wade Page may have been motivated by white supremacist beliefs and Christian extremism to attack Sikh worshippers, other assailants may have attacked Sikh Americans because Sikhs do not fit the perpetrators' image of true Americans, regardless of whether they are mistaken for Muslims.

This possibility applies to many other victims of bias-motivated violence after 9/11, including some Muslim victims. Hostility toward racial and religious minorities among segments of American society has a long tradition in the nation's history. As Muslims, Sikhs, and other minority groups grow in numbers and gain increased visibility, they are more likely to encounter aggression inspired by biased attitudes. Especially for Muslims and people who resemble common American images of Muslims, 9/11 may have accelerated this process, as fear and anger sparked by al-Qaeda's terrorist attacks are subsumed under broader racist outlooks. In an expansion of Stanley Cohen's concept of widening the net, many minorities—especially Muslims—may find themselves targeted by those who see 9/11 as part of a larger assault on "white" and "Christian" America.

Choosing Violence

Even after an enemy group is defined and the boundaries that delineate that group are established, other factors are necessary to mobilize hate crime offenders to violent action. As discussed, most acts of intolerance fall short of physical violence, and most bigots do not regularly engage in violent attacks. Additional incentives other than bias are required. In the early 1990s, criminologists Jack Levin and Jack McDevitt developed a hate crime typology to identify and categorize such additional motives. Their typology, which was based on an analysis of bias-motivated crimes committed in Boston over an 18-month period, grouped offenses into three categories: defensive hate crimes, mission-driven hate crimes, and thrill-seeking hate crimes. In collaboration with sociologist Susan Bennett, they updated this typology in 2002 to include a fourth category: retaliatory hate crimes.[126] This categorization system has been used widely in subsequent years by sociologists and police departments.

The latter of these categories, retaliatory hate crimes, appears to explain the sharp increase in anti-Muslim violence in the first several weeks after 9/11. In this type of attack, an assailant (or group of assailants) seeks revenge for a real or perceived attack on his social group by members of another group.[127] Following the 9/11 terrorist attacks, hate-crime perpetrators engaged in retaliatory violence against Muslims and people they mistook for Muslims in regions across the United States. Anger and outrage over the terrorist attacks impelled assailants to seek revenge for an attack on a group—Americans—with which they personally identified. As is usually true for retaliatory hate crimes, offenders did not seek out those who were responsible for the attacks, which would have been impossible in any case since the hijackers were dead and other al-Qaeda members out of reach. Instead, assailants targeted members of what they perceived to be the attackers' group. The suspicion that Muslim extremists were to blame, which was quickly confirmed, led many to assign guilt by association to all Muslims.

In defensive hate crimes, assailants are galvanized into action by their perception that another group is threatening to take a valuable resource away from them or is invading their territory. Perpetrators are often mobilized to commit violent attacks on property or persons as a means of protecting their neighborhood or workplace from the encroachment of another group.[128] This category of hate crimes points to a motive for many attacks on Islamic institutions in the years after 9/11, especially against mosques and Islamic community centers in neighborhoods resistant to the presence of Muslims. In one emblematic case, vandals painted "Not Welcome" at the construction site of the highly contested Islamic center in Murfreesboro, Tennessee, and then set fire to construction equipment.[129] In addition, across the country, attacks on homes and businesses owned by Muslim Americans may often stem from assailants signaling their opposition to a Muslim presence in their neighborhoods.

Mission-driven hate crimes, the rarest type according to Levin's and McDevitt's research, occur when assailants are impelled to eliminate a group they believe to be evil or a threat. Such individuals are often deeply disturbed and sometimes psychotic.[130] This motive may partially explain a number of killing sprees and apparent random homicides targeting Muslims. In the immediate aftermath of 9/11, shooting sprees carried out by Frank Roque and Mark Stroman may have contained elements of mission-driven violence. Stroman carried out his crimes over several weeks, indicated a strong commitment to murdering Muslims. Roque, whose family history of mental illness spared him the death penalty, indicated that he believed all Muslims were responsible for 9/11 and that Muslim children should be killed to prevent them from growing up to be like their parents.[131] Similarly, Larme Price and Salvatore Perrone, both guilty of killing sprees over several weeks in New York City, may have been pursuing missions to punish or eliminate people they believed to be evil.

By contrast, thrill-seeking hate crimes appear to be the most common type, comprising two-thirds of all hate crimes committed in the 18-month period of the Levin-McDevitt study. In most cases, such acts are committed by teenagers or young men looking for excitement, the exhilaration of displaying power, or the opportunity to impress peers. Offenders tend to have little commitment to bias against their victims, often telling police after their apprehension that they were just bored or looking for fun.[132] Nevertheless, bigotry remains an underlying factor, as assailants typically select victims from social groups that society has identified as deserving of hostility.[133] In the minds of thrill-seekers, even those without strong personal bias, negative stereotypes and unfavorable public attitudes about the victimized group often justify the group's punishment. Relatively small but growing pockets of American society began to view Muslim Americans in this light during the decades before 9/11. In the years afterward, after a brief increase in favorable views of Muslim Americans, negative public attitudes toward Muslims in the country hardened and spread, leaving them increasingly vulnerable to being labeled a group that deserves punishment or is safe to victimize.

This aspect of thrill-seeking hate crimes underscores a common element found in all types of bias-motivated crimes: the role of culture and society in defining groups that deserve punishment and, in some cases, offering rewards for delivering retribution. Retaliatory hate crimes and defensive hate crimes targeting Muslim Americans require the assailants to view Muslims as an enemy "other," different from the rest of Americans and posing a threat to the community or the larger society. Perpetrators of mission-driven hate crimes, even those suffering from psychosis, require social cues to tell them which group is a threat. Similarly, without direction from society, assailants who commit thrill-seeking hate crimes would not know which groups are safe to attack or which groups to victimize to gain peer approval and respect.

Moreover, other acts of intolerance, including constitutionally pro-tected actions such as delivering anti-Muslim hate speech and protest-ing against mosques and Islamic centers, are facilitated by aspects of society that communicate approval for such behavior. The mobilization of hundreds of people to march on the Bridgeview Mosque Foundation in Illinois during the first few days after 9/11 was facilitated by negative stereotypes of Muslims, endemic in Western culture, and by disparaging images presented in popular media. These and other social cues aid the process of connecting fellow Americans who happened to be Muslim to an attack on the country by a foreign terrorist organization. Similarly, the countless acts of anti-Muslim bigotry across the country in the years afterward are based, in part, on the framing of Muslims as a threat and a group that deserves contempt.

CHAPTER 6

Muslim Americans and the Homeland Security Enterprise

L ike most immigrant communities in America, upon their arrival in the United States, Muslim immigrants began organizing informally at the local level to aid their transition into American society. Designed primarily to help new citizens adjust to their environment while maintaining valued aspects of their cultures, nascent community-building efforts formed the basis for what would become a diverse and thriving civil-society infrastructure. A parallel trend in political and social organization on the part of African American Muslims, although conceived in part as a means of constructing a collective identity removed from American society, contributed to Muslim civic mobilization. Moreover, Muslim citizens increasingly participated in American public life through the same pathways that Americans of almost all faiths become engaged in, and a part of, American society. Today, this formal and informal Muslim civic mobilization provides a powerful, yet underutilized, resource for America's homeland security enterprise.

Muslim Americans and American Civil Society

At least as far back as the late 19th century, as significant numbers of Muslim immigrants began to arrive on American shores, Muslims in America started organizing community groups and informal associations to help them navigate American culture and society.[1] Such groups and gatherings were directed primarily at solving local community concerns, and they often revolved around mosques and efforts to construct new mosques. Muslim immigrant-based organizations remained divided largely along ethnic lines, with immigrant communities maintaining varying degrees of cohesion based on their countries or regions of origin. In the early 20th century, a parallel trend developed among African American Muslims as some African Americans began turning to Islam as an alternative identity set apart from mainstream American society. Most prominently, the Moorish Science Temple and the Nation of Islam emerged as vehicles to pursue political and social goals centered on the African American experience.

Shortly after World War II, Muslim activists initiated the first major effort to form an organization representing Muslims nationwide. In 1952, the International Muslim Society held its first convention in Cedar Rapids, Iowa, attracting about 400 participants. The principal organizers, led by a second-generation Arab American and World War II veteran named Abdallah Igram, were Muslims working to forge a place for Muslim identity in mainstream American society. They focused primarily on the immigrant Muslim population and second-generation Muslim Americans and, to a lesser extent, on Muslims in Canada. Their efforts led to the creation of the Federation of Islamic Associations of the United States and Canada, an umbrella organization that became the principal vehicle for connecting local Muslim groups across the nation throughout the 1950s and 1960s. Its primary constituency remained Muslim diaspora communities.[2]

In later years, as the number of foreign students coming to North America from predominantly Muslim countries increased, a demand arose among Muslim students from abroad for a vehicle to provide unity and to aid in cultural expression during their stay in America and Canada. In 1963, student leaders formed the Muslim Students Association of the United States and Canada, with 10 local affiliates at various universities. During the following decades, the organization established local chapters in most major universities in the United States. Especially during the early years of this expansion, the Muslim Students Association catered primarily to foreign students who planned to reside in the United States temporarily as they completed their studies, with the intent of returning to their home countries.[3] This focus contrasted with the Federation of Islamic Associations' mission of providing a source of unity for Muslims who planned to stay in the United States, including many who were native-born Americans.

The Muslim Student Association's focus on young foreign nationals who planned relatively brief stays in the United States began to change as growing numbers of foreign students made America their home after their studies. Combined with the increased flow of immigrants to the United States from Muslim countries following the immigration reforms of 1965, this trend gave rise to demands for organizations that could effectively represent the interests of permanent Muslim residents and citizens in the United States. These demands resulted in the creation of new organizations focused on a permanent Muslim presence in the country. The Islamic Circle of North America (ICNA), formed in 1968, directed its main efforts at encouraging Muslims to follow Islamic traditions and, especially in later years, community building at the local level.[4] Almost 15 years later, the Islamic Society of North America (ISNA) emerged as an offshoot of the Muslim Students Association, with the mission of developing educational and social programs for Muslims living permanently in the United States and Canada.[5]

Other organizations emerged soon afterward to enhance Muslim participation in American public life and to advance the interests of a growing Muslim population. In 1982, United Muslims of America arose as a national organization dedicated to educating Muslim Americans about civic engagement and encouraging their active participation in mainstream social, economic, and political activities.[6] Four years later, activists in Southern California formed the Muslim Political Action Committee, changing the organization's name two years later to the Muslim Public Affairs Council (MPAC). Over the years, this organization became one on the most widely recognized national Muslim advocacy groups in the country. In 1992, the Muslim Women's League emerged as a spin-off of MPAC.[7]

Throughout the 1990s, the increase in Muslim immigration and the resulting diversification of America's Muslim population accelerated both the growth of Muslim civic organizations and an expansion in the range of their missions and activities. New Muslim organizations arising during the decade included spiritual institutions like the Islamic Supreme Council of America, community development organizations such as the Muslim American Society, and groups dedicated to interfaith cooperation and cultural exchange such as the American Society for Muslim Advancement. Other new groups focused more strongly on mobilizing Muslim Americans for political engagement and social activism, such as the American Muslim Political Coordinating Council, the American Muslim Alliance, and American Muslims Intent on Learning and Activism. They were joined by new associations dedicated to the professional advancement of their members, including the Council for the Advancement of Muslim Professionals, the National Association of Muslim

Lawyers, the Association of Muslim Scientists and Engineers, the Islamic Medical Association of North America, and numerous others.

In 1994, a group of Muslim activists established the Council on American-Islamic Relations (CAIR) in Washington, D.C., as a civil rights and Muslim advocacy organization. The following year, CAIR gained national exposure as an organization representing Muslim Americans after the Oklahoma City bombing. Leaders of the organization held a press conference at the site of the bombing and delivered a donation for the bombing victims, collected from Muslims living in Oklahoma, to the state's governor. Later that year, CAIR released *A Rush to Judgment*, a report chronicling civil rights abuses perpetrated on Muslims around the country after the bombing. In subsequent years, CAIR established dozens of local chapters across the United States to advocate on behalf of Muslim Americans.[8]

Alongside these national organizations, citywide and local community groups catering to Muslims arose across the United States. Following the path taken by immigrant communities throughout American history, hundreds of Muslim institutions and informal groups emerged to address the local needs of a steadily growing Muslim population, including a rising number of converts to Islam. This civil society infrastructure grew in capacity as mosques, Islamic community centers, local clubs, self-help groups, Islamic charities, and local chapters of national Muslim organizations proliferated. In April 2001, the efforts of the Muslim community in Jackson, Mississippi, led to the opening of the International Museum of Muslim Cultures, the first American museum dedicated to Muslim history and culture.[9]

Toward the close of the 20th century, native-born African American Muslims began gradually establishing ties to this civil society infrastructure, which remained largely aimed at the needs of more recent arrivals from the Middle East and South Asia. Upon the death of Elijah Mohammad, leader of the Nation of Islam since the 1930s, his son, Warith Deen Mohammad, took charge of the organization. Abandoning his father's race-based and separatist agenda, Deen Mohammad changed the name of the organization and gradually moved his followers' religious practices toward traditional Sunni Islam. Louis Farrakhan subsequently reclaimed the name Nation of Islam for a revived African American–centric organization, but this new Nation of Islam never attracted the numbers who remained loyal to Deen Mohammad. Along with some other notable African American Muslim leaders, such as Zaid Shakir and Siraj Wahhaj, Deen Mohammad began participating in the activities of mainstream Muslim organizations. The African American Muslim identity remained distinct from the rest of America's Muslim population. However, to some degree, a convergence of interests was slowly beginning to take shape.[10]

Throughout this period of Muslim civic mobilization, several ethnic-based civil society organizations with large Muslim constituencies, especially Arab Americans, emerged across the country. In 1972, activists in Dearborn, Michigan, established the Arab Community Center for Economic and Social Services (ACCESS) to serve as a community building and social service organization.[11] Eight years later, former U.S. Senator James Abourezk founded the American-Arab Anti-Discrimination Committee (ADC) to defend the rights of American citizens of Arab descent.[12] In 1985, the Arab American Institute opened its doors in Washington, D.C., to serve as a policy institute and to encourage Arab American participation in American politics.[13] At the close of the century, activists founded the civic organization South Asian American Leaders of Tomorrow in Tacoma Park, Maryland, to serve as an advocacy organizations for people of South Asian heritage. The organization later changed its name to South Asian Americans Leading Together (SAALT).[14]

By the beginning of the 21st century, Muslims in America were represented by at least 300 ethnic associations with large Muslim constituencies, 200 Muslim student groups, 200 Islamic schools, and 100 community media outlets catering to Muslims.[15] Across the country, mosques, Islamic centers, and local community groups supported a wide diversity of social, economic, political, and religious goals pursued by an increasingly diverse Muslim American population. In addition, Muslim Americans integrated into U.S. society through all the same informal avenues that Americans of all faiths and ethnicities use to participate in public life. Along with their fellow Americans, Muslims contributed to American society and culture as students, professionals, volunteers in non-Muslim civic groups, members of the Armed Services, police officers, firefighters, teachers, local politicians, civil servants, professional athletes, actors, authors, and individuals adopting countless other social roles.

Muslim Civic Engagement and Civil Rights after 9/11

By the time of the 9/11 attacks, Muslim Americans had built the foundations of a potentially influential civil-society infrastructure to represent and support their interests. After the terrorist attacks, Muslim organizations and associations that comprised this infrastructure turned their attention to the needs of Muslim Americans in the post-9/11 environment.

Muslim advocacy groups and politically oriented organizations offered relevant experience and expertise as Muslim Americans adjusted to the new political and social landscape. Joining them were Muslim community organizations, professional associations, and religious groups that—although they often lacked experience in social activism—quickly adapted to meet the needs of their members and constituents. Social scientists Anny Bakalian and Mehd Bozorgmehr at the Middle East and Middle Eastern American Center conducted interviews with the leaders of 50 civic organizations catering to Muslims and people of Middle Eastern descent. They found that most of the organizations in their study took steps to meet the post-9/11 needs of Muslim Americans, regardless of the organizations' mandates and formal mission statements.[16]

As Muslim organizations mobilized after 9/11, among the first issues they sought to address was the growing threat to the safety and civil rights of Muslims in America. The Muslim Public Affairs Council and the Council on American-Islamic Relations began separately documenting hate crimes and other acts of aggression directed at Muslims. In subsequent years, CAIR released annual reports on the status of Muslim civil rights in America. The American-Arab Anti-Discrimination Committee and South Asian Americans Leading Together initiated similar efforts to document abuses suffered by people of Middle Eastern and South Asian origin. In addition, ICNA Relief, a charitable organization established by the Islamic Circle of North America, began documenting civil rights cases and providing services to Muslims detained by authorities as part of the nationwide investigation of 9/11.[17]

Other efforts to counter civil rights abuses and hate crimes followed. In 2004, a coalition of Muslim organizations founded the American Muslim Task Force on Civil Rights and Elections, an advocacy organization designed to encourage Muslim political participation and to defend the rights of Muslim citizens. The founding coalition of this task force included the most influential Muslim organizations in America, such as MPAC, CAIR, the Islamic Society of North America, the Islamic Circle of North America, the Muslim American Society, and the Muslim Students Association-National. That same year, the Muslim American Society established the MAS Freedom Foundation to engage in civil rights and public policy advocacy. The new foundation created a Human and Civil Rights Division to address human and civil rights violations in the United States and abroad. One year later, the National Association of Muslim Lawyers established a charitable arm, called Muslim Advocates, to provide legal assistance for Muslim Americans and to counter hate crimes and discrimination targeting Muslims.[18]

Throughout the years following 9/11, CAIR engaged in a wide range of activities to advance its core mission of defending the rights of Muslim Americans and presenting Islam as a mainstream American religion. Alongside its annual reports on civil rights and hate crime abuses, the organization produced a series of public service announcements carried on television, radio, and national newspapers. These announcements featured Muslim Americans of various backgrounds, including first responders present at the World Trade Center on 9/11, describing how they have served their nation.[19] To educate Muslim Americans about how best to protect their civil rights, the organization produced a series of guides, including handbooks advising Muslims of their rights as American citizens, advising communities on how to protect themselves against hate crimes and discrimination, and advising Muslim leaders on how best to counter anti-Islam legislation at the state level.[20] Also, CAIR provided legal counsel to Muslims claiming civil rights violations by the U.S. government and filed suits against government agencies on behalf of Muslims subjected to warrantless surveillance and having their names placed on the No Fly List.[21]

The Muslim Public Affairs Council also embraced the task of countering hate crimes, civil rights violations, and other acts of intolerance directed at Muslim Americans. To empower Muslims at the grassroots level, MPAC developed a series of training sessions and workshops called "Truth over Fear: Countering Islamophobia." This training course was designed to give participants the skills to effectively engage local news media outlets about the topic of anti-Muslim hostility, to work with elected officials and government representatives on this issue, and to build interfaith and civic alliances. Also, through its Hollywood Bureau, MPAC began working to reduce reliance on stereotypes and negative depictions of Islam and Muslims prevalent in the entertainment industry. Since its creation, the Hollywood Bureau has shared expertise with a large pool of producers, directors, and screenwriters, while advising studios and production companies regarding film and television productions depicting Islam or Muslims.[22]

Numerous other Muslim organizations mobilized to address civil rights issues and other challenges related to being Muslim in post-9/11 America, from providing legal advice and political advocacy to countering intolerance and discrimination at the community level. In addition, many Muslim organizations joined with non-Muslim civic groups to promote civil rights and combat anti-Muslim bigotry. Organizations experienced in human and civil rights advocacy—such as the American Civil Liberties Union, Human Rights Watch, and the Southern Poverty

Law Center—proved to be valuable allies. Additionally, interfaith groups provided support to Muslim outreach and coalition-building efforts. The World Council of Churches, the World Jewish Congress, the Interfaith Alliance, and numerous other interfaith groups joined with Muslim organizations to promote tolerance and mutual respect. In 2006, a national coalition of religious groups and congregations formed the National Religious Campaign against Torture. Several Muslim organizations joined this effort, including the Islamic Society of North America, the Islamic Circle of North America, the Muslim Public Affairs Council, and others. This coalition eventually gained more than 320 member organizations of various religious affiliations.[23]

Alongside these efforts by established Muslim organizations, new civic groups and associations arose after 9/11 to address the civil rights needs of Muslim Americans. Advocacy groups such as the Human Rights Education Law Project (HELP), created to provide legal assistance to Muslims detained during the investigation of the 9/11 attacks, directed their efforts at especially vulnerable populations. Other new organizations, such as the American Islamic Congress, focused on encouraging Muslim civic engagement. Among the most prominent Muslim organizations founded after 9/11 was the Institute for Social Policy and Understanding (ISPU), a research and policy institute focused primarily on issues related to Muslim Americans in the post-9/11 environment and other issues affecting Muslim communities around the world. While working on these issues, ISPU produced reports on U.S. post-9/11 policies, analyses of anti-Sharia legislation at the state level, and strategies for overcoming opposition to mosques and Islamic centers in local communities.[24] Through these and other new organizations, Muslim Americans expanded the breadth and reach of civil rights advocacy available to them in the years after 9/11.

Muslim Civic Engagement and Homeland Security after 9/11

Parallel to Muslim civic mobilization on behalf of civil rights, several Muslim organizations initiated efforts to contribute to homeland security. Among the most common activities, pursued by most national and major regional Muslim organizations, was to condemn terrorism and those who engage in it. Before the end of the day on 9/11, several Muslim organizations joined together to issue a condemnation of the terrorist attacks. The condemnation stated: "American Muslims utterly condemn what are apparently vicious and cowardly acts of terrorism against innocent civilians. We join all Americans in calling for the swift apprehension and punishment for the perpetrators. No political cause could ever be assisted by such immoral acts." The statement was signed by several national Muslim organizations, including the Muslim Public Affairs Council, the Council on American-Islamic Relations, the Islamic Society of North America, the Islamic Circle of North America, the Muslim American Society, the American Muslim Alliance, and the American Muslim Council. A few days later, this joint statement appeared in a full-page ad in the *Washington Post*.[25]

In subsequent years, Muslim groups jointly and individually issued numerous condemnations of terrorism and acts of violence by Muslim extremist groups.[26] Many Muslim organizations issued statements on several occasions condemning specific acts of terrorism committed by Muslim extremists both abroad and in the United States. The Council on American-Islamic Relations, in addition to issuing such statements frequently, launched an online petition drive condemning terrorism as un-Islamic. According to CAIR, the petition gained several hundred thousand signatures over the next several years. In 2005, the Fiqh Council of North America, a body of Islamic scholars, issued a religious ruling (fatwa) after al-Qaeda-trained terrorists bombed targets in London, killing 52 people. The fatwa stated: "Islam strictly condemns religious extremism and the use of violence against innocent lives. There is no justification in Islam for extremism and terrorism. Targeting civilians' lives and property through suicide bombings or any other method of attack is forbidden—and those who commit these barbarous acts are criminals, not martyrs."[27]

Alongside these efforts to debunk religious justifications for acts of terrorism, several Muslim organizations launched initiatives to combat extremist influences. Among the most active was the Muslim Public Affairs Council, which initiated a series of projects and activities to counter extremism and radicalization. In 2005, MPAC launched its National Grassroots Campaign to Fight Terrorism. Through this campaign, MPAC developed and disseminated recommendations to mosques and Islamic centers on how to recognize criminal activity and prevent radical elements from infiltrating their facilities. Among the recommendations, MPAC emphasized the need to maintain accurate financial records and sources of income, to ban unauthorized private events and speeches, to vet guest speakers and the content of their presentations, and to maintain relationships with regional FBI offices and local law enforcement.[28] As part of this campaign, MPAC invited mosques and Islamic centers around the country to implement these recommendations and to provide feedback on how to improve them.

Shortly after beginning this grassroots antiterrorism campaign, MPAC released a report on the root causes of extremism, with recommendations on how to address them while fostering the healthy participation of young Muslims in society.[29] Later, MPAC hosted a briefing about online radicalization for policy makers, federal officials, Congressional staff members, and representatives from civil society organizations. Following this briefing, MPAC and the Muslim youth group MakeSpace jointly hosted a public forum on violent extremism, which attracted more than 250 participants.[30] Along with these events, MPAC launched another grassroots campaign, the "Safe Spaces" initiative, this time directed at preventing radicalization among youth. Through this initiative, MPAC worked with imams, councilors, and youth workers to develop a strategy for community leaders to recognize the signs of radicalization and to intervene to prevent it. The cornerstone of this strategy was a three-tiered approach to address the underlying problems that make young people vulnerable to extremist ideologies and to intervene if they begin to adopt extremist beliefs. As a last resort, the strategy called for removing radicalized individuals from mosque congregations and contacting law enforcement authorities.[31]

In a similar effort to counter radicalizing influences among youth, Project Nur, a student-led initiative sponsored by the American Islamic Congress, launched a grassroots campaign called "Voices Against Radicalism" in 2014. Through this campaign, students at universities and colleges across the country began organizing events to discuss the causes of radicalization and to identify means to counter extremist ideologies. Students also began developing videos featuring interviews with victims of extremism on campus. As part of a coordinated nationwide effort, the American Islamic Congress and Project Nur headquarters in Washington, D.C., announced plans to disseminate these videos online in order to demonstrate the damaging effects of violent extremism. This nationwide campaign also called for presentations from students telling the personal stories of victims of extremism, outlining campus community efforts focused on prevention and education, and describing interfaith initiatives to condemn extremism.[32]

In the years after 9/11, the World Organization for Resource Development and Education (WORDE), an organization dedicated to countering extremism in the United States and Muslim societies abroad, initiated several homeland-security-related activities. Along with a report on countering radicalization, titled *A Community-Based Approach to Countering Radicalization: A Partnership for America*, WORDE issued a series of reports on peace building and on countering violent extremism in Afghanistan and Pakistan. Also, under the leadership of Muslim scholar Hedieh Mirahmadi, WORDE developed working relationships with law enforcement and intelligence agencies to educate local communities and government officials about key aspects of radicalization and extremism. In cooperation with the National Counterterrorism Center (NCTC), WORDE hosted Community Awareness Briefings for local community members on the threat of radicalization in the United States, abroad, and online. Working with policy makers and law enforcement personnel, WORDE also conducted workshops and briefings to strengthen the cultural and religious proficiency of officials with responsibility for engaging Muslim communities.[33]

Other Muslim organizations arose after 9/11 specifically to address the problems of radicalization and violent extremism. Similar to counter-radicalization activities undertaken by MPAC and WORDE, the Muslim organization Muflehun (Arabic for "those who will succeed") began developing programs to prevent violent extremism from gaining a foothold in communities within the United States and overseas. Basing its programs on Islamic principles, Muflehun designed a strategy of prevention, intervention when prevention fails, and reintegration of individuals back into society after they have abandoned extremist ideas. At the same time, the organization Muslims Against Terrorism undertook interfaith efforts to promote common American values as a means of delegitimizing violent extremism. Meanwhile, the Free Muslims Coalition and the American Islamic Forum for Democracy took secular approaches, staunchly supporting the separation of religion and the state as the best avenue for countering ideologies promoted by Muslim extremists.[34]

Alongside these formal organized efforts to promote homeland security, Muslim Americans contributed to American security through individual initiatives as volunteers and professionals. Imams and Muslim leaders undertook efforts to address the needs of young people vulnerable to extremist ideas and recruitment by terrorist groups.[35] Muslim citizens took the initiative to report extremist or suspicious activities. By the end of 2013, in nearly 30 percent of terrorist plots in the United States involving Muslim extremists, authorities thwarted attacks after receiving tips from Muslim Americans.[36] Moreover, thousands of Muslim Americans joined the armed forces, federal law enforcement agencies, and intelligence services. From 2001 through 2011, more than 6,000 U.S. service members who declared their religion to be Islam served in overseas deployments in the U.S. military, including 14 who were killed in action.[37] Other Muslim Americans joined police forces across the country. From 2002 through 2007, a Muslim American named Sylvester

Johnson served as Philadelphia Police Commissioner. Similarly, for several years after 9/11, the director of the CIA's Counterterrorism Center was a Muslim career CIA officer.[38]

Joining these Muslim Americans serving their country after 9/11 were the first two Muslims to be elected to the U.S. Congress. In 2006, Keith Ellison won a seat in the House of Representatives, representing the Fifth Congressional District of Minnesota. Two years later, another Muslim, Andre Carson, joined him in Congress after winning a seat representing the Seventh Congressional District of Indiana. Both men have since won reelection several times. In 2015, Representative Carson became a member of the House Permanent Select Committee on Intelligence, charged with overseeing the activities of the 17 agencies that comprise the U.S. intelligence community.

Muslim Americans and Community-Focused Security

Despite the expansion of America's homeland security capabilities, both throughout the federal government and across state and municipal governments, the effectiveness of the nation's homeland security enterprise relies largely on the active participation of citizens. The state cannot implement and enforce public safety rules and laws, including those designed to counter the threat of terrorism, without the informed consent and cooperation of the American public. Similarly, federal, state, and local governments cannot formulate effective policies to protect the countless local communities and neighborhoods across the nation without input from residents regarding local needs, vulnerabilities, and criminal activities. Security and law enforcement agencies at all levels of government require information and knowledge from America's 320 million citizens to take effective action to prevent and respond to terrorism. This need is reflected in the Nationwide Suspicious Activities Reporting Initiative, managed by the Department of Justice, and the Department of Homeland Security's "If You See Something, Say Something" campaign.

In turn, active and willing public participation in the homeland security enterprise rests largely on the perceived legitimacy of homeland security strategies and tactics as well as the unbiased and fair implementation of policies by security and law enforcement officials. Perceptions of discriminatory policies and practices risk alienating individuals, communities, and entire social groups whose active engagement benefits all Americans. Such alienation fosters passive noncompliance and nonparticipation, a lack of cooperation with law enforcement out of fear, and even active resistance to policies. In addition to undermining homeland security, this type of mistrust between security and law enforcement professionals and the communities they serve raises obstacles to effective policing and crime prevention, including protecting vulnerable minorities from discrimination and hate crimes. Without cooperative security arrangements, built on collaboration between government officials and the citizenry to define security goals and formulate policies to meet them, avoidable risks to security and public safety inevitably arise.

In the post-9/11 environment, Muslim American participation is an essential component of homeland security. Only a small fraction of America's Muslim population, along with a handful of non-Muslims looking for an ideological justification for violence, are receptive to extremist and violent interpretations of Islam. However, as demonstrated by Nidal Hasan's attack on fellow soldiers at Fort Hood in 2009 and the Tsarnaev brothers' attack at the Boston Marathon in 2013, lone actors and small groups can inflict substantial destruction and mass casualties. Islamic scholars and religious leaders, through written works and religious rulings, help delegitimize religious justifications for such acts. Similarly, Muslim participation in interfaith initiatives and secular intercommunal activities helps to counter clash-of-civilization narratives and to stigmatize extremist beliefs that justify violence against civilians. Moreover, immigrants from predominantly Muslim countries and many second-generation and third-generation Muslim Americans have language skills and cultural knowledge that are highly valued by law enforcement and homeland security professionals. Along with their input, residents of communities with large Muslim populations often have valuable information and observations about their neighborhoods that could aid homeland security efforts.

At the same time, Muslim mobilization to protect civil rights, both from government encroachment and from bias-motivated elements of society, keeps the concerns of Muslim citizens on the public agenda. Addressing these concerns helps safeguard America's democratic principles, particularly the commitment to freedom of religion, protection of minority rights, and equal protection under the law. Additionally, protecting the rights of Muslims as American citizens, rather than targeting them as a suspect group, is essential to fostering trust and cooperation to achieve the shared objectives of policy makers, homeland security and law enforcement officials, and Muslim individuals and communities across the nation. Such collaboration is undermined by laws and policies that target Muslims and by unfair and coercive practices. Muslim civic engagement to counter such measures, especially when integrated into American civil society and joined by non-Muslim citizens, helps prevent the marginalization of Muslim Americans and their exclusion from participating in the homeland security enterprise.

Community-Focused Security

The success of cooperative security arrangements, and whether such arrangements are even attempted, depends first and foremost on the models of security adopted at the national level and in the nation's urban centers and local communities. In this respect, a fundamental choice for policy makers, homeland security officials, and law enforcement at all levels of government is whether to rely on a community-targeted approach or a community-focused approach to security. As defined by criminologist Basia Spalek, a community-targeted approach prioritizes national security over the interests and security needs of communities, which are targeted as potential safe spaces in which terrorists may attempt to blend into society. By contrast, a community-focused approach relies on collaboration and community participation to identify threats to the community and formulate policies to address these threats. This approach capitalizes on the benefits of working with communities rather than treating them as theaters of operation.[39]

Both community-targeted and community-focused approaches are most often directed at geographically defined communities, especially when local law enforcement is the primary provider of security. However, particularly when federal authorities take the lead, these approaches may also be directed toward communities of interest—defined by common ethnic, religious, or other shared identities—that span across local communities in the United States and across international borders. In either case, community targeting often involves passing broad legislation and developing strategies without input from the targeted community. It also frequently relies heavily on surveillance, informants, stop-and-search practices, and other intrusive measures without the community's knowledge or consent. Community-focused security may also involve the use of intrusive techniques but includes consultation with community members about the circumstances under which they are used. Community targeting without such consultation offers advantages, including relative freedom of action and a high degree of secrecy regarding methods employed by security agencies, but such benefits come at the risk of limiting meaningful community participation in providing security.[40]

The damaging impact of community targeting, or the perception among community members that they are being targeted, is apparent in the findings of a 2006 study conducted by the Vera Institute of Justice.

To assess relationships between Arab Americans and law enforcement officials, researchers at the Vera Institute conducted surveys in 16 local communities in the United States with large Arab American populations. When asked to identify the main concerns of their communities, 62 percent of community members pointed to federal government policies such as immigration enforcement, detention and deportation, and racial profiling. Only 22 percent identified hate crimes, harassment, and discrimination as their primary concerns. Throughout the surveys, Arab American community members, local law enforcement officers, and FBI officials consistently identified the community's distrust of law enforcement as the single most important barrier to greater cooperation.[41]

Another study, this time focused specifically on Muslim Americans, produced similar findings. For this study, criminologist Tony Gaskew, director of the Criminal Justice program at the University of Pittsburgh and a former police detective, conducted 443 interviews with native-born Muslim Americans and Muslim immigrants living in central Florida. His interviews, conducted over a 12-month period in 2005 and 2006, revealed a pervasive belief among participants that Muslims were the targets of policies and practices designed to combat terrorism, including racial profiling and harassment by police. Along with fear and mistrust of police and the legal system in general, Gaskew found a widespread fear that contact with police could lead to deportation or indefinite confinement. He also uncovered a strong sense among participants that Islam was under attack by the U.S. criminal justice system. Several participants indicated that they would avoid contact with police under any circumstance.[42]

Community-targeted approaches that foster such sentiments contradict the basic tenets of community policing, a philosophy of law enforcement that has gained wide acceptance among policy makers and law enforcement professionals since its emergence in the 1970s. The Department of Justice established an Office of Community-Oriented Policing Services (COPS) in the 1990s to help local police forces adopt community-focused approaches. According to the COPS definition, community policing is the "systematic use of partnerships and problem-solving techniques to proactively address the immediate conditions that give rise to public safety issues."[43] Many police departments have struggled with the design and implementation of effective strategies based on this approach, resulting in a diversity of outcomes. However, aspects of community policing are present in security and law enforcement agencies throughout America, sometimes in federal agencies but particularly in local police departments. Such aspects include collaboration through neighborhood watch groups, regular forums and community meetings to facilitate the exchange of ideas between citizens and law enforcement officials, and decision-making bodies that allow community members to participate in identifying threats to the community, determining best strategies for countering these threats, and evaluating the results.[44]

Fundamental to community policing is the belief that members of the community are often better able than police to identify security threats and recognize suspicious activities that may be precursors to criminal activity, including acts of terrorism.[45] The advantage that community residents have in this respect makes them potentially valuable assets in the development of criminal intelligence, which consists of information related to crime that has been collected, analyzed, and refined for use by policy makers and law enforcement professionals. Good intelligence is critical for sound strategic planning and policy formulation as well as criminal investigations and efforts to deter and prevent criminal activity.[46] The collection of raw, unanalyzed information that becomes the basis of good criminal intelligence relies heavily on the participation of community members who report suspicious activity, provide tips and leads to police, and recognize unusual occurrences in their neighborhoods that police often miss.

Members of a particular social group—whether the group is defined by ethnicity, religion, political views, or some other social identity—often interact frequently with one another, giving them more opportunities to notice unusual and potentially dangerous behavior on the part of other members of the group. Similarly, cultural and linguistic knowledge unique to a social group may enable members of the group to detect suspicious activities by other group members that outsiders would miss. As a result of such advantages, Muslim members of a particular community are often best able to detect signs that extremist views are gaining acceptance among a Muslim youth or that an outsider who promotes such views has infiltrated the community. After years of practicing law enforcement as a police officer and studying the interaction between Muslims and police as a criminologist, Tony Gaskew reached the following conclusion:

A trustworthy and positive relationship with the local community is one of the most valuable resources available to law enforcement officials today who are involved in counterterrorism operations . . . The community is truly the eyes and ears of police agencies around the country and the means by which the overwhelming majority of crimes are either prevented or solved.[47]

Community confidence in law enforcement and security officials is essential to facilitate the consistent flow of information from community residents. Policing that does not address problems identified by the community or that is perceived as biased against certain groups within the community is detrimental to collaboration. This fact is underscored by the results of a study of Muslim attitudes in New York City. In 2009, a team of researchers from New York University and the University of Chicago evaluated attitudes among New York City's Muslim residents toward cooperating with police to combat terrorism. They found a strong correlation between a willingness to cooperate with police and a perception that the police exercised procedural justice in performing their duties. Procedural justice in the study was defined as the degree to which authorities sought and considered the views of people in the community when making policies about how to combat terrorism as well as the overall fairness with which policies were implemented. By contrast, the study found little correlation between a willingness to cooperate and either the cultural backgrounds, political beliefs, or degree of religious observance among Muslim residents.[48]

A similar study, this one examining law enforcement relations with Muslim residents in Britain, further highlighted the importance of community confidence in law enforcement to maintain collaborative police-community relations. For this study of the British experience, an interdisciplinary team at the University of Birmingham examined the correlation between the willingness of Muslims to work with police and their impressions about the fairness of counterterrorism policies and practices. The team found that police reliance on intrusive and coercive tactics—such as stop-and-search practices, high-profile police raids that do not result in terrorism-related convictions, and aggressive attempts to recruit informants—fostered a sense among Muslims that they were a suspect group and reduced their motivation to work with police. The research team further found that police-community partnerships that allowed community members to become involved in decision making were highly effective in promoting constructive engagement to aid counterterrorism policing.[49]

Along with these benefits, community policing and the community-focused approach that underlies it also lead to more effective prevention, investigation, and prosecution of hate crimes and other acts of intolerance.[50] With improved knowledge of local neighborhoods, including their vulnerabilities and potential problem areas, police are better able to deter bias-motivated attacks on vulnerable minorities. The findings of a Human Rights Watch study of policing practices in six large cities in the United States underline these advantages. This study revealed that previously established working relationships between police and Arab and Muslim community members were central to mitigating backlash violence after 9/11. Human Rights Watch researchers found that cooperative police-community relations were especially effective in Dearborn, Michigan.

A city with 30,000 Arab American residents, Dearborn experienced just two violent hate crimes related to 9/11 during the national surge in anti-Muslim violence that followed the terrorist attacks. This outcome rested primarily on positive working relationships that allowed police to develop detailed knowledge of the city's neighborhoods before 9/11 and, as a result, to quickly identify and deploy officers to areas vulnerable to backlash violence after the terrorist attacks.[51] By contrast, in many law enforcement jurisdictions elsewhere in the country, especially in jurisdictions without significant relationships between police and vulnerable communities, police found themselves in a reactive posture, responding to hate crime incidents after the fact rather than preventing them.[52]

The Winding Path to Community-Focused Security

During the first several months after 9/11, government authorities across the country adopted aspects of a community-focused approach to security that recognized the interests of Muslim Americans. At the federal level, President Bush publically denounced acts of intolerance against Muslims, and the U.S. Congress passed a resolution condemning acts of discrimination and violence targeting Muslim Americans and Americans of Arab and South Asian origin. Several federal agencies took steps to back up these sentiments. The secretary of education sent letters to school administrators and university presidents across the nation, calling on educators to take preventive steps to protect Muslim and Arab students, while the U.S. Commission on Civil Rights established a hotline to receive claims of discrimination and harassment against Muslim, Arab, and South Asian Americans.[53] The Equal Employment Opportunity Commission (EEOC) took similar action, creating a new designation to track employment discrimination related to 9/11. Over the next decade, the EEOC filed nearly 90 lawsuits against employers for discriminating against Muslims, Sikhs, and people of Middle Eastern and South Asian heritage.[54]

Federal law enforcement agencies also took community-focused steps to combat post-9/11 backlash crimes and to prevent the social marginalization of Muslim Americans. In late 2001, the Community Relations Service at the Department of Justice issued guidance for local law enforcement agencies to prevent violence targeting Muslims. This guidance placed a strong emphasis on community outreach, including establishing partnerships with community-based organizations and creating community task forces.[55] Early the following year, the FBI launched an outreach program that included regular meetings with Muslim civic organizations and community leaders. As part of this initiative, FBI Director Robert Mueller and other FBI officials met regularly with the leadership of the Muslim Public Affairs Council, the Council on American-Islamic Relations, and other Muslim organizations.[56] Later, the Civil Rights Division at the Department of Justice established the formal Initiative to Combat Post-9/11 Discriminatory Backlash, which placed a priority on cases involving discrimination against Arab, Sikh, Muslim, and South Asian Americans in employment, housing, education, and access to public accommodations.[57]

Outside of Washington, several law enforcement agencies initiated outreach and partnership-building efforts. Officials in many jurisdictions appointed community liaison officers, organized forums and town-hall meetings, formed working groups and community advisory boards, and assigned officers to visit mosques, Islamic community centers, and local Muslim-owned businesses.[58] During the years after 9/11, the Los Angeles County Sheriff's Department proved to be especially successful at institutionalizing elements of community-focused security. At the invitation of Sheriff Leroy Baca, several Muslim community members and leaders of Muslim organizations participated in discussions about how best to prevent a terrorist attack in Los Angeles County. These discussions led to the creation of the Muslim American Homeland Security Congress, which brought together elected officials, law enforcement officers, and representatives of Muslim organizations and interfaith groups to develop strategies for preventing terrorism, hate crimes, and acts of discrimination. Sheriff Baca also established a Muslim Community Affairs Unit to foster wider collaboration with Muslim community members. This unit grew over time, eventually comprising a team of Muslim American deputies who spoke various relevant languages, including Arabic, Farsi, Urdu, and Pashtu.[59]

Despite some significant successes, these government efforts to protect the rights of Muslim Americans and foster constructive engagement were often overshadowed by policies and practices based on a community-targeting approach. The federal government's use of immigration laws to confine Muslim foreign nationals as special-interest detainees, alongside the designation of thousands of foreign visitors from predominantly Muslim countries as potential security threats under the NSEERS program, signaled an emerging pattern of viewing Muslims as suspect. This pattern became more entrenched with the rapid expansion of the No Fly List to mark thousands of Muslims—U.S. citizens and foreign nationals alike—as potential terrorists. The use of aggressive tactics by federal authorities to recruit Muslim informants, including use of the No Fly List to intimidate potential recruits, further distanced federal homeland security measures from the partnership-building approach essential to community-focused security.

Highly publicized actions within the U.S. Congress also contributed to a sense that Muslim Americans were being targeted as suspects rather than approached as potential partners. Among the most contentious was a series of congressional hearings convened by Representative Peter King, chairman of the House Committee on Homeland Security. Acting on his belief that Muslim Americans were not doing enough to help in the fight against terrorism, Representative King held five hearings in 2011 and 2012 to examine the threat of radicalization among Muslim Americans. The first hearing, titled "The Extent of Radicalization in the American Muslim Community and that Community's Response," set the dominant theme throughout the hearings—that Muslim Americans were not cooperating sufficiently with law enforcement. In setting this tone, Representative King downplayed the numerous instances of Muslim cooperation with police since 9/11, while also missing an opportunity to explore new avenues of collaboration, rather than casting blame for perceived noncooperation.[60]

In April 2011, one month after Representative King convened his first hearing on radicalization among Muslim Americans, Representative Sue Myrick held a congressional hearing with a similar theme. Representative Myrick, who chaired a subcommittee within the House Permanent Select Committee on Intelligence responsible for terrorism and counterintelligence, convened the hearing to explore the activities of the Egypt-based Muslim Brotherhood, along with the group's supposed ties to Muslim organizations in America.[61] The following year, Michele Bachmann of Minnesota and four other members of Congress sent letters to several government agencies expressing concern that the Muslim Brotherhood could be infiltrating the federal government.

Many governments at the state and local levels also pursued policies that, in contrast to the Los Angeles County Sheriff's Department's approach, treated Muslim Americans as potential threats to society. The New York Police Department initiated several intrusive and coercive practices characteristic of community targeting, including clandestine surveillance, infiltrating mosque congregations, spying on Muslim student groups, and using intimidation to recruit Muslim informants. Elsewhere in the country, state legislators attempted to malign Islam and Muslim religious practices through various bans on Sharia. By the end of 2014, supporters of such measures had introduced anti-Sharia bills in two-thirds of the nation's state legislatures and had success passing such laws in 11 states. Meanwhile, several municipalities and local governments in various regions of the country attempted to ban Muslim houses of worship. Occasionally, such efforts were accompanied by open expressions of bigotry and fear of Muslims.

During the years after 9/11, as policy makers and government agencies employed a wide range of (often contradictory) homeland security policies and practices, several Muslim organizations and groups with large Muslim constituencies took leading roles in developing community-focused approaches to security. In the immediate aftermath of 9/11, the American-Arab Anti-Discrimination Committee joined with federal law enforcement officials to establish a vehicle for dialogue and joint problem solving. Imad Hamad, the regional director of the American-Arab Anti-Discrimination Committee in Michigan, and John Bell, the special agent in charge of the FBI office in Detroit, initiated the process by bringing together government and community leaders in the Detroit metropolitan area to address anti-Arab and anti-Muslim discrimination and violence.[62] After several months of frequent meetings, the participants established a permanent structure, called Building Respect in Diverse Groups to Enhance Sensitivity (BRIDGES), to institutionalize and expand collaboration.[63]

Under the leadership of Imad Hamad and Jeffrey Collins, Unites States attorney for the Eastern District of Michigan, BRIDGES grew to include representatives of several federal agencies. Along with the FBI and the Department of Justice, officials with the Department of Homeland Security, Immigration and Customs Enforcement, Customs and Border Protection, and other federal agencies began to regularly participate. From local communities in the Detroit area, Arab, Muslim, and Sikh residents attended to communicate their concerns. Still active more than a decade after its creation, BRIDGES continues to serve as a problem-solving forum to address issues related to border crossings, No Fly Lists, Islamic charities, hate crimes, and law enforcement policies and procedures.[64]

With a greater focus on building local-level partnerships, the Minnesota-area chapter of the Muslim American Society (MAS-MN) initiated efforts to strengthen relations with the St. Paul Police Department. To reduce crime that was targeting Muslims residents in the community, particularly among the large Somali immigrant population, MAS-MN agreed to introduce police officers to the local community through a series of structured events. The effort grew into a larger project, funded by a federal grant, to expand cooperative relations between the St. Paul police and Somali and Muslim community members. Through workshops and community events, police officers educated residents about detecting drug use in families and countering gang activity in their neighborhoods. In turn, MAS-MN offered training to strengthen cultural awareness among law enforcement officials.[65]

Later, the St. Paul Police Department took the lead and developed a much broader project called the African Immigrant Muslim Coordinated Outreach Program (AIMCOP). This initiative generated controversy concerning initial plans to use some of the outreach activities to gather information on residents, highlighting the need to maintain a clear separation between outreach and surveillance. This misstep appeared be the result of carelessness in the program design rather than an attempt at deception, and the St. Paul Police Department claimed the information-gathering component was never implemented. In any case, AIMCOP grew to include nearly 50 police officers engaged in community relations throughout the Minnesota-St. Paul region. With funding from this program, MAS-MN continued to organize meetings at various locations to introduce families and youth to members of their local police force, while law enforcement officials engaged residents on topics important to the community, such as warning signs of youth substance abuse and gang involvement.[66]

In another initiative aimed at partnering with local law enforcement, the World Organization for Resource Development and Education joined with the Montgomery County Police Department in Maryland to develop a community-focused strategy for countering violent extremism. The resulting strategy, the Montgomery County Model, cultivates local expertise and capability to recognize the precursors to radicalization. Through this model, parents, teachers, principals, religious leaders of all faiths, and other members of the community are trained to recognize signs of radicalization and contributing factors, such as social alienation, domestic violence, trauma of war, and various psychiatric conditions. Law enforcement officials also receive training to recognize when individuals are susceptible to extremist ideas, with an emphasis on increasing the cultural competency of police officers. To foster timely intervention, the Montgomery County Model develops the expertise needed by social workers, psychologists, councilors, clergy, and others within the community to come to the aid of individuals vulnerable to extremist views before they turn to violence.[67]

To develop a set of guidelines for these types of collaborative efforts, the Muslim Public Affairs Council released a report titled *Building Bridges to Strengthen America: Forging an Effective Counterterrorism Enterprise between Muslim Americans and Law Enforcement.* This report, which provided a blueprint based on community policing, focused primarily on local law enforcement, with advice for strengthening coordination with the FBI and other federal agencies. It called for a division of labor, with law enforcement focused on criminal behavior associated with terrorism, while Muslim community members focused on the ideological and social aspects of radicalization. The report emphasized the advantages of community-focused law enforcement methods to gather information, rather than relying heavily on informants, wiretaps, and other intrusive measures that risk alienating community members and undermining cooperation. The report underlined the importance of Muslim community members, in turn, helping police officials acquire better understanding of the community ("community knowledge"), which aids authorities in identifying and addressing community vulnerabilities and potential problems.[68]

In June 2011, the Obama administration embraced elements of a community-focused approach to homeland security with its public release of a strategy for defeating al-Qaeda and affiliated groups as well as individuals inspired by al-Qaeda's ideology. Titled *National Strategy for Counterterrorism*, this document presented a multidimensional approach involving the use of military force, intelligence, law enforcement, diplomacy, and the private sector to counter terrorism at home and abroad. The strategy document briefly mentioned the need to strengthen the ability of communities across the United States to combat radicalization, terrorist recruitment, and mobilization to violence. Two months later, the White House released a second document, *Empowering Local Partners to Prevent Violent Extremism in the United States*, describing the administration's strategy for aiding local communities to realize this goal. This strategy, along with a detailed Strategic Implementation Plan released later the same year, outlined steps to support local communities that may be targeted by violent extremists and to foster partnerships between local law enforcement agencies and the communities they serve.

Three years later, Attorney General Eric Holder announced a new initiative to develop community-led efforts to counter the influence of extremist ideas and curb radicalization among individuals susceptible of such beliefs. The cornerstone of this initiative was a set of pilot projects in three cities—Los Angeles, Minneapolis, and Boston—to test collaborative efforts to build community capacity and strengthen collaboration between the federal government, local officials, local law enforcement, and community organizations and residents.[69] In February 2015, five months after the initiation of these pilot projects, the White House hosted a three-day international summit on countering violent extremism. The summit brought together local stakeholders, government officials, and leaders from more than 60 countries to identify best practices for developing community-oriented approaches to counter extremism and radicalization. Along with city officials working on the three pilot projects, representatives of similar initiatives in the United States and abroad outlined their efforts to build local capacities to counter extremism.[70]

An underlying premise of the summit and the local-level efforts it highlighted was the necessity of a community-focused approach. As spelled out in the White House strategy for countering violent extremism:

> The best defenses against violent extremist ideologies are well-informed and equipped families, local communities, and local institutions . . . Communities are best placed to recognize and confront the threat because violent extremists are targeting their children, families, and neighbors. Rather than blame particular communities, it is essential that we find ways to help them protect themselves. To do so, we must continue to ensure that all Americans understand that they are an essential part of our civic life and partners in our efforts to combat violent extremist ideologies and organizations that seek to weaken our society.[71]

The Obama administration's push for building local communities' capacities to counter extremist influences underscores a trend toward integrating community-focused approaches into the homeland security enterprise, with an emphasis on engaging Muslim citizens, local groups, and national organizations. Efforts within various federal, state, and municipal agencies to develop such approaches date back to the early months following 9/11, but they were largely overshadowed by more coercive and intrusive policies, from broad surveillance to indefinite detention. Also, many elements of community targeting directed primarily at Muslim Americans remain in use nearly 15 years after 9/11, such as the liberal use of material witness warrants and aggressive recruitment of informants. Moreover, as critics of President Obama's approach toward countering extremism have pointed out, focusing on Muslim radicalization as a security threat risks further stigmatizing Muslim Americans.

Nevertheless, a shift toward community-focused security, which recognizes the unique capabilities of the nation's Muslim citizens while addressing their concerns in post-9/11 America, offers the advantages of enhancing national security in a manner that increases the resilience and health of local communities. Central to the success of such a shift is the ability of agencies and officials at all levels of government to build effective partnerships with Muslim civic organizations and local groups that, like the rest of American civil society, serve to strengthen local communities and American society as a whole. In addition, encouraging Muslims as individuals to participate in American civic life, rather than attempting to marginalize them through discriminatory laws or alienate them with intimidating policing practices, removes obstacles to more effective engagement with the nation's Muslim population. Federal, state, and (some) municipal governments have substantial resources and powers— including the use of force—at their disposal to combat terrorism. However, without the trust and cooperation of America's Muslim citizens, they risk forfeiting one of the nation's most important assets for enhancing homeland security.

Epilogue: Aligning Security and Civil Rights

A mong the most contentious and difficult issues for any liberal democracy facing domestic security challenges is balancing the need for public safety with the civil rights and liberties of its citizens. Addressing both is a critical function of the state, a dual responsibility that can lead to policy changes and broader political reforms as the push and pull between these two interests demand attention. As demonstrated by episodes in U.S. history, security concerns frequently take precedence in times of acute crisis or when the civil rights of social groups with relatively little social or political influence are at risk. The 1919 Palmer Raids to round up political dissidents and the internment of Japanese Americans during World War II underscore this trend. Also, when security or law enforcement agencies amass disproportionate power in the political system, overzealous and misguided execution of their security function without sufficient oversight may result, as highlighted by the FBI's domestic counterintelligence operations during the civil rights era.

Since 9/11, aspects of all of these tendencies have been on display. Within days of the terrorist attacks, Congress passed the Authorization for Use of Military Force, granting the president extraordinary authority to use military force against nonstate actors and, as later interpreted, to detain enemy combatants indefinitely without trial. Six weeks later, Congress passed the Patriot Act, expanding the federal government's powers to conduct surveillance of citizens and clandestine searches of their homes and places of work. The FBI sharply increased its use of National Security Letters without search warrants, while the

Department of the Treasury seized the assets of charities with (sometimes tenuous or unclear) connections to terrorist organizations abroad. Meanwhile, the National Security Agency launched a series of surveillance programs that captured data from the wireless communications of millions of Americans. Along with these policy changes, the federal government initiated the creation and expansion of a homeland security enterprise centered in Washington but spread out across the country and beyond U.S. borders.

These counterterrorism policies and practices have focused heavily on Muslims in America. Through the use of immigration laws and material witness warrants, federal authorities have practiced preventive detention, confining Muslim foreign nationals and U.S. citizens while the FBI investigated them for terrorist connections, even though authorities lacked probable cause to charge them with crimes. Through informants, undercover officers, and electronic surveillance, federal and municipal law enforcement authorities have spied on mosque congregations and Muslim groups without having evidence of criminal activity. The federal government has also placed Muslim Americans on the No Fly List while they were traveling abroad and participated in the arrest and interrogation of Muslim Americans by foreign governments. In addition, Muslim Americans have endured discriminatory government actions that have no connection to homeland security, including attempts to ban mosques from local communities and efforts to denigrate Islam through bans on Sharia.

At the same time, Muslims have been essential participants in America's homeland security enterprise. Through individual initiative, as members of Muslim civic organizations, and as civil servants, they have provided highly valued cultural knowledge and language capabilities to homeland security officials, while aiding local police in understanding and engaging Muslim communities. They have served their country as members of the armed forces, intelligence services, and police forces around the nation. Moreover, law enforcement authorities have made dozens of terrorism-related arrests after being informed of suspicious activities by Muslim citizens. These actions underscore the desire of most Muslim Americans, like most Americans in general, to aid homeland security efforts when possible and to help secure their communities.

Of course, Muslim Americans are U.S. citizens entitled to the same civil rights and liberties claimed by all American citizens. Although contested in the years after 9/11, these rights include protection from government actions that circumvent due process, including arrest and detention without probable cause, indefinite detention without charge or trial, and proxy detention by foreign governments acting in coopera-tion with U.S. officials. These rights also include freedom from intrusive police surveillance based on religious and ethnic profiling rather than evidence of criminal activity. In addition, Muslim Americans also have the right to protection from discrimination in public schools, the work-place, and public spaces as well as from hate crimes and other illegal acts of intolerance.

These three roles assigned to Muslims in post-9/11 America—the subject of counterterrorism polices, valued contributors to homeland security, and U.S. citizens entitled to constitutionally protected rights—underlie the need to align homeland security and civil rights, rather than viewing them as competing objectives. Such an alignment requires security and law enforcement authorities to recognize the essential role Muslim Americans play in homeland security and to encourage their participation, often forgoing potential short-term gains in security for the sake of protecting the rights of Muslim citizens. Central to this task is curtailing abusive government practices that target Muslims, discour-age cooperation, and risk delegitimizing homeland security policies in the eyes of Muslim Americans and much of the public. Also essential to this goal is combating anti-Muslim discrimination, hate crimes, and other acts of intolerance aimed at alienating Muslim Americans from society.

Aligning homeland security and civil rights does not entail completely eliminating the conflict between the demands of counterterrorism and protecting the rights of American citizens. Difficult policy decisions will be necessary, at times, for the foreseeable future. Nevertheless, such alignment is based on the recognition that, over the long term, homeland security and civil rights are mutually reinforcing complements. Ensur-ing the rights of Muslim citizens, in addition to safeguarding America's democratic principles, is essential to encouraging Muslim American participation in the nation's homeland security enterprise. Muslim par-ticipation in this enterprise—as security professionals, law enforcement officers, elected officials, policy makers in government, and concerned citizens aiding police and other security providers—contributes enor-mously to American security. In turn, by helping to counter terrorist activity in the United States, Muslim participation in homeland security efforts reduces prospects for the type of crises that, throughout Ameri-can history, have led to the erosion of civil rights and an increase in intolerance toward vulnerable minorities. Capitalizing on this mutually beneficial relationship is one of the cornerstones of an effective home-land security strategy.

Timeline of Major Policies and Government Actions Affecting Muslims in America

1931

The FBI begins investigating the Moorish Science Temple and its founder, Noble Drew Ali, in the first FBI domestic operation targeting Muslims in America.

1942

The FBI initiates RACON, an investigation of African American organizations suspected of having pro-Japanese sympathies. Targets of the investigation include the Moorish Science Temple, the Nation of Islam, and other African American Muslim groups.

1967

The FBI launches a counterintelligence program against "black nationalist hate groups" (COINTELPRO-BNHG) to disrupt and neutralize dissident African American organizations and their allies. Along with civil rights organizations and left-wing activist groups, the FBI targets the Nation of Islam and Elijah Muhammad.

1972

Following the massacre of Israeli athletes at the Olympics in Munich by Palestinian terrorists, the Nixon administration initiates Operation

Boulder to disrupt pro-Palestinian groups and other politically active Arab groups in the United States.

1979

Following the seizure of the U.S. embassy and American diplomats in Tehran by Iranian revolutionaries, the Carter administration authorizes the Iranian Control Program. This program requires Iranian nationals studying at universities in the United States (approximately 57,000 students) to register with immigration authorities.

1990

As the U.S. military begins operations to counter Iraq's invasion of Kuwait, President George H.W. Bush authorizes a program requiring all foreign visitors bearing Iraqi or Kuwaiti passports to register with immigration officials and to be fingerprinted and photographed.

1993

The Clinton administration renews special registration requirements for Iraqi nationals visiting the United States and extends these requirements to visitors from Sudan.

1996

The Clinton administration extends special registration requirements to visitors from Iran and Libya.

September 2001

The FBI begins its investigation of the 9/11 terrorist attacks (the PENTT-BOM investigation). Authorities arrest more than 1,200 people in the United States, including 762 Muslim foreign nationals who are designated as being of interest to the PENTTBOM investigation. These special interest detainees, all guilty of immigration violations, are detained until investigators clear them of any connection to terrorism.

September 2001

Congress passes the Authorization for the Use of Military Force, giving the president broad powers to use military force against unspecified nations and nonstate actors he determines planned, committed, authorized, or aided the 9/11 terrorist attacks. This authorization is used as one of the legal rationales for holding enemy combatants indefinitely without trial and conducting drone strikes against suspected terrorists abroad.

October 2001

Congress passes the Patriot Act, giving federal authorities expanded powers to engage in electronic surveillance, conduct clandestine searches of private property, and access the personal records of U.S. citizens without search warrants.

November 2001

Congress passes the Aviation and Transportation Security Act, which establishes the Transportation Security Administration. The law also gives the new agency the authority to maintain lists of individuals suspected of being a threat to civilian aviation and to prevent identified individuals from boarding aircraft.

November 2001

The FBI and cooperating agencies begin interviewing thousands of foreign nationals residing in the United States, all of whom are from predominantly Muslim countries.

December 2001

Federal agents begin raids on Islamic charities suspected of channeling funds to terrorist organizations abroad. Over the next several years, nine Islamic charities are forced to close after federal authorities seize their assets.

January 2002

The Department of Justice launches the Absconder Apprehension Initiative, a nationwide effort to detain, question, and deport more than 300,000 foreign nationals without legal immigration status who, despite being issued orders to leave the country, remain in the United States. The attorney general orders the FBI, the U.S Marshals Service, and immigration authorities to prioritize the apprehension of 6,000 foreign nationals from predominantly Muslim countries.

January 2002

The U.S. military transfers Yaser Hamdi, a dual U.S.-Saudi citizen captured in Afghanistan, to the Guantanamo Bay detention facility. Upon discovering that Hamdi has U.S. citizenship three months later, authorities transfer him to a military prison in South Carolina and, in June 2002, declare him an enemy combatant. Hamdi is the only known U.S. citizen interned at Guantanamo Bay and the only known U.S. citizen captured abroad to be designated an enemy combatant.

May 2002

Authorities arrest Jose Padilla, a U.S. citizen working with al-Qaeda, at Chicago O'Hare International Airport as he arrives from Pakistan. One month later, the Bush administration declares Padilla an enemy combatant and transfers him to military custody. Padilla is the only known U.S. citizen arrested in the United States to be declared an enemy combatant.

September 2002

Authorities arrest Canadian citizen Maher Arar at JFK International Airport, where he was transferring to a flight bound for Canada as part of a return trip from travels abroad. Officials then deport Arar to Syria, where he is imprisoned and tortured for more than a year. Syrian authorities release Arar after determining that he has no ties to terrorists. Arar is the only known person arrested in the United States to be subjected to extraordinary rendition.

September 2002

The Bush administration initiates the National Security Entry-Exit Registration System (NSEERS), which imposes special registration requirements on foreign nationals visiting the United States from 24 predominantly Muslim countries. The program is suspended in December 2003 and officially terminated in 2011.

November 2002

The CIA carries out its first known targeted killing via drone-fired missile. The target, a senior al-Qaeda leader named Abu Ali al-Harithi, is killed while traveling down a desert road in Yemen. Several other passengers in al-Harithi's vehicle are killed in the attack, including Kamal Derwish, a U.S. citizen and member of al-Qaeda. The death of Derwish as a collateral casualty marks the first killing of a U.S. citizen via drone strike.

February 2003

A federal judge grants New York City officials the authority to modify an 18-year-old consent decree restricting the New York Police Department's ability to investigate political activity (the Handschu Guidelines). The judge's ruling allows the NYPD to expand its surveillance and intelligence operations, including actions directed at Muslims across the New York City metropolitan area.

March 2003

As the U.S. military prepares to invade Iraq, the FBI begins Operation Darkening Clouds, an effort to interview approximately 11,000 people of Iraqi origin residing in the United States.

June 2003

The Bush administration declares Ali Saleh Kahlah al-Marri, a dual Qatari-Saudi national, to be an enemy combatant and transfers him to military custody. Arrested in December 2001 on a material witness warrant, al-Marri is the only foreign national arrested on U.S. soil to be designated an enemy combatant.

May 2004

The FBI begins interviewing Muslim and Arab Americans in the Washington, D.C., area and elsewhere in the country to gather information about potential terrorist attacks during the Republican and Democratic National Conventions and the presidential election.

May 2004

Federal authorities launch Operation Front Line, which prioritizes the arrest of more than 2,500 people guilty of immigration violations, the large majority of whom are from predominantly Muslim countries. The operation is designed to disrupt any potential terrorist plots timed to coincide with the 2004 presidential election and 2005 presidential inauguration.

June 2004

The Supreme Court rules that the 2001 Authorization for the Use of Military Force grants the president authority to detain U.S. citizens captured in Afghanistan for the duration of the conflict. However, the Court also rules that U.S. citizens, even when detained as enemy combatants, have the right to contest their detention in court.

July 2005

The Los Angeles County Sheriff's Department establishes the Muslim-American Homeland Security Congress to foster collaboration between the sheriff's department and Muslims in Los Angeles County.

January 2007

Kenyan authorities detain U.S. citizen Amir Mohamed Meshal as he attempts to cross the Somalia-Kenya border. While incarcerated in a Nairobi prison, Meshal is questioned by FBI agents. The following month, Kenyan authorities hand him over to Ethiopian forces operating in Somalia. Ethiopian authorities subsequently transfer Meshal to a prison in Addis Ababa, where FBI agents again question him. He is released in May 2007. This incident may be the first case in which a U.S. citizen is subjected to detention by proxy, through which cooperating foreign governments detain individuals on behalf of or in cooperation with the United States.

July 2007

The Los Angeles County Sheriff's Department establishes a Muslim Community Affairs Unit, which eventually grows to include several deputies who, together, speak at least five languages relevant to the Muslim population of Los Angeles County.

January 2009

Two days after his inauguration, President Barack Obama issues a series of executive orders to end the CIA's secret detention program and close CIA black sites, ban the use of brutal interrogation techniques, and close the Guantanamo Bay detention facility within one year. Congress blocks his efforts to close the Guantanamo facility, and the U.S. retains control of a detention facility for enemy combatants in Afghanistan until 2014.

President Obama also retains the option of transferring suspected terrorists to the custody of foreign governments, with greater oversight from the State Department to ensure that detainees are not abused.

April 2010

The Oklahoma state legislature votes to conduct a referendum on a proposed amendment to the state constitution (the Save Our State Amendment) that would ban state courts from considering Sharia during their proceedings. This act is the first anti-Sharia measure passed by a state legislature. In November, the amendment is approved with 70 percent of the vote. A federal court later voids the measure as a violation of the U.S. Constitution. To avoid this result, other state legislatures adopt various prohibitions on foreign law that, while aimed primarily at banning Sharia, do not mention Sharia or Islam.

March 2011

The House Homeland Security Committee, under the leadership of Republican Representative Peter King, begins a series of hearings to examine the threat of radicalization among Muslim Americans. A dominant theme of the hearings is Representative King's belief that Muslim Americans are not doing enough to help law enforcement and security officials counter Muslim extremists.

April 2011

As the U.S. and allied forces begin air strikes in Libya to aid rebels seeking to overthrow Muammar el-Qaddafi, the FBI begins interviewing more than 800 people of Libyan origin residing in the United States. This effort is designed to uncover any spies working for the el-Qaddafi regime or terrorists affiliated with Libyan extremist groups.

September 2011

A drone-fired missile kills Anwar al-Awlaki, a U.S. citizen suspected of playing a key leadership role in al-Qaeda in the Arabian Peninsula (AQAP). Another American working with AQAP, Samir Khan, is killed in the missile strike, although he is not the intended target. Al-Awlaki is the first American intentionally targeted for assassination via drone strike.

October 2011

In an attempt to assassinate Ibrahim al-Banna, a senior al-Qaeda leader from Egypt, the CIA conducts a drone strike against a site in Yemen, killing a dozen people. Among those killed in the strike is U.S. citizen Abdulrahman Anwar al-Awlaki, the 16-year-old son of Anwar al-Awlaki. The intelligence behind the operation proves faulty, and al-Banna remains unharmed. The unintended killing of the younger al-Awlaki marks the fourth known death of an American via drone strike.

November 2011

A drone strike in Pakistan kills a group of suspected Taliban insurgents, including U.S. citizen Jude Kenan Mohammad.

July 2012

Five members of the U.S. House of Representatives—Michele Bachmann, Trent Franks, Louie Gohmert, Tom Rooney, and Lynn Westmoreland—send letters to the inspectors general of the State Department, the Defense Department, the Justice Department, and other government agencies expressing concern that the Muslim Brotherhood could be infiltrating the federal government.

January 2015

Three Americans are killed in two separate drone strikes in Pakistan. The first drone strike kills Adam Gadahn, an American serving as a propagandist for al-Qaeda. The second drone strike kills Ahmed Farouq, a senior member of al-Qaeda in the Indian Subcontinent (AQIS), an al-Qaeda-affiliated terrorist group. The second strike also kills two aid workers who were being held hostage by al-Qaeda: U.S. citizen Warren Weinstein and Italian citizen Giovanni Lo Porto.

Notes

Chapter 1

1. Jonathan Lyons, *Islam through Western Eyes: From the Crusades to the War on Terrorism* (New York: Columbia University Press, 2012) 64, 70–72.

2. David R. Blanks and Michael Frassetto, *Western Views of Islam in Medieval and Early Modern Europe* (New York: St. Martin's Press, 1999), 208–209.

3. David R. Blanks and Michael Frassetto, *Western Views of Islam in Medieval and Early Modern Europe* (New York: St. Martin's Press, 1999), 214.

4. Jonathan Lyons, *Islam through Western Eyes: From the Crusades to the War on Terrorism* (New York: Columbia University Press, 2012), 113, 133–135.

5. Denise Spellberg, *Thomas Jefferson's Qur'an: Islam and the Founders* (New York: Alfred A. Knopf, 2013), 17.

6. Peter Gottschalk and Gabriel Greenberg, "Common Heritage, Uncommon Fear: Islamophobia in the United States and British India," in *Islamophobia in America: The Anatomy of Intolerance*, ed. Carl Ernst (New York: Palgrave Macmillan, 2013), 24; Thomas Kidd, *American Christians and Islam: Evangelical Culture and Muslims from the Colonial Period to the Age of Terrorism* (Princeton: Princeton University Press, 2009), 7–9.

7. Robert Allison, *The Crescent Obscured: The United States and the Muslim World 1776–1815* (Oxford: Oxford University Press, 1995), 43; Peter Gottschalk and Gabriel Greenberg, "Common Heritage, Uncommon Fear: Islamophobia in the United States and British India," in *Islamophobia in America: The Anatomy of Intolerance*, ed. Carl Ernst (New York: Palgrave Macmillan, 2013), 24.

8. Timothy Marr, *The Cultural Roots of American Islamicism* (Cambridge: Cambridge University Press, 2006), 35–36.

9. Paul Baepler, *White Slaves, African Masters: An Anthology of American Barbary Captivity Narratives* (Chicago: University of Chicago Press, 1999), 2, 4, 6–7, 24.

10. Michael Kitzen, *Tripoli and the United States at War: A History of American Relations with the Barbary States* (London: McFarland & Company, 1962), 14; Frederick Leiner, *The End of Barbary Terror: America's 1815 War Against the Pirates of North Africa* (Oxford: Oxford University Press, 2006), 8, 13.

11. Michael Kitzen, *Tripoli and the United States at War: A History of American Relations with the Barbary States* (London: McFarland & Company, 1962), 8.

12. Robert Allison, *The Crescent Obscured: The United States and the Muslim World 1776–1815* (Oxford: Oxford University Press, 1995), xiv.

13. Michael Kitzen, *Tripoli and the United States at War: A History of American Relations with the Barbary States* (London: McFarland & Company, 1962), 10.

14. Russell D. Buhite, *Lives at Risk: Hostages and Victims in American Foreign Policy* (Wilmington, DE: Scholarly Resources, Inc., 1995), 4, 30.

15. Timothy Marr, *The Cultural Roots of American Islamicism* (Cambridge: Cambridge University Press, 2006), 30.

16. Ray Irwin, *The Diplomatic Relations of the United States with the Barbary Powers 1776–1816* (New York: Russell & Russell, 1931), 32–33.

17. Michael Kitzen, *Tripoli and the United States at War: A History of American Relations with the Barbary States* (London: McFarland & Company, 1962), 19, 21.

18. Ray Irwin, *The Diplomatic Relations of the United States with the Barbary Powers 1776–1816* (New York: Russell & Russell, 1931), 98; Michael Kitzen, *Tripoli and the United States at War: A History of American Relations with the Barbary States* (London: McFarland & Company, 1962), 44.

19. Max Boot, *The Savage Wars of Peace: Small Wars and the Rise of American Power* (New York: Basic Books, 2002), 20–26.

20. Max Boot, *The Savage Wars of Peace: Small Wars and the Rise of American Power* (New York: Basic Books, 2002), 27–28.

21. Russel D. Buhite, *Lives at Risk: Hostages and Victims in American Foreign Policy* (Wilmington, DE: Scholarly Resources, Inc., 1995), 16.

22. Max Boot, *The Savage Wars of Peace: Small Wars and the Rise of American Power* (New York: Basic Books, 2002), 47–48.

23. Max Boot, *The Savage Wars of Peace: Small Wars and the Rise of American Power* (New York: Basic Books, 2002), 49.

24. "The Philippine-American War," Department of State, Office of the Historian, November 1, 2013, https://history.state.gov/milestones/1899-1913/war.

25. Charles A. Byler, "Pacifying the Moros: American Military Government in the Southern Philippines, 1899–1913," *Military Review*, May–June 2005, 41.

26. James R. Arnold, *The Moro War: How America Battled a Muslim Insurgency in the Philippine Jungle, 1902–1913* (New York: Bloomsbury, 2011), 2; Najeeb Mitry Saleeby, *The History of Sulu* (London: Forgotten Books, 2012, reprint of 1908 edition), 208–214.

27. James R. Arnold, *The Moro War: How America Battled a Muslim Insurgency in the Philippine Jungle, 1902–1913* (New York: Bloomsbury, 2011), 9.

28. Robert Fulton, *Moroland: The History of Uncle Sam and the Moros* (Bend, Oregon: Tumalo Creek Press, 2009), 62.

29. Charles A. Byler, "Pacifying the Moros: American Military Government in the Southern Philippines, 1899–1913," *Military Review*, May-June 2005, 41.

30. Charles A. Byler, "Pacifying the Moros: American Military Government in the Southern Philippines, 1899–1913," *Military Review*, May–June 2005, 41–43.

31. Charles A. Byler, "Pacifying the Moros: American Military Government in the Southern Philippines, 1899–1913," *Military Review*, May–June 2005, 43–44.

32. "The Philippine-American War, 1899–1902," Department of State, Office of the Historian, November 2013, https://history.state.gov/milestones/1899-1913/war.

33. Russell D. Buhite, *Lives at Risk: Hostages and Victims in American Foreign Policy* (Wilmington, DE: Scholarly Resources, 1995), 72, 75–76.

34. Russell D, Buhite, *Lives at Risk: Hostages and Victims in American Foreign Policy* (Wilmington, DE: Scholarly Resources, 1995), 77, 79.

35. "A Guide to the United States' History of Recognition, Diplomatic, and Consular Relations 1776–2008: Turkey," United States Embassy, Ankara, http://turkey.usembassy.gov/us_diplomatic_interaction_turkey.html (accessed August 4, 2014).

36. Justin McCarthy, *The Turk in America: The Creation of an Enduring Prejudice* (Salt Lake City: University of Utah Press, 2010), 94, 106, 116, 118.

37. Guenter Lewy, *The Armenian Massacres in Ottoman Turkey: A Disputed Genocide* (Salt Lake City: University of Utah Press, 2007), 20–26.

38. Douglas Howard, *The History of Turkey* (Westport, CT: Greenwood Press, 2001), 82; Justin McCarthy, *The Ottoman Turks: An Introductory History to 1923* (London: Longman Ltd. 1997), 83.

39. Roger Trask, *The United States Response to Turkish Nationalism and Reform, 1914–1939* (Minneapolis: University of Minnesota Press, 1971), 11.

40. Roger Trask, *The United States Response to Turkish Nationalism and Reform, 1914–1939* (Minneapolis: University of Minnesota Press, 1971), 9–10.

41. John A. DeNovo, *American Interests and Policies in the Middle East: 1900–1939* (Minneapolis: University of Minnesota Press, 1963), 101; Roger Trask, *The United States Response to Turkish Nationalism and Reform, 1914–1939* (Minneapolis: University of Minnesota Press, 1971), 21.

42. Thomas Kidd, *American Christians and Islam: Evangelical Culture and Muslims from the Colonial Period to the Age of Terrorism* (Princeton: Princeton University Press, 2009), 21, 26; Douglas Little, *American Orientalism: The United States and the Middle East since 1945* (Chapel Hill: University of North Carolina Press, 2008), 11–12.

43. Paul Baepler, "Introduction," in *White Slaves, African Masters: An Anthology of American Barbary Captivity Narratives*, ed. Paul Baepler (Chicago: University of Chicago Press, 1999), 10. Robert Fulton, *Moroland: The History of Uncle Sam and the Moros* (Bend, OR: Tumalo Creek Pres, 2009), vi; "Topics in Chronicling America: The Perdicaris Affair," Library of Congress, February 13, 2013, www.loc.gov/rr/news/topics/perdicaris.html.

44. Thomas Kidd, *American Christians and Islam: Evangelical Culture and Muslims from the Colonial Period to the Age of Terrorism* (Princeton: Princeton University Press, 2009), 21, 26; Justin McCarthy, *The Turk in America: The Creation of an Enduring Prejudice* (Salt lake City: University of Utah, 2010), 158.

45. Peter Charles Hoffer, *The Brave New World: A History of Early America* (Baltimore, MD: Johns Hopkins University Press, 2006), 83–85.

46. Kambiz GhaneaBassiri, *A History of Islam in America* (Cambridge: Cambridge University Press, 2010), 10–12; Richard Brent Turner, *Islam in the African American Experience* (Bloomington: Indiana University Press, 1997), 11.

47. Frank E. Gizzard, *Jamestown Colony: A Political, Social, and Cultural History* (Santa Barbara: ABC-CLIO, 2007), 198–199.

48. Michael A. Gomez, *Black Crescent: The Experience and Legacy of African Muslims in America* (Cambridge: Cambridge University Press, 2005), 166.

49. Edward Curtis, "The Black Muslim Scare of the Twentieth Century: Religious Stereotyping and Out-grouping of Muslims in the United States," in *Islamophobia in America: The Anatomy of Intolerance*, ed. Carl Ernst (New York: Palgrave Macmillan, 2013), 78.

50. Kambiz GhaneaBassiri, *A History of Islam in America* (Cambridge: Cambridge University Press, 2010), 30–31; Richard Brent Turner, *Islam in the African American Experience* (Bloomington: Indiana University Press, 1997), 25.

51. Richard Brent Turner, *Islam in the African American Experience* (Bloomington: Indiana University Press, 1997), 20, 28, 30–32.

52. Richard Brent Turner, *Islam in the African American Experience* (Bloomington: Indiana University Press, 1997), 26, 32–40.

53. Denise Spellberg, *Thomas Jefferson's Qur'an: Islam and the Founders* (New York: Alfred A. Knopf, 2013), 5.

54. Denise Spellberg, *Thomas Jefferson's Qur'an: Islam and the Founders* (New York: Alfred A. Knopf, 2013), 238.

55. Thomas Kidd, *American Christians and Islam: Evangelical Culture and Muslims from the Colonial Period to the Age of Terrorism* (Princeton: Princeton University Press, 2009), 1; Denise Spellberg, *Thomas Jefferson's Qur'an: Islam and the Founders* (New York: Alfred A. Knopf, 2013), 3–6.

56. Steven G. Koven and Frank Gotzke, *American Immigration Policy: Confronting the Nation's Challenges* (New York: Springfield, 2010), 9.

57. Anny Bakalian and Mehdi Bozorgmehr, *Backlash 9/11: Middle Eastern and Muslim Americans Respond* (Berkeley: University of California Press, 2009), 70.

58. Geneive Abdo, *Mecca and Main Street: Muslim Life in America after 9/11* (Oxford: Oxford University Press, 2006), 70.

59. Kambiz GhaneaBassiri, *A History of Islam in America* (Cambridge: Cambridge University Press, 2010), 140–150.

60. Kambiz GhaneaBassiri, *A History of Islam in America* (Cambridge: Cambridge University Press, 2010), 163.

61. Steven G. Koven and Frank Gotzke, *American Immigration Policy: Confronting the Nation's Challenges* (New York: Springfield, 2010), 10.

62. Kambiz GhaneaBassiri, *A History of Islam in America* (Cambridge: Cambridge University Press, 2010), 151.

63. Roger Daniels, *The Golden Door: American Immigration Policy and Immigrants since 1882* (New York: Hill and Wang, 2005), 33, 46.

64. Steven G. Koven and Frank Gotzke, *American Immigration Policy: Confronting the Nation's Challenges* (New York: Springfield, 2010), 11.

65. Nicholas Lemann, *The Promised Land: The Great Black Migration and How It Changed America* (New York: Vintage Books, 1992), 6; Isabel Wilkerson, *The Warmth of Other Suns: The Epic Story of America's Great Migration* (New York: Vintage Books, 2010), 9–10.

66. Geneive Abdo, *Mecca and Main Street: Muslim Life in America after 9/11* (Oxford: Oxford University Press, 2006), 72, 77.

67. Richard Brent Turner, *Islam in the African American Experience* (Bloomington: Indiana University Press, 1997), 123–124.

68. Edward Curtis, "The Black Muslim Scare of the Twentieth Century: Religious Stereotyping and Out-grouping of Muslims in the United States," in *Islamophobia in America: The Anatomy of Intolerance*, ed. Carl Ernst (New York: Palgrave Macmillan, 2013), 85–86; Kambiz GhaneaBassiri, *A History of Islam in America* (Cambridge: Cambridge University Press, 2010), 210.

69. Patrick D. Bowen, "Satti Majid: A Sudanese Founder of American Islam," in *Journal of Africana Religions* 1, no. 2 (2013), 194; Kambiz GhaneaBassiri, *A History of Islam in America* (Cambridge: Cambridge University Press, 2010), 176.

70. Kambiz GhaneaBassiri, *A History of Islam in America* (Cambridge: Cambridge University Press, 2010), 204.

71. Jane Smith, *Islam in America* (New York: Columbia University Press, 2010), 80; Richard Brent Turner, *Islam in the African American Experience* (Bloomington: Indiana University Press, 1997), 92.

72. Michael A. Gomez, *Black Crescent: The Experience and Legacy of African Muslims in America* (Cambridge: Cambridge University Press, 2005), 206.

73. Jane Smith, *Islam in America* (New York: Columbia University Press, 2010), 80; Richard Brent Turner, *Islam in the African American Experience* (Bloomington: Indiana University Press, 1997), 71–72, 92–93.

74. Michael A. Gomez, *Black Crescent: The Experience and Legacy of African Muslims in America* (Cambridge: Cambridge University Press, 2005), 271–272.

75. Kambiz GhaneaBassiri, *A History of Islam in America* (Cambridge: Cambridge University Press, 2010), 222–223.

76. Michael A. Gomez, *Black Crescent: The Experience and Legacy of African Muslims in America* (Cambridge: Cambridge University Press, 2005), 276.

77. Jane Smith, *Islam in America* (New York: Columbia University Press, 2010), 82; Richard Brent Turner, *Islam in the African American Experience* (Bloomington: Indiana University Press, 1997), 148–151.

78. Kambiz GhaneaBassiri, *A History of Islam in America* (Cambridge: University of California Press, 2010), 224.

79. Jane Smith, *Islam in America* (New York: Columbia University Press, 2010), 83.

80. Richard Brent Turner, *Islam in the African American Experience* (Bloomington: Indiana University Press, 1997), 151, 154.

81. Richard Brent Turner, *Islam in the African American Experience* (Bloomington: Indiana University Press, 1997), 167.

82. Geneive Abdo, *Mecca and Main Street: Muslim Life in America after 9/11* (Oxford: Oxford University Press, 2006), 77.

83. Tim Weiner, *Enemies: A History of the FBI* (New York: Random House, 2012), 10–11.

84. Tim Weiner, *Enemies: A History of the FBI* (New York: Random House, 2012), 13–16.

85. Tim Weiner, *Enemies: A History of the FBI* (New York: Random House, 2012), 19–20.

86. Tim Weiner, *Enemies: A History of the FBI* (New York: Random House, 2012), 29–31.

87. David Cunningham, *There's Something Happening Here: The New Left, the Klan, and FBI Counterintelligence* (Berkeley: University of California Press, 2004), 16–20; Federal Bureau of Investigation, "A Brief History of the FBI," www.fbi.gov/about-us/history/brief-history (accessed August 10, 2014).

88. Richard Brent Turner, *Islam in the African American Experience* (Bloomington: Indiana University Press, 1997), 99.

89. Edward Curtis, "The Black Muslim Scare of the Twentieth Century: Religious Stereotyping and Out-grouping of Muslims in the United States," in *Islamophobia in America: The Anatomy of Intolerance*, ed. Carl Ernst (New York: Palgrave Macmillan, 2013), 90; Federal Bureau of Investigation, "Moorish Science Temple of America," *FBI Records: The Vault*, http://vault.fbi.gov/Moorish%20Science%20Temple%20of%20America (accessed August 10, 2014).

90. Ronald Fritze, *Invented Knowledge: False History, Fake Science, and Pseudo-Religions* (London: Reaktion Books, 2009), 135–166; Richard Brent Turner, *Islam in the African American Experience* (Bloomington: Indiana University Press, 1997), 167.

91. Michael A. Gomez, *Black Crescent: The Experience and Legacy of African Muslims in America* (Cambridge: Cambridge University Press, 2005), 284.

92. Richard Brent Turner, *Islam in the African American Experience* (Bloomington: Indiana University Press, 1997), 163.

93. Martha F. Lee, "The Nation of Islam and Violence," in *Violence and New Religious Movements*, ed. James R. Lewis (Oxford: Oxford University Press, 2011), 295–306.

94. Edward Curtis, "The Black Muslim Scare of the Twentieth Century: Religious Stereotyping and Out-grouping of Muslims in the United States," in *Islamophobia in America: The Anatomy of Intolerance*, ed. Carl Ernst (New York: Palgrave Macmillan, 2013), 90.

95. Robert A. Hill, ed., *The FBI's RACON: Racial Conditions in the United States during World War II* (Boston: Northeastern University Press, 1995), 4, 15.

96. Edward Curtis, "The Black Muslim Scare of the Twentieth Century: Religious Stereotyping and Out-grouping of Muslims in the United States," in *Islamophobia in America: The Anatomy of Intolerance*, ed. Carl Ernst (New York: Palgrave Macmillan, 2013), 91.

97. Robert A. Hill, ed., *The FBI's RACON: Racial Conditions in the United States during World War II* (Boston: Northeastern University Press, 1995), 4, 29.

98. Edward Curtis, "The Black Muslim Scare of the Twentieth Century: Religious Stereotyping and Out-grouping of Muslims in the United States," in *Islamophobia in America: The Anatomy of Intolerance*, ed. Carl Ernst (New York: Palgrave Macmillan, 2013), 92.

99. Richard Brent Turner, *Islam in the African American Experience* (Bloomington: Indiana University Press, 1997), 167.

100. Richard Brent Turner, *Islam in the African American Experience* (Bloomington: Indiana University Press, 1997), 168.

101. Richard Brent Turner, *Islam in the African American Experience* (Bloomington: Indiana University Press, 1997), 103, 168–169.

102. Richard Brent Turner, *Islam in the African American Experience* (Bloomington: Indiana University Press, 1997), 103, 168; Edward Curtis, "The Black Muslim Scare of the Twentieth Century: Religious Stereotyping and Out-grouping of Muslims in the United States," in *Islamophobia in America: The Anatomy of Intolerance*, ed. Carl Ernst (New York: Palgrave Macmillan, 2013), 92–93.

103. Edward Curtis, "The Black Muslim Scare of the Twentieth Century: Religious Stereotyping and Out-grouping of Muslims in the United States," in *Islamophobia in America: The Anatomy of Intolerance*, ed. Carl Ernst (New York: Palgrave Macmillan, 2013), 93.

104. Robert A. Hill, ed., *The FBI's RACON: Racial Conditions in the United States during World War II* (Boston: Northeastern University Press, 1995), 17.

105. Tim Weiner, *Enemies: A History of the FBI* (New York: Random House, 2012), 195.

106. Jay Feldman, *Manufacturing Hysteria: A History of Scapegoating, Surveillance, and Secrecy in Modern America* (New York: Anchor Books, 2011), 255, 285.

107. Jay Feldman, *Manufacturing Hysteria: A History of Scapegoating, Surveillance, and Secrecy in Modern America* (New York: Anchor Books, 2011), 271.

108. Tim Weiner, *Enemies: A History of the FBI* (New York: Random House, 2012), 197–198.

109. Jay Feldman, *Manufacturing Hysteria: A History of Scapegoating, Surveillance, and Secrecy in Modern America* (New York: Anchor Books, 2011), 264; Tim Weiner, *Enemies: A History of the FBI* (New York: Random House, 2012), 235–236, 250.

110. Federal Bureau of Investigation, *Nation of Islam: The FBI Files* (Lexington, KY: Filiquarian Publishing/Qontro, 2013), 1.

111. Federal Bureau of Investigation, *Nation of Islam: The FBI Files* (Lexington, KY: Filiquarian Publishing/Qontro, 2013), iii.

112. Ward Churchill and Jim Vander Wall, *The COINTELPRO Papers: Documents from the FBI's Secret Wars Against Domestic Dissent* (Boston: South End Press, 1990), 103; Edward Curtis, "The Black Muslim Scare of the Twentieth Century: Religious Stereotyping and Out-grouping of Muslims in the United States," in *Islamophobia in America: The Anatomy of Intolerance*, ed. Carl Ernst (New York: Palgrave Macmillan, 2013), 95.

113. Richard Brent Turner, *Islam in the African American Experience* (Bloomington: Indiana University Press, 1997), 167.

114. Edward Curtis, "The Black Muslim Scare of the Twentieth Century: Religious Stereotyping and Out-grouping of Muslims in the United States," in *Islamophobia in America: The Anatomy of Intolerance*, ed. Carl Ernst (New York: Palgrave Macmillan, 2013), 98; Richard Brent Turner, *Islam in the African American Experience* (Bloomington: Indiana University Press, 1997), 165.

115. Edward Curtis, "The Black Muslim Scare of the Twentieth Century: Religious Stereotyping and Out-grouping of Muslims in the United States," in *Islamophobia in America: The Anatomy of Intolerance*, ed. Carl Ernst (New York: Palgrave Macmillan, 2013), 95.

116. Federal Bureau of Investigation, *Nation of Islam: The FBI Files* (Lexington, KY: Filiquarian Publishing/ Qontro, 2013), 1.

117. David Cunningham, *There's Something Happening Here: The New Left, the Klan, and FBI Counterintelligence* (Berkeley: University of California Press, 2004), 32–33.

118. Jay Feldman, *Manufacturing Hysteria: A History of Scapegoating, Surveillance, and Secrecy in Modern America* (New York: Anchor Books, 2011), 275.

119. James Kirkpatrick Davis, *Spying on America: The FBI's Domestic Counterintelligence Program* (Westport, CT: Praeger, 1992), 101.

120. Jay Feldman, *Manufacturing Hysteria: A History of Scapegoating, Surveillance, and Secrecy in Modern America* (New York: Anchor Books, 2011), 278–279; James Kirkpatrick Davis, *Spying on America: The FBI's Domestic Counterintelligence Program* (Westport, CT: Praeger, 1992), 102.

121. Edward Curtis, "The Black Muslim Scare of the Twentieth Century: Religious Stereotyping and Out-grouping of Muslims in the United States," in *Islamophobia in America: The Anatomy of Intolerance*, ed. Carl Ernst (New York: Palgrave Macmillan, 2013), 98.

122. Jay Feldman, *Manufacturing Hysteria: A History of Scapegoating, Surveillance, and Secrecy in Modern America* (New York: Anchor Books, 2011), 280–281.

123. David Cunningham, *There's Something Happening Here: The New Left, the Klan, and FBI Counterintelligence* (Berkeley: University of California Press, 2004), 35–36; Jay Feldman, *Manufacturing Hysteria: A History of Scapegoating, Surveillance, and Secrecy in Modern America* (New York: Anchor Books, 2011), 292–293.

124. David Cunningham, *There's Something Happening Here: The New Left, the Klan, and FBI Counterintelligence* (Berkeley: University of California Press, 2004), 113; Jay Feldman, *Manufacturing Hysteria: A History of Scapegoating, Surveillance, and Secrecy in Modern America* (New York: Anchor Books, 2011), 293.

125. Steven G. Koven and Frank Gotzke, *American Immigration Policy: Confronting the Nation's Challenges* (New York: Springfield, 2010), 12.

126. Yvonne Yazbeck Haddad, *Becoming American? The Forging of Arab and Muslim Identity in Pluralist America* (Waco, Texas: Baylor University Press, 2011), 4–5.

127. Kambiz GhaneaBassiri, *A History of Islam in America* (Cambridge: Cambridge University Press, 2010), 293.

128. Theodore Caplow, et al., *The First Measured Century: An Illustrated Guide to Trends in America: 1900–2000* (Washington, D.C.: AEI Press, 2001), accessed at www.pbs.org/fmc/book/7leisure6.htm.

129. Helen D. Hazen and Heike C. Alberts, "Visitors or Immigrants? International Students in the United States," *Population, Space and Place* 12, no. 3 (2006): 201.

130. Kambiz GhaneaBassiri, *A History of Islam in America* (Cambridge: Cambridge University Press, 2010), 264.

131. Anny Bakalian and Mehdi Bozorgmehr, *Backlash 9/11: Middle Eastern and Muslim Americans Respond* (Berkeley: University of California Press, 2009), 72.

132. *Open Doors 2010: Report on International Educational Exchange* (New York: International Institute for Education, 2011), http://www.iie.org/Research-and-Publications/Open-Doors.

133. C. Augustus Martin, *The Sage Encyclopedia of Terrorism* (Los Angeles: Sage Publications, 2011), 209–211; "Olympics Massacre: Munich—The Real Story," *The Independent*, January 22, 2006, www.independent.co.uk.

134. Yvonne Yazbeck Haddad, "The Shaping of Arab and Muslim Identity in the United States," in *Immigration and Religion in America: Comparative and Historical Perspective*, ed. Richard Alba, et al. (New York: New York University Press, 2008), 262.

135. L. Patrick Gray, III, *In Nixon's Web: A Year in the Crosshairs of Watergate* (New York: Henry Holt and Company, 2008), 15; Tim Weiner, *Enemies: A History of the FBI* (New York: Random House, 2012), 313–314.

136. "FBI Records Reveal Details of Nixon-Era Racial Profiling Program Targeting Arabs," *IntelWire*, December 4, 2010, http://news.intelwire.com/2010/12/fbi-records-reveal-details-of-nixon-era.html.

137. Marvin Wingfield, "The Impact of 9/11, Middle East Conflicts, and Anti-Arab Discrimination," in *Daily Life of Arab Americans in the 21st Century*, ed. Anan Ameri and Holly Arida (Santa Barbara: Greenwood, 2012), 41.

138. Russell D. Buhite, *Lives at Risk: Hostages and Victims in American Foreign Policy* (Wilmington, DE: Scholastic Resources, 1995), 166–167; Harvey W. Kushner, *Encyclopedia of Terrorism* (Thousand Oaks, California: Sage Publications, 2003), 179–180; "Timeline: A Modern History of Iran," PBS *Newshour*, February 11, 2010, www.pbs.org/newshour.

139. Russell D. Buhite, *Lives at Risk: Hostages and Victims in American Foreign Policy* (Wilmington, DE: Scholastic Resources, 1995), 179–180, 183–167; Harvey W. Kushner, *Encyclopedia of Terrorism* (Thousand Oaks, California: Sage Publications, 2003), 179–180.

140. Anny Bakalian and Mehdi Bozorgmehr, *Backlash 9/11: Middle Eastern and Muslim Americans Respond* (Berkeley: University of California Press, 2009), 38.

141. Mehdi Bozorgmehr, Anny Bakalian, Sara Salman, "Host Hostility and Nativism," in *The Routledge International Handbook of Migration Studies* (New York: Routledge, 2013), 194–195.

142. Anny Bakalian and Mehdi Bozorgmehr, *Backlash 9/11: Middle Eastern and Muslim Americans Respond* (Berkeley: University of California Press, 2009), 57.

143. Central Intelligence Agency, "FLASHBACK: April 18, 1983: U.S. Embassy Attacked in Beirut," April 17, 2014, www.cia.gov.

144. British Broadcasting Corporation, "Thirty Years Later, a Bombing in Lebanon still Echoes," October 22, 2013, http://www.bbc.com/news/.

145. Harvey W. Kushner, *Encyclopedia of Terrorism* (Thousands Oaks, CA: Sage Publications, 2003), 166.

146. "Terrorist Attacks on Americans: 1979–1988," PBS *Frontline*, www.pbs.org/frontline, accessed September 30, 2014.

147. Central Intelligence Agency, "Terrorist Bombing of Pan Am Flight 103," July 23, 2012, www.cia.gov.

148. Louise A. Cainkar, *Homeland Insecurity: The Arab American and Muslim American Experience after 9/11* (New York: Russell Sage Foundation, 2009), 132, 140; Louise A. Cainkar, "Targeting Muslims, at Ashcroft's Discretion," Middle East Research and Information Project, March 14, 2003, http://www.merip.org/mero/mero031403.

149. Joseph McCann, *Terrorism on American Soil* (Boulder, Colorado: Sentient Publications, 2006), 178–179, 186–187.

150. Joseph Fried, "Sheik and 9 Followers Guilty," *New York Times*, October 1995; Chitra Ragavan, "Tracing Terror's Roots: How the First World Trade Center Plot Sowed the Seeds for 9/11," *U.S. News and World Report*, February 16, 2003.

151. Louise A. Cainkar, *Homeland Insecurity: The Arab American and Muslim American Experience after 9/11* (New York: Russell Sage Foundation, 2009), 132, Louise A. Cainkar, "Targeting Muslims, at Ashcroft's Discretion," Middle East Research and Information Project, March 14, 2003, http://www.merip.org/mero/mero031403.

152. Lawrence Wright, *The Looming Tower: Al-Qaeda and the Road to 9/11* (New York: Vintage Books, 2007), 150.

153. Roy Gutman, *How We Missed the Story: Osama bin Laden, the Taliban, and the Hijacking of Afghanistan* (Washington, D.C.: United States Institute of Peace, 2008), 85.

154. Louise A. Cainkar, *Homeland Insecurity: The Arab American and Muslim American Experience after 9/11* (New York: Russell Sage Foundation, 2009), 132.

155. Jerry Gray, "Foreigners Investing In Libya or in Iran Face U.S. Sanctions," *New York Times*, July 24, 1996.

156. Louise A. Cainkar, *Homeland Insecurity: The Arab American and Muslim American Experience after 9/11* (New York: Russell Sage Foundation, 2009), 132.

157. Assaf Moghadam, *The Gobalization of Martyrdom* (Baltimore: Johns Hopkins University Press, 2008), 86–88; Lawrence Wright, *The Looming Tower: Al-Qaeda and the Road to 9/11* (New York: Vintage Books, 2007), 306–308, 360–361, 336–337.

Chapter 2

1. Senate Joint Resolution 23, 107th Congress (2001).

2. Transportation Security Administration, last updated January 10, 2014, http://www.tsa.gov/.

3. Charles Nemeth, *Homeland Security: An Introduction to Principles and Practice* (Boca Raton: CRC Press, 2013), 407–408.

4. David Cole and James X. Dempsey, *Terrorism and the Constitution* (New York: The New Press, 2006), 38, 51, 60.

5. Charles Nemeth, *Homeland Security: An Introduction to Principles and Practice* (Boca Raton: CRC Press, 2013), 54–55, 371, 522.

6. Charles Nemeth, *Homeland Security: An Introduction to Principles and Practice* (Boca Raton: CRC Press, 2013), 352–356.

7. Robert S. Mueller, III, "Statement Before the House Permanent Select Committee on Intelligence," October 6, 2011, http://www.fbi.gov/news/testimony/the-state-of-intelligence-reform-10-years-after-911.

8. Dana Priest and William Arkin, *Top Secret America: The Rise of the New American Security State* (New York: Little, Brown & Company, 2011), 86.

9. Bureau of Counterterrorism, Department of State, accessed January 28, 2015, http://www.state.gov/j/ct/about/mission/index.htm.

10. "DNI Clapper Established National Counterintelligence and Security Center," ODNI News Release No. 46-14, December 1, 2014, http://www.dni.gov/index.php/newsroom/press-releases.

11. David F. Kettl, *Systems Under Stress: Homeland Security and American Politics* (Washington, D.C.: Congressional Quarterly Press, 2007), 106–107; Charles Nemeth, *Homeland Security: An Introduction to Principles and Practice* (Boca Raton: CRC Press, 2013), 83–84.

12. Susan Herman, *Taking Liberties: The War on Terror and the Erosion of American Democracy* (Oxford: Oxford University Press, 2011), 137–138, 144, 152–54.

13. Kam Wong, *The Impact of USA Patriot Act on American Society: An Evidence Based Approach* (New York: Nova Science Publishers, 2007), 202–204.

14. Barton Gellman, "U.S. Surveillance Architecture Includes Collection of Revealing Internet, Phone Metadata," *Washington Post*, June 15, 2013; Ryan Lizza, "State of Deception," *The New Yorker*, December 16, 2013.

15. Dana Priest and William Arkin, *Top Secret America: The Rise of the New American Security State* (New York: Little, Brown & Company, 2011), 144–145, 148.

16. Anny Bakalian and Mehdi Bozorgmehr, *Backlash 9/11: Middle Eastern and Muslim Americans Respond* (Berkeley: University of California, 2009), 257; Student and Exchange Visitor Program (Immigration and Customs Enforcement, Department of Homeland Security), http://www.ice.gov/sevis/, accessed June 17, 2014.

17. Charles Nemeth, *Homeland Security: An Introduction to Principles and Practice* (Boca Raton: CRC Press, 2013), 86, 398.

18. Office of the Inspector General, Department of Justice, *The September 11 Detainees: A Review of the Treatment of Aliens Held on Immigration Charges in Connection with the Investigation of the September 11 Attacks* (April 2003), 1; Tim Weiner, *Enemies: A History of the FBI* (New York: Random House, 2012), 419.

19. Office of the Inspector General, Department of Justice, *The September 11 Detainees: A Review of the Treatment of Aliens Held on Immigration Charges in Connection with the Investigation of the September 11 Attacks* (April 2003), 41.

20. Nancy Murray, "Profiled: Arabs, Muslims, and the Post-9/11 Hunt for the Enemy Within," in *Civil Rights in Peril: The Targeting of Arabs and Muslims*, ed. Elaine C. Hagopian (Chicago: Haymarket Books, 2004), 31.

21. Office of the Inspector General, Department of Justice, *The September 11 Detainees: A Review of the Treatment of Aliens Held on Immigration Charges in Connection with the Investigation of the September 11 Attacks* (April 2003), 165.

22. Nancy Murray, "Profiled: Arabs, Muslims, and the Post-9/11 Hunt for the Enemy Within," in *Civil Rights in Peril: The Targeting of Arabs and*

Muslims, ed. Elaine C. Hagopian (Chicago: Haymarket Books, 2004), 33; Office of the Inspector General, Department of Justice, *The September 11 Detainees: A Review of the Treatment of Aliens Held on Immigration Charges in Connection with the Investigation of the September 11 Attacks* (April 2003), 15, 72. 91.

23. Office of the Inspector General, Department of Justice, *The September 11 Detainees: A Review of the Treatment of Aliens Held on Immigration Charges in Connection with the Investigation of the September 11 Attacks* (April 2003), 37, 104.

24. Louise A. Cainkar, *Homeland Insecurity: The Arab American and Muslim American Experience after 9/11* (New York: Russell Sage Foundation, 2009), 120; Tram Nguyen, *We Are All Suspects Now: Untold Stories from Immigrant Communities after 9/11* (Boston: Beacon Press, 2005), 14.

25. Office of the Inspector General, Department of Justice, *The September 11 Detainees: A Review of the Treatment of Aliens Held on Immigration Charges in Connection with the Investigation of the September 11 Attacks* (April 2003), 105, 111, 121, 142–143; Michael Welch, *Scapegoats of September 11th: Hate Crimes and State Crimes in the War on Terror* (New Brunswick, NJ: Rutgers University Press, 2006), 95–96.

26. Office of the Inspector General, Department of Justice, *The September 11 Detainees: A Review of the Treatment of Aliens Held on Immigration Charges in Connection with the Investigation of the September 11 Attacks* (April 2003), 46, 52.

27. Louise A. Cainkar, *Homeland Insecurity: The Arab American and Muslim American Experience after 9/11* (New York: Russell Sage Foundation, 2009), 120.

28. Michael Welch, *Scapegoats of September 11th: Hate Crimes and State Crimes in the War on Terror* (New Brunswick, NJ: Rutgers University Press, 2006), 93; Tram Nguyen, *We Are All Suspects Now: Untold Stories from Immigrant Communities after 9/11* (Boston: Beacon Press, 2005), 2.

29. "Guidance for Absconder Apprehension Initiative," Memorandum from the Deputy Attorney General to the Commissioner of the Immigration and Naturalization Service, Director of the Federal Bureau of Investigation, Director of the U.S. Marshals Service, and the United States Attorneys, January 25, 2002, accessed through FindLaw.com, news.findlaw.com/hdocs/docs/doj/abscndr 012502mem.pdf.

30. "Official Warns of 'Multiple' al Qaeda Attacks," CNN, March 19, 2003, http://www.cnn.com.

31. Anny Bakalian and Mehdi Bozogmehr, *Backlash 9/11: Middle Eastern and Muslim Americans Respond* (Berkeley: University of California Press, 2009), 260; Michael Welch, *Scapegoats of September 11th: Hate Crimes and State Crimes in the War on Terror* (New Brunswick: Rutgers University Press, 2006), 97–98.

32. Eric Lichtblau, "Inquiry Targeted 2000 Foreign Muslims in 2004," *New York Times*, October 31, 2008.

33. Louise A. Cainkar, *Homeland Insecurity: The Arab American and Muslim American Experience after 9/11* (New York: Russell Sage Foundation, 2009), 146.

34. Susan Herman, *Taking Liberties: The War on Terror and the Erosion of American Democracy* (Oxford: Oxford University Press, 2011), 34–35.

35. Joaquin Sapien, "Are Prosecutors Taking Advantage of Material Witness Orders?," *Salon*, August 17, 2013.

36. Anjana Malhotra, *Witness to Abuse: Human Rights Abuses under the Material Witness Law since September 11* (New York: Human Rights Watch, June 2005), 2–5, 16, 97.

37. Nina Totenberg, "Court Considers Ashcroft's Liability In Terror Case," *Morning Edition*, National Public Radio (Washington, D.C.: WAMU, March 2, 2011).

38. "Ashcroft v. al-Kidd," *Harvard Law Review* 145 (2011): 222–223.

39. Tim Weiner, *Enemies: A History of the FBI* (New York: Random House, 2012), 436–437.

40. Susan Herman, *Taking Liberties: The War on Terror and the Erosion of American Democracy* (Oxford: Oxford University Press, 2011), 103, 106–109.

41. Richard M. Stana, et al., *Justice Department's Project to Interview Aliens after September 11, 2001* (Washington, D.C.: General Accounting Office, April 2003), 5.

42. Geneive Abdo, *Mecca and Main Street: Muslim Life in America after 9/11* (Oxford: Oxford University Press, 2006), 84; Richard M. Stana, et al., *Justice Department's Project to Interview Aliens after September 11, 2001* (Washington, D.C.: General Accounting Office, April 2003), 3–5, 12.

43. Richard M. Stana, et al., *Justice Department's Project to Interview Aliens after September 11, 2001* (Washington, D.C.: General Accounting Office, April 2003), 5, 9; Marvin Wingfield, "The Impact of 9/11, Middle East Conflicts, and Anti-Arab Discrimination," in *Daily Life of Arab Americans in the 21st Century* (Santa Barbara: Greenwood, 2012), 23.

44. Devlin Barrett, "FBI Questioning Libyans," *Wall Street Journal*, April 5, 2011; NYCLU Sues Over Secret FBI Data-Mining Program 'Operation Darkening Clouds," New York Civil Liberties Union, June 28, 2008, www.nyclu.org.

45. Devlin Barrett, "FBI Questioning Libyans," *Wall Street Journal*, April 5, 2011.

46. Richard Schmitt and Donna Horowitz, "FBI Starts to Question Muslim in U.S. About Possible Attacks," *Los Angeles Times*, July 2004.

47. Mary Beth Sheridan, "Interviews of Muslims to Broaden," *Washington Post*, July 17, 2004.

48. Devlin Barrett, "FBI Questioning Libyans," *Wall Street Journal*, April 5, 2011; Richard Esposito and Jason Ryan, "FBI Has Interviewed 800 Libyans about Terror Threat," ABC News, April 2011, http://abcnews.go.com.

49. Anny Bakalian and Medhi Bozorgmehr, *Backlash 9/11: Middle Eastern and Muslim Americans Respond* (Berkeley: University of California Press,

2009), 257; Lori Peek, *Behind the Backlash: Muslim Americans after 9/11* (New Delhi: Social Science Press, 2012), 192.

50. Anny Bakalian and Medhi Bozorgmehr, *Backlash 9/11: Middle Eastern and Muslim Americans Respond* (Berkeley: University of California Press, 2009), 54, 258–259; Louise A. Cainkar, *Homeland Insecurity: The Arab American and Muslim American Experience after 9/11* (New York: Russell Sage Foundation, 2009), 131, 133.

51. Louise A. Cainkar, *Homeland Insecurity: The Arab American and Muslim American Experience after 9/11* (New York: Russell Sage Foundation, 2009), 128.

52. Michael Welch, *Scapegoats of September 11th: Hate Crimes and State Crimes in the War on Terror* (New Brunswick: Rutgers University Press, 2006), 84.

53. "DHS Removes Designated Countries from NSEERS Registration," Department of Homeland Security, May 2011, http://www.dhs.gov/dhs-removes-designated-countries-nseers-registration-may-2011.

54. Mark Clayton, "Too Much Terrorism Data? Connecting the Dots May Be Getting Harder," NBC News, May 23, 2013, http://investigations.nbcnews.com

55. Susan Herman, *Taking Liberties: The War on Terror and the Erosion of American Democracy* (Oxford: Oxford University Press, 2011), 66.

56. William J. Krouse and Bart Elias, *Terrorist Watchlist Checks and Air Passenger Prescreening* (Washington, D.C.: Congressional Research Service, December 30, 2009), 11–12.

57. Kevin Anderson, "Cat Stevens to Be Deported after Jet Diversion,' *USA Today*, September 21, 2004; "Cat Stevens in the Dark Over No-Fly List," ABC News, October 1, 2004, www.abcnews.go.com.

58. Omar Sacirbey, "Judge Rules in Favor of Muslim Woman on No-Fly List," *Washington Post*, January 16, 2014.

59. Eileen R. Larence, et al., *Terrorist Watchlist: Routinely Assessing Impact of Agency Actions since the December 25, 2009 Attempted Attack Could Help Inform Future Efforts* (Washington, D.C.: Government Accountability Office, May 2012), 12.

60. Brian Ross and John Solomon, "US Apologizes to Billionaire Added to Terror No-fly List," ABC News, May 21, 2010, http://abcnews.go.com.

61. *Unleashed and Unchained: The FBI's Unchecked Abuse of* Authority (New York: American Civil Liberties Union, September 2013), 47.

62. Douglas Hopper, "The Terrorist Screening Center Defends No Fly List," *Tell Me More* (National Public Radio), August 13, 2010, www.npr.org.

63. "Latif, et al. v. Holder, et al. - ACLU Challenge to Government No Fly List," American Civil Liberties Union, accessed on June 11, 2014, www.aclu.org.

64. Peter Finn, "ACLU Mounts First Legal Challenge to No-Fly List," *Washington Post*, June 30, 2010.

65. Samreen Hooda, "Muslims on the No-Fly List now Suing FBI Pressured to Be Informants," *Huffington Post*, May 17, 2013.

66. Nick Baumann, "American Muslim Alleges FBI Had a Hand in His Torture," *Mother Jones*, April 17, 2012; *Unleashed and Unchained: The FBI's Unchecked Abuse of* Authority (New York: American Civil Liberties Union, September 2013), 47.

67. Martin Von Krogh, "American Seeks Political Asylum in Sweden, Alleging Torture, FBI Coercion," NBC News, April 18, 2012, www.usnews.nbcnews.com.

68. Ellen Rolfes, "Lawsuit Alleges FBI Misused No-Fly List to Recruit Would-Be Muslim Informants," *PBS Newshour* (Public Broadcasting Service), April 23, 2014, http://www.pbs.org/newshour; *Tanvir v. Holder*, United States District Court for the Southern District of New York, April 22, 2014, accessed through the Center for Constitutional Rights, www.ccrjustice.org/Tanvir.

69. Amanda Vicinanzo, "Justice Department Revises Procedures for Contesting Inclusion on the No Fly List," *Homeland Security Today*, April 20, 2015, http://www.hstoday.us; Adam Goldman, "U.S. to Inform Americans Whether They Are on 'No-Fly' List, and Possibly Why," *Washington Post*, April 2015.

70. "Executive Order 13224," U.S. Department of State, Office of the Coordinator for Counterterrorism, September 23, 2001, www.state.gov; "Executive Order on Terrorist Financing," The White House," September 24, 2001, http://georgewbush-whitehouse.archives.gov/.

71. "Blocking Faith, Freezing Charities: Chilling Muslim Charitable Giving in the War on Terrorism Financing," American Civil Liberties Union, June 2009, 27–36; Susan Herman, *Taking Liberties: The War on Terror and the Erosion of American Democracy* (Oxford: Oxford University Press, 2011), 28–29.

72. Gretel Kovach, "Muslim Charity Convicted in Terrorism Financing Case," *New York Times*, October 25, 2008; Susan Herman, *Taking Liberties: The War on Terror and the Erosion of American Democracy* (Oxford: Oxford University Press, 2011), 54, 59.

73. "Blocking Faith, Freezing Charities: Chilling Muslim Charitable Giving in the War on Terrorism Financing," American Civil Liberties Union, June 2009, 50–52.

74. "Blocking Faith, Freezing Charities: Chilling Muslim Charitable Giving in the War on Terrorism Financing," American Civil Liberties Union, June 2009, 59; Susan Herman, *Taking Liberties: The War on Terror and the Erosion of American Democracy* (Oxford: Oxford University Press, 2011), 55.

75. Zahra N. Jamal, "Charitable Giving Among Muslim Americans: Ten Years after 9/11," Institute for Social Policy and Understanding, Policy Brief No. 46, September 2011.

76. "Blocking Faith, Freezing Charities: Chilling Muslim Charitable Giving in the War on Terrorism Financing," American Civil Liberties Union, June 2009, 64.

77. "Blocking Faith, Freezing Charities: Chilling Muslim Charitable Giving in the War on Terrorism Financing," American Civil Liberties Union, June 2009, 11, 59, 63.

78. Barbar Bradley Hagerty, "Muslims Face Risks in Giving to Charities," *Morning Edition* (National Public Radio), June 16, 2009, www.npr.org.

79. Karen Greenberg, et al., *Terrorism Trial Report Card: September 11, 2001 — September 11, 2011* (New York: Center on Law and Security, New York University School of Law, 2011).

80. Jonathan Hafetz, *Habeas Corpus after 9/11: Confronting America's New Global Detention System* (New York: New York University Press, 2011).

81. Jonathan Hafetz, *Habeas Corpus after 9/11: Confronting America's New Global Detention System* (New York: New York University Press, 2011), 18, 20, 29, 31.

82. "The Guantanamo Docket," *New York Times* and National Public Radio, updated May 21, 2014, http://projects.nytimes.com/guantanamo.

83. Jonathan Hafetz, *Habeas Corpus after 9/11: Confronting America's New Global Detention System* (New York: New York University Press, 2011), 49.

84. Kevin Sieff, "In Afghanistan, a Second Guantanamo," *Washington Post*, August 4, 2013; *Remaking Bagram: The Creation of an Afghan Internment Regime and the Divide over U.S. Detention Power* (New York: Open Society Foundations, 2012), 5–7, 27–30.

85. *Globalizing Torture: CIA Secret Detention and Extraordinary Rendition* (New York: Open Society Foundations, 2013), 6, 12, 15.

86. Jonathan Hafetz, *Habeas Corpus after 9/11: Confronting America's New Global Detention System* (New York: New York University Press, 2011), 38–42; Greg Miller, Adam Goldman, and Julie Tate, "Senate Report on CIA Program Details Brutality, Dishonesty," *Washington Post*, December 9, 2014.

87. *Globalizing Torture: CIA Secret Detention and Extraordinary Rendition*, Open Society Justice Initiative (New York: Open Society Foundations, 2013), 14.

88. *Globalizing Torture: CIA Secret Detention and Extraordinary Rendition* (New York: Open Society Foundations, 2013), 14–15; Jonathan Hafetz, *Habeas Corpus after 9/11: Confronting America's New Global Detention System* (New York: New York University Press, 2011), 53.

89. Jane Mayer, *The Dark Side: The Inside Story of How the War on Terror Turned into a War on American Ideals* (New York: Doubleday, 2008), 110.

90. Jennifer K. Elsea, *Detention of American Citizens as Enemy Combatants* (Washington, D.C.: Congressional Research Service, February 2005), 3–4; Jonathan Hafetz, *Habeas Corpus after 9/11: Confronting America's New Global Detention System* (New York: New York University Press, 2011), 77.

91. J.M. Berger, *Jihad Joe: Americans Who Go to War in the Name of Islam* (Washington, D.C.: Potomac Books, 2011), 98–99; Amanda Ripley, "The Case of the Dirty Bomber," *Time*, June 16, 2002.

92. Jonathan Hafetz, *Habeas Corpus after 9/11: Confronting America's New Global Detention System* (New York: New York University Press, 2011), 47.

93. Jennifer K. Elsea, *Detention of U.S. Persons as Enemy Belligerents* (Washington, D.C.: Congressional Research Service, July 2013), 2.

94. Jerry Markton, "Hamdi Returned to Saudi Arabia," *Washington Post*, October 12, 2004.

95. Jennifer K. Elsea, *Detention of U.S. Persons as Enemy Belligerents* (Washington, D.C.: Congressional Research Service, July 2013), 38–40.

96. "Ali Al-Marri Pleads Guilty to Conspiracy to Provide Material Support to Al-Qaeda," *Justice News*, Department of Justice, April 30, 2009, www.justice. gov/opa; Eric Lichtblau, "Bush Declared Student an Enemy Combatant," *New York Times*, June 24, 2003.

97. Jennifer K. Elsea, *Detention of U.S. Persons as Enemy Belligerents* (Washington, D.C.: Congressional Research Service, July 2013), 43.

98. David Cole and Jules Lobel, *Less Safe, Less Free: Why America Is Losing the War on Terror* (New York: The New Press, 2009), 24; *Globalizing Torture: CIA Secret Detention and Extraordinary Rendition* (New York: Open Society Foundations, 2013), 32.

99. Nick Baumann, "Locked Up Abroad - for the FBI," *Mother Jones*, September/October 2011.

100. Raymond Bonner, "New Jersey Man Who Fled Somalia Ends Up in an Ethiopian Jail," *New York Times*, April 23, 2007; Jonathan Hafetz, *Habeas Corpus after 9/11: Confronting America's Global Detention System* (New York: New York University Press, 2011), 199.

101. Jonathan Landay, "Imprisoned American Denies Being al-Qaeda Operative," *McClatchy Newspapers*, March 24, 2007.

102. Anna Louie Sussman, "Naji Hamdan's Nightmare," *The Nation*, March 4, 2010; Kark Vick, "U.S. Muslim's Case Poses Test for New Administration," *Washington Post*, March 23, 2009.

103. Barack Obama, "Executive Order - Closure of Guantanamo Detention Facilities," The White House, January 22, 2009; www.whitehouse.gov; Barack Obama, "Executive Order 13493 - Review of Detention Policy Options," The White House, January 22, 2009, www.whitehouse.gov; Barack Obama, Executive Order 13491 - Ensuring Lawful Interrogations," The White House, January 22, 2009, www.whitehouse.gov; Jonathan Hafetz, *Habeas Corpus after 9/11: Confronting America's New Global Detention System* (New York: New York University Press, 2011).

104. David Johnston, "US Says Rendition to Continue, but with more Oversight," *New York Times*, August 24, 2009.

105. Carol Rosenberg, "Why Obama Hasn't Closed Guantanamo Camps," *Miami Herald*, January 7, 2012.

106. Helene Cooper, "Five Guantánamo Prisoners Are Released to Kazakhstan," *New York Times*, December 31, 2014; Missy Ryan and Adam Goldman, "U.S. prepares to Accelerate Detainee Transfers from Guantanamo Bay Prison," *Washington Post*, December 24, 2014.

107. Adam Goldman, "U.S. quietly Whittles Down Foreign Detainee Population at Facility in Afghanistan," *Washington Post*, February 25, 2014.

108. Sudarsan Raghavan, "U.S. Closes last Detainee Site in Afghanistan as Troop Pullout Advances," *Washington Post*, December 12, 2014.

109. David Johnston, "US Says Rendition to Continue, but with more Oversight," *New York Times*, August 24, 2009.

110. Karen DeYoung, Greg Miller, and Greg Jaffe, "U.S. Indicts Somali on Terrorism Charges," *Washington Post*, July 5, 2011.

111. Deborah Feyerick and Lateef Mungin, "Alleged al Qaeda Operative Abu Anas al Libi Pleads Not Guilty," CNN, October 15, 2013, www.cnn.com; Adam Goldman, "Video Shows U.S. Abduction of Accused al-Qaeda Terrorist on Trial for Embassy Bombings," *Washington Post*, January 10, 2014.

112. Peter Finn, "The Post-9/11 Life of an American Charged with Murder," *Washington Post*, September 4, 2010; Anna Gearan, "American Jailed in Yemen, Sharif Mobley, Has Disappeared and Is in Danger, His Lawyers Say," *Washington Post*, April 11, 2014.

113. Keir Simmons and Charlene Gubash, "American Sharif Mobley Hasn't Appeared in Yemen Court for a Year," NBC News, January 20, 2014, http://www.nbcnews.com/news/world/american-sharif-mobley-hasnt-appeared-yemen-court-year-n288856.

114. Peter Finn and Kafia A. Hosh, "I Felt Like I was Getting Kidnapped," *Washington Post*, January 22, 2011; Mark Mazzetti, "Detained American Says He Was Beaten in Kuwait," *New York Times*, January 5, 2011.

115. Nick Baumann, "American Muslim Alleges FBI Had a Hand in His Torture," *Mother Jones*, April 17, 2012; Martin Von Krogh, "American Seeks Political Asylum in Sweden, Alleging Torture, FBI Coercion," NBC News, April, 2012, www.usnews.nbcnews.com.

116. Dana Priest and William Arkin, *Top Secret America: The Rise of the New American Security State* (New York: Little, Brown and Company, 2011), 14.

117. Micah Zenko, "The Long Third War," *Foreign Policy*, October 30, 2012.

118. James Sandler, "Kemal Derwish: The Life and Death of an American Terrorist," *Frontline* (Public Broadcasting Service), October 16, 2003, www.pbs.org.

119. Bill Roggio and Alexander Mayor, "Charting the Data for U.S. Drone Strikes in Pakistan," *Long War Journal*, December 13, 2013, www.longwarjournal.org.

120. Eric Schmitt and David Sanger, "Pakistan Shift Could Curtail Drone Strikes," *Washington Post*, February 22, 2008.

121. Chris Woods, "Militants and Civilians Killed in Multiple U.S. Somalia Strikes," Bureau of Investigative Journalism, February 22, 2012, www.thebureauinvestigates.com.

122. Bill Roggio and Alexander Mayor, "Charting the Data for U.S. Drone Strikes in Pakistan," *Long War Journal*, December 13, 2013, www.longwarjournal.org; "Drone Wars Yemen: Analysis," New America, accessed November 23, 2014, http://securitydata.newamerica.net/drones/yemen/analysis.

123. "Drone Wars Pakistan: Analysis," New America, accessed November 23, 2014, http://securitydata.newamerica.net; "Drone Wars Yemen: Analysis," New America, accessed November 23, 2014, http://securitydata.newamerica.net; "Get the Data: Drone Wars," Bureau of Investigative Journalism, accessed November 23, 2014, www.thebureauinvestigates.com.

124. J.M. Berger, *Jihad Joe: Americans Who Go to War in the Name of Islam* (Washington, D.C.: Potomac Books, 2011), 115–126, 133–148.

125. Peter Finn, "Awlaki Directed Christmas 'Underwear Bomber' Plot, Justice Department Memo Says," *Washington Post*, February 10, 2012.

126. Charlie Savage, "Secret U.S. Memo Made Legal Case to Kill a Citizen," *New York Times*, October 8 2011.

127. Mark Hosenball and Matt Spetalnick, "Drone Strike Ends Long Hunt for U.S.-Born Awlaki," Reuters, September 30, 2011, www.reuters.com; Mark Mazzetti, Charlie Savage, and Scott Shane, "How a U.S. Citizen Came to Be in America's Cross Hairs, *New York Times*, March 9, 2013.

128. Aaron Y. Zelin, "American Jihadi," *Foreign Policy*, September 30, 2011.

129. Tom Finn and Noah Browning, "An American Teenager in Yemen Paying for the Sins of His Father," *Time*, October 27, 2011; Mark Mazzetti, Charlie Savage, and Scott Shane, "How a U.S. Citizen Came to Be in America's Crosshairs," *New York Times*, March 9, 2013.

130. Scott Shane and Eric Schmitt, "One Drone Victim's Trail From Raleigh to Pakistan," *New York Times*, May 22, 2013.

131. Adam Entous, Damian Paletta, and Felicia Schwartz, "American, Italian Hostages Killed in CIA Drone Strike in January," *Wall Street Journal*, April 23, 2015.

132. Eric Schmitt, "Adam Gadahn Was Propagandist for al-Qaeda Who Sold Terror in English," *New York Times*, April 23, 2015.

Chapter 3

1. Charles Nemeth, *Homeland Security: An Introduction to Principles and Practice* (Boca Raton: CRC Press, 2013), 255.

2. "State Counterterrorism Profiles," in *Top Secret America: A Washington Post Investigation*, accessed July 14, 2014, http://projects.washingtonpost.com/top-secret-america/states.

3. Charles Nemeth, *Homeland Security: An Introduction to Principles and Practice* (Boca Raton: CRC Press, 2013), 270; "State and Major Urban Area Fusion Centers," Department of Homeland Security, accessed July 1, 2014, www.dhs.gov/state-and-major-urban-area-fusion-centers.

4. Lois Davis, et al., *Long-Term Effect of Law Enforcement's Post-9/11 Focus on Counterterrorism and Homeland Security* (Santa Monica: RAND Corporation, 2010), 52; Charles Nemeth, *Homeland Security: An Introduction to Principles and Practice* (Boca Raton: CRC Press, 2013), 340.

5. Charles Nemeth, *Homeland Security: An Introduction to Principles and Practice* (Boca Raton: CRC Press, 2013) 340–342, "Protecting America from Terrorist Attack: Our Joint Terrorism Task Forces," Federal Bureau of Investigation, accessed July 14, 2014, www.fbi.gov/about-us/investigate/terrorism/terrorism_jttfs.

6. "State Counterterrorism Profiles," in *Top Secret America: A Washington Post Investigation*, accessed July 14, 2014, http://projects.washingtonpost.com/top-secret-america/states.

7. Brian A. Reaves, "Federal Law Enforcement Officers, 2008," Department of Justice, Bureau of Justice Statistics, June 2012, www.bjs.gov.

8. Brian A. Reaves, "Census of State and Local Law Enforcement Agencies," Bureau of Justice Statistics, Department of Justice, July 2012, www.bjs.gov.

9. Brian A. Reaves, "Census of State and Local Law Enforcement Agencies," Bureau of Justice Statistics, Department of Justice, July 2012, www.bjs.gov.

10. Lois David, et al., *Long-Term Effects of Law Enforcement's Post-9/11 Focus on Counterterrorism and Homeland Security* (Santa Monica: RAND Corporation, 2010), 39, 111–112.

11. Radley Balko, *Rise of the Warrior Cop: The Militarization of America's Police Forces* (New York: PublicAffairs, 2014), Kindle edition, chapter 7.

12. Christopher Ingraham, "The Pentagon Gave Nearly Half a Billion Dollars of Military Gear to Local Law Enforcement Last Year," *Washington* Post, August 14, 2014; David Welna, "Drawing on Pentagon Surplus, Police Now Wield Weapons of War," *All Things Considered* (National Public Radio), August 15, 2014, http://www.npr.org.

13. Radley Balko, *Rise of the Warrior Cop: The Militarization of America's Police Forces* (New York: PublicAffairs, 2014), Kindle edition, chapter 7.

14. Brian A. Reaves, "Census of State and Local Law Enforcement Agencies," Department of Justice, Bureau of Justice Statistics, July 2012, www.bjs.gov.

15. Matt Apuzzo and Adam Goldman, *Enemies Within: Inside the NYDP's Secret Spying Unit and Bin Laden's Final Plot against America* (New York: Simon and Schuster, 2013), 15, 30; *Learning from 9/11: Organizational Change in the New York City and Arlington County, Va. Police Departments* (Washington, D.C.: National Institute of Justice, Department of Justice, 2009), 3.

16. Matt Apuzzo and Adam Goldman, *Enemies Within: Inside the NYDP's Secret Spying Unit and Bin Laden's Final Plot against America* (New York: Simon and Schuster, 2013), 47–48.

17. Michael Daly, "NYPD on the Real 'Enemies Within': Going Undercover With Jihadis," *Daily Beast*, September 9, 2013, http://www.thedailybeast.com.

18. Ramzi Kassem, "The Long Roots of the NYPD Spying Program," *The Nation*, June 13, 2013.

19. Matt Apuzzo and Adam Goldman, *Enemies Within: Inside the NYDP's Secret Spying Unit and Bin Laden's Final Plot against America* (New York: Simon and Schuster, 2013), 52, 128, 180.

20. Matt Apuzzo and Adam Goldman, "With CIA Help, NYPD Moves Covertly into Muslim Areas," in *AP's Probe into NYPD Intelligence Operations* (Associated Press), August 23, 2011, www.ap.org/media-center/nypd/investigation.

21. Grey Fisher, "The New NYPD: Pushing Civil Liberty Bounds to Keep the City Safe," *National Security Journal* (Cambridge, MA: Harvard Law School, September 20, 2011), http://harvardnsj.org.

22. Chris Hawley, "NYPD Monitored Muslims All Over the Northeast," in *AP's Probe Into NYPD Intelligence Operations* (Associated Press), February 18, 2012, www.ap.org/media-center/nypd/investigation.

23. Matt Apuzzo and Adam Goldman, *Enemies Within: Inside the NYDP's Secret Spying Unit and Bin Laden's Final Plot against America* (New York: Simon and Schuster, 2013), 140.

24. Adam Goldman and Matt Apuzzo, "With Cameras, Informants, NYPD Eyed Mosques," in *AP's Probe Into NYPD Intelligence Operations* (Associated Press), February 23, 2012, www.ap.org/media-center/nypd/investigation.

25. Matt Apuzzo and Adam Goldman, *Enemies Within: Inside the NYDP's Secret Spying Unit and Bin Laden's Final Plot against America* (New York: Simon and Schuster, 2013), 191.

26. Matt Apuzzo and Adam Goldman, *Enemies Within: Inside the NYDP's Secret Spying Unit and Bin Laden's Final Plot against America* (New York: Simon and Schuster, 2013), 180.

27. Matt Apuzzo and Adam Goldman, *Enemies Within: Inside the NYDP's Secret Spying Unit and Bin Laden's Final Plot against America* (New York: Simon and Schuster, 2013), 181; Adam Goldman and Matt Apuzzo, "NYPD Designates Mosques as Terrorist Organizations," in *AP's Probe Into NYPD Intelligence Operations* (Associated Press), August 28, 2013, www.ap.org/media-center/nypd/investigation.

28. Adam Goldman and Matt Apuzzo, "NYPD Built Secret Files on Mosques outside NY," in *AP's Probe Into NYPD Intelligence Operations* (Associated Press), February 22, 2012, www.ap.org/media-center/nypd/investigation; Adam Goldman and Matt Apuzzo, "With CIA Help, NYPD Moves Covertly in Muslim Areas," in *AP's Probe Into NYPD Intelligence Operations* (Associated Press), August 23, 2011, www.ap.org/media-center/nypd/investigation.

29. Chris Hawley, "NYPD Monitored Muslims All Over the Northeast," in *AP's Probe Into NYPD Intelligence Operations*, February 18, 2012, www.ap.org/media-center/nypd/investigation.

30. Ion Bogdan Vasi and David Strang, "Civil Liberty in America: The Diffusion of Municipal Bill of Rights Resolutions after the Passage of the USA PATRIOT Act," *American Journal of Sociology* 114, no. 6 (May 2009), 1716–1764.

31. Susan Herman, *Taking Liberties: The War on Terror and the Erosion of American Democracy* (Oxford: Oxford University Press, 2011), 213.

32. Tung Yin, "Joint Terrorism Task Forces as a Window into the Security vs. Civil Liberties Debate," *Florida Coastal Law Review* 13, no. 1 (2012), 1–32.

33. *Muslim Americans: No Signs of Growth in Alienation or Support for Extremism* (Washington, D.C.: Pew Research Center, August 2011), 31.

34. "Initiative to Combat Post-9/11 Backlash," Civil Rights Division, Department of Justice, accessed July 3, 2014, www.justice.gov/crt/legalinfo/

discrimupdate.php; "Title VII: Religious Accommodation Provisions, the MTA, and Fairness," *New York Times*, June 3, 2013.

35. "Court Enters Consent Decree Granting Muslim Girl's Right to Wear Headscarf to School," *Religious Freedom in Focus* 4 (May 2004), www.justice.gov; "United States v. Muskogee Public School District," United States District Court, Eastern District of Oklahoma, accessed July 3, 2014, www .justice.gov.

36. "Suit Filed Against County that Barred Corrections Worker from Wearing Headscarf," *Religious Freedom in Focus* 39 (June/July 2009), www.justice.gov.

37. "ACLU Files Lawsuit on Behalf of Muslim Woman Forced to Remove Head Covering in Georgia Courthouse," American Civil Liberty Union, December 14, 2010, www.aclu.org; Josh Levs, "Police to Get Training after Head-scarf Wearer's Arrest," CNN, December 23, 2008, www.cnn.com.

38. "Georgia Policy Change to Allow Religious Headcoverings in Court; DOJ Closes Inquiry," *Religious Freedom in Focus* 39 (June/July 2009), www.justice.gov.

39. "DOJ Sues New York Corrections Department Over Refusal to Make Religious Accommodations," *Religious Freedom in Focus* 23 (March 2007), www.justice.gov.

40. "Justice Department Files Suit against School District over Failure to Accommodate Muslim School Police Officer," *Religious Freedom in Focus* 60 (May 2014), www.justice.gov.

41. Sophia Pearson, "Philadelphia Tells Muslim Police to Trim Beards or Lose Jobs," Bloomberg News, October 19, 2005, www.bloomberg.com; "Pennsylvania Judge Upholds Muslim Firefighter's Religious Liberty in ACLU Lawsuit," American Civil Liberties Union, June 1, 2005, www.aclu.org.

42. *Confronting Discrimination in the Post-9/11 Era: Challenges and Opportunities Ten Years Later* (Washington, D.C.: Department of Justice, October 2011), 11.

43. "Civil Rights Division Settles Muslim Student Prayer Case," *Religious Freedom in Focus* 25 (May 2007), www.justice.gov.

44. Manya A. Brachear, "Settlement Reached in Muslim's Suit over Denial of Time Off for Hajj," *Chicago Tribune*, October 19, 2011; Pete Yost, "Muslim School Teacher Denied Hajj, U.S. Sues Illinois School District," *Christian Science Monitor*, December 14, 2010.

45. "The Religious Land Use and Institutionalized Persons Act," Civil Rights Division, Department of Justice, accessed July 11, 2014, www.justice.gov/crt.

46. *Enforcing Religious Freedom in Prison* (Washington, D.C.: United States Commission on Civil Rights, September 2008), 85.

47. Matt Coker, "Souhair Katib Can Sue County of Orange for Forcing Her to Remove Her Hijab: Supreme Court," *OC Weekly*, October 3, 2011; "Court Holding Facility Is Covered by RLUIPA, En Banc Court Rules," *Religious Freedom in Focus* 45 (March 2011), www.justice.gov.

48. "MCSO Implements Muslim Head Scarf Policy in County Jails," American Civil Liberties Union of Arizona, February 4, 2010, www.acluaz.org.

49. "Appeals Court Upholds Prisoner's Right to Wear Quarter-Inch Beard," *Religious Freedom in Focus* 56 (April 2013), www.justice.gov.

50. Eugene Volokh, "Supreme Court Will Hear Muslim Prisoner's Religious Challenge to Prison No-Beards Policy," *Washington Post*, March 3, 2014.

51. Adam Liptak, "Ban on Prison Beards Violates Muslim Rights, Supreme Court Rules," *New York Times*, January 20, 2015.

52. James Shea, "Feds Speak with Sullivan County Sheriff about Religious Complaints," *Bristol Herald Courier*, December 20, 2012; "United States Closes Investigation over Access to Religious Literature after County Jail Implements Changes," *Religious Freedom in Focus* 56 (April 2013), www.justice.gov.

53. "Prisoners Gain Access to Religious Materials, Resolving DOJ Lawsuit," *Religious Freedom in Focus* 50 (January 2012), www.justice.gov; United States Application for Intervention, United States v. Berkeley County Sheriff's Office, Civil Action 2:10-02594-MBS (United States District Court, District of South Carolina, Charleston Division, April 2011).

54. *Report on the Tenth Anniversary of the Religious Land Use and Institutionalized Persons Act* (Washington, D.C.: Department of Justice, September 2010), 3.

55. *Report on the Tenth Anniversary of the Religious Land Use and Institutionalized Persons Act* (Washington, D.C.: Department of Justice, September 2010), 4.

56. Ihsan Bagby, *The American Mosque 2011: Basic Characteristics of the American Mosque and Attitudes of Mosque Leaders* (Hartford, CT: Faith Communities Today, Cooperative Congregational Studies Partnership, January 2012), 5.

57. *Confronting Discrimination in the Post-9/11 Era: Challenges and Opportunities Ten Years Later* (Washington, D.C.: Department of Justice, October 2011), 12.

58. Brief of the United States as Amicus Curiae, Albanian Association Fund v. Wayne Township, Civil Action 2:06-cv-3217 (United States District Court, District of New Jersey, October 2007); "Township Taking of Mosque's Property Implicates RLUIPA, United States Argues," *Religious Freedom in Focus* 28 (June/July 2007), www.justice.gov.

59. Complaint of the United States, United States v. County of Henrico, Civil Action No. 3:11-cv-583-HEH (United States District Court, Eastern District of Virginia, September 2011); *Confronting Discrimination in the Post-9/11 Era: Challenges and Opportunities Ten Years Later* (Washington, D.C.: Department of Justice, October 2011), 12.

60. Mike Esterl, "Mosque Zoning Row Draws Scrutiny," *Wall Street Journal*, August 13, 2011; DOJ Reaches Settlement in Georgia Mosque Dispute," *Religious Freedom in Focus* 47 (August 2011), www.justice.gov.

61. Amanda Vogt and Rachel Osterman, "Morton Grove, Muslim Group OK Mosque Deal," *Chicago Tribune*, June 9, 2004; *Confronting Discrimination in the Post-9/11 Era: Challenges and Opportunities Ten Years Later*

(Washington, D.C.: Department of Justice, October 2011), 12; "Morton Grove, IL Settles Lawsuit with School after DOJ Mediation," *Religious Freedom in Focus* 5 (June/July 2004), www.justice.gov.

62. "DOJ Closes RLUIPA Investigation after Illinois Village Allows Mosque Expansion," *Religious Freedom in Focus* 32 (March/April 2008), www.justice .gov; *Report on the Tenth Anniversary of the Religious Land Use and Institutionalized Persons Act* (Washington, D.C.: Department of Justice, September 2010), 4.

63. "Agreement Reached to Resolve Mosque Construction Dispute in Lomita, California," *Religious Freedom in Focus* 56 (April 2013), www.justice .gov; Ruben Vives, "Complaint Filed over Lomita's Denial of Bid for New Mosque," *Los Angeles Times*, March 22, 2012.

64. "Court Dismisses RLUIPA Appeal after Settlement," *Religious Freedom in Focus* 59 (February 2014), www.justice.gov.

65. "Justice Department Files Suit Against City of St. Anthony Village over Denial of Permit for Mosque," *Justice News*, August 27, 2014, www.justice.gov/ opa; John Croman (KARE 11 News), "Justice Department Sues Minnesota City over Mosque Permit," *USA Today*, August 28, 2014.

66. Matthew Grimley, "Meet the Abu Hiraira Islamic Center," *Twin Cities Daily Planet*, January 28, 2015.

67. Andrea Elliot, "The Man Behind the Anti-Sharia Movement," *New York Times*, July 30, 2011.

68. "Applying God's Law: Religious Courts and Mediation in the U.S.," Pew Research Center, April 2013, http://www.pewforum.org/2013/04/08/applying-gods-law-religious-courts-and-mediation-in-the-us; Faiza Patel, Matthew Duss, and Amos Toh, *Foreign Law Bans: Legal Uncertainties and Practical Problems* (Washington, D.C.: Center for American Progress and the Brennan Center for Justice, May 2013), 5–6, 50.

69. Faiza Patel, Matthew Duss, and Amos Toh, *Foreign Law Bans: Legal Uncertainties and Practical Problems* (Washington, D.C.: Center for American Progress and the Brennan Center for Justice, May 2013), 7.

70. Asma T. Uddin and Dave Pantzer, *A First Amendment Analysis of Anti-Sharia Initiatives* (Washington, D.C.: Institute for Social Policy and Understanding, May 2012), 23.

71. Faiza Patel, Matthew Duss, and Amos Toh, *Foreign Law Bans: Legal Uncertainties and Practical Problems* (Washington, D.C.: Center for American Progress and the Brennan Center for Justice, May 2013), 7.

72. Mary Wisniewski, "U.S. Judge Bars Oklahoma from Implementing Anti-Sharia Law," Reuters, August 17, 2013.

73. Asma T. Uddin and Dave Pantzer, *A First Amendment Analysis of Anti-Sharia Initiatives* (Washington, D.C.: Institute for Social Policy and Understanding, May 2012), 14.

74. "Applying God's Law: Religious Courts and Mediation in the U.S.," Pew Research Center, April 2013, http://www.pewforum.org/2013/04/08/applying-gods-law-religious-courts-and-mediation-in-the-us/.

75. Faiza Patel, Matthew Duss, and Amos Toh, *Foreign Law Bans: Legal Uncertainties and Practical Problems* (Washington, D.C.: Center for American Progress and the Brennan Center for Justice, May 2013), 15–16.

76. Faiza Patel, Matthew Duss, and Amos Toh, *Foreign Law Bans: Legal Uncertainties and Practical Problems* (Washington, D.C.: Center for American Progress and the Brennan Center for Justice, May 2013), 34–35.

77. Omar Sacirbey, "Anti-Shari'ah Movement Changes Tactics and Gains Success," *Religious News Service*, May 16, 2013, www.religionnews.com.

78. Omar Sacirbey, "Citing Risk to Adoptions, Missouri Gov. Vetoes Anti-Shariah Bill," *Religious News Service*, June 4, 2013, www.religionnews.com.

79. "State Legislation Restricting Use of Foreign or Religious Law," Pew Research Center, April 2013, http://www.pewforum.org/2013/04/08/state-legislation-restricting-use-of-foreign-or-religious-law/.

80. "Alabama Foreign Laws in Court, Amendment 1(2014)," BallotPedia, accessed February 11, 2015, http://ballotpedia.org/Alabama_Foreign_Laws_in_Court,_Amendment_1_(2014); Julia Edwards (Reuters), "Alabama Voters Pass Sharia Law Ban," *Huffington Post*, November 5, 2014.

Chapter 4

1. "Islam Rising: What Do We Think of Islam," *Los Angeles Times*, April 6, 1993, http://articles.latimes.com/1993-04-06/news/wr-19921_1_islam.

2. "National Day of Prayer and Remembrance," Washington National Cathedral, September 14, 2001, www.nationalcathedral.org.

3. "Islam Is Peace, Says President" (remarks by President George W. Bush, Islamic Center of Washington), The White House, Office of the Press Secretary, September 17, 2001, http://georgewbush-whitehouse.archives.gov/news/releases/2001/09/20010917-11.html.

4. Christopher Bail, *Terrified: How Anti-Muslim Fringe Organizations Became Mainstream* (Princeton: Princeton University Press, 2015), Kindle edition (chapter 7).

5. Washington Post-ABC News Poll, August 2010, available through the Washington Post Public Opinion Poll Archive, http://www.washingtonpost.com/wp-srv/politics/polls/poll-archive.html.

6. Washington Post-ABC News Poll, August 2010, available through the Washington Post Public Opinion Poll Archive, www.washingtonpost.com/wp-srv/politics/polls/poll-archive.html.

7. Washington Post-ABC News Poll, August 2010, available through the Washington Post Public Opinion Poll Archive, www.washingtonpost.com/wp-srv/politics/polls/poll-archive.html.

8. Pew Research Center and Pew Forum on Religion and Public Life, *Public Remains Conflicted Over Islam* (Washington, D.C.: Pew Research Center for People and the Press, August 2010), 2.

9. "Time Poll Results: Americans' View on the Campaign, Religion and the Mosque Controversy," *Time*, August 18, 2010, http://content.time.com/time/politics/article/0,8599,2011680,00.html.

10. Lori Peek, *Behind the Backlash: Muslim Americans after 9/11* (New Delhi: Social Science Press, 2012), 13–14.

11. Robert Wuthnow, *America and the Challenges of Religious Diversity* (Princeton: Princeton University Press, 2007), 216.

12. Arab American Institute and Zogby International, *American Views of Arab and Muslim Americans* (Washington, D.C.: Arab American Institute), September 2010, 6–7.

13. Pew Research Center, *Growing Concern about Rise of Islamic Extremism at Home and Abroad* (Washington, D.C.: Pew Research Center for People and the Press, September 2014), 6.

14. Pew Research Center and Pew Forum on Religion and Public Life, *Post-9/11 Attitudes: Religion More Prominent, Muslim-Americans More Accepted* (Pew Research Center for People and the Press, December 2001), 1.

15. Pew Research Center and Pew Forum on Religion and Public Life, *Religion and Politics: Contention and Consensus* (Pew Research Center for People and the Press, July 2003), 24; Pew Research Center and Pew Forum on Religion and Public Life, *Views of Muslim Americans Hold Steady after London Bombings* (Pew Research Center for People and the Press, July 2005), 1; Pew Research Center and Pew Forum on Religion and Public Life, *Public Expresses Mixed Views of Islam, Mormons* (Pew Research Center for People and the Press, September 2007), 1.

16. "Time Poll Results: Americans' View on the Campaign, Religion and the Mosque Controversy," *Time*, August 18, 2010, http://content.time.com/time/politics/article/0,8599,2011680,00.html.

17. Arab American Institute and Zogby Analytics, *American Attitudes Toward Arabs and Muslims*, July 2014, www.aaiusa.org/reports/american-attitudes-toward-arabs-and-muslims-2014.

18. Pam Belluck, "Unrepentant Shoe Bomber Is Given a Life Sentence," *New York Times*, January 31, 2003; Jenny Booth, "Gloucester Shoebomber Jailed for 13 Years," *The Times*, April 22, 2005.

19. *EU Terrorism Situation and Trends Report 2007* (The Hague: Europol, 2007), 19; "UK 2006 Liquid Explosives Plot Trial Overview," Transportation Security Administration, September 8, 2008, http://www.tsa.gov/press/releases/2008/09/08/uk-2006-liquid-explosives-plot-trial-overview.

20. Scott Shane and Eric Lipton, "Passengers' Quick Action Halted Attack," *New York Times*, December 26, 2009; "Summary of the White House Review of the December 25, 2009 Attempted Terrorist Attack," The White House, Office of the Press Secretary, January 8, 2009, http://www.whitehouse.gov/the-press-office/white-house-review-summary-regarding-12252009-attempted-terrorist-attack.

21. Spencer S. Hsu, "Al-Qaeda Operative Is Charged in N.Y. Subway Plot," *Washington Post*, July 8, 2010; G. Sulzberger, "Two More Men Charged In Plot to Bomb Subways," *New York Times*, February 25, 2010.

22. Al Baker and William Rashbaum, "Police Find Car Bomb in Times Square," *New York Times*, May 1, 2010; Mark Mazzetti, Sabrina, Tavernise, and Jack Healy, "Suspect, Charged, Said to Admit to Role in Plot," *New York Times*, May 4, 2010.

23. Gene Johnson, "Naveed Haq Guilty in Jewish Center Trial," *Seattle Times*, December 15, 2009; Jennifer Sullivan, "Seattle Jewish Center Shooter Gets Life Sentence," *Los Angeles Times*, January 15, 2010.

24. James Dao, "Man Claims Terror Ties in Little Rock Shooting," *New York Times*, January 22, 2010.

25. Philip Rucker and Ellen Nakashima, "Hasan Charged with 13 Counts of Murder," *Washington Post*, November 13, 2009; Eric Schmitt and Eric Lipton, "Focus on Internet Imams as Al Qaeda Recruiters," *New York Times*, December 31, 2009.

26. John Eligon and Michael Cooper, "Blasts at Boston Marathon Kill 3," *New York Times*, April 15, 2013; Scott Wilson, Greg Miller, and Sari Horwitz, "Boston Bombing Suspect Cites U.S. Wars as Motivation," *Washington Post*, April 23, 2013.

27. Mark Murray, "ISIS Threat: Fear of Terrorist Attack Soars to 9/11 High, NBC News/WSJ Poll Finds," NBC News, http://www.nbcnews.com/politics/first-read/isis-threat-fear-terror-attack-soars-9-11-high-nbc-n199496.

28. Arab American Institute and Zogby Analytics, *American Attitudes Toward Arabs and Muslims*, July 2014, www.aaiusa.org/reports/american-attitudes-toward-arabs-and-muslims-2014.

29. Robert M. Entman, "Framing: Towards Clarification of a Fractured Paradigm," *Journal of Communication* 43, no. 4 (1993): 54–55; Maxwell McCombs, "A Look at Agenda-Setting: Past, Present and Future," *Journalism Studies* 6, no. 4 (2005): 546.

30. Brigitte L. Nacos and Oscar Torres-Reyna, *Fueling Our Fears: Stereotyping, Media Coverage, and Public Opinion of Muslim Americans* (Lanham, MD: Rowman and Littlefield, 2007), 7–8.

31. Brigitte L. Nacos and Oscar Torres-Reyna, *Fueling Our Fears: Stereotyping, Media Coverage, and Public Opinion of Muslim Americans* (Lanham, MD: Rowman and Littlefield, 2007), 14–15.

32. Brigitte L. Nacos and Oscar Torres-Reyna, *Fueling Our Fears: Stereotyping, Media Coverage, and Public Opinion of Muslim Americans* (Lanham, MD: Rowman and Littlefield, 2007), 15, 17–18.

33. Brigitte L. Nacos and Oscar Torres-Reyna, *Fueling Our Fears: Stereotyping, Media Coverage, and Public Opinion of Muslim Americans* (Lanham, MD: Rowman and Littlefield, 2007), 25–27.

34. Brigitte L. Nacos and Oscar Torres-Reyna, *Fueling Our Fears: Stereotyping, Media Coverage, and Public Opinion of Muslim Americans* (Lanham, MD: Rowman and Littlefield, 2007), 25–27.

35. "Anti-Muslim Stereotypes Increase on TV, Hampering Understanding," Media Tenor, http://us.mediatenor.com/en/library/newsletters/162/anti-muslim-stereotypes-increase-on-tv-hampering-understanding, accessed January 14, 2015; Roland Schatz, "U.S. TV Primetime News Prefer Stereotypes: Muslims Framed mostly as Criminals" (presentation, *Muslim-Christian Relations in the 21st Century: Challenges and Opportunities*, Alwaleed Bin Talal Center for Muslim Christian Understanding, Georgetown University, Washington, D.C., November 21, 2013).

36. Peter Gottschalk and Gabriel Greenberg, *Islamophobia: Making Muslims the Enemy* (Lanham, MD. Rowman and Littlefield, 2008), 1.

37. Enayat Najafizada and Rod Nordland, "Afghans Avenge Florida Koran Burning, Killing 12," *New York Times*, April 1, 2011.

38. Ian Lloyd Neubauer, "Harsh Sentence a Warning to Australia's Young Muslim Zealots," *Time*, May 14, 2013.

39. *Newsweek*, September 17, 2012.

40. Charles Kurzman, *Muslim-American Terrorism in 2013* (Raleigh, NC: Duke University, February 2013), 4.

41. Charles Kurzman, "Islamic Statements Against Terrorism," http://kurzman.unc.edu/islamic-statements-against-terrorism, updated March 15, 2012; Sheila Musaji, "Muslim Voices Against Extremism and Terrorism," *The American Muslim*, June 1, 2007, http://theamericanmuslim.org.

42. Brigitte L. Nacos and Oscar Torres-Reyna, *Fueling Our Fears: Stereotyping, Media Coverage, and Public Opinion of Muslim Americans* (Lanham, MD: Rowman and Littlefield, 2007), 29–31; "Study Shows Increase in Negative Messages About Muslims in the Media," University of North Carolina, Chapel Hill, accessed December 11, 2014, http://college.unc.edu/2012/11/29/bailstudy.

43. Jack G. Shaheen, *Reel Bad Arabs: How Hollywood Vilifies a People* (Northampton, MA: Olive Branch Press, 2001), 2, 7, 10–12, 27. Shaheen's original study analyzed more than 950 films. In an updated study, released in 2012, he analyzed an additional 125 pre-9/11 movies.

44. Jack G. Shaheen, *Guilty: Hollywood's Verdict on Arabs after 9/11* (Northampton, MA: Olive Branch Press, 2008), 32, 121–122, 127–131, 154–155, 158, 165–166, 178–179.

45. Jack G. Shaheen, *Guilty: Hollywood's Verdict on Arabs after 9/11* (Northampton, MA: Olive Branch Press, 2008), 25, 35.

46. Jack G. Shaheen, *Guilty: Hollywood's Verdict on Arabs after 9/11* (Northampton, MA: Olive Branch Press, 2008), 45–49.

47. Evelyn Alsultany, *Arabs and Muslims in the Media: Race and Representation after 9/11* (New York: New York University Press, 2012), 21–27.

48. Evelyn Alsultany, *Arabs and Muslims in the Media: Race and Representation after 9/11* (New York: New York University Press, 2012), 20, 28.

49. Bernard Lewis, "The Roots of Muslim Rage," *The Atlantic*, September 1990, 60.

50. Samuel Huntington, "The Clash of Civilizations?" *Foreign Affairs* 73, no. 3 (Summer 1993), 22, 31–32.

51. Daniel Pipes, "The Muslims Are Coming! The Muslims Are Coming!" *The National Review*, November 1990, reproduced with revisions by the Middle EastForum, http://www.danielpipes.org/198/the-muslims-are-coming-the-muslims-are-coming.

52. Daniel Pipes, "Distinguishing between Islam and Islamism" (presentation, Center for Strategic and International Studies, June 30, 1998), http://www.danielpipes.org/954/distinguishing-between-islam-and-islamism.

53. Daniel Pipes, "The New Anti-Semitism," *The Jewish Exponent*, October 16, 1997.

54. Daniel Pipes, "The Danger Within: Militant Islam in America," *Commentary*, November 2001, reproduced by the Middle East Forum, http://www.danielpipes.org/77/the-danger-within-militant-islam-in-america.

55. Daniel Pipes, "The Danger Within: Militant Islam in America," *Commentary*, November 2001, reproduced by the Middle East Forum, http://www.danielpipes.org/77/the-danger-within-militant-islam-in-america.

56. "About Campus Watch," Campus Watch, accessed January 20, 2015, http://www.campus-watch.org/about.php; Wajahat Ali, *Fear, Inc.: The Roots of the Islamophobia Network in America* (Washington, D.C.: Center for American Progress, 2011), 41.

57. "About Islamist Watch," Islamist Watch, accessed January 20, 2015, http://www.islamist-watch.org/about.php; Wajahat Ali, *Fear, Inc.: The Roots of the Islamophobia Network in America* (Washington, D.C.: Center for American Progress, 2011), 42.

58. Christina Sterbenz, "New York Times Published Anti-Islamist Ad the Same Day the 9/11 Museum Opened," *Business Insider*, May 22, 2014, http://www.businessinsider.com/ipt-new-york-times-ad-2014-5.

59. "About the David Horowitz Freedom Center," David Horowtiz Freedom Center, http://www.horowitzfreedomcenter.org/about, accessed January 21, 2015.

60. Fern Sidman, "FrontPage Editor at Bklyn College: Palestinians Are Morally Sick," Arutz Sheva-7 (Israeli National News), accessed January 21, 2015, http://www.israelnationalnews.com/News/News.aspx/142844#.VL_WYr4-B0p.

61. "About the David Horowitz Freedom Center," David Horowtiz Freedom Center, http://www.horowitzfreedomcenter.org/about, accessed January 21, 2015.

62. Wajahat Ali, *Fear Inc.: The Roots of the Islamophobia Network in America* (Washington, D.C.: Center for American Progress, 2011), 27.

63. "Pam Geller," Southern Poverty Law Center, accessed January 21, 2015, http://www.splcenter.org/get-informed/intelligence-files/profiles/pamela-geller.

64. "Pam Geller," Southern Poverty Law Center, accessed January 21, 2015, http://www.splcenter.org/get-informed/intelligence-files/profiles/pamela-geller.

65. Nathan Lean, *The Islamophobia Industry: How the Right Manufactures Fear of Muslims* (London: Pluto Press, 2012), 46, 51, 53.

66. Evelyn Alsultany, *Arabs and Muslims in the Media: Race and Representation after 9/11* (New York: New York University Press, 2012), 167; Shani McManus, "Community Reacts to Mosque," *Sun Sentinel*, July 27, 2010.

67. Anti-Defamation League, *Stop Islamization of America* (New York: Anti-Defamation League, September 2012), 6.

68. The American Freedom Defense Initiative (AFDI), accessed January 12, 2015, http://freedomdefense.typepad.com/about.html.

69. Stav Ziv, "Controversial Anti-Muslim Ads Coming to New York City Transit," *Newsweek*, September 24, 2014, http://www.newsweek.com/controversial-anti-muslim-ads-coming-new-york-city-transit-272975.

70. Paul Duggan, "In Metro Ads, Pro-Israel Group Features Photo of Hitler," *Washington Post*, May 15, 2014.

71. William G. Boykin, et al., *Sharia: The Threat to America* (Washington, D.C.: Center for Security Policy, 2010), 17–18, 27–33, 77–79

72. David Yerushalmi, "David Yerushalmi's Strategic Analysis of Lawfare: How to Stop the Sharia Threat" (video presentation), PipeLineNews. org, November 30, 2011, http://www.pipelinenews.org/2011/nov/30/David-Yerushalmis-Strategic-Analysis-Of-Lawfare-How.html.

73. Wajahat Ali, *Fear Inc.: The Roots of the Islamophobia Network in America* (Washington, D.C.: Center for American Progress, 2011), 36; Asma T. Uddin and Dave Pantzer, *A First Amendment Analysis of Anti-Sharia Initiatives* (Washington, D.C.: Institute for Social Policy and Understanding, 2012), 11.

74. Mordechai Kedar and David Yerushalmi, "Correlations between Sharia Adherence and Violent Dogma in U.S. Mosques," Mapping Sharia (website), accessed January 22, 2015, http://mappingsharia.com.

75. Andrea Elliott, "The Man Behind the Anti-Shariah Movement," *New York Times*, July 30, 2011.

76. "About the Clarion Project," The Clarion Project, accessed January 22, 2015, http://www.clarionproject.org/about; Wajahat Ali, *Fear Inc.: The Roots of the Islamophobia Network in America* (Washington, D.C.: Center for American Progress, 2011), 100–101.

77. "Progressive Muslim Organizations," The Clarion Project, accessed January 22, 2015, http://www.clarionproject.org/Progressive-Muslim-Organizations

78. "Islamist Organization in America," The Clarion Project, accessed January 22, 2015, http://www.clarionproject.org/islamist-organizations

79. *Obsession: Radical Islam's War against the West*, directed by Wayne Kopping (Clarion Fund, 2007).

80. Kimberly Kindy, "Group Swamps Swing States With Movie on Radical Islam," *Washington Post*, October 26, 2008; Peter Overby, "Charity Floods Swing States with Anti-Islam DVD," *Morning Edition* (National Public Radio), September 26, 2008.

81. *The Third Jihad: Radical Islam's Vision for America*, directed by Wayne Kopping (Clarion Fund, 2008).

82. Wajahat Ali, *Fear Inc.: The Roots of the Islamophobia Network in America* (Washington, D.C.: Center for American Progress, 2011), 65.

83. Laurie Goodstein, "Drawing U.S. Crowds with Anti-Islam Message," *New York Times*, March 7, 2011.

84. Laurie Goodstein, "Drawing U.S. Crowds with Anti-Islam Message," *New York Times*, March 7, 2011.

85. Act for America website, accessed January 22, 2015, https://www.actfor america.org.

86. Nathan Lean, *The Islamophobia Industry: How the Right Manufactures Fear of Muslims* (London: Pluto Press, 2012), 101, 106–107.

87. "Act! Accomplishments," Act! for America, accessed September 23, 2015, https://actforamericaeducation.com/index.php/learn/accomplishments.

88. Christopher Bail, *Terrified: How Anti-Muslim Fringe Organizations Became Mainstream* (Princeton: Princeton University Press, 2015), Kindle edition.

89. Nathan Lean, *The Islamophobia Industry: How the Right Manufactures Fear of Muslims* (London: Pluto Press, 2012), 10, 13.

90. Robert Steinback, "The Anti-Muslim Inner Circle," *Intelligence Report* 142 (Southern Poverty Law Center, Summer 2011), http://www .splcenter.org/get-informed/intelligence-report/browse-all-issues/2011/summer/ the-anti-muslim-inner-circle.

91. Wajahat Ali, *Fear, Inc.: The Roots of the Islamophobia Network in America* (Washington, D.C.: Center for American Progress, 2011), 2; *The Right Wing Playbook on Anti-Muslim Extremism* (Washington, D.C.: People for the American Way, 2011), 2–7.

92. Christopher Bail, *Terrified: How Anti-Muslim Fringe Organizations Became Mainstream* (Princeton: Princeton University Press, 2015), Kindle edition.

93. Anne Barnard, "In Lower Manhattan, 2 Mosques Have Firm Roots," *New York Times*, August 13, 2010.

94. Alex Altman, "Time Poll: Majority Oppose Mosque, Many Distrust Muslims," *Time*, August 19, 2010.

95. Pew Research Center and Pew Forum on Religion and Public Life, *Public Remains Conflicted over Islam* (Washington, D.C.: Pew Research Center for People and the Press, 2010), 3.

96. "Nationwide Anti-Mosque Activity," American Civil Liberties Union, accessed January 23, 2015, https://www.aclu.org/maps/ map-nationwide-anti-mosque-activity.

97. Pew Forum on Religion and Public Life, *Controversies Over Mosques and Islamic Centers Across the U.S.* (Washington, D.C.: Pew Research Center for People and the Press, 2012), 2–22.

98. Department of Justice, Civil Right Division, *Religious Freedom in Focus* 53 (August 2012), http://www.justice.gov/crt/spec_topics/religiousdiscrimination/ newsletter/focus_53.html.

99. Blake Farmer, "A Fight to the Finish for Tennessee Mosque," *All Things Considered* (National Public Radio), June 21, 2010, http://www.npr.org/2012/06/21/155432158/a-fight-to-the-finish-for-tennessee-mosque.

100. Andrea Elliot, "The Man Behind the Anti-Shariah Movement," *New York Times*, July 30, 2011.

101. Phyllis B. Gerstenfeld, *Hate Crimes: Causes, Controls, and Controversies* (Los Angeles: Sage Publications, 2013), 119.

102. Lori Peek, *Behind the Backlash: Muslim Americans after 9/11* (New Delhi: Social Science Press, 2012), 5.

103. Wajahat Ali, *Fear, Inc.: The Roots of the Islamophobia Network in America* (Washington, D.C.: Center for American Progress, 2011), 111.

104. "Tancredo: Threats On Islam Sites Could Deter Terrorists," *Denver Post*, August 3, 2007.

105. Mucahit Bilici, *Finding Mecca in America: How Islam Became an American Religion* (Chicago: Chicago University Press, 2012), 151.

106. "Anatomy of a Smear: Sorting Fact from Fiction in the 2008 Election Campaign," *NOW* (Public Broadcasting Service), January 4, 2008, http://www.pbs.org/now/shows/401/political-smears.html.

107. Perry Bacon, Jr., "Foes Use Obama's Muslim Ties to Fuel Rumors about Him," *Washington Post,* November 29, 2007.

108. "No Mosque At Ground Zero," Renee Ellmers for Congress, posted November 15, 2010, https://www.youtube.com/watch?v=dc_xu7xoT6c.

109. "No Mosque At Ground Zero," Renee Ellmers for Congress, posted November 15, 2010, https://www.youtube.com/watch?v=dc_xu7xoT6c.

110. Ilario Pantano, "A Mosque at Ground Zero? Forsaking Israel? What's Next . . . a Nuclear Iran?," Pantano for Congress, June 17, 2010, http://www.pantanoforcongress.com/posts/a-mosque-at-ground-zero-forsaking-israel-what-s-nexta-nuclear-iran.

111. MSNBC Staff, "Bye-bye Allen West: Remembering His 10 Most Impressive Moments," MSNBC, November 20, 2012, http://www.msnbc.com/the-last-word/bye-bye-allen-west-remembering-his-10-most-i.

112. "A Mosque in the Middle," Pew Research Center, July 13, 2010, http://www.pewforum.org/2010/07/13/a-mosque-in-the-middle.

113. Scott Keyes, "Herman Cain Tells ThinkProgress 'I Will Not' Appoint a Muslim in My Administration," ThinkProgress, March 26, 2011, http://thinkprogress.org/politics/2011/03/26/153625/herman-cain-muslims.

114. Tanya Somanader, "Herman Cain: Americans Have the Right to Ban Mosques," ThinkProgress, July 17, 2011, http://thinkprogress.org/politics/2011/07/17/271216/herman-cain-americans-have-the-right-to-ban-mosques.

115. Associated Press, "Cain Apologizes after Meeting with Muslim Leaders," *USA Today*, July 28, 2011; Conor Friedersdorf, "Herman Cain's Anti-Muslim Prejudice Returns," *The Atlantic*, November 14, 2011, http://www.theatlantic.com/politics/archive/2011/11/herman-cains-anti-muslim-prejudice-returns/248471.

116. Scott Shane, "In Islamic Law, Gingrich Sees a Moral Threat," *New York Times*, December 21, 2011.

117. Andy Barr, "Newt Gingrich Compares Mosque to Nazis," *Politico*, August 16, 2010, http://www.politico.com/news/stories/0810/41112.html.

118. Lauren Fox, "Michele Bachmann Sticks to Accusations about Muslim Brotherhood," *U.S. News and World Report*, July 19, 2012.

119. Sameera Hafiz and Suman Raghunathan, *Under Suspicion, Under Attack: Xenophobic Political Rhetoric and Hate Violence against South Asian, Muslim, Sikh, Hindu, Middle Eastern, and Arab Communities in the United States* (Tacoma Park, MD: SAALT, 2014), 3, 10.

120. Dianna Dandridge, "Bennett Stands His Ground," *Sequoyah County Times*, September 17, 2014.

Chapter 5

1. Don Terry, "Community Ties Fray for Muslims," *Chicago Tribune*, September 25, 2001.

2. Don Terry and Noreen S. Ahmed-Ullah, "Protesters Turn Anger on Muslim Americans," *Chicago Tribune*, September 14, 2001.

3. Louise A. Cainkar, *Homeland Insecurity: The Arab American and Muslim American Experience after 9/11* (New York: Russell Sage Foundation, 2009), 206.

4. Don Terry, "Community Ties Fray for Muslims," *Chicago Tribune*, September 25, 2001.

5. Robert A. Baron and Deborah R. Richardson, *Human Aggression* (New York: Plenum Press, 1994), 7.

6. Federal Bureau of Investigation, *Hate Crime Statistics 2001* (Washington, D.C.: Department of Justice), 9.

7. Federal Bureau of Investigation, *Hate Crime Statistics 2001* (Washington, D.C.: Department of Justice), 9, 12–13.

8. *Confronting Discrimination in the Post-9/11 Era: Challenges and Opportunities Ten Years Later* (Washington, D.C.: Department of Justice, April 2012), 4.

9. Anti-Defamation League, "Comparison of FBI Hate Crime Statistics (2000–2012)," March 2014, http://www.adl.org/combating-hate.

10. *Confronting Discrimination in the Post-9/11 Era: Challenges and Opportunities Ten Years Later* (Washington, D.C.: Department of Justice, April 2012), 6–7.

11. Federal Bureau of Investigation, *Hate Crimes Statistics 2012*, Table 1, November 25, 2013, http://www.fbi.gov/about-us/cjis/ucr/hate-crime/2012.

12. Howard Ehrlich, *Hate Crimes and Ethnoviolence: The History, Current Affairs, and Future of Discrimination in America* (Boulder, CO: Westview Press, 2009), 18–19; Barbara Perry, *In the Name of Hate: Understanding Hate Crimes* (New York: Routledge, 2001), 9; "Hate Crimes," Department of Justice, Civil Rights Division, accessed October 29, 2014, http://www.justice.gov/crt/.

13. Beth Shuster, "Crimes of Hate or just Crimes," *Los Angeles Times*, October 11, 2001.

14. Anny Bakalian and Mehdi Bozorgmehr, *Backlash 9/11: Middle Eastern and Muslim Americans Respond* (Berkeley: University of California Press, 2009), 126–127; Barbara Perry, *In the Name of Hate: Understanding Hate Crimes* (New York: Routledge, 2001), 8, 11–12.

15. Richard A. Berk, Elizabeth A. Boyd, and Karl M. Hamner, "Thinking More Clearly About Hate-Motivated Crimes," *Hate and Bias Crime: A Reader*, ed. Barbara Perry (New York: Routledge, 2003), 55.

16. Lynn Langton, Michael Planty, and Nathan Sandhultz, *Hate Crime Victimization, 2003–2011* (Washington, D.C.: Bureau of Justice Statistics, Department of Justice, 2013), 5.

17. "Data Collection: National Crime Victimization Survey (NCVS)," Bureau of Justice Statistics, Department of Justice, accessed October 29, 2014, http://www.bjs.gov.

18. Lynn Langton, Michael Planty, and Nathan Sandhultz, *Hate Crime Victimization, 2003–2011* (Washington, D.C.: Bureau of Justice Statistics, Department of Justice, 2013), 1, 3; Meagan Meuchel Wilson, *Hate Crime Victimization, 2004–2012, Statistical Tables* (Washington, D.C.: Bureau of Justice Statistics, Department of Justice, 2013), 1.

19. Calculations based on data from the FBI's annual Unified Crime Reports, accessed October 29, 2014, http://www.fbi.gov/about-us/investigate/civilrights/hate_crimes.

20. Federal Bureau of Investigation, *Hate Crimes Statistics 2012*, Table 1, November 25, 2013, www.fbi.gov/about-us/cjis/ucr/hate-crime/2012.

21. Howard Ehrlich, *Hate Crimes and Ethnoviolence: The History, Current Affairs, and Future of Discrimination in America* (Boulder, CO: Westview Press, 2009), 17; Howard Ehrlich, "Ethnoviolence," *Encyclopedia of Race, Ethnicity, and Society*, ed. Richard Schaefer (Thousand Oaks, California: Sage Publications, 2008), 471–473.

22. Howard Ehrlich, *Hate Crimes and Ethnoviolence: The History, Current Affairs, and Future of Discrimination in America* (Boulder, CO: Westview Press, 2009), 18–19.

23. Debasish Mishra and Deepa Iyer, *American Backlash: Terrorists Bring War Home in more Ways than One* (Tacoma Park, MD: SAALT, 2001), 6–7. After this publication, SAALT changed its name from "South Asian Leaders of Tomorrow" to "South Asian Americans Leading Together," maintaining the same acronym (www.saalt.org).

24. Barbara Perry, "Anti-Muslim Retaliatory Violence Following the 9/11 Terrorist Attacks," *Hate and Bias Crime: A Reader*, ed. Barbara Perry (New York: Routledge, 2003), 184.

25. *The USA Patriot Act: Impact on the Arab and Muslim Community*, Institute for Social Policy and Understanding (Clinton Township, Michigan: ISPU, 2004), 13–15.

26. Amardeep Singh, *We Are Not the Enemy: Hate Crimes Against Arabs, Muslims, and Those Perceived to Be Arab or Muslim After September 11* (New York: Human Rights Watch, 2002), 3.

27. Sameera Hafiz and Suman Raghunathan, *Under Suspicion, Under Attack: Xenophobic Political Rhetoric and Hate Violence against South Asian, Muslim, Sikh, Hindu, Middle Eastern, and Arab Communities in the United States* (Tacoma Park, MD: SAALT, 2014), 18.

28. Lori Peek, *Behind the Backlash: Muslim Americans after 9/11* (New Delhi: Social Science Press, 2012), 64, 71–77.

29. Lori Peek, *Behind the Backlash: Muslim Americans after 9/11* (New Delhi: Social Science Press, 2012), 86.

30. Debasish Mishra and Deepa Iyer, *American Backlash: Terrorists Bring War Home in more Ways than One* (Tacoma Park, MD: SAALT, 2014), 41.

31. Nicoletta Karam, *The 9/11 Backlash: A Decade of U.S. Hate Crimes Targeting the Innocent* (Berkeley, CA: Beatitude Press, 2012), Kindle edition, chapter 5.

32. John de León, "Burien Woman Pleads Not Guilty in Alleged Attack on Muslims," *Seattle Times*, November 2, 2010.

33. Nicoletta Karam, *The 9/11 Backlash: A Decade of U.S. Hate Crimes Targeting the Innocent* (Berkeley, CA: Beatitude Press, 2012), Kindle edition, chapter 5; Seattle Times Staff, "Edmonds Man Sentenced in Cross-Burning Outside Home," *Seattle Times*, February 17, 2006.

34. Nicoletta Karam, *The 9/11 Backlash: A Decade of U.S. Hate Crimes Targeting the Innocent* (Berkeley, CA: Beatitude Press, 2012), Kindle edition, chapter 5.

35. Nicoletta Karam, *The 9/11 Backlash: A Decade of U.S. Hate Crimes Targeting the Innocent* (Berkeley, CA: Beatitude Press, 2012), Kindle edition, chapter 5; Lori Peek, *Behind the Backlash: Muslim Americans after 9/11* (New Delhi: Social Science Press, 2012), 29; Debasish Mishra and Deepa Iyer, *American Backlash: Terrorists Bring War Home in more Ways than One* (Tacoma Park, MD: SAALT, 2014), 38, 40.

36. Lori Peek, *Behind the Backlash: Muslim Americans after 9/11* (New Delhi: Social Science Press, 2012), 30.

37. Nicoletta Karam, *The 9/11 Backlash: A Decade of U.S. Hate Crimes Targeting the Innocent* (Berkeley, CA: Beatitude Press, 2012), Kindle edition, chapter 7.

38. Debasish Mishra and Deepa Iyer, *American Backlash: Terrorists Bring War Home in more Ways than One* (Tacoma Park, MD: SAALT, 2014), 39.

39. Nicoletta Karam, *The 9/11 Backlash: A Decade of U.S. Hate Crimes Targeting the Innocent* (Berkeley, CA: Beatitude Press, 2012), Kindle edition, chapter 5; Debasish Mishra and Deepa Iyer, *American Backlash: Terrorists Bring War Home in more Ways than One* (Tacoma Park, MD: SAALT, 2014), 34–35.

40. *Confronting Discrimination in the Post-9/11 Era: Challenges and Opportunities Ten Years Later* (Washington, D.C.: Department of Justice, April 2012), 7.

41. Debasish Mishra and Deepa Iyer, *American Backlash: Terrorists Bring War Home in more Ways than One* (Tacoma Park, MD: SAALT, 2014), 25.

42. Debasish Mishra and Deepa Iyer, *American Backlash: Terrorists Bring War Home in more Ways than One* (Tacoma Park, MD: SAALT, 2014), 25–26.

43. Nicoletta Karam, *The 9/11 Backlash: A Decade of U.S. Hate Crimes Targeting the Innocent* (Berkeley, CA: Beatitude Press, 2012), Kindle edition, chapter 6.

44. Debasish Mishra and Deepa Iyer, *American Backlash: Terrorists Bring War Home in more Ways than One* (Tacoma Park, MD: SAALT, 2014), 30.

45. Jack Levin and Jack McDevitt, *Hate Crimes Revisited: America's War On Those Who Are Different* (Boulder, CO: Westview Press, 2002), 17.

46. Nicoletta Karam, *The 9/11 Backlash: A Decade of U.S. Hate Crimes Targeting the Innocent* (Berkeley, CA: Beatitude Press, 2012), Kindle edition, chapter 4.

47. Nicoletta Karam, *The 9/11 Backlash: A Decade of U.S. Hate Crimes Targeting the Innocent* (Berkeley, CA: Beatitude Press, 2012), Kindle edition, chapter 7.

48. Nicoletta Karam, *The 9/11 Backlash: A Decade of U.S. Hate Crimes Targeting the Innocent* (Berkeley, CA: Beatitude Press, 2012), Kindle edition, chapter 9.

49. *Confronting Discrimination in the Post-9/11 Era: Challenges and Opportunities Ten Years Later* (Washington, D.C.: Department of Justice, April 2012), 4.

50. Debasish Mishra and Deepa Iyer, *American Backlash: Terrorists Bring War Home in more Ways than One* (Tacoma Park, MD: SAALT, 2014), 7.

51. Nicoletta Karam, *The 9/11 Backlash: A Decade of U.S. Hate Crimes Targeting the Innocent* (Berkeley, CA: Beatitude Press, 2012), Kindle edition, chapter 5.

52. "Man Who Slashed Cabbie in Anti-Muslim Tirade, Sentenced to Nearly 10 Years in Prison," CBS News, June 25, 2013, http://wwwnewyork.cbslocal.com.

53. Nicoletta Karam, *The 9/11 Backlash: A Decade of U.S. Hate Crimes Targeting the Innocent* (Berkeley, CA: Beatitude Press, 2012), Kindle edition, chapter 5, Debasish Mishra and Deepa Iyer, *American Backlash: Terrorists Bring War Home in more Ways than One* (Tacoma Park, MD: SAALT, 2014), 37; Mohammed Nimer, "Muslims in the American Body Politic," *Muslims' Place in the American Public Square: Hopes, Fears, and Aspirations,* ed. Zahid H. Bukhari, et al. (Walnut Creek, CA: AltaMira Press, 2004), 147.

54. Debasish Mishra and Deepa Iyer, *American Backlash: Terrorists Bring War Home in more Ways than One* (Tacoma Park, MD: SAALT, 2014), 39.

55. Nicoletta Karam, *The 9/11 Backlash: A Decade of U.S. Hate Crimes Targeting the Innocent* (Berkeley, CA: Beatitude Press, 2012), Kindle edition, chapter 5.

222 Notes

56. Jonathan Cooper and Nigel Duara, "Arson Suspected at Islamic Center in Oregon," *Washington Post*, November 28, 2010; Sheila Musaji, "Islamophobia: Prejudice, Racist, or Violent Incidents at Mosques," *The American Muslim*, June 5, 2013; "Twenty Year Sentence in Mosque Arson Case," *Religious Freedom in Focus* 56 (April 2013), http://wwwjustic.gov; Debasish Mishra and Deepa Iyer, *American Backlash: Terrorists Bring War Home in more Ways than One* (Tacoma Park, MD: SAALT, 2014), 38; *Confronting Discrimination in the Post-9/11 Era: Challenges and Opportunities Ten Years Later* (Washington, D.C.: Department of Justice, April 2012), 8; Nicoletta Karam, *The 9/11 Backlash: A Decade of U.S. Hate Crimes Targeting the Innocent* (Berkeley, CA: Beatitude Press, 2012), Kindle edition, chapter 5.

57. Nicoletta Karam, *The 9/11 Backlash: A Decade of U.S. Hate Crimes Targeting the Innocent* (Berkeley, CA: Beatitude Press, 2012), Kindle edition, chapter 5.

58. *Confronting Discrimination in the Post-9/11 Era: Challenges and Opportunities Ten Years Later* (Washington, D.C.: Department of Justice, April 2012), 7.

59. Mohammed Nimer, "Muslims in the American Body Politic," *Muslims' Place in the American Public Square: Hopes, Fears, and Aspirations*, ed. Zahid H. Bukhari et al. (Walnut Creek, CA: AltaMira Press, 2004), 147; "Man Rams Car into Ohio Mosque," *Toledo Blade*, September 18, 2001

60. Associated Press, "Decade after 9/11, Muslims more Engaged," *Goshen News*, September 10, 2011; Jodi Wilgoren, "The Pakistani Americans: Isolated Family Finds Support and Reason to Worry in Illinois," *New York Times*, October 2001.

61. *Confronting Discrimination in the Post-9/11 Era: Challenges and Opportunities Ten Years Later* (Washington, D.C.: Department of Justice, April 2012), 7, Mohammed Nimer, "Muslims in the American Body Politic," *Muslims' Place in the American Public Square: Hopes, Fears, and Aspirations*, ed. Zahid H. Bukhari, et al. (Walnut Creek, CA: AltaMira Press, 2004), 147; Associated Press, "Man Who Rammed Mosque Guilty of Hate Crime," St. *Petersburg Times*, November 2, 2002.

62. Nicoletta Karam, *The 9/11 Backlash: A Decade of U.S. Hate Crimes Targeting the Innocent* (Berkeley, CA: Beatitude Press, 2012), Kindle edition, chapter 8.

63. *Confronting Discrimination in the Post-9/11 Era: Challenges and Opportunities Ten Years Later* (Washington, D.C.: Department of Justice, April 2012), 8.

64. *Confronting Discrimination in the Post-9/11 Era: Challenges and Opportunities Ten Years Later* (Washington, D.C.: Department of Justice, April 2012), 7; Nicoletta Karam, *The 9/11 Backlash: A Decade of U.S. Hate Crimes Targeting the Innocent* (Berkeley, CA: Beatitude Press, 2012), Kindle edition, chapter 7.

65. Anny Bakalian and Mehdi Bozorgmehr, *Backlash 9/11: Middle Eastern and Muslim Americans Respond* (Berkeley: University of California Press,

2009), 1; Lori Peek, *Behind the Backlash: Muslim Americans after 9/11* (New Delhi: Social Science Press, 2012), 28.

66. Nicoletta Karam, *The 9/11 Backlash: A Decade of U.S. Hate Crimes Targeting the Innocent* (Berkeley, CA: Beatitude Press, 2012), Kindle edition, chapter 10.

67. South Asian Americans Leading Together, *In Our Own Words: Narratives of South Asian New Yorkers Affected by Racial and Religious Profiling* (Tacoma Park, MD: SAALT, 2012), 17.

68. Lori Peek, *Behind the Backlash: Muslim Americans after 9/11* (New Delhi: Social Science Press, 2012), 28.

69. Anny Bakalian and Mehdi Bozorgmehr, *Backlash 9/11: Middle Eastern and Muslim Americans Respond* (Berkeley: University of California Press, 2009), 2–3; Lori Peek, *Behind the Backlash: Muslim Americans after 9/11* (New Delhi: Social Science Press, 2012), 29.

70. South Asian Americans Leading Together, *In Our Own Words: Narratives of South Asian New Yorkers Affected by Racial and Religious Profiling* (Tacoma Park, MD: SAALT, 2012), 17.

71. Nicoletta Karam, *The 9/11 Backlash: A Decade of U.S. Hate Crimes Targeting the Innocent* (Berkeley, CA: Beatitude Press, 2012), Kindle edition, chapter 10; Robert F. Worth, "Police Arrest Brooklyn Man in Slayings of 4 Shopkeepers," *New York Times*, March 31, 2003.

72. Amardeep Sing, *We Are not the Enemy* (New York: Human Rights Watch, 2002), 17–18; "Man Gets Life in Murder of Arab American," *Los Angeles Times*, July 16, 2002.

73. John H. Richardson, "Not Guilty by Reason of Afghanistan," *Esquire*, February 1, 2003; Dinitia Smith, "Tragedy Haunts Film on Afghan Diaspora; Friends of a Murdered Filmmaker Struggle to Finish His Work," *New York Times*, October 2, 2002.

74. *Compounding the Tragedy: The Other Victims of September 11th* (Los Angeles: Los Angeles County Commission on Human Relations, 2002), 16.

75. Nicoletta Karam, *The 9/11 Backlash: A Decade of U.S. Hate Crimes Targeting the Innocent* (Berkeley, CA: Beatitude Press, 2012), Kindle edition, chapter 10; "Anti-Muslim Incidents Since Sept. 11, 2001," Southern Poverty Law Center, March 29, 2011, http://wwwsplc.org.

76. "Merchant Killed in Sylmar," *Los Angeles Times*, October 19, 2001.

77. Nicoletta Karam, *The 9/11 Backlash: A Decade of U.S. Hate Crimes Targeting the Innocent* (Berkeley, CA: Beatitude Press, 2012), Kindle edition, chapter 10; Amardeep Singh, *We Are Not the Enemy: Hate Crimes Against Arabs, Muslims, and Those Perceived to Be Arab or Muslim After September 11* (New York: Human Rights Watch, 2002), 18–19.

78. David Kelley, "FBI Investigating Fatal Blast at a San Bernardino County Home as a Hate Crime," *Los Angeles Times*, July 10, 2009.

79. Lydia Polgreen and Al Baker, "Men Kill Student, 18, on Brooklyn Street," *New York Times*, November 13, 2002; Tina Susman, "Federal Hate Crime Figures Tell Little," *Baltimore Sun*, December 13, 2002.

80. Nicoletta Karam, *The 9/11 Backlash: A Decade of U.S. Hate Crimes Targeting the Innocent* (Berkeley, CA: Beatitude Press, 2012), Kindle edition, chapter 10; Courtney Dentch, "SE Queens Man Arrested in Slaying of Bangladeshi," *Times Ledger*, August 22, 2002, http://www.timesledger.com/stories/2002/34/20020822-archive308.html.

81. Tomas Rowan, "Man Sentenced for Killing Afghan Mom," ABC News, April 15, 2008, http://wwwabclocal.go.com; "SF Court Upholds Conviction in Possible Hate Crime Shooting of Woman," *The San Francisco Appeal*, February 5, 2010.

82. "Detectives Call Home Depot Shooting Racially Motivated," KCRA-TV News March 27, 2014, http://wwwkcra.com: Stephen Magagnini, "Suspect in Killing of Iraqi Refugee in Sacramento Pleads Guilty," *Sacramento Bee*, October 8, 2014.

83. J. David Goodman, "Suspect in Three Killings Faced Financial Troubles," *New York Times*, November 22, 2012; Colin Moynihan and Christopher Maag, "Same .22-Caliber Pistol Was Used to Kill Three Merchants in Brooklyn, Police Say," *New York Times*, November 17, 2012; NBC-New York and the Associate Press, "Man Charged in Slayings of Brooklyn Shopkeepers," NBC News, November 21, 2012, http://wwwusnews.nbcnews.com.

84. Heather Hollingsworth (Associated Press), "Driver Charged With Murder in Somali Teen's Death," ABC News, December 5, 2014, http://abcnews.go.com/US/wireStory/teen-pedestrian-dies-missouri-hit-run-27386013; Mark Morris, Eric Adler, and Tony Rizzothe, "Man Charged with Murder for Allegedly Charging Teen with SUV outside Kansas City Mosque," *Kansas City Star*, December 5, 2014.

85. David Rosenzweig, "JDL Officials Pleads Guilty in Bomb Plot," *Los Angeles Times*, February 5, 2003; Sherri Day, "F.B.I. Arrests Members of Militant Anti-Arab Group," *New York Times*, December 12, 2001; Greg Winter, "2 Held in Plot to Attack Mosque and Congressman," *New York Times*, December 13, 2001.

86. Southern Poverty Law Center, "Jewish Defense League," accessed November 5, 2014, http://www.splcenter.org/get-informed/intelligence-files/groups/jewish-defense-league.

87. Paloma Esquivel, "In Alex Odeh's 1985 Slaying, Still Seeking Answers," *Los Angeles Times*, October 20, 2013; National Counterterrorism Center, "Terrorist Associated Assassination Incidents in the United States, accessed November 5, 2014, http://www.nctc.gov/site/technical/assassination_incidents.html.

88. "Bomb Plot Charge only latest JDL Controversy," ABC News, March 19, 2002, http://wwwabcnews.go.com; Harvey W. Kushner, *Encyclopedia of Terrorism* (Thousand Oaks, California: Sage Publications, 2003), 192–193.

89. Sherri Day, "F.B.I. Arrests Members of Militant Anti-Arab Group," *New York Times*, December 12, 2001; Greg Winter, "2 Held in Plot to Attack Mosque and Congressman," *New York Times*, December 13, 2001.

90. Jean Guccione, "JDL Chief Dies; Suit Threatened," *Los Angeles Times*, November 15, 2002.

91. David Pierson and Greg Krikorian, "Former JDL Activist Slain in Federal Prison," *Los Angeles Times,* November 6, 2005; David Rosenzweig, "JDL Officials Pleads Guilty in Bomb Plot," *Los Angeles Times*, February 5, 2003.

92. "Florida Muslims Are on Alert After Arrest," *New York Times*, August 25, 2002; Leanora Minai and Maureen Byrne Ahern, "Podiatrist's Arsenal Part of Blueprint for Terror," *St. Petersburg Times*, August 24, 2002; Tanya Weinberg, "Pinellas Doctor Gets 12 1/2 Years For Bomb Plot," *Sun Sentinel,* June 20, 2003.

93. Leanora Minai and Maureen Byrne Ahern, "Podiatrist's Arsenal Part of Blueprint for Terror," *St. Petersburg Times*, August 24, 2002.

94. Department of Justice, "Initiative to Combat Post-9/11 Discriminatory Backlash," accessed November 5, 2014, http://www.justice.gov/crt/legalinfo/discrimupdate.php.

95. Associated Press, "Tenn. Man Pleads Guilty to Plotting Attack on Muslims," CBS News, May 20, 2015, http://www.cbsnews.com/news/tennessee-man-pleads-guilty-to-plotting-attack-on-muslims; Barbara Goldberg, "Tennessee Man Plotted to Attack Muslims, Burn Down Mosque in New York's Islamberg," Reuters, May 19, 2015, www.reuters.com/article/2015/05/19/us-usa-muslim-threat-idUSKBN0O41Y820150519.

96. Rafaela M. Dancygier and Donald P. Green, "Hate Crimes," in *The Sage Handbook of Prejudice, Stereotyping and Discrimination*, ed. John F. Dovidio, et al. (London: Sage Publications, 2010), 298–299; Nathan Hall, *Hate Crime* (London: Routledge, 2013), 119–120.

97. National Institute of Justice, "Terrorism," September 13, 2011, http://wwwnij.gov/topics/crime/terrorism.

98. National Consortium for the Study of Terrorism and Responses to Terrorism, "Global Terrorism Database - Data Collection Methodology," accessed November 12, 2014, http://www.start.umd.edu/gtd/using%2Dgtd/.

99. Victor Asal, et al., *Analysis of Factors Related to Hate Crimes and Terrorism* (College Park, MD: START, University of Maryland, 2012), 6, 8.

100. Kellina M. Craig, "A Review of the Social Psychological Literature on Hate Crimes as a Distinct Form of Aggression," *Hate and Bias Crime: A Reader*, ed. Barbara Perry (New York: Routledge, 2003), 117.

101. Pew Forum on Religion and Public Life, *The Global Religious Landscape* (Washington, D.C.: Pew Research Center, 2010), 21.

102. Pew Forum on Religion and Public Life, *The World's Muslims: Unity and Diversity* (Washington, D.C.: Pew Research Center, 2012), 9.

103. Pew Forum on Religion and Public Life, *Muslim Americans: No Signs of Growth in Alienation or Support for Extremism* (Washington, D.C.: Pew Research Center, 2012), 13–14, 16, 20.

104. Coexist Foundation and Gallup, *Muslim Americans: A National Portrait* (Washington, D.C.: Gallup, Inc., 2009), 21.

105. Stanley Cohen, *Folk Devils and Moral Panics: The Creation of the Mods and Rockers* (New York: Routledge, 2002), 1, 27, 59.

106. Lu-Win Wang, "Hate Crimes and Everyday Discrimination: Influences of and on the Social Contexts," in *Crimes of Hate: Selected Readings*, ed. Phyllis B. Gerstenfeld and Diana R. Grant (Thousand Oaks, CA: Sage Publications, 2004), 161–162.

107. South Asian Americans Leading Together, *In Our Own Words: Narratives of South Asian New Yorkers Affected by Racial and Religious Profiling* (Tacoma Park, MD: SAALT, 2012), 10.

108. South Asian Americans Leading Together, *In Our Own Words: Narratives of South Asian New Yorkers Affected by Racial and Religious Profiling* (Tacoma Park, MD: SAALT, 2012), 11; Marvin Wingfield, "The Impact of 9/11, Middle East Conflicts, and Anti-Arab Discrimination," in *Daily Life of Arab Americans in the 21st Century*, ed. Anan Ameri and Holly Arida (Santa Barbara: Greenwood, 2012), 40.

109. South Asian Americans Leading Together, *In Our Own Words: Narratives of South Asian New Yorkers Affected by Racial and Religious Profiling* (Tacoma Park, MD: SAALT, 2012), 11; Lori Peek, *Behind the Backlash: Muslim Americans after 9/11* (New Delhi: Social Science Press, 2012), 23.

110. Federal Bureau of Investigation, "Terror Hits Home: The Oklahoma City Bombing," accessed November 19, 2014, http://www.fbi.gov/about-us/history/famous-cases/oklahoma-city-bombing.

111. Mohammed Nimer, "Muslims in the American Body Politic," *Muslims' Place in the American Public Square: Hopes, Fears, and Aspirations*, ed. Zahid H. Bukhari, et al. (Walnut Creek, CA: AltaMira Press, 2004), 146; Council for American-Islamic Relations, *A Rush to Judgment* (Washington, D.C.: CAIR, 1995), http://www.cair.com/civil-rights/civil-rights-reports/1995.html.

112. Council for American-Islamic Relations, *The Price of Ignorance* (Washington, D.C.: CAIR, 1996), 18.

113. Stanley Cohen, *Folk Devils and Moral Panics: The Creation of the Mods and Rockers* (New York: Routledge, 2002), 64.

114. Louise Cainkar, "American Muslims at the Dawn of the 21st Century: Hope and Pessimism in the Drive for Civic and Political Inclusion," in *Muslims in the West after 9/11: Religion, Politics and Law*, ed. Jocelyne Cesari (London: Routledge, 2010), 182.

115. Victoria Munro, *Hate Crime in the Media: A History* (Santa Barbara: Praeger, 2014), 55.

116. Robin S. Toma, et al., *Compounding the Tragedy: The Other Victims of September 11th* (Los Angeles: Los Angeles County Commission on Human Relations, 2002), 3.

117. Marc Santora and Sarah Maslin Nir, "Woman Sought after 2nd Fatal Shove onto Subway Tracks this Month, *New York Times*, December 28, 2012; Marc Santora, "Woman Is Charged with Murder as a Hate Crime in a Fatal Subway Push," *New York Times*, December 29, 2012.

118. South Asian Americans Leading Together, *In Our Own Words: Narratives of South Asian New Yorkers Affected by Racial and Religious Profiling* (Tacoma Park, MD: SAALT, 2012), 20; Nicoletta Karam, *The 9/11 Backlash: A Decade of U.S. Hate Crimes Targeting the Innocent* (Berkeley, CA: Beatitude Press, 2012), Kindle edition, chapter 5.

119. South Asian Americans Leading Together, *In Our Own Words: Narratives of South Asian New Yorkers Affected by Racial and Religious Profiling* (Tacoma Park, MD: SAALT, 2012), 19.

120. "History of Hate: Crimes Against Sikhs since 9/11," *Huffington Post*, August 7, 2012.

121. Jaxon Van Derbeken (San Francisco Chronicle), "American Nightmare: Sukhpal Singh Sodhi Came to S.F. to Help His Village in India. Now, a Year after his Brother's Death, His Family Mourns Again, *SFGate*, August 6, 2002, http://www.sfgate.com/news/article/AMERICAN-NIGHTMARE-Sukhpal-Singh-Sodhi-came-to-2813583.php.

122. *Confronting Discrimination in the Post-9/11 Era: Challenges and Opportunities Ten Years Later* (Washington, D.C.: Department of Justice, April 2012), 7; Nicoletta Karam, *The 9/11 Backlash: A Decade of U.S. Hate Crimes Targeting the Innocent* (Berkeley, CA: Beatitude Press, 2012), Kindle edition, chapter 10; "History of Hate: Crimes Against Sikhs since 9/11," *Huffington Post*, August 7, 2012.

123. Lee Romney, "Attack on Sikh Men Triggers Outcry in Elk Grove, Calif., and Beyond," *Los Angeles Times*, April 11, 2011.

124. Federal Bureau of Investigation, "Oak Creek Sikh Temple Shooting Investigation Conclusion," November 20, 2012, http://www.fbi.gov/milwaukee/press-releases/2012/oak-creek-sikh-temple-shooting-investigation-conclusion; Joe Heim, "Wade Michael Page Was Steeped in Neo-Nazi 'Hate Music' Movement," *Washington Post*, August 7, 2012.

125. Stanford Peace Innovation Lab, *Turban Myths: The Opportunity and Challenges for Reframing a Cultural Symbol for Post-9/11 America* (Stanford, CA: SPIL, 2013), 32–35.

126. Jack McDevitt, Jack Levin, and Susan Bennett, "Hate Crime Offenders: An Expanded Typology," *Crimes of Hate: Selected Readings*, ed. Phyllis B. Gerstenfeld and Diana R. Grant (Thousand Oaks, CA: Sage Publications, 2003), 110.

127. Jack McDevitt, Jack Levin, and Susan Bennett, "Hate Crime Offenders: An Expanded Typology," *Hate and Bias Crime: A Reader*, ed. Barbara Perry (New York: Routledge, 2003), 114–115.

128. Jack McDevitt, Jack Levin, and Susan Bennett, "Hate Crime Offenders: An Expanded Typology," *Crimes of Hate: Selected Readings*, ed. Phyllis B. Gerstenfeld and Diana R. Grant (Thousand Oaks, CA: Sage Publications, 2003), 110–111.

129. Robbie Brown and Christine Hauser, "After a Struggle, Mosque Opens in Tennessee," *New York Times*, August 10, 2012.

130. Phyllis B. Gerstenfeld, *Hate Crimes: Causes, Controls, and Controversies* (Los Angeles: Sage Publications, 2013), 94–95; Jack McDevitt, Jack Levin, and Susan Bennett, "Hate Crime Offenders: An Expanded Typology," *Crimes of Hate: Selected Readings*, ed. Phyllis B. Gerstenfeld and Diana R. Grant (Thousand Oaks, CA: Sage Publications, 2003), 111.

131. Simran Jeet Singh, "A Unique Perspective on Hate Crimes: The Story of a Convicted Killer," *Huffington Post*, July 20, 2012.

132. Jack McDevitt, Jack Levin, and Susan Bennett, "Hate Crime Offenders: An Expanded Typology," *Crimes of Hate: Selected Readings*, ed. Phyllis B. Gerstenfeld and Diana R. Grant (Thousand Oaks, CA: Sage Publications, 2003), 110, 113.

133. Neil Chakraborti and Jon Garland, *Hate Crime: Impact, Causes, and Responses* (Los Angeles: Sage Publications, 2009), 127.

Chapter 6

1. Anny Bakalian and Mehdi Bozorgmehr, *Backlash 9/11: Middle Eastern and Muslim Americans Respond* (Berkeley: University of California Press, 2009), 100–101.

2. Kambiz GhaneaBassiri, *A History of Islam in America* (Cambridge: Cambridge University Press, 2010), 238–239.

3. Geneive Abdo, *Mecca and Main Street: Muslim Life in America after 9/11* (Oxford: Oxford University Press, 2006), 197; Kambiz GhaneaBassiri, *A History of Islam in America* (Cambridge: Cambridge University Press, 2010), 265–266.

4. Islamic Circle of North America, accessed February 15, 2015, http://www.icna.org; Kambiz GhaneaBassiri, *A History of Islam in America* (Cambridge: Cambridge University Press, 2010), 353.

5. Kambiz GhaneaBassiri, *A History of Islam in America* (Cambridge: Cambridge University Press, 2010), 320, 353; Task Force on Muslim American Civic and Political Engagement, *Strengthening America: The Civic and Political Integration of Muslim Americans* (Chicago: Chicago Council on Global Affairs, 2007), 77.

6. United Muslims of America, accessed February 11, 2015, http://www.umanet.org.

7. Kambiz GhaneaBassiri, *A History of Islam in America* (Cambridge: Cambridge University Press, 2010), 314–315, 345.

8. Mucahit Bilici, *Finding Mecca in America: How Islam Became an American Religion* (Chicago: Chicago University Press, 2012), 127–128.

9. Scott Bohlinger, "First U.S. Museum Devoted to Islam Based in Jackson, Mississippi," *The Washington File*, March 27, 2003.

10. Edward E. Curtis, *Islam in Black America: Identity, Liberty, and Difference in African-American Thought* (Albany: State University of New York, 2002), 113–117; Kambiz GhaneaBassiri, *A History of Islam in America* (Cambridge: Cambridge University Press, 2010), 284–291, 319.

11. Arab Community Center for Economic and Social Services, accessed February 12, 2015, https://www.accesscommunity.org; Kambiz GhaneaBassiri, *A History of Islam in America* (Cambridge: Cambridge University Press, 2010), 345.

12. American-Arab Anti-Discrimination Committee, accessed February 15, 2015, http://www.adc.org.

13. Arab American Institute, accessed February 15, 2015, http://www.aai usa.org.

14. South Asian Americans Leading Together, accessed February 12, 2015, http://saalt.org.

15. Mohammed Nimer, "Muslims in the American Body Politic," *Muslims' Place in the American Public Square: Hopes, Fears, and Aspirations*, ed. Zahid H. Bukhari, et al. (Walnut Creek, CA: AltaMira Press, 2004), 145.

16. Anny Bakalian and Mehdi Bozorgmehr, *Backlash 9/11: Middle Eastern and Muslim Americans Respond* (Berkeley: University of California Press, 2009), 97, 117–118.

17. Task Force on Muslim American Civic and Political Engagement, *Strengthening America: The Civic and Political Integration of Muslim Americans* (Chicago: Chicago Council on Global Affairs, 2007), 77.

18. Task Force on Muslim American Civic and Political Engagement, *Strengthening America: The Civic and Political Integration of Muslim Americans* (Chicago: Chicago Council on Global Affairs, 2007), 72, 78, 80.

19. Anny Bakalian and Mehdi Bozorgmehr, *Backlash 9/11: Middle Eastern and Muslim Americans Respond* (Berkeley: University of California Press, 2009), 182; Council for American-Islamic Relations, accessed February 13, 2015, http://www.cair.com/american-muslims/cair-public-service-announce ments.html.

20. CAIR guides and handbooks: *Know Your Rights and Responsibilities as an American Muslim, Community Safety Kit, Securing Religious Liberty,* and *Challenging Islamophobia Pocket Guide,* http://www.cair.com/american -muslims/guides-and-toolkits.html.

21. Council for American-Islamic Relations, "In the Courts," March 28, 2013, http://www.cair.com/civil-rights/in-the-courts.html.

22. Muslim Public Affairs Council, "Hollywood Bureau," accessed February 13, 2015, http://www.mpac.org/programs/hollywood-bureau.php; Muslim Public Affairs Council, "Truth over Fear," accessed February 13, 2015, http://www .mpac.org/programs/truth-over-fear.php.

23. National Religious Campaign Against Torture, accessed February 13, 2015, http://www.nrcat.org.

24. Institute for Social Policy and Understanding, accessed February 13, 2015, http://www.ispu.org.

25. Council for American-Islamic Relations, "CAIR's Condemnation of Terrorism," June 2011, https://www.cair.com/about-us/cair-anti-terrorism-cam paigns.html; Task Force on Muslim American Civic and Political Engagement, *Strengthening America: The Civic and Political Integration of Muslim Americans* (Chicago: Chicago Council on Global Affairs, 2007), 38.

26. Charles Kurzman, "Islamic Statements Against Terrorism," accessed February 18, 2015, http://kurzman.unc.edu/islamic-statements-against-terrorism; Sheila Musaji, "Fatwas and Statements by Muslim Scholars and Organizations," *The American Muslim*, July 20, 2015, http://theamericanmuslim.org/tam.php/features/articles/muslim_voices_against_extremism_and_terrorism_part_i_fatwas.

27. Anny Bakalian and Mehdi Bozorgmehr, *Backlash 9/11: Middle Eastern and Muslim Americans Respond* (Berkeley: University of California Press, 2009), 97, 117–118.

28. Muslim Public Affairs Council, *Grassroots Campaign to Fight Terrorism Handbook* (Los Angeles: MPAC, 2005), http://www.mpac.org/assets/docs/publications/campaign-to-fight-terrorism-brochure.pdf.

29. Muslim Public Affairs Council, *The Impact of 9/11 on Muslim American Young People: National and Religious Identity Formation in the Age of Terrorism and Islamophobia* (Los Angeles: MPAC, 2007), http://www.mpac.org/assets/docs/publications/MPAC-Special-Report---Muslim-Youth.pdf.

30. Muslim Public Affairs Council, "MPAC Tackles Violent Extremism and Online Radicalization at Two DC Events," May 30, 2013, http://www.mpac.org/programs/government-relations/mpac-tackles-violent-extremism-and-online-radicalization-at-two-dc-events.php; New American Foundation, "Online Radicalization: Myths and Realities," accessed February 19, 2015, http://www.newamerica.net/events/2013/online_radicalization_myths_realities.

31. Muslim Public Affairs Council, "Safe Spaces Initiative: Tools for Developing Healthy Communities," accessed February 19, 2015, http://www.mpac.org/safespaces.

32. Project Nur, "Voices Against Radicalization," accessed February 19, 2015, http://projectnur.org/voices-against-radicalism.

33. World Organization for Resource Development and Education, "US Government Outreach," accessed February 19, 2015, http://www.worde.org/programs/1013-2.

34. Qamar-ul Huda, *The Diversity of Muslims in the United States: Views as Americans* (Washington, DC: United States Institute of Peace, 2006), 13–14.

35. Laurie Goodstein, "U.S. Muslims Take On ISIS' Recruiting Machine," *New York Times*, February 19, 2015.

36. Charles Kurzman, *Muslim-American Terrorism: Declining Further* (Chapel Hill: University of North Carolina, 2013), http://kurzman.unc.edu/files/2011/06/Kurzman_Muslim-American_Terrorism_February_1_2013.pdf.

37. *Homegrown Terrorism: The Threat to Military Communities inside the United States*, Majority Investigative Report, Committee on Homeland Security, U.S. House of Representatives, December 2011.

38. Greg Miller, "At CIA, a Convert to Islam Leads the Terrorism Hunt," *Washington Post*, March 24, 2012.

39. Basia Spalek, "Community-Based Approaches to Counter-Terrorism," *Counter-Terrorism: Community-Based Approaches to Preventing Terror Crime*, ed. Basia Spalek (London: Palgrave Macmillan, 2012), 37.

40. Basia Spalek, "Community-Based Approaches to Counter-Terrorism," *Counter-Terrorism: Community-Based Approaches to Preventing Terror Crime*, ed. Basia Spalek (London: Palgrave Macmillan, 2012), 31–37, 42.

41. Nicole J. Henderson, et al., *Law Enforcement and Arab American Community Relations after September 11, 2001: Engagement in a Time of Uncertainty* (New York: Vera Institute of Justice, 2006), 13, 21–22.

42. Tony Gaskew, *Policing Muslim American Communities* (Lewiston, NY: The Edwin Mellen Press, 2008), 162, 165, 179.

43. "Community Policing Defined," *Community Policing Dispatch* (Washington, D.C.: Department of Justice, 2014), 1.

44. Lee P. Brown, *Policing in the 21st Century: Community Policing* (Bloomington: AuthorHouse, 2012), 150; Deborah Ramiriz, et al., "Community Partnerships Thwart Terrorism," *Preventing Ideological Violence: Communities, Police, and Case Studies of "Success,"* ed. P. Daniel Silk, et al. (New York: Palgrave Macmillan, 2013), 153–154.

45. Deborah Ramirez, et al., "Community Partnerships to Thwart Terrorism," *Preventing Ideological Violence: Communities, Police, and Case Studies of "Success,"* ed. P. Daniel Silk, et al. (New York: Palgrave Macmillan, 2013), 153.

46. David L. Carter, *Law Enforcement Intelligence: A Guide for State, Local, and Tribal Law Enforcement Agencies* (Washington, D.C.: Department of Justice, 2009), 9, 80.

47. Tony Gaskew, *Policing Muslim American Communities* (Lewiston, NY: The Edwin Mellen Press, 2008), 161.

48. Tom Tyler, Stephen J. Schulhofer, and Aziz R. Huq, "Legitimacy and Deterrence Effects in Counter-Terrorism Policing: A Study of Muslim Americans," Pubic Law and Legal Theory Research Paper Series (Chicago and New York: The Law School at Chicago University and New York University School of Law, 2009), 3, 16–18.

49. Basia Spalek, Salwa El Awa, and Laura Zahra McDonald, *Police-Muslim Engagement and Partnerships for the Purposes of Counter-Terrorism: An Examination* (Birmingham, UK: University of Birmingham, 2008), 9, 11–12, 14–15.

50. Basia Spalek, "Policing within Counter-Terrorism," *Counter-Terrorism: Community-Based Approaches to Preventing Terror Crime* (London: Palgrave Macmillan, 2012), 53.

51. Amardeep Singh, *We Are Not the Enemy: Hate Crimes Against Arabs, Muslims, and Those Perceived to Be Arab or Muslim after September 11, 2001* (Washington, D.C.: Human Rights, 2002), 27–28.

52. Heather J. Davies and Gerald R. Murphy, *Protecting Your Communities from Terrorism: Strategies for Local Law Enforcement* (Washington, D.C.: Department of Justice, 2004), 37.

53. Lori Peek, *Behind the Backlash: Muslim Americans after 9/11* (Philadelphia: Temple University Press, 2012), 27.

54. Equal Employment Opportunity Commission, "What You Should Know about the EEOC and Religious and National Origin Discrimination

Involving the Muslim, Sikh, Arab, Middle Eastern and South Asian Communities," accessed February 25, 2015, http://www.eeoc.gov/eeoc/newsroom/wysk/religion_national_origin_9-11.cfm.

55. Community Relations Service, Department of Justice, "Twenty Plus Things Law Enforcement Agencies Can Do to Prevent or Respond to Hate Incidents Against Arab-Americans, Muslims, and Sikhs," November 16, 2001, http://www.justice.gov/archive/crs/pubs/twentyplus.htm.

56. Christopher Bail, *Terrified: How Anti-Muslim Fringe Groups Became Mainstream* (Princeton: Princeton University Press, 2015), Kindle edition, chapter 6.

57. Civil Rights Division, Department of Justice, "Initiative to Combat Post-9/11 Discriminatory Backlash," accessed February 25, 2015, http://www.justice.gov/crt/legalinfo/nordwg_mission.php.

58. Debbie A Ramirez, Sasha Cohen O'Connell, and Rabia Zafar, *Developing Partnerships Between Law Enforcement and American Muslim, Arab, and Sikh Communities: A Promising Practices Guide* (Boston: Partnering for Prevention and Community Safety Initiative Publications, Northeastern University Law School, 2004), 57–59, 72.

59. Mike Abdeen, "Lessons Learned and Best Practices: The Outreach Efforts of the Los Angeles County Sheriff's Department Community Policing Method with Emphasis on the Muslim Community," in *Preventing Ideological Violence: Communities, Police, and Case Studies of "Success,"* ed. P. Daniel Silk, et al. (New York: Palgrave Macmillan, 2013), 227–229; Los Angeles County Sheriff's Department, Muslim Public Affairs Unit, accessed February 25, 2015, http://shq.lasdnews.net/content/uoa/MCA/MCAOverviewJan2010_LoRes.pdf; Muslim American Homeland Security Congress, accessed February 25, 2015, http://www.lasdhq.org/sites/muslimoutreach_new/Files/MAHSC%20Brochure.pdf.

60. David A. Fahrenthold and Michelle Boorstein, "Rep. Peter King's Muslim Hearings: A Key Moment in an Angry Conversation," *Washington Post*, March 9, 2011; *Hearing on the Extent of Radicalization in the Muslim American Community and that Community's Response*, Committee on Homeland Security, U.S. House of Representatives, March 10, 2011.

61. Wajahat Ali, *Fear, Inc.: The Roots of the Islamophobia Network in America* (Washington, D.C.: Center for American Progress, 2011), 113.

62. United States Attorney's Office, Eastern District of Michigan, "Community Engagement," accessed February 26, 2015, http://www.justice.gov/usao/mie/programs/commtrust.html.

63. Ihsan Alkhatib, "Building Bridges: The Experience of Leaders in Detroit, Michigan," *Preventing Ideological Violence: Communities, Police, and Case Studies of "Success,"* ed. P. Daniel Silk, et al. (New York: Palgrave Macmillan, 2013), 212.

64. Ihsan Alkhatib, "Building Bridges: The Experience of Leaders in Detroit, Michigan," *Preventing Ideological Violence: Communities, Police, and Case Studies of "Success,"* ed. P. Daniel Silk, et al. (New York: Palgrave Macmillan,

2013), 213–214; Department of Homeland Security, "Detroit Community Celebrates 10 Years of Building BRIDGES," September 2011, http://www.dhs.gov/detroit-community-celebrates-10-years-building-bridges.

65. Muslim American Society, "MAS MN Statement on Relations with Law Enforcement," February 8, 2015, http://www.muslimamericansociety.org/content/mas-mn-statement-on-relations-with-law-enforcement.

66. Cora Currier, "Spies Among Us: How Community Outreach Programs to Muslims Blur Lines Between Outreach and Intelligence," *The Intercept*, January 21, 2015; Devin Henry, "Minnesotans Focus on Stopping Terrorist Recruitment at Hill Hearing," *Minnesota Post*, July 27, 2011; Muslim American Society, "MAS MN Statement on Relations with Law Enforcement," February 8, 2015, http://www.muslimamericansociety.org/content/mas-mn-statement-on-relations-with-law-enforcement.

67. Margaret Brennan, "Can a Community Program Help Stop Homegrown Radicals," *CBS This Morning*, October 23, 2014; Washington Institute for Near East Policy, "New Strategies for Countering Homegrown Violent Extremism," November 21, 2013, http://www.washingtoninstitute.org/policy-analysis/view/new-strategies-for-countering-homegrown-violent-extremism; WORDE, "The Montgomery County Model," accessed February 26, 2015, http://www.worde.org/programs/the-montgomery-county-model.

68. Alejandro J. Beutel, *Building Bridges to Strengthen America: Forging an Effective Counterterrorism Enterprise between Muslim Americans and Law Enforcement* (Los Angeles: Muslim Public Affairs Council, 2009), 36–42.

69. Department of Justice, "Attorney General Holder Announces Pilot Program to Counter Violent Extremists," September 15, 2014, http://www.fbi.gov/news/pressrel/press-releases/attorney-general-holder-announces-pilot-program-to-counter-violent-extremists; Executive Staff of the FBI's National Security Branch, "A New Approach to Countering Violent Extremism: Sharing Expertise and Empowering Local Communities," *FBI Law Enforcement Bulletin*, October 7, 2014, http://leb.fbi.gov/2014/october/a-new-approach-to-countering-violent-extremism-sharing-expertise-and-empowering-local-communities.

70. Julie Hirschfield Davis, "Obama Urges Global United Front Against Extremist Groups Like ISIS," *New York Times*, February 15, 2015; Juliet Eilperin, "Trying to Counter Extremism at Home, U.S. Faces a Risk: Sowing More Distrust," *Washington Post*, February 16, 2015.

71. The White House, *Empowering Local Partners to Prevent Violent Extremism in the United States*, August 2011, 2–3.

Selected Bibliography

Books

Abdo, Geneive. *Mecca and Main Street: Muslim Life in America after 9/11.* Oxford: Oxford University Press, 2006.

Ahmed, Akbar. *Journey into America: The Challenge of Islam.* Washington, D.C.: Brookings Institution Press, 2011.

Allison, Robert. *The Crescent Obscured: The United States and the Muslim World 1776–1815.* Oxford: Oxford University Press, 1995.

Alsultany, Evelyn. *Arabs and Muslims in the Media: Race and Representation after 9/11.* New York: New York University Press, 2012.

Apuzzo, Matt and Adam Goldman. *Enemies Within: Inside the NYDP's Secret Spying Unit and bin Laden's Final Plot against America.* New York: Simon and Schuster, 2013.

Arnold, James R. *The Moro War: How America Battled a Muslim Insurgency in the Philippine Jungle, 1902–1913.* New York: Bloomsbury, 2011.

Bail, Christopher. *Terrified: How Anti-Muslim Fringe Organizations Became Mainstream.* Princeton: Princeton University Press, 2015.

Bakalian, Anny and Mehdi Bozorgmehr. *Backlash 9/11: Middle Eastern and Muslim Americans Respond.* Berkeley: University of California Press, 2009.

Balko, Radley. *Rise of the Warrior Cop: The Militarization of America's Police Forces.* New York: PublicAffairs, 2014.

Baron, Robert A., and Deborah R. Richardson. *Human Aggression.* New York: Plenum Press, 1994.

Bayoumi, Moustafa. *How Does It Feel to Be a Problem? Being Young and Arab in America.* New York: Penguin Books, 2008.

Berger, J.M. *Jihad Joe: Americans Who Go to War in the Name of Islam.* Washington, D.C.: Potomac Books, 2011.

Bilici, Mucahit. *Finding Mecca in America: How Islam Is Becoming an American Religion.* Chicago: University of Chicago Press, 2012.

Blanks, David R., and Michael Frassetto, eds. *Western Views of Islam in Medieval and Early Modern Europe: Perceptions of the Other.* New York: St. Martin's Press, 1999.

Boot, Max. *The Savage Wars of Peace: Small Wars and the Rise of American Power.* New York: Basic Books, 2002.

Buhite, Russell D. *Lives at Risk: Hostages and Victims in American Foreign Policy.* Wilmington, DE: Scholarly Resources, Inc., 1995.

Cainkar, Louise A. *Homeland Insecurity: The Arab American and Muslim American Experience after 9/11.* New York: Russell Sage Foundation, 2009.

Churchill, Ward and Jim Vander Wall. *The COINTELPRO Papers: Documents from the FBI's Secret Wars Against Domestic Dissent.* Boston: South End Press, 1990.

Cohen, Stanley. *Folk Devils and Moral Panics: The Creation of the Mods and Rockers.* New York: Routledge, 2002.

Cole, David, and James Dempsey. *Terrorism and the Constitution.* New York: The New Press, 2006.

Cole, David, and Jules Lobel. *Less Safe, Less Free: Why America Is Losing the War on Terror.* New York: The New Press, 2009.

Cunningham, David. *There's Something Happening Here: The New Left, the Klan, and FBI Counterintelligence.* Berkeley: University of California Press, 2004.

Daniels, Roger. *The Golden Door: American Immigration Policy and Immigrants since 1882.* New York: Hill and Wang, 2005.

Davis, James Kirkpatrick. *Spying on America: The FBI's Domestic Counterintelligence Program.* Westport, CT: Praeger, 1992.

DeNovo, John A. *American Interests and Policies in the Middle East: 1900–1939.* Minneapolis: University of Minnesota Press, 1963.

Federal Bureau of Investigation, *Nation of Islam: The FBI Files.* Lexington, KY: Filiquarian Publishing/Qontro, 2013.

Feldman, Jay. *Manufacturing Hysteria: A History of Scapegoating, Surveillance, and Secrecy in Modern America.* New York: Anchor Books, 2011.

Fulton, Robert. *Moroland: The History of Uncle Sam and the Moros.* Bend, Oregon: Tumalo Creek Press, 2009.

Gaskew, Tom. *Policing Muslim American Communities: A Compendium of Post-9/11 Interviews.* Lewiston, NY: Edwin Mellen Press, 2008.

Gerstenfeld, Phyllis B. *Hate Crimes: Causes, Controls, and Controversies.* Los Angeles: Sage Publications, 2013.

GhaneaBassiri, Kambiz. *A History of Islam in America.* Cambridge: Cambridge University Press, 2010.

Gomez, Michael A. *Black Crescent: The Experience and Legacy of African Muslims in America.* Cambridge: Cambridge University Press, 2005.

Gottschalk, Peter, and Gabriel Greenberg. *Islamophobia: Making Muslims the Enemy.* Lanham, MD: Rowman and Littlefield Publishers, 2007.

Gray, L. Patrick, *In Nixon's Web: A Year in the Crosshairs of Watergate.* New York: Henry Holt and Company, 2008.

Gutman, Roy. *How We Missed the Story: Osama bin Laden, the Taliban, and the Hijacking of Afghanistan.* Washington, D.C.: United States Institute of Peace, 2008.

Haddad, Yvonne Yazbeck. *Becoming American? The Forging of Arab and Muslim Identity in Pluralist America.* Waco, Texas: Baylor University Press, 2011.

Hafetz, Jonathan. *Habeas Corpus after 9/11: Confronting America's New Global Detention System.* New York: New York University Press, 2011.

Hall, Nathan. *Hate Crime.* London: Routledge, 2013.

Herman, Susan N. *Taking Liberties: The War on Terror and the Erosion of American Democracy.* Oxford: Oxford University Press, 2011.

Hill, Robert A., ed. *The FBI's RACON: Racial Conditions in the United States during World War II.* Boston: Northeastern University Press, 1995.

Hoffer, Peter Charles. *The Brave New World: A History of Early America.* Baltimore, MD: Johns Hopkins University Press, 2006.

Howard, Douglas. *The History of Turkey.* Westport, CT: Greenwood Press, 2001.

Irwin, Ray. *The Diplomatic Relations of the United States with the Barbary Powers 1776–1816.* New York: Russell and Russell, 1931.

Karam, Nicoletta. *The 9/11 Backlash: A Decade of U.S. Hate Crimes Targeting the Innocent.* Berkeley, CA: Beatitude Press, 2012.

Kettl, David F. *Systems Under Stress: Homeland Security and American Politics.* Washington, D.C.: Congressional Quarterly Press, 2007.

Kidd, Thomas. *American Christians and Islam: Evangelical Culture and Muslims from the Colonial Period to the Age of Terrorism.* Princeton: Princeton University Press, 2009.

Kitzen, Michael. *Tripoli and the United States at War: A History of American Relations with the Barbary States.* London: McFarland & Company, 1962.

Koven, Steven G. and Frank Gotzke. *American Immigration Policy: Confronting the Nation's Challenges.* New York: Springfield, 2010.

Kushner, Harvey W. *Encyclopedia of Terrorism.* Thousands Oaks, CA: Sage Publications, 2003.

Lean, Nathan. *The Islamophobia Industry: How the Right Manufactures Fear of Muslims.* London: Pluto Press, 2012.

Leiner, Frederick. *The End of Barbary Terror: America's 1815 War Against the Pirates of North Africa.* Oxford: Oxford University Press, 2006.

Lemann, Nicholas. *The Promised Land: The Great Black Migration and How It Changed America.* New York: Vintage Books, 1992.

Levin, Jack and Jack McDevitt. *Hate Crimes Revisited: America's War on Those Who Are Different.* Boulder, CO: Westview Press, 2002.

Lewy, Guenter. *The Armenian Massacres in Ottoman Turkey: A Disputed Genocide.* Salt Lake City: University of Utah Press, 2007.

Little, Douglas. *American Orientalism: The United States and the Middle East since 1945.* Chapel Hill: University of North Carolina Press, 2008.

Lyons, Jonathan. *Islam through Western Eyes: From the Crusades to the War on Terrorism.* New York: Columbia University Press, 2012.

Marr, Timothy. *The Cultural Roots of American Islamicism*. Cambridge: Cambridge University Press, 2006.

Martin, C. Augustus. *The Sage Encyclopedia of Terrorism*. Los Angeles: Sage Publications, 2011.

Mayer, Jane. *The Dark Side: The Inside Story of How the War on Terror Turned into a War on American Ideals*. New York: Doubleday, 2008.

McCann, Joseph. *Terrorism on American Soil*. Boulder, Colorado: Sentient Publications, 2006.

McCarthy, Justin. *The Ottoman Turks: An Introductory History to 1923*. London: Longman Ltd., 1997.

McCarthy, Justin. *The Turk in America: The Creation of an Enduring Prejudice*. Salt Lake City: University of Utah Press, 2010.

Moghadam, Assaf. *The Gobalization of Martyrdom*. Baltimore: Johns Hopkins University Press, 2008.

Munro, Victoria. *Hate Crime in the Media: A History*. Santa Barbara: Praeger, 2014.

Nacos, Brigitte L., and Oscar Torres-Reyna. *Fueling Our Fears: Stereotyping, Media Coverage, and Public Opinion of Muslim Americans*. Lanham, MD: Rowman and Littlefield, 2007.

Nemeth, Charles. *Homeland Security: An Introduction to Principles and Practice*. Boca Raton: CRC Press, 2013.

Nguyen, Tram. *We Are All Suspects Now: Untold Stories from Immigrant Communities after 9/11*. Boston: Beacon Press, 2005.

Peek, Lori. *Behind the Backlash: Muslim Americans after 9/11*. New Delhi: Social Science Press, 2012.

Perry, Barbara. *In the Name of Hate: Understanding Hate Crimes*. New York: Routledge, 2001.

Priest, Dana, and William Arkin. *Top Secret America: The Rise of the New American Security State*. New York: Little, Brown and Company, 2011.

Saleeby, Najeeb Mitry. *The History of Sulu*. London: Forgotten Books, 2012, reprint of 1908 edition.

Semmerling, Tim Jon. *"Evil" Arabs in American Popular Film: Orientalist Fear*. Austin: University of Texas Press, 2006.

Shaheen, Jack G. *Guilty: Hollywood's Verdict on Arabs after 9/11*. Northampton, MA: Olive Branch Press, 2008.

Shaheen, Jack G. *Reel Bad Arabs: How Hollywood Vilifies a People*. Northampton, MA: Olive Branch Press, 2012.

Smith, Jane. *Islam in America*. New York: Columbia University Press, 2010.

Spellberg, Denise. *Thomas Jefferson's Qur'an: Islam and the Founders*. New York: Alfred A. Knopf, 2013.

Trask, Roger. *The United States Response to Turkish Nationalism and Reform, 1914–1939*. Minneapolis: University of Minnesota Press, 1971.

Turner, Richard Brent. *Islam in the African American Experience*. Bloomington: Indiana University Press, 1997.

Weiner, Tim. *Enemies: A History of the FBI*. New York: Random House, 2012.

Welch, Michael. *Scapegoats of September 11th: Hate Crimes and State Crimes in the War on Terror*. New Brunswick: Rutgers University Press, 2006.

Wilkerson, Isabel. *The Warmth of Other Suns: The Epic Story of America's Great Migration*. New York: Vintage Books, 2010.

Wong, Kam. *The Impact of USA Patriot Act on American Society: An Evidence Based Assessment*. New York: Nova Science Publishers, 2007.

Wright, Lawrence. *The Looming Tower: Al-Qaeda and the Road to 9/11*. New York: Vintage Books, 2007.

Wuthnow, Robert. *America and the Challenges of Religious Diversity*. Princeton: Princeton University Press, 2007.

Reports and Official Documents

Ali, Wajahat. *Fear, Inc.: The Roots of the Islamophobia Network in America*. Washington, D.C.: Center for American Progress, 2011.

American Attitudes Toward Arabs and Muslims. Washington, D.C.: Arab American Institute, 2014.

Asal, Victor, Kathleen Deloughery, Ryan D. King, R. Karl Rethemeyer. *Analysis of Factors Related to Hate Crimes and Terrorism*. College Park, MD: National Consortium for the Study of Terrorism and Responses to Terrorism, University of Maryland, 2012.

Bagby, Ihsan. *The American Mosque 2011: Basic Characteristics of the American Mosque and Attitudes of Mosque Leaders*. Hartford, CT: Faith Communities Today, Cooperative Congregational Studies Partnership, 2012.

Beutel, Alejandro J. *Building Bridges to Strengthen America: Forging an Effective Counterterrorism Enterprise between Muslim Americans and Law Enforcement*. Los Angeles: Muslim Public Affairs Council, 2009.

Boykin, William J., et al. *Sharia: The Threat to America*. Washington, D.C.: Center for Security Policy, 2010.

Carter, David L. *Law Enforcement Intelligence: A Guide for State, Local, and Tribal Law Enforcement Agencies*. Washington, D.C.: Department of Justice, 2009.

Compounding the Tragedy: The Other Victims of September 11th. Los Angeles: Los Angeles County Commission on Human Relations, 2002.

Confronting Discrimination in the Post-9/11 Era: Challenges and Opportunities Ten Years Later. Washington, D.C.: Department of Justice, October 2011.

Controversies Over Mosques and Islamic Centers Across the U.S. Washington, D.C.: Pew Research Center, 2012.

Davies, Heather J., and Gerald R. Murphy, *Protecting Your Communities from Terrorism: Strategies for Local Law Enforcement*, Washington, D.C.: Department of Justice, 2004.

Davis, Lois, et al. *Long-Term Effect of Law Enforcement's Post-9/11 Focus on Counterterrorism and Homeland Security*. Santa Monica: RAND Corporation, 2010.

Elsea, Jennifer K. *Detention of American Citizens as Enemy Combatants.* Washington, D.C.: Congressional Research Service, February 2005.

Empowering Local Partners to Prevent Violent Extremism in the United States, Washington, D.C.: The White House, August 2011.

Enforcing Religious Freedom in Prison, Washington, D.C.: United States Commission on Civil Rights, September 2008.

EU Terrorism Situation and Trends Report 2007. The Hague: Europol, 2007.

The Global Religious Landscape. Washington, D.C.: Pew Research Center, 2010.

Globalizing Torture: CIA Secret Detention and Extraordinary Rendition. New York: Open Society Foundations, 2013.

Grassroots Campaign to Fight Terrorism Handbook. Los Angeles: Muslim Public Affairs Council, 2005.

Greenberg, Karen, editor-in-chief. *Terrorism Trial Report Card: September 11, 2001–September 11, 2011.* New York: Center on Law and Security, New York University School of Law, 2011.

Growing Concern about Rise of Islamic Extremism at Home and Abroad. Washington, D.C.: Pew Research Center, September 2014.

Hafiz, Sameera, and Suman Raghunathan. *Under Suspicion, Under Attack: Xenophobic Political Rhetoric and Hate Violence against South Asian, Muslim, Sikh, Hindu, Middle Eastern, and Arab Communities in the United States.* Tacoma Park, MD: South Asian Americans Leading Together, 2014.

Henderson, Nicole J., Christopher W. Orwitz, Naomi F. Sugie, and Joel Miller. *Law Enforcement and Arab American Community Relations after September 11, 2001: Engagement in a Time of Uncertainty.* New York: Vera Institute of Justice, 2006.

Homegrown Terrorism: The Threat to Military Communities inside the United States, Majority Investigative Report, Committee on Homeland Security, U.S. House of Representatives, December 2011.

Huda, Qamar-ul. *The Diversity of Muslims in the United States: Views as Americans.* Washington, D.C.: United States Institute of Peace, 2006.

The Impact of 9/11 on Muslim American Young People: National and Religious Identity Formation in the Age of Terrorism and Islamophobia. Los Angeles: Muslim Public Affairs Council, 2007.

In Our Own Words: Narratives of South Asian New Yorkers Affected by Racial and Religious Profiling. Tacoma Park, MD: South Asian Americans Leading Together, 2012.

Justice Department's Project to Interview Aliens after September 11, 2001. Washington, D.C.: Government Accountability Office, April 2003.

Krouse, William J., and Bart Elias. *Terrorist Watchlist Checks and Air Passenger Prescreening.* Washington, D.C.: Congressional Research Service, December 30, 2009.

Kurzman, Charles. *Muslim-American Terrorism: Declining Further.* Chapel Hill: University of North Carolina, 2013.

Kurzman, Charles. *Muslim-American Terrorism in 2013*. Raleigh, NC: Duke University, February 2013.

Langton, Lynn, Michael Planty, and Nathan Sandhultz. *Hate Crime Victimization, 2003–2011*. Washington, D.C.: Bureau of Justice Statistics, Department of Justice, 2013.

Learning from 9/11: Organizational Change in the New York City and Arlington County, VA, Police Departments. Washington, D.C.: National Institute of Justice, Department of Justice, 2009.

Malhotra, Anjana. *Witness to Abuse: Human Rights Abuses under the Material Witness Law since September 11*. New York: Human Rights Watch, June 2005.

Mishra, Debasish, and Deepa Iyer. *American Backlash: Terrorists Bring War Home in More Ways than One*. Tacoma Park, MD: South Asian American Leaders of Tomorrow, 2001.

Muslim Americans: A National Portrait. Washington, D.C.: Gallup, Inc., 2009.

Muslim Americans: No Signs of Growth in Alienation or Support for Extremism. Washington, D.C.: Pew Research Center, 2012.

The Price of Ignorance. Washington, D.C.: Council for American-Islamic Relations, 1996.

Post-9/11 Attitudes: Religion More Prominent, Muslim-Americans More Accepted, Washington, D.C.: Pew Research Center, December 2001.

Priest, Dana and William Arkin. *Top Secret America: A Washington Post Investigation*, http://projects.washingtonpost.com/top-secret-america.

Public Expresses Mixed Views of Islam, Mormons. Washington, D.C.: Pew Research Center, September 2007.

Public Remains Conflicted Over Islam. Washington, D.C.: Pew Research Center, August 2010.

Ramirez, Debbie A., Sasha Cohen O'Connell, and Rabia Zafar, *Developing Partnerships Between Law Enforcement and American Muslim, Arab, and Sikh Communities: A Promising Practices Guide*. Boston: Partnering for Prevention and Community Safety Initiative Publications, Northeastern University Law School, 2004.

Religion and Politics: Contention and Consensus. Washington, D.C.: Pew Research Center, July 2003.

Remaking Bagram: The Creation of an Afghan Internment Regime and the Divide over U.S. Detention Power. New York: Open Society Foundations, 2012.

Report on the Tenth Anniversary of the Religious Land Use and Institutionalized Persons Act. Washington, D.C.: Department of Justice, September 2010.

The Right Wing Playbook on Anti-Muslim Extremism. Washington, D.C.: People for the American Way, 2011.

The September 11 Detainees: A Review of the Treatment of Aliens Held on Immigration Charges in Connection with the Investigation of the September 11 Attacks. Washington, D.C.: Office of the Inspector General, Department of Justice, 2003.

Sing, Amardeep. *We Are Not the Enemy: Hate Crimes Against Arabs, Muslims, and Those Perceived to Be Arab or Muslim After September 11.* New York: Human Rights Watch, 2002.

Spalek, Basia, Salwa El Awa, and Laura Zahra McDonald. *Police-Muslim Engagement and Partnerships for the Purposes of Counter-Terrorism: An Examination.* Birmingham, UK: University of Birmingham, 2008.

Task Force on Muslim American Civic and Political Engagement. *Strengthening America: The Civic and Political Integration of Muslim Americans.* Chicago: Chicago Council on Global Affairs, 2007.

Terrorist Watchlist: Routinely Assessing Impact of Agency Actions since the December 25, 2009 Attempted Attack Could Help Inform Future Efforts. Washington, D.C.: Government Accountability Office, May 2012.

Turban Myths: The Opportunity and Challenges for Reframing a Cultural Symbol for Post-9/11 America. Stanford, CA: Stanford Peace Innovation Lab, 2013.

Tyler, Tom, Stephen J. Schulhofer, and Aziz R. Huq. "Legitimacy and Deterrence Effects in Counter-Terrorism Policing: A Study of Muslim Americans." Pubic Law and Legal Theory Research Paper Series. Chicago and New York: University of Chicago Law School and New York University School of Law, 2009.

Unleashed and Unchained: The FBI's Unchecked Abuse of Authority. New York: American Civil Liberties Union, September 2013.

The USA Patriot Act: Impact on the Arab and Muslim Community. Clinton Township, Michigan: Institute for Social Policy and Understanding, 2004.

Views of Muslim Americans Hold Steady after London Bombings. Washington, D.C.: Pew Research Center, July 2005.

Washington Post-ABC News Polls, available through the *Washington Post* Public Opinion Poll Archive.

Wilson, Meagan Meuchel. *Hate Crime Victimization, 2004–2012.* Washington, D.C.: Bureau of Justice Statistics, Department of Justice, 2013.

The World's Muslims: Unity and Diversity. Washington, D.C.: Pew Research Center, 2012.

Book Chapters and Journal Articles

Abdeen, Mike. "Lessons Learned and Best Practices: The Outreach Efforts of the Los Angeles County Sheriff's Department Community Policing Method with Emphasis on the Muslim Community." In *Preventing Ideological Violence: Communities, Police, and Case Studies of "Success,"* edited by P. Daniel Silk, Basia Spalek, Mary O'Rawe, 227–238. New York: Palgrave Macmillan, 2013.

Alkhatib, Ihsan. "Building Bridges: The Experience of Leaders in Detroit, Michigan." In *Preventing Ideological Violence: Communities, Police, and Case Studies of "Success,"* edited by P. Daniel Silk, Basia Spalek, and Mary O'Rawe, 209–226. New York: Palgrave Macmillan, 2013.

Baepler, Paul. "Introduction." In *White Slaves, African Masters: An Anthology of American Barbary Captivity Narratives*, edited by Paul Baepler, 1–58. Chicago: University of Chicago Press, 1999.

Berk, Richard A., Elizabeth A. Boyd, and Karl M. Hamner. "Thinking More Clearly About Hate-Motivated Crimes." In *Hate and Bias Crime: A Reader*, edited by Barbara Perry, 49–60. New York: Routledge, 2003.

Bowen, Patrick D. "Satti Majid: A Sudanese Founder of American Islam." *Journal of Africana Religions* 1, no. 2 (2013).

Byler, Charles A. "Pacifying the Moros: American Military Government in the Southern Philippines, 1899–1913." *Military Review*, May–June 2005.

Bozorgmehr, Mehdi, Anny Bakalian, and Sarah Salman. "Host Hostility and Nativism." In *The Routledge International Handbook of Migration Studies*, edited by Steven J. Gold and Stephanie J. Nawyn, 189–201. New York: Routledge, 2013.

Cainkar, Louise. "American Muslims at the Dawn of the 21st Century: Hope and Pessimism in the Drive for Civic and Political Inclusion." In *Muslims in the West after 9/11: Religion, Politics and Law*, edited by Jocelyne Cesari, 176–197. London: Routledge, 2010.

Craig, Kellina M. "A Review of the Social Psychological Literature on Hate Crimes as a Distinct Form of Aggression." In *Hate and Bias Crime: A Reader*, edited by Barbara Perry, 117–130. New York: Routledge, 2003.

Curtis, Edward. "The Black Muslim Scare of the Twentieth Century: Religious Stereotyping and Out-grouping of Muslims in the United States." In *Islamophobia in America: The Anatomy of Intolerance*, edited by Carl Ernst, 75–106. New York: Palgrave Macmillan, 2013.

Dancygier, Rafaela M., and Donald P. Green. "Hate Crimes." In *The Sage Handbook of Prejudice, Stereotyping and Discrimination*, edited by John F. Dovidio, Miles Hewstone, Peter Glick, and Victoria M. Esses, 294–311. London: Sage Publications, 2010.

Entman, Robert M. "Framing: Towards Clarification of a Fractured Paradigm." *Journal of Communication* 43, no. 4 (1993), 51–58.

GhaneaBassiri, Kambiz. "Islamophobia in American History: Religious Stereotyping and Out-grouping of Muslims in the United States." In *Islamophobia in America: The Anatomy of Intolerance*, edited by Carl Ernst, 53–74. New York: Palgrave Macmillan, 2013.

Gottschalk, Peter, and Gabriel Greenberg. "Common Heritage, Uncommon Fear: Islamophobia in the United States and British India." In *Islamophobia in America: The Anatomy of Intolerance*, edited by Carl Ernst, 21–52. New York: Palgrave Macmillan, 2013.

Haddad, Yvonne Yazbeck. "The Shaping of Arab and Muslim Identity in the United States." In *Immigration and Religion in America: Comparative and Historical Perspective*, edited by Richard Alba, Albert J. Raboteau, Josh DeWind, 246–276. New York: New York University Press, 2008.

Hazen, Helen D., and Heike C. Alberts. "Visitors or Immigrants? International Students in the United States," *Population, Space and Place* 12, no. 3 (2006).

Huntington, Samuel. "The Clash of Civilizations?" *Foreign Affairs* 73, no. 3 (Summer 1993).

Lee, Martha F. "The Nation of Islam and Violence." In *Violence and New Religious Movements*, edited by James R. Lewis. Oxford: Oxford University Press, 2011.

Lizza, Ryan. "State of Deception." *The New Yorker*, December 16, 2013.

McCombs, Maxwell. "A Look at Agenda-Setting: Past, Present and Future." *Journalism Studies* 6, no. 4 (2005), 543–557.

Murray, Nancy. "Profiled: Arabs, Muslims, and the Post-9/11 Hunt for the Enemy Within." In *Civil Rights in Peril: The Targeting of Arabs and Muslims*, edited by Elaine C. Hagopian. Chicago: Haymarket Books, 2004.

Nimer, Mohammed. "Muslims in the American Body Politic." In *Muslims' Place in the American Public Square: Hopes, Fears, and Aspirations*, edited by Zahid H. Bukhari, Sulayman S. Nyang, Mumtaz Ahmad, and John L. Esposito. Walnut Creek, CA: AltaMira Press, 2004.

Perry, Barbara. "Anti-Muslim Retaliatory Violence Following the 9/11 Terrorist Attacks." In *Hate and Bias Crime: A Reader*, edited by Barbara Perry, 183–202. New York: Routledge, 2003.

Ramirez, Deborah, Tara Lai Quinlan, Sean P. Mal, and Taylor Shutt. "Community Partnerships to Thwart Terrorism." In *Preventing Ideological Violence: Communities, Police, and Case Studies of "Success,"* edited by P. Daniel Silk, Basia Spalek, and Mary O'Rawe, 151–170. New York: Palgrave Macmillan, 2013.

Spalek, Basia. "Community-Based Approaches to Counter-Terrorism." In *Counter-Terrorism: Community-Based Approaches to Preventing Terror Crime*, edited by Basia Spalek, 27–49. London: Palgrave Macmillan, 2012.

Spalek, Basia. "Policing within Counter-Terrorism." In *Counter-Terrorism: Community-Based Approaches to Preventing Terror Crime*, edited by Basia Spalek, 50–73. London: Palgrave Macmillan, 2012.

Steinback, Robert "The Anti-Muslim Inner Circle," *Intelligence Report* 142 (Southern Poverty Law Center, Summer 2011), http://www.splcenter.org.

Vasi, Ion Bogdan, and David Strang. "Civil Liberty in America: The Diffusion of Municipal Bill of Rights Resolutions after the Passage of the USA PATRIOT Act." *American Journal of Sociology* 114, no. 6 (May 2009), 1716–1764.

Wang, Lu-Win. "Hate Crimes and Everyday Discrimination: Influences of and on the Social Contexts." In *Crimes of Hate: Selected Readings*, edited by Phyllis B. Gerstenfeld and Diana R. Grant, 156–168. Thousand Oaks, CA: Sage Publications, 2004.

Wingfield, Marvin. "The Impact of 9/11, Middle East Conflicts, and Anti-Arab Discrimination." In *Daily Life of Arab Americans in the 21st Century*, edited by Anan Ameri and Holly Arida, 29–55. Santa Barbara: Greenwood, 2012.

Yin, Tung. "Joint Terrorism Task Forces as a Window into the Security vs. Civil Liberties Debate," *Florida Coastal Law Review* 13, no. 1 (2012), 1–32.

Zelin, Aaron Y. "American Jihadi." *Foreign Policy*, September 30, 2011.

Zenko, Micah. "The Long Third War." *Foreign Policy*, October 30, 2012.

Newspaper Articles and Other News Sources

"Agreement Reached to Resolve Mosque Construction Dispute in Lomita, California." *Religious Freedom in Focus* 56 (April 2013), http://www.justice.gov/crt/spec_topics/religiousdiscrimination/newsletters.php.

"Appeals Court Upholds Prisoner's Right to Wear Quarter-Inch Beard." *Religious Freedom in Focus* 56 (April 2013), http://www.justice.gov/crt/spec_topics/religiousdiscrimination/newsletters.php.

"Applying God's Law: Religious Courts and Mediation in the U.S." Pew Research Center, April 2013, http://www.pewforum.org.

Apuzzo, Matt, and Adam Goldman. "With CIA Help, NYPD Moves Covertly into Muslim Areas." *AP's Probe into NYPD Intelligence Operations* (Associated Press), August 23, 2011, www.ap.org/media-center/nypd/investigation.

Associated Press. "Cain Apologizes after Meeting with Muslim Leaders." *USA Today*, July 28, 2011.

Associated Press. "Man Who Rammed Mosque Guilty of Hate Crime." St. *Petersburg Times*, November 2, 2002.

Bacon, Perry. "Foes Use Obama's Muslim Ties to Fuel Rumors about Him." *Washington Post,* November 29, 2007.

Baker, Al, and William Rashbaum. "Police Find Car Bomb in Times Square." *New York Times*, May 1, 2010.

Barnard, Anne. "In Lower Manhattan, 2 Mosques Have Firm Roots." *New York Times*, August 13, 2010.

Barr, Andy. "Newt Gingrich Compares Mosque to Nazis." *Politico*, August 16, 2010, http://www.politico.com.

Barrett, Devlin. "FBI Questioning Libyans." *Wall Street Journal*, April 5, 2011.

Baumann, Nick. "American Muslim Alleges FBI Had a Hand in His Torture." *Mother Jones*, April 17, 2012.

Belluck, Pam. "Unrepentant Shoe Bomber Is Given a Life Sentence." *New York Times*, January 31, 2003.

Bohlinger, Scott. "First U.S. Museum Devoted to Islam Based in Jackson, Mississippi." *The Washington File* (Washington, D.C.: Department of State), March 27, 2003.

Bonner, Raymond. "New Jersey Man Who Fled Somalia Ends Up in an Ethiopian Jail." *New York Times,* April 23, 2007.

Booth, Jenny. "Gloucester Shoebomber Jailed for 13 Years." *The Times*, April 22, 2005.

Brachear, Manya A. "Settlement Reached in Muslim's Suit over Denial of Time Off for Hajj." *Chicago Tribune*, October 19, 2011.

Brennan, Margaret. "Can a Community Program Help Stop Homegrown Radicals." *CBS This Morning*, October 23, 2014.

Brown, Robbie, and Christine Hauser. "After a Struggle, Mosque Opens in Tennessee." *New York Times*, August 10, 2012.

"Bye-bye Allen West: Remembering His 10 Most Impressive Moments." MSNBC, November 20, 2012, http://www.msnbc.com.

"Civil Rights Division Settles Muslim Student Prayer Case." *Religious Freedom in Focus* 25 (May 2007), http://www.justice.gov/crt/spec_topics/religiousdis crimination/newsletters.php.

Clayton, Mark. "Too Much Terrorism Data? Connecting the Dots May Be Getting Harder." NBC News, May 23, 2013, http://investigations.nbcnews.com.

Coker, Matt. "Souhair Katib Can Sue County of Orange for Forcing Her to Remove Her Hijab: Supreme Court." *OC Weekly*, October 3, 2011.

Cooper, Helene. "Five Guantánamo Prisoners Are Released to Kazakhstan." *New York Times*, December 31, 2014.

Cooper, Jonathan and Nigel Duara. "Arson Suspected at Islamic Center in Oregon." *Washington Post*, November 28, 2010.

"Court Dismisses RLUIPA Appeal after Settlement." *Religious Freedom in Focus* 59 (February 2014), http://www.justice.gov/crt/spec_topics/religiousdiscrimi nation/newsletters.php.

"Court Enters Consent Decree Granting Muslim Girl's Right to Wear Headscarf to School." *Religious Freedom in Focus* 4 (May 2004), http://www.justice .gov/crt/spec_topics/religiousdiscrimination/newsletters.php.

"Court Holding Facility Is Covered by RLUIPA, En Banc Court Rules." *Religious Freedom in Focus* 45 (March 2011), http://www.justice.gov/crt/spec_ topics/religiousdiscrimination/newsletters.php.

Croman, John (KARE 11 News). "Justice Department Sues Minnesota City over Mosque Permit." *USA Today*, August 28, 2014.

Currier, Cora. "Spies Among Us: How Community Outreach Programs to Muslims Blur Lines Between Outreach and Intelligence." *The Intercept*, January 21, 2015.

Daly, Michael. "NYPD on the Real Enemies Within: Going Undercover With Jihadis." *Daily Beast*. September 9, 2013, http://www.thedailybeast.com.

Dandridge-Rystrom, Dianna. "Bennett Stands His Ground." *Sequoyah County Times*, September 17, 2014.

Dao, James. "Man Claims Terror Ties in Little Rock Shooting." *New York Times*, January 22, 2010.

Davis, Julie Hirschfield. "Obama Urges Global United Front Against Extremist Groups Like ISIS." *New York Times*, February 15, 2015.

Day, Sherri. "F.B.I. Arrests Members of Militant Anti-Arab Group." *New York Times*, December 12, 2001.

Dentch, Courtney. "SE Queens Man Arrested in Slaying of Bangladeshi." *Times Ledger*, August 22, 2002.

DeYoung, Karen, Greg Miller, and Greg Jaffe. "U.S. Indicts Somali on Terrorism Charges." *Washington Post*, July 5, 2011.

"DOJ Closes RLUIPA Investigation after Illinois Village Allows Mosque Expansion." *Religious Freedom in Focus* 32 (March/April 2008), http://www .justice.gov/crt/spec_topics/religiousdiscrimination/newsletters.php.

"DOJ Reaches Settlement in Georgia Mosque Dispute." *Religious Freedom in Focus* 47 (August 2011), http://www.justice.gov/crt/spec_topics/religiousdis crimination/newsletters.php.

"DOJ Sues New York Corrections Department Over Refusal to Make Religious Accommodations." *Religious Freedom in Focus* 23 (March 2007), http://www.justice.gov/crt/spec_topics/religiousdiscrimination/newsletters.php.

Duggan, Paul. "In Metro Ads, Pro-Israel Group Features Photo of Hitler." *Washington Post*, May 15, 2014.

"Edmonds Man Sentenced in Cross-Burning Outside Home." *Seattle Times*, February 17, 2006.

Eilperin, Juliet. "Trying to Counter Extremism at Home, U.S. Faces a Risk: Sowing More Distrust." *Washington Post*, February 16, 2015.

Eligon, John, and Michael Cooper. "Blasts at Boston Marathon Kill 3." *New York Times*, April 15, 2013.

Elliot, Andrea. "The Man Behind the Anti-Sharia Movement." *New York Times*, July 30, 2011.

Esposito, Richard, and Jason Ryan. "FBI Has Interviewed 800 Libyans about Terror Threat." ABC News, April 2011, http://abcnews.go.com.

Esquivel, Paloma. "In Alex Odeh's 1985 Slaying, Still Seeking Answers." *Los Angeles Times*, October 20, 2013.

Esterl, Mike. "Mosque Zoning Row Draws Scrutiny." *Wall Street Journal*, August 13, 2011.

Fahrenthold, David A., and Michelle Boorstein. "Rep. Peter King's Muslim Hearings: A Key Moment in an Angry Conversation." *Washington Post*, March 9, 2011.

Farmer, Blake. "A Fight to the Finish for Tennessee Mosque." *All Things Considered* (National Public Radio), June 21, 2010, http://www.npr.org.

"FBI Records Reveal Details of Nixon-Era Racial Profiling Program Targeting Arabs." *IntelWire*, December 4, 2010, http://news.intelwire.com.

Federal Bureau of Investigation. "Moorish Science Temple of America." *FBI Records: The Vault*, http://vault.fbi.gov.

Feyerick, Deborah, and Lateef Mungin. "Alleged al Qaeda Operative Abu Anas al Libi Pleads Not Guilty." CNN, October 15, 2013, www.cnn.com.

Finn, Peter. "ACLU Mounts First Legal Challenge to No-Fly List." *Washington Post*, June 30, 2010.

Finn, Peter. "Awlaki Directed Christmas 'Underwear Bomber' Plot, Justice Department Memo Says." *Washington Post*, February 10, 2012.

Finn, Peter. "The Post-9/11 Life of an American Charged with Murder." *Washington Post*, September 4, 2010.

Finn, Peter, and Kafia A. Hosh. "I Felt Like I Was Getting Kidnapped." *Washington Post*, January 22, 2011.

Finn, Tom, and Noah Browning. "An American Teenager in Yemen Paying for the Sins of His Father." *Time*, October 27, 2011.

Fisher, Grey. "The New NYPD: Pushing Civil Liberty Bounds to Keep the City Safe." *National Security Journal*. Cambridge, MA: Harvard Law School, September 20, 2011.

"Florida Muslims Are on Alert After Arrest." *New York Times*, August 25, 2002.

Fox, Lauren. "Michele Bachmann Sticks to Accusations about Muslim Brotherhood." *U.S. News and World Report*, July 19, 2012.

Friedersdorf, Conor. "Herman Cain's Anti-Muslim Prejudice Returns." *The Atlantic*, November 14, 2011.

Gearan, Anna. "American Jailed in Yemen, Sharif Mobley, Has Disappeared and Is in Danger, His Lawyers Say." *Washington Post*, April 11, 2014.

Gellman, Barton. "U.S. Surveillance Architecture Includes Collection of Revealing Internet, Phone Metadata." *Washington Post*, June 15, 2013.

"Georgia Policy Change to Allow Religious Headcoverings in Court; DOJ Closes Inquiry." *Religious Freedom in Focus* 39 (June/July 2009), http://www.justice.gov/crt/spec_topics/religiousdiscrimination/newsletters.php.

Goldman, Adam, and Matt Apuzzo. "NYPD Built Secret Files on Mosques outside NY." *AP's Probe Into NYPD Intelligence Operations* (Associated Press), February 22, 2012, www.ap.org/media-center/nypd/investigation.

Goldman, Adam, and Matt Apuzzo. "NYPD Designates Mosques as Terrorist Organizations." *AP's Probe Into NYPD Intelligence Operations* (Associated Press), August 28, 2013, www.ap.org/media-center/nypd/investigation.

Goldman, Adam. "U.S. Quietly Whittles Down Foreign Detainee Population at Facility in Afghanistan." *Washington Post*, February 25, 2014.

Goldman, Adam. "Video Shows U.S. Abduction of Accused al-Qaeda Terrorist on Trial for Embassy Bombings." *Washington Post*, January 10, 2014.

Goldman, Adam, and Matt Apuzzo. "With Cameras, Informants, NYPD Eyed Mosques." *AP's Probe Into NYPD Intelligence Operations* (Associated Press), February 23, 2012, www.ap.org/media-center/nypd/investigation.

Goldman, Adam, and Matt Apuzzo. "With CIA Help, NYPD Moves Covertly in Muslim Areas." *AP's Probe Into NYPD Intelligence Operations* (Associated Press), August 23, 2011, www.ap.org/media-center/nypd/investigation.

Goodman, J. David. "Suspect in Three Killings Faced Financial Troubles." *New York Times*, November 22, 2012.

Goodstein, Laurie. "Drawing U.S. Crowds with Anti-Islam Message." *New York Times*, March 7, 2011.

Goodstein, Laurie. "U.S. Muslims Take On ISIS' Recruiting Machine." *New York Times*, February 19, 2015.

Gray, Jerry. "Foreigners Investing In Libya or in Iran Face U.S. Sanctions." *New York Times*, July 24, 1996.

Grimley, Matthew. "Meet the Abu Hiraira Islamic Center." *Twin Cities Daily Planet*, January 28, 2015.

Guccione, Jean. "JDL Chief Dies; Suit Threatened." *Los Angeles Times*, November 15, 2002.

Hagerty, Barbara Bradley. "Muslims Face Risks in Giving to Charities." *Morning Edition* (National Public Radio), June 16, 2009.

Hawley, Chris. "NYPD Monitored Muslims All Over the Northeast." *AP's Probe Into NYPD Intelligence Operations* (Associated Press), February 18, 2012, www.ap.org/media-center/nypd/investigation.

Heim, Joe. "Wade Michael Page Was Steeped in Neo-Nazi Hate Music Movement." *Washington Post*, August 7, 2012.

Henry, Devin. "Minnesotans Focus on Stopping Terrorist Recruitment at Hill Hearing." *Minnesota Post*, July 27, 2011.

"History of Hate: Crimes Against Sikhs since 9/11." *Huffington Post*, August 7, 2012.

Hollingsworth, Heather (Associated Press). "Driver Charged With Murder in Somali Teen's Death." ABC News, December 5, 2014, http://abcnews.go.com.

Hooda, Samreen. "Muslims on the No-Fly List now Suing FBI Pressured to Be Informants." *Huffington Post*, May 17, 2013, http://www.huffingtonpost.com.

Hopper, Douglas. "The Terrorist Screening Center Defends No Fly List." *Tell Me More* (National Public Radio), August 13, 2010, www.npr.org.

Hosenball, Mark, and Matt Spetalnick. "Drone Strike Ends Long Hunt for U.S.-Born Awlaki." Reuters, September 30, 2011, www.reuters.com.

Hsu, Spencer S. "Al-Qaeda Operative Is Charged in N.Y. Subway Plot." *Washington Post*, July 8, 2010.

Ingraham, Christopher. "The Pentagon Gave Nearly Half a Billion Dollars of Military Gear to Local Law Enforcement Last Year." *Washington* Post, August 14, 2014.

"Islam Rising: What Do We Think of Islam." *Los Angeles Times*, April 6, 1993.

Jamal, Zahra N. "Charitable Giving Among Muslim Americans: Ten Years after 9/11." Institute for Social Policy and Understanding, Policy Brief No. 46, September 2011.

Johnson, Gene. "Naveed Haq Guilty in Jewish Center Trial." *Seattle Times*, December 15, 2009.

Johnston, David. "US Says Rendition to Continue, But with More Oversight." *New York Times*, August 24, 2009.

"Justice Department Files Suit against School District over Failure to Accommodate Muslim School Police Officer." *Religious Freedom in Focus* 60 (May 2014), http://www.justice.gov/crt/spec_topics/religiousdiscrimination/newsletters.php.

Kassem, Ramzi. "The Long Roots of the NYPD Spying Program." *The Nation*, June 13, 2013.

Kelley, David. "FBI Investigating Fatal Blast at a San Bernardino County Home as a Hate Crime." *Los Angeles Times*, July 10, 2009.

Keyes, Scott. "Herman Cain Tells ThinkProgress 'I Will Not' Appoint a Muslim in My Administration." ThinkProgress, March 26, 2011, http://thinkprogress.org.

Kindy, Kimberly. "Group Swamps Swing States With Movie on Radical Islam." *Washington Post*, October 26, 2008.

Kovach, Gretel. "Muslim Charity Convicted in Terrorism Financing Case." *New York Times*, October 25, 2008.

Krogh, Martin Von. "American Seeks Political Asylum in Sweden, Alleging Torture, FBI Coercion." NBC News, April 18, 2012, www.usnews.nbcnews.com.

Leon, John de. "Burien Woman Pleads Not Guilty in Alleged Attack on Muslims." *Seattle Times*, November 2, 2010.

Levs, Josh. "Police to Get Training after Head-scarf Wearer's Arrest." CNN. December 23, 2008, www.cnn.com.

Lewis, Bernard. "The Roots of Muslim Rage." *The Atlantic*, September 1990, 60.

Lichtblau, Eric. "Bush Declared Student an Enemy Combatant." *New York Times*, June 24, 2003.

Lichtblau, Eric. "Inquiry Targeted 2000 Foreign Muslims in 2004." *New York Times*, October 31, 2008.

Liptak, Adam. "Ban on Prison Beards Violates Muslim Rights, Supreme Court Rules." *New York Times*, January 20, 2015.

Magagnini, Stephen. "Suspect in Killing of Iraqi Refugee in Sacramento Pleads Guilty." *Sacramento Bee*, October 8, 2014.

"Man Charged in Slayings of Brooklyn Shopkeepers." NBC News, November 21, 2012, http://wwwusnews.nbcnews.com.

"Man Gets Life in Murder of Arab American." *Los Angeles Times*, July 16, 2002.

"Man Who Slashed Cabbie in Anti-Muslim Tirade, Sentenced to Nearly 10 Years in Prison." CBS News, June 25, 2013, http://wwwnewyork.cbslocal.com.

Markton, Jerry. "Hamdi Returned to Saudi Arabia." *Washington Post*, October 12, 2004.

Mazzetti, Mark. "Detained American Says He Was Beaten in Kuwait." *New York Times*, January 5, 2011.

Mazzetti, Mark, Charlie Savage, and Scott Shane. "How a U.S. Citizen Came to Be in America's Cross Hairs." *New York Times*, March 9, 2013.

Mazzetti, Mark, Sabrina Tavernise, and Jack Healy. "Suspect, Charged, Said to Admit to Role in Plot." *New York Times*, May 4, 2010.

"Merchant Killed in Sylmar." *Los Angeles Times*, October 19, 2001.

Miller, Greg. "At CIA, a Convert to Islam Leads the Terrorism Hunt." *Washington Post*, March 24, 2012.

Miller, Greg, Adam Goldman, and Julie Tate. "Senate Report on CIA Program Details Brutality, Dishonesty." *Washington Post*, December 9, 2014.

Minai, Leonora, and Maureen Byrne Ahern. "Podiatrist's Arsenal Part of Blueprint for Terror." *St. Petersburg Times*, August 24, 2002.

Morris, Mark, Eric Adler, and Tony Rizzothe. "Man Charged with Murder for Allegedly Charging Teen with SUV outside Kansas City Mosque." *Kansas City Star*, December 5, 2014.

"Morton Grove, IL, Settles Lawsuit with School after DOJ Mediation." *Religious Freedom in Focus* 5 (June/July 2004), http://www.justice.gov/crt/spec_topics/religiousdiscrimination/newsletters.php.

Moynihan, Colin, and Christopher Maag. "Same .22-Caliber Pistol Was Used to Kill Three Merchants in Brooklyn, Police Say." *New York Times*, November 17, 2012.

Murray, Mark. "ISIS Threat: Fear of Terrorist Attack Soars to 9/11 High, NBC News/WSJ Poll Finds." NBC News, http://www.nbcnews.com.

Musaji, Sheila. "Islamophobia: Prejudice, Racist, or Violent Incidents at Mosques." *The American Muslim*, June 5, 2013.

Najafizada, Enayat, and Rod Nordland. "Afghans Avenge Florida Koran Burning, Killing 12." *New York Times*, April 1, 2011.

Neubauer, Ian Lloyd. "Harsh Sentence a Warning to Australia's Young Muslim Zealots." *Time*, May 14, 2013.

Overby, Peter. "Charity Floods Swing States with Anti-Islam DVD." *Morning Edition* (National Public Radio), September 26, 2008.

Pearson, Sophia. "Philadelphia Tells Muslim Police to Trim Beards or Lose Jobs." Bloomberg News, October 19, 2005, www.bloomberg.com.

Pierson, David, and Greg Krikorian. "Former JDL Activist Slain in Federal Prison." *Los Angeles Times,* November 6, 2005.

Pipes, Daniel. "The Danger Within: Militant Islam in America." *Commentary*, November 2001, reproduced by the Middle East Forum, http://www.daniel pipes.org.

Pipes, Daniel. "The Muslims Are Coming! The Muslims Are Coming!" *The National Review*, November 1990, reproduced with revisions by the Middle East Forum, http://www.danielpipes.org.

Pipes, Daniel. "The New Anti-Semitism." *The Jewish Exponent*, October 16, 1997.

Polgreen, Lydia, and Al Baker. "Men Kill Student, 18, on Brooklyn Street." *New York Times*, November 13, 2002.

"Prisoners Gain Access to Religious Materials, Resolving DOJ Lawsuit." *Religious Freedom in Focus* 50 (January 2012), http://www.justice.gov/crt/spec_topics/religiousdiscrimination/newsletters.php.

Raghavan, Sudarsan. "U.S. Closes last Detainee Site in Afghanistan as Troop Pullout Advances." *Washington Post*, December 12, 2014.

Reaves, Brian A. "Census of State and Local Law Enforcement Agencies." Bureau of Justice Statistics, Department of Justice, July 2012, www.bjs.gov.

Reaves, Brian A. "Federal Law Enforcement Officers, 2008." Bureau of Justice Statistics, Department of Justice, June 2012, www.bjs.gov.

Richardson, John H. "Not Guilty by Reason of Afghanistan." *Esquire*, February 1, 2003.

Ripley, Amanda. "The Case of the Dirty Bomber." *Time*, June 16, 2002.

Roggio, Bill, and Alexander Mayor. "Charting the Data for U.S. Drone Strikes in Pakistan." *Long War Journal*, December 13, 2013, www.longwarjournal.org.

Rolfes, Ellen. "Lawsuit Alleges FBI Misused No-Fly List to Recruit Would-Be Muslim Informants." *PBS Newshour* (Public Broadcasting Service), April 23, 2014, http://www.pbs.org/newshour.

Romney, Lee. "Attack on Sikh Men Triggers Outcry in Elk Grove, Calif., and Beyond." *Los Angeles Times*, April 11, 2011.

Rosenberg, Carol. "Why Obama Hasn't Closed Guantanamo Camps." *Miami Herald*, January 7, 2012.

Rosenzweig, David. "JDL Officials Pleads Guilty in Bomb Plot." *Los Angeles Times*, February 5, 2003.

Ross, Brian, and John Solomon. "US Apologizes to Billionaire Added to Terror No-fly List." ABC News, May 21, 2010, http://abcnews.go.com.

Rowan, Tomas. "Man Sentenced for Killing Afghan Mom." ABC News, April 15, 2008, http://wwwabclocal.go.com.

Rucker, Philip, and Ellen Nakashima. "Hasan Charged with 13 Counts of Murder." *Washington Post*, November 13, 2009.

Ryan, Missy, and Adam Goldman. "U.S. Prepares to Accelerate Detainee Transfers from Guantanamo Bay Prison." *Washington Post*, December 24, 2014.

Sacirbey, Omar. "Anti-Shari'ah Movement Changes Tactics and Gains Success." *Religious News Service*, May 16, 2013, www.religionnews.com.

Sacirbey, Omar. "Citing Risk to Adoptions, Missouri Gov. Vetoes Anti-Shariah Bill." *Religious News Service*, June 4, 2013, www.religionnews.com.

Sacirbey, Omar. "Judge Rules in Favor of Muslim Woman on No-Fly List." *Washington Post*, January 16, 2014.

Santora, Marc. "Woman Is Charged with Murder as a Hate Crime in a Fatal Subway Push." *New York Times*, December 29, 2012.

Santora, Marc, and Sarah Maslin Nir. "Woman Sought after 2nd Fatal Shove onto Subway Tracks this Month." *New York Times*, December 28, 2012.

Sapien, Joaquin. "Are Prosecutors Taking Advantage of Material Witness Orders?" *Salon*, August 17, 2013.

Savage, Charlie. "Secret U.S. Memo Made Legal Case to Kill a Citizen." *New York Times*, October 8 2011.

"SF Court Upholds Conviction in Possible Hate Crime Shooting of Woman." *The San Francisco Appeal*, February 5, 2010.

Shane, Scott. "In Islamic Law, Gingrich Sees a Mortal Threat to U.S." *New York Times*, December 21, 2011.

Shane, Scott, and Eric Lipton. "Passengers' Quick Action Halted Attack." *New York Times*, December 26, 2009.

Shane, Scott, and Eric Schmitt. "One Drone Victim's Trail From Raleigh to Pakistan." *New York Times*, May 22, 2013.

Shea, James. "Feds Speak with Sullivan County Sheriff about Religious Complaints." *Bristol Herald Courier*. December 20, 2012.

Schmitt, Eric, and Eric Lipton. "Focus on Internet Imams as Al Qaeda Recruiters." *New York Times*, December 31, 2009.

Schmitt, Eric, and David Sanger. "Pakistan Shift Could Curtail Drone Strikes." *Washington Post*, February 22, 2008.

Schmitt, Richard, and Donna Horowitz. "FBI Starts to Question Muslims in U.S. About Possible Attacks." *Los Angeles Times*, July 2004.

Sheridan, Mary Beth. "Interviews of Muslims to Broaden." *Washington Post*, July 17, 2004.

Shuster, Beth. "Crimes of Hate or just Crimes." *Los Angeles Times*, October 11, 2001.

Sieff, Kevin. "In Afghanistan, a Second Guantanamo." *Washington Post*, August 4, 2013.

Simmons, Keir, and Charlene Gubash. "American Sharif Mobley Hasn't Appeared in Yemen Court for a Year." NBC News, January 20, 2014, http://www.nbcnews.com.

Singh, Simran Jeet. "A Unique Perspective on Hate Crimes: The Story of a Convicted Killer." *Huffington Post*, July 20, 2012.

Smith, Dinitia. "Tragedy Haunts Film on Afghan Diaspora; Friends of a Murdered Filmmaker Struggle to Finish His Work." *New York Times*, October 2, 2002.

Somanader, Tanya. "Herman Cain: Americans Have the Right to Ban Mosques." ThinkProgress, July 17, 2011, http://thinkprogress.org.

"State Legislation Restricting Use of Foreign or Religious Law," Pew Research Center, April 2013, http://www.pewforum.org.

"Suit Filed Against County that Barred Corrections Worker from Wearing Headscarf." *Religious Freedom in Focus* 39 (June/July 2009), http://www.justice.gov/crt/spec_topics/religiousdiscrimination/newsletters.php.

Sullivan, Jennifer. "Seattle Jewish Center Shooter Gets Life Sentence." *Los Angeles Times*, January 15, 2010.

Sulzberger, G. "Two More Men Charged In Plot to Bomb Subways." *New York Times*, February 25, 2010.

Susman, Tina. "Federal Hate Crime Figures Tell Little." *Baltimore Sun*, December 13, 2002.

Sussman, Anna Louie. "Naji Hamdan's Nightmare." *The Nation*, March 4, 2010.

"Tancredo: Threats On Islam Sites Could Deter Terrorists." *Denver Post*, August 3, 2007.

Terry, Don "Community Ties Fray for Muslims." *Chicago Tribune*, September 25, 2001.

Terry, Don and Noreen S. Ahmed-Ullah. "Protesters Turn Anger on Muslim Americans." *Chicago Tribune*, September 14, 2001.

"Time Poll Results: Americans' View on the Campaign, Religion and the Mosque Controversy." *Time*, August 18, 2010.

Totenberg, Nina. "Court Considers Ashcroft's Liability In Terror Case." *Morning Edition* (National Public Radio), March 2, 2011, www.npr.org.

"Township Taking of Mosque's Property Implicates RLUIPA, United States Argues." *Religious Freedom in Focus* 28 (June/July 2007), http://www.justice.gov/crt/spec_topics/religiousdiscrimination/newsletters.php.

"Twenty Year Sentence in Mosque Arson Case," *Religious Freedom in Focus* 56 (April 2013), http://www.justice.gov/crt/spec_topics/religiousdiscrimination/newsletters.php.

"United States Closes Investigation over Access to Religious Literature after County Jail Implements Changes." *Religious Freedom in Focus* 56 (April 2013), http://www.justice.gov/crt/spec_topics/religiousdiscrimination/newsletters.php.

Vick, Karl. "U.S. Muslim's Case Poses Test for New Administration." *Washington Post*, March 23, 2009.

Vives, Ruben "Complaint Filed over Lomita's Denial of Bid for New Mosque." *Los Angeles Times*, March 22, 2012.

Vogt, Amanda, and Rachel Osterman. "Morton Grove, Muslim Group OK Mosque Deal." *Chicago Tribune*, June 9, 2004.

Volokh, Eugene. "Supreme Court Will Hear Muslim Prisoner's Religious Challenge to Prison No-Beards Policy." *Washington Post*, March 3, 2014.

Weinberg, Tanya. "Pinellas Doctor Gets 12 1/2 Years For Bomb Plot." *Sun Sentinel*, June 20, 2003.

Welna, David. "Drawing on Pentagon Surplus, Police Now Wield Weapons of War." *All Things Considered* (National Public Radio), August 15, 2014, http://www.npr.org.

Wilgoren, Jodi. "The Pakistani Americans: Isolated Family Finds Support and Reason to Worry in Illinois." *New York Times*, October 2001.

Wilson, Scott, Greg Miller, and Sari Horwitz. "Boston Bombing Suspect Cites U.S. Wars as Motivation." *Washington Post*, April 23, 2013.

Winter, Greg. "2 Held in Plot to Attack Mosque and Congressman." *New York Times*, December 13, 2001.

Wisniewski, Mary. "U.S. Judge Bars Oklahoma from Implementing Anti-Sharia Law." Reuters, August 17, 2013, http://www.reuters.com.

Woods, Chris. "Militants and Civilians Killed in Multiple U.S. Somalia Strikes." Bureau of Investigative Journalism, February 22, 2012, www.thebureau investigates.com.

Worth, Robert F. "Police Arrest Brooklyn Man in Slayings of 4 Shopkeepers." *New York Times*, March 31, 2003.

Yost, Pete. "Muslim School Teacher Denied Hajj, U.S. Sues Illinois School District." *Christian Science Monitor*, December 14, 2010.

Ziv, Stav. "Controversial Anti-Muslim Ads Coming to New York City Transit." *Newsweek*, September 24, 2014.

Further Reading

Perceptions of Islam in Western and American Culture

Alsultany, Evelyn. *Arabs and Muslims in the Media: Race and Representation after 9/11*. New York: New York University Press, 2012.

Bail, Christopher. *Terrified: How Anti-Muslim Fringe Organizations Became Mainstream*. Princeton: Princeton University Press, 2015.

Blanks, David R., and Michael Frassetto, eds. *Western Views of Islam in Medieval and Early Modern Europe: Perceptions of the Other*. New York: St. Martin's Press, 1999.

Ernst, Carl, ed. *Islamophobia in America: The Anatomy of Intolerance*. New York: Palgrave Macmillan, 2013.

Gottschalk, Peter, and Gabriel Greenberg. *Islamophobia: Making Muslims the Enemy*. Lanham, MD: Rowman and Littlefield Publishers, 2007.

Kidd, Thomas. *American Christians and Islam: Evangelical Culture and Muslims from the Colonial Period to the Age of Terrorism*. Princeton: Princeton University Press, 2009.

Lyons, Jonathan. *Islam through Western Eyes: From the Crusades to the War on Terrorism*. New York: Columbia University Press, 2012.

McCarthy, Justin. *The Turk in America: The Creation of an Enduring Prejudice*. Salt Lake City: University of Utah Press, 2010.

Nacos, Brigitte L., and Oscar Torres-Reyna. *Fueling Our Fears: Stereotyping, Media Coverage, and Public Opinion of Muslim Americans*. Lanham, MD: Rowman and Littlefield, 2007.

Said, Edward. *Covering Islam: How the Media and the Experts Determine How We See the Rest of the World*. New York: Vintage Books, 1997.

Said, Edward. *Orientalism*. New York: Vintage Books, 1979.

Semmerling, Tim Jon. *"Evil" Arabs in American Popular Film: Orientalist Fear*. Austin: University of Texas Press, 2006.

Shaheen, Jack G. *Guilty: Hollywood's Verdict on Arabs after 9/11.* Northampton, MA: Olive Branch Press, 2008.

Shaheen, Jack G. *Reel Bad Arabs: How Hollywood Vilifies a People.* Northampton, MA: Olive Branch Press, 2012.

History of Muslims in America

Bilici, Mucahit. *Finding Mecca in America: How Islam Is Becoming an American Religion.* Chicago: University of Chicago Press, 2012.

Curtis, Edward E., ed. *The Columbia Sourcebook of Muslims in the United States.* New York: Columbia University Press, 2009.

Curtis, Edward E. *Islam in Black America.* Albany: State University of New York Press, 2002.

Diouf, Sylviane A. *Servants of Allah: African Muslims Enslaved in the Americas.* New York: New York University Press, 1998.

GhaneaBassiri, Kambiz. *A History of Islam in America.* Cambridge: Cambridge University Press, 2010.

Gomez, Michael A. *Black Crescent: The Experience and Legacy of African Muslims in America.* Cambridge: Cambridge University Press, 2005.

Hammer, Juliane, and Omid Safi, eds. *The Cambridge Companion to American Islam.* Cambridge: Cambridge University Press, 2013.

Smith, Jane. *Islam in America.* New York: Columbia University Press, 2010.

Spellberg, Denise. *Thomas Jefferson's Qur'an: Islam and the Founders.* New York: Alfred A. Knopf, 2013.

Turner, Richard Brent. *Islam in the African American Experience.* Bloomington: Indiana University Press, 1997.

Muslim American Experience after 9/11

Abdo, Geneive. *Mecca and Main Street: Muslim Life in America after 9/11.* Oxford: Oxford University Press, 2006.

Ahmed, Akbar. *Journey into America: The Challenge of Islam.* Washington, DC: Brookings Institution Press, 2010.

Bakalian, Anny and Mehdi Bozorgmehr. *Backlash 9/11: Middle Eastern and Muslim Americans Respond.* Berkeley: University of California Press, 2009.

Bayoumi, Moustafa. *How Does It Feel to Be a Problem? Being Young and Arab in America.* New York: Penguin Books, 2008.

Bukhari, Zahid H., et al., eds. *Muslims' Place in the American Public Square: Hopes, Fears, and Aspirations.* Walnut Creek, CA: AltaMira Press, 2004.

Cainkar, Louise A. *Homeland Insecurity: The Arab American and Muslim American Experience after 9/11.* New York: Russell Sage Foundation, 2009.

Kundnani, Arun. *The Muslims Are Coming: Islamophobia, Extremism, and the Domestic War on Terror.* London: Verso, 2014.

Lean, Nathan. *The Islamophobia Industry: How the Right Manufactures Fear of Muslims*. London: Pluto Press, 2012.

Peek, Lori. *Behind the Backlash: Muslim Americans after 9/11*. New Delhi: Social Science Press, 2012.

Welch, Michael. *Scapegoats of September 11th: Hate Crimes and State Crimes in the War on Terror*. New Brunswick: Rutgers University Press, 2006.

Security Policy and Muslim Americans

Aaronson, Trevor. *The Terror Factory: Inside the FBI's Manufactured War on Terrorism*. New York: Ig Publishing, 2013.

Apuzzo, Matt, and Adam Goldman. *Enemies Within: Inside the NYDP's Secret Spying Unit and bin Laden's Final Plot against America*. New York: Simon and Schuster, 2013.

Awan, Imran, and Brian Blakemore, eds. *Extremism, Counter-Terrorism and Policing*. Burlington, VT: Ashgate Publishing, 2013.

Churchill, Ward, and Jim Vander Wall. *The COINTELPRO Papers: Documents from the FBI's Secret Wars against Domestic Dissent*. Boston: South End Press, 1990.

Davis, James Kirkpatrick. *Spying on America: The FBI's Domestic Counterintelligence Program*. Westport, CT: Praeger, 1992.

Federal Bureau of Investigation, *Nation of Islam: The FBI Files*. Lexington, KY: Filiquarian Publishing/Qontro, 2013.

Gaskew, Tom. *Policing Muslim American Communities: A Compendium of Post-9/11 Interviews*. Lewiston, NY: Edwin Mellen Press, 2008.

Hafetz, Jonathan. *Habeas Corpus after 9/11: Confronting America's New Global Detention System*. New York: New York University Press, 2011.

Herman, Susan N. *Taking Liberties: The War on Terror and the Erosion of American Democracy*. Oxford: Oxford University Press, 2011.

Hill, Robert A., ed. *The FBI's RACON: Racial Conditions in the United States during World War II*. Boston: Northeastern University Press, 1995.

Silk, P. Daniel, Basia Spalek, and Mary O'Rawe, eds. *Preventing Ideological Violence: Communities, Police, and Case Studies of "Success."* New York: Palgrave Macmillan, 2013.

Spalek, Basia, ed. *Counter-Terrorism: Community-Based Approaches to Preventing Terror Crime*. London: Palgrave Macmillan, 2012.

Index

About the Author

JEFFREY L. THOMAS is a security policy analyst with more than 20 years of experience examining homeland security and counterterrorism policies, U.S. relations with the Muslim world, and the experience of Muslims in America. He has served as senior fellow for Homeland Security and Threat Assessment at the Center for the Study of the Presidency and Congress (CSPC) as well as research associate in the Russia and Eurasia Program and the Islamic Studies Program at the Center for Strategic and International Studies (CSIS). He is a contributing author to the CSPC report *Strengthening U.S.-Muslim Communications* and to the book *Islam in Russia: The Politics of Identity and Security*.